Oxford Moral Theory

Series Editor
David Copp, University of California, Davis

Commonsense Consequentialism

Wherein Morality Meets Rationality

DOUGLAS W. PORTMORE

OXFORD
UNIVERSITY PRESS

#691927979

OXFORD
UNIVERSITY PRESS

Oxford University Press, Inc., publishes works that further
Oxford University's objective of excellence
in research, scholarship, and education.

Oxford   New York
Auckland   Cape Town   Dar es Salaam   Hong Kong   Karachi
Kuala Lumpur   Madrid   Melbourne   Mexico City   Nairobi
New Delhi   Shanghai   Taipei   Toronto

With offices in
Argentina   Austria   Brazil   Chile   Czech Republic   France   Greece
Guatemala   Hungary   Italy   Japan   Poland   Portugal   Singapore
South Korea   Switzerland   Thailand   Turkey   Ukraine   Vietnam

Copyright © 2011 Oxford University Press

Published by Oxford University Press, Inc.
198 Madison Avenue, New York, New York 10016

www.oup.com

Oxford is a registered trademark of Oxford University Press

Library of Congress Cataloging-in-Publication Data
Portmore, Douglas W.
Commonsense consequentialism: wherein morality meets rationality / Douglas W. Portmore.
p.   cm.—(Oxford moral theory)
Includes bibliographical references and index.
ISBN 978-0-19-979453-9 (alk. paper)
1. Consequentialism (Ethics)   2. Ethics.   3. Practical reason.   I. Title.
BJ1031.P67 2011
171'.5—dc22   2010050743

ISBN-13: 9780199794539

1 3 5 7 9 8 6 4 2
Printed in the United States of America
on acid-free paper

For my wife and daughter, Erin and Fiona Portmore

CONTENTS

ACKNOWLEDGMENTS

Consequentialism is typically taken to be an agent-neutral theory: a theory that gives each agent the exact same set of aims. Unfortunately, no agent-neutral theory can accommodate all of our commonsense moral intuitions. For instance, no agent-neutral theory can accommodate the intuition that it would be wrong to break a promise even so as to prevent two others from each breaking a comparable promise, for the only way to accommodate such an intuition is to give each agent the distinct aim of, say, minimizing his or her own promise-breakings—thus, giving me the aim of minimizing *my* promise-breakings and you the aim of minimizing *your* promise-breakings.

In a graduate seminar taught by Jamie Dreier at Monash University in 1994, I was first introduced to the possibility of combining a consequentialist moral theory with an agent-relative ranking of outcomes. I found this to be an intriguing possibility, for it has the prospect of bringing consequentialism in line with our commonsense moral intuitions. I have, ever since, been trying to work out how this might best be done. My first attempt came in the form of the dissertation that I wrote at the University of California, Santa Barbara, with Matthew Hanser supervising and Christopher McMahon and Burleigh Wilkins rounding out the committee. I thank them for their guidance during those early years.

After graduate school, I continued to work in this area, publishing a number of articles. This brought on a small but formidable wave of critics, which included Michael Byron, Betsy Postow, Ben Sachs, Mark Schroeder, and Jussi Suikkanen. I have learned a lot from these critics, and my views have changed substantially due to their influence. My greatest debt is owed to Mark Schroeder. If it were not for his penetrating criticisms of my earlier views, this book would have never taken shape. It was by grappling with his criticisms that I came to the conclusion that consequentialists should rank outcomes, not according to their agent-neutral (or even their agent-relative) value, but according to how much reason each agent has to desire that those outcomes obtain. And it was this conclusion that led to my making certain crucial connections between my views about morality and my views about practical reasons, the very connections that lie at the heart of this book.

Besides these critics, I thank Anne Baril, Steve Campbell, Erik Carlson, Richard Yetter Chappell, Josh Glasgow, Peter Graham, Paul Hurley, Andrew Khoury, Paul McNamara, Toni Rønnow-Rasmussen, Jacob Ross, S. Andrew Schroeder, Russ Shafer-Landau, Dave Shoemaker, David Sobel, Andy Specht, and Jean-Paul Vessel for helpful comments on some portion of the manuscript itself. And I thank especially Peter de Marneffe, G. Shyam Nair, Robert Neal, Ben Sachs, and Travis Timmerman, who each read and commented on the entire manuscript.

In helping me work through my views on what we ought to do when our future actions are not under our present deliberative control, I thank Richard Yetter Chappell and Jacob Ross. Richard convinced me that I was on the wrong path (viz., the path to possibilism) in my first attempt to deal with the issue, and Jacob convinced me that, although I was generally on the right track in my second attempt, some substantial revisions were needed. Their insightful criticisms on earlier drafts of chapters 6 and 7 led to some of the most substantial revisions of the manuscript as well as to my first experiences with heart palpitations, brought on by the anxiety over how best to deal with their criticisms. Peter Graham also sent me some very helpful comments on chapter 6, but, unfortunately, they came after I had already submitted the final pre-copyedited version of the manuscript, and so I have not been able to address them except in the most superficial way.

For many helpful discussions, I thank the commentators on my posts at *PEA Soup*, http://peasoup.typepad.com/peasoup/, as well as Richard Yetter Chappell and the commentators on his blog, *Philosophy, et cetera*, http://www .philosophyetc.net/. Many of the ideas in this book were first presented as blog posts on *PEA Soup*. By participating on blogs, I have been able to get the sort of feedback on my ideas that, a few decades ago, could only have been gotten from one's colleagues. With the advent of the internet and blogging, the circle of people whom you can bounce ideas off of transcends all geographical barriers. I am fortunate to live in such times.

For financial support while working on this book, I thank Arizona State University and the Center for Ethics and Public Affairs at the Murphy Institute, Tulane University. Their financial support enabled me to spend the 2008–2009 academic year as a Faculty Fellow in residence at the Center. This was the year in which much of the book was written. Special thanks are owed to the Institute's previous director, Richard F. Teichgraeber III, and to the Center's coordinator, Margaret M. Keenan. They went well beyond what anyone could rightfully expect in terms of helping me during some minor crises that I encountered when I first took up residence in New Orleans, Louisiana (if Hurricane Gustav and an attempted robbery can be considered minor). But lest the reader get the wrong impression, I had a wonderful time in New Orleans despite those initial hiccups and am happy to return there every chance that I get.

I thank Brad Hooker and Mark Schroeder for their helpful comments on the manuscript that I initially submitted to Oxford University Press. And I thank Peter Ohlin (the philosophy editor at Oxford University Press, New York) and

David Copp (the series editor) for their help and encouragement along the way to bringing this book to print.

Precursors of several chapters have been published elsewhere. Chapter 2 is an expanded version of PORTMORE FORTHCOMINGa. Chapter 3 is a slightly revised version of PORTMORE FORTHCOMINGc. Chapter 4 is a much revised and expanded version of PORTMORE 2009 and includes some ideas from PORTMORE 1998. Chapter 5 combines material from PORTMORE 2008a and PORTMORE 2008b. Chapter 6 is a substantially revised version of PORTMORE FORTHCOMINGb. (Unfortunately, PORTMORE FORTHCOMINGb reflects my earlier thinking about what we ought to do when our future actions are not under our present delibera-tive control, the views that Richard Yetter Chappell later convinced me were mistaken.)

For permission to borrow material from these publications, I thank the editors and publishers of the journals in which they appeared. And, for helpful comments and discussions on early ancestors of these articles and some other pertinent arti-cles, I thank Richard Arneson, David Benatar, Noell Birondo, Dan Boisvert, Ben Bradley, Campbell Brown, Michael Byron, Cheshire Calhoun, Andrew Cochrane, Stew Cohen, Peter de Marneffe, Dale Dorsey, Jamie Dreier, Julia Driver, Nir Eyal, Fred Feldman, J. L. A. Garcia, Josh Gert, Josh Glasgow, Pat Greenspan, Matthew Hanser, Caspar Hare, Chris Heathwood, Brad Hooker, Frances Howard-Snyder, Thomas Hurka, Shelly Kagan, Sharon Lloyd, Errol Lord, Jennie Louise, Eric Mack, John Maier, Peter Marchetto, Chris McMahon, Paul McNamara, David McNaughton, Christian Miller, G. Shyam Nair, Robert Noggle, Howard Nye, Sven Nyholm, Jonas Olson, Derek Parfit, Betsy Postow, Peter Railton, Jacob Ross, Ben Sachs, Geoffrey Sayre-McCord, Mark Schroeder, David Shoemaker, Ted Sider, David Sobel, Jussi Suikkanen, Sergio Tenenbaum, Valerie Tiberius, Mark Timmons, Mark van Roojen, Pekka Väyrynen, Jean-Paul Vessel, Steven Wall, Michael J. Zimmerman, numerous anonymous referees, students in my Spring 2008 sem-inar on consequentialism, and audiences at Tulane University, Arizona State University, Florida State University, the 2008 Bellingham Summer Philosophy Conference, the 2008 Rocky Mountain Ethics Congress, the 2006 Pacific APA Meeting, the 2010 Arizona Workshop on Normative Ethics, and the 2000 and 2005 International Society for Utilitarian Studies conferences.

Lastly, for their love and constant support while working on this book, I thank my wife and daughter, Erin and Fiona Portmore, and my parents: Linda Hills, Pakinee Portmore, and Ralph Portmore.

ABBREVIATIONS

AC   The view that an act's deontic status is determined by the agent's reasons for and against preferring its outcome to those of the available alternatives, such that, if S is morally required to perform x, then, of all the outcomes that S could bring about, S has most (indeed, decisive) reason to desire that x's outcome obtains.

BET   Outcome o_i is better than outcome o_j.

CR   An act is morally permissible if and only if its outcome is not (on the agent's ranking) outranked by that of any available alternative.

CSC   The view according to which all the following are true: (a) it is, as of t_i, objectively morally permissible for S to perform a non-maximal set of actions, α_j, beginning at t_j ($t_i < t_j$) if and only if, and because, it is, as of t_i, objectively morally permissible for S to perform a maximal set of actions, MSA_i, that involves S's performing α_j; (b) it is, as of t_i, objectively morally permissible for S to perform a maximal set of actions, MSA_i, if and only if, and because, MSA_i is one of the optimal MSAs that is, as of t_i, scrupulously securable by S; (c) MSA_i is one of the optimal MSAs that is, as of t_i, scrupulously securable by S if and only if, and because, MSA_i's outcome is not, on S's evaluative ranking, outranked by that of any alternative MSA that is, as of t_i, scrupulously securable by S; and (d) MSA_i's outcome is not, on S's evaluative ranking, outranked by that of any alternative MSA that is, as of t_i, scrupulously securable by S if and only if, and because, there is no alternative MSA that is, as of t_i, scrupulously securable by S whose outcome S has both more requiring reason and more reason, all things considered, to want to obtain.

CSC*   The view according to which all the following are true: (a) it is, as of t_i, objectively morally permissible for S to perform a non-maximal set of actions, α_j, beginning at t_j $(t_i < t_j)$ if and only if, and because, it is, as of t_i, objectively morally permissible for S to perform a maximal set of actions, MSA_j, that involves S's performing α_j; (b) it is, as of t_i, objectively morally permissible for S to perform a maximal set of actions, MSA_i, if and only if, and because, MSA_i is one of the optimal MSAs that is, as of t_i, scrupulously securable by S; (c) MSA_i is one of the optimal MSAs that is, as of t_i, scrupulously securable by S if and only if, and because, MSA_i's prospect is not, on S's t_i-relative evaluative ranking, outranked by that of any alternative MSA that is, as of t_i, scrupulously securable by S; and (d) MSA_i's prospect is not, on S's t_i-relative evaluative ranking, outranked by that of any alternative MSA that is, as of t_i, scrupulously securable by S if and only if, and because, there is no alternative MSA that is, as of t_i, scrupulously securable by S whose prospect S has at t_i both more requiring reason and more reason, all things considered, to desire.

CSU   The view according to which all the following are true: (a) it is, as of t_i, objectively morally permissible for S to perform a non-maximal set of actions, α_j, beginning at t_j $(t_i < t_j)$ if and only if, and because, it is, as of t_i, objectively morally permissible for S to perform a maximal set of actions, MSA_j, that involves S's performing α_j; (b) it is, as of t_i, objectively morally permissible for S to perform a maximal set of actions, MSA_i, if and only if, and because, MSA_i is one of the optimal MSAs that is, as of t_i, scrupulously securable by S; (c) MSA_i is one of the optimal MSAs that is, as of t_i, scrupulously securable by S if and only if, and because, MSA_i's outcome is not, on S's evaluative ranking, outranked by that of any alternative MSA that is, as of t_i, scrupulously securable by S; and (d) MSA_i's outcome is not, on S's evaluative ranking, outranked by that of any alternative MSA that is, as of t_i, scrupulously securable by S if and only if, and because, there is no alternative MSA that is, as of t_i, scrupulously securable by S whose outcome contains both more constraint-adjusted utility and more comprehensively adjusted utility than MSA_i's outcome does.

DES   S has more reason to desire that o_i obtains than to desire that o_j obtains.

DET   For any remotely plausible nonconsequentialist theory, there is a substantive version of consequentialism that is deontically equivalent to it.

DRAC   S's performing x is morally permissible if and only if, and because, there is no available act alternative that would produce an outcome that S has both more moral reason and more reason, all things considered, to want to obtain than to want x's outcome to obtain.

DRAC$_{cr}$ S's performing x is morally permissible if and only if there is no available act alternative that would produce an outcome that S has both more moral reason and more reason, all things considered, to want to obtain than to want x's outcome to obtain.

EGO   It is, as of t_i, objectively rationally permissible for S to perform φ if and only if, and because, there is no alternative act that is, as of t_i, personally possible for S that would produce more utility for S than φ would.

LR   If S is legally required to perform x, then S has decisive reason to perform x, all things considered.

MAU   The view both (1) that traditional act-consequentialism is true and (2) that an act maximizes the good if and only if it maximizes aggregate utility.

MAU$_{cr}$ It is objectively morally permissible for S to perform an act, x, if and only if there is no alternative act that is personally possible for S that would produce more aggregate utility than x would.

META   S's performing φ is morally permissible if and only if there is no available alternative, ψ, that S has both more requiring reason and more reason, all things considered, to perform.

MO   If S has more moral reason to perform x than to perform y ($y \neq x$), then S is not morally permitted to perform y. And, thus, if S has most moral reason to perform x, then S is morally required to perform x.

MODSU   The view according to which all the following hold: (1) dual-ranking act-consequentialism is true; (2) S has more moral reason to want o_i to obtain than to want o_j ($j \neq i$) to obtain if and only if o_i contains more constraint-adjusted utility than o_j does; and (3) S has more reason, all things considered, to want o_i to obtain than to want o_j to obtain if and only if o_i contains more comprehensively adjusted utility than o_j does.

MODSU$_{cr}$ S's performing x is morally permissible if and only if there is no available act alternative that would produce both more constraint-adjusted utility and more comprehensively adjusted utility than x would, where the constraint-adjusted utility of an outcome is just the sum of the utility for others, adjusted by multiplying any disutility (or loss of utility) resulting from S's infringement of an agent-centered constraint by five hundred, and where the comprehensively adjusted utility of an outcome is just its constraint-adjusted utility added to the product of S's utility times ten.

MPU   The view according to which all the following are true: (*a*) it is, as of t_p objectively morally permissible for S to perform a non-maximal set of actions, α_j, beginning at t_j ($t_i < t_j$) if and only if, and because, it is, as of t_p objectively morally permissible for S to perform a maximal set of actions, MSA_p that involves S's performing α_j; (*b*) it is, as of t_p objectively morally permissible for S to perform a maximal set of actions, MSA_p if and only if, and because, MSA_i is one of the optimal MSAs that is, as of t_p personally possible for S; (*c*) MSA_i is one of the optimal MSAs that is, as of t_p personally possible for S if and only if, and because, MSA_i's outcome is not, on S's evaluative ranking, outranked by that of any alternative MSA that is, as of t_p personally possible for S; and (*d*) MSA_i's outcome is not, on S's evaluative ranking, outranked by that of any alternative MSA that is, as of t_p personally possible for S if and only if, and because, there is no alternative MSA that is, as of t_p personally possible for S whose outcome contains more aggregate utility than MSA_i's outcome does.

MR   If a subject, S, is morally required to perform an act, *x*, then S has most (indeed, decisive) reason to perform *x*, all things considered.

MR¹   The deontic status of a non-maximal set of actions, α_j, beginning at t_j ($t_i < t_j$) is determined by the agent's reasons for and against performing α_j, such that, if S is, as of t_p morally required to perform α_j, then S has most reason, all things considered, to perform α_j.

MR*   The deontic status of α_j is determined by the agent's reasons for and against performing α_j, such that, if S is, as of t_p morally required to perform α_j, then S has at t_i most (indeed, decisive) reason, all things considered, to perform α_j.

MR~MRS   Some *moral reasons* have absolutely no (~) *moral requiring strength*.

MS   It is, as of t_p objectively morally permissible for S to perform a non-maximal set of actions, α_j, beginning at t_j ($t_i < t_j$) if and only if, and because, at least one of the objectively morally permissible maximal sets of actions that are, as of t_p scrupulously securable by S involves S's performing α_j.

MSA   A maximal set of actions—a set of actions, α_j, that is, as of t_p available to S (i.e., available either in the sense of being personally possible for S or in the sense of being scrupulously securable by S) is a maximal set of actions if and only if there is no other set of actions, α_p that is, as of t_p available to S such that performing α_i involves performing α_j but not vice versa.

MSU   The view according to which all the following are true: (*a*) it is, as of t_p objectively morally permissible for S to perform a non-maximal set of actions, α_j, beginning at t_i $(t_i < t_j)$ if and only if, and because, it is, as of t_i, objectively morally permissible for S to perform a maximal set of actions, MSA_i, that involves S's performing α_j; (*b*) it is, as of t_i, objectively morally permissible for S to perform a maximal set of actions, MSA_i, if and only if, and because, MSA_i is one of the optimal MSAs that is, as of t_i, scrupulously securable by S; (*c*) MSA_i is one of the optimal MSAs that is, as of t_i, scrupulously securable by S if and only if, and because, MSA_i's outcome is not, on S's evaluative ranking, out-ranked by that of any alternative MSA that is, as of t_i, scrupulously securable by S; and (*d*) MSA_i's outcome is not, on S's evaluative ranking, outranked by that of any alternative MSA that is, as of t_i, scrupulously securable by S if and only if, and because, there is no alternative MSA that is, as of t_i, scrupulously securable by S whose outcome contains more aggregate utility than MSA_i's outcome does.

NMR+MJS   *Non-moral reasons* have some (+) *moral justifying strength*. And, thus, non-moral reasons can, and sometimes do, prevent moral reasons, even those with considerable moral requiring strength, from generating moral requirements.

PAC $[P(S, t_i, x_1), P(S, t_i, x_2), \ldots, \& P(S, t_i, x_n)] \rightarrow P[S, t_i, (x_1, x_2, \ldots, \& x_n)]$, where "$P(S, t_i, x_i)$" stands for "S is, as of t_i, permitted to perform x_i."

PDC $P[S, t_i, (x_1, x_2, \ldots, \& x_n)] \rightarrow [P(S, t_i, x_1), P(S, t_i, x_2), \ldots, \& P(S, t_i, x_n)]$, where "$P(S, t_i, x_i)$" stands for "S is, as of t_i, permitted to perform x_i."

PER   S has more reason to perform a_i than to perform a_j.

RMAU$_{cr}$ It is, as of t_i, objectively morally permissible for S to perform a set of actions, α_j, beginning at t_j $(t_i < t_j)$ if and only if there is no alternative set of actions that is, as of t_i, personally possible for S that would produce more aggregate utility than α_j would.

RO   If S has more moral reason to perform x than to perform y ($y \neq x$), then S is not rationally permitted to perform y. And, thus, if S has most moral reason to perform x, then S is rationally required (i.e., has decisive reason, all things considered) to perform x.

RP   The fact that S is morally required to perform x constitutes (and, thus, provides) an overriding (and, hence, decisive) reason for S to perform x.

SC   The deontic status of a non-maximal set of actions, α_j, beginning at t_j $(t_i < t_j)$ is determined by the reasons there are for and against the agent's preferring certain outcomes to others, such that, if S is, as of t_i, morally required to perform α_j, then, of all the outcomes that S could bring about by performing some MSA that is, as of t_i, scrupulously securable by S, S has most reason to desire some subset of those that would result from S's performing an MSA that involves S's performing α_j.

SEC   It is, as of t_i, objectively rationally permissible for S to perform a non-maximal set of actions, α_j, beginning at t_j ($t_i < t_j$) if and only if, and because, at least one of the objectively rationally permissible maximal sets of actions that are, as of t_i, scrupulously securable by S involves S's performing α_j.

SOU   S's performing x is morally permissible if and only if there is no available act alternative that would produce both more utility for others and more overall utility than x would.

SR   If S is schmorally required to perform x, then S has decisive reason to perform x, all things considered.

SU   The view according to which all the following hold: (1) dual-ranking act-consequentialism is true; (2) S has more moral reason to want o_i to obtain than to want o_j ($j \neq i$) to obtain if and only if o_i contains more utility for others (i.e., for those other than S) than o_j does; and (3) S has more reason, all things considered, to want o_i to obtain than to want o_j to obtain if and only if o_i contains more egoistically adjusted utility than o_j does.

SU$_{cr}$ S's performing x is morally permissible if and only if there is no available act alternative that would produce both more utility for others (i.e., for those other than S) and more egoistically adjusted utility than x would, where egoistically adjusted utility includes everyone's utility but adjusts the overall total by giving S's utility, say, ten times the weight of anyone else's.

SupDC $\text{SUP}[S, t_i, (\alpha_1, \alpha_2, \ldots, \& \alpha_n)] \rightarrow [\text{SUP}(S, t_i, \alpha_1), \text{SUP}(S, t_i, \alpha_2), \ldots, \& \text{SUP}(S, t_i, \alpha_n)]$, where "$\text{SUP}(S, t_i, \alpha_i)$" stands for "S's performing α_i is, as of t_i, supererogatory."

SUPER   It is, as of t_i, supererogatory for S to perform a set of actions, α_j, beginning at t_j ($t_i < t_j$) if and only if, and because, both of the following hold: (1) in performing α_j, S does not thereby only minimally or partially fulfill some positive duty, and (2) there is some alternative set of actions, α_i, also beginning at t_j ($t_i < t_j$) such that: (*a*) it is, as of t_i, both objectively morally permissible for S to perform α_j and objectively morally permissible for S to perform α_i and (*b*) S has more moral reason to perform α_j than to perform α_i.

SUPER-MAX It is, as of t_i, supererogatory for S to perform a maximal set of actions, MSA$_j$, beginning at t_j ($t_i < t_j$) if and only if, and because, there is some alternative maximal set of actions, MSA$_i$, also beginning at t_j ($t_i < t_j$) such that: (*a*) it is, as of t_i, both objectively morally permissible for S to perform MSA_j and objectively morally permissible for S to perform MSA_i and (b) S has more moral reason to perform MSA_j than to perform MSA_i.

SUPERF   It is, as of t_i, superperfecterogatory for S to perform a set of actions, α_j, beginning at t_j $(t_i < t_j)$ if and only if, and because, there is some alternative set of actions, α_i, also beginning at t_j $(t_i < t_j)$ such that: (a) it is, as of t_i, both objectively morally permissible for S to perform α_j and objectively morally permissible for S to perform α_i and (b) S has more moral reason to perform α_j than to perform α_i.

TAC   The view both (1) that act-consequentialism is true and (2) that an act produces an outcome that the agent has optimal reason to want to obtain if and only if it maximizes the good (impersonally construed).

TAC$_{cr}$ S's performing x is morally permissible if and only if S's performing x would maximize the good (impersonally construed).

TCR   (1) S has more reason to perform a_i than to perform a_j if S has more reason to desire that o_i obtains than to desire that o_j obtains; (2) S has more reason to perform a_i than to perform a_j only if S has more reason to desire that o_i obtains than to desire that o_j obtains; and (3) if S has more reason to perform a_i than to perform a_j, then this is so in virtue of the fact that S has more reason to desire that o_i obtains than to desire that o_j obtains.

TCR–1   S has more reason to perform a_i than to perform a_j if S has more reason to desire that o_i obtains than to desire that o_j obtains.

TCR–2   S has more reason to perform a_i than to perform a_j only if S has more reason to desire that o_i obtains than to desire that o_j obtains.

TCR–3   If S has more reason to perform a_i than to perform a_j, then this is so in virtue of the fact that S has more reason to desire that o_i obtains than to desire that o_j obtains.

TCR–1+2   S has more reason to perform a_i than to perform a_j if and only if S has more reason to desire that o_i obtains than to desire that o_j obtains.

TCR^1   (1) S has more reason to perform a_i than to perform a_j if S has more reason to desire p_i than to desire p_j; (2) S has more reason to perform a_i than to perform a_j only if S has more reason to desire p_i than to desire p_j; and (3) if S has more reason to perform a_i than to perform a_j, then this is so in virtue of the fact that S has more reason to desire p_i than to desire p_j.

TCR^2   S has more reason to perform a_i than to perform a_j if and only if, and because, the set of all the *non-pragmatic reasons* that S has for desiring that o_i obtains is weightier than the set of all the *non-pragmatic reasons* that S has for desiring that o_j obtains.

TCR³ S has at t_i more reason to perform a_i than to perform a_j just when, and because, S has at t_i more reason to desire that o_i obtains than to desire that o_j obtains.

TCR⁴ An agent's reasons for and against performing α_j are determined by her reasons for and against preferring certain outcomes to others, such that if S has most reason to perform α_j, then, of all the outcomes that S could bring about by performing some MSA that is, as of t_i, scrupulously securable by S, S has most reason to desire some subset of those that would result from S's performing an MSA that involves S's performing α_j.

TCR* An agent's reasons for and against performing α_j are determined by her reasons for and against preferring certain outcomes to others, such that S has at t_i more reason to perform a_i than to perform a_j just when, and because, S has at t_i more reason to desire p_i than to desire p_j, where p_i and p_j are the prospects of a_i and a_j, respectively.

TMS The view according to which all the following are true: (*a*) it is, as of t_i, objectively rationally permissible for S to perform a non-maximal set of actions, α_j, beginning at t_j $(t_i < t_j)$ if and only if, and because, it is, as of t_i, objectively rationally permissible for S to perform a maximal set of actions, MSA_i, that involves S's performing α_j; (*b*) it is, as of t_i, objectively rationally permissible for S to perform a maximal set of actions, MSA_i, if and only if, and because, MSA_i is one of the optimal MSAs that is, as of t_i, scrupulously securable by S; (*c*) MSA_i is one of the optimal MSAs that is, as of t_i, scrupulously securable by S if and only if, and because, MSA_i's prospect is not, on S's t_i-relative evaluative ranking, outranked by that of any alternative MSA that is, as of t_i, scrupulously securable by S; and (*d*) MSA_i's prospect is not, on S's t_i-relative evaluative ranking, outranked by that of any alternative MSA that is, as of t_i, scrupulously securable by S if and only if, and because, there is no alternative MSA that is, as of t_i, scrupulously securable by S whose prospect S has at t_i more reason, all things considered, to desire.

Commonsense Consequentialism

1

Why I Am Not a Utilitarian

§1.1 Utilitarianism: The good, the bad, and the ugly

Let me start with a confession. I used to be a hardcore utilitarian. According to utilitarianism, an act is morally permissible if and only if it maximizes aggregate utility.[1] And I held, rather simplistically, that aggregate utility just consists in the net sum of pleasure minus pain. What made me a *hardcore* utilitarian was my unapologetic stance regarding utilitarianism's counterintuitive implications. Someone would ask: Do you really think that it is permissible to torture an innocent child if that would produce the most aggregate utility? And I would respond: It is not just permissible; it is *obligatory*! That is the kind of simplistic and unapologetic utilitarian that I was. My views have, I would like to think, matured since then. Eventually, utilitarianism's counterintuitive implications were too much for even me to stomach.

What led to my conversion? It was not, as one might suppose, the sorts of counterintuitive implications that are typically cited in today's philosophy lectures and textbooks. Although it is often cited as one of utilitarianism's most counterintuitive implications, I do not find it utterly absurd to suppose that agents are, other things being equal, permitted to commit one murder (which I will define as the intentional killing of an innocent person) so as to prevent five murders. After all, the state of affairs in which five murders have been committed is, other things being equal, five times as bad as the one in which only one murder has been committed. Nor do I find it utterly absurd to suppose that agents are morally required to do some very demanding things—such as, to donate all their disposable income to hunger-relief organizations—if this will save hundreds of children from starving to death. After all, an agent's material wealth is not nearly as important as the lives of hundreds of children.

---

[1] The aggregate utility produced by an act is the sum of all the utility it produces minus the sum of all the disutility it produces, where utility is a measure of whatever it is that enhances a subject's welfare, and disutility is a measure of whatever it is that diminishes a subject's welfare. An act would maximize aggregate utility if and only if there is no available alternative act that would produce more aggregate utility than it would. And note that I use "utilitarianism" as shorthand for "maximizing act-utilitarianism."

3

What soured me on utilitarianism were not these counterintuitive implications (the bad), but the following two (the ugly). First, utilitarianism implies that agents are morally required to commit murder whenever doing so will produce the most aggregate utility, and, thus, even when the net gain would be quite small, as small as, say, one *utile*.[2] And let me just stipulate that a utile is the smallest possible unit of utility: equivalent to someone's experiencing the mildest of pleasures for the briefest of moments. Second, utilitarianism implies that agents should sacrifice, not only their disposable income, but even their own lives and the lives of those whom they love most whenever doing so will produce the most aggregate utility, and, thus, even when the net gain would be as small as one utile.[3] I find these implications utterly absurd.

I find them utterly absurd, for I find it incredible to suppose that such miniscule gains in aggregate utility could be sufficient to make it reasonable to perform such acts. Of course, I acknowledge that agents have some reason to maximize aggregate utility, but it seems that they have other reasons as well. For instance, it seems that I have a reason to preserve my own life apart from whether or not my doing so would maximize aggregate utility. And it seems that I also have a reason to refrain from murder apart from whether or not my doing so would maximize aggregate utility. What's more, it seems that these other reasons sometimes decisively oppose the reason that I have to maximize aggregate utility. If, for instance, my choice is between saving my own life (and let me tell you that it is a good one) and saving some stranger's life, and the only thing that speaks in favor of saving the stranger is that this would result in there being one more utile overall, then it seems that I have not just sufficient, but decisive, reason to save my own life. The reason that I have to favor my own life over that of some stranger's outweighs the reason that I have to maximize aggregate utility, for a net gain of one utile is simply not enough to rationally justify sacrificing my own life. Yet utilitarianism requires that I make such unreasonable sacrifices.

The fact that utilitarianism sometimes requires agents to act contrary to what they have decisive reason to do leads me to reject utilitarianism, for I believe that morality is rationally authoritative—that is, I believe that moral requirements are requirements of reason. Moral requirements seem to do more than just tell us how we must act in order to comply with certain rules. More importantly, they tell us how we must act if we are to act as we ought to act, all things considered. In this respect, morality differs from many other codes of conduct. Take the law, for instance. The law tells us how we must act in order to comply with certain legal rules, but it does not necessarily tell us how we ought, or have most reason, to act—at least, not all things considered. Indeed, there are times when we ought, all things considered, to violate the rules of law, as when one needs to get one's

---

[2] For a similar objection, see W. D. Ross 1930, p. 35.
[3] This objection comes from HOOKER 2000, pp. 151–152.

injured child to the emergency room as quickly as possible and can safely proceed through some intersection against the red light. But, unlike legal requirements, moral requirements seem to specify requirements of reason. Thus, I reject any moral theory, such as utilitarianism, that requires agents to act contrary to the requirements of reason.

Although I reject utilitarianism, there is, I admit, something quite compelling about it (the good). At utilitarianism's core is a certain compelling idea that explains why I and others have been led to accept it in spite of its wildly counterintuitive implications. The compelling idea seems to be that an act's deontic status is determined by the agent's reasons for preferring its outcome (where this includes everything that would be the case were the act to be performed) to those of the available alternatives such that it can never be morally wrong for her to act so as to bring about the outcome that she has most reason to want to obtain.[4] Since actions are the means by which agents affect how things go, it is only natural to suppose that how an agent should act depends on how she should want things to go. Thus, if she has most reason to want the world to turn out one way rather than another way, then she has most reason to act so as to ensure that it turns out that way rather than the other way.[5] If, for instance, she ought to prefer the world in which she has performed x to the one in which she has performed y, then she has more reason to perform x than to perform y. When this teleological conception of reasons is combined with the idea that moral requirements are requirements of reason such that it is never morally wrong for an agent to do that which she has most reason to do, we get the compelling idea that it is never morally wrong for an agent to act so as to bring about the outcome that she has most reason to want to obtain.

So I am torn. On the one hand, it seems to me that utilitarianism cannot be right insofar as it sometimes requires agents to act in ways that are contrary to reason. On the other hand, I find utilitarianism's core idea—that how we ought to act is determined by how we ought to want things to go—compelling. This book attempts to resolve the conflict. My hope is that the conflict can be resolved by accepting utilitarianism's teleological conception of reasons while rejecting its view that what each agent has most reason to want is that aggregate utility be

---

[4] Initially, this may not seem to be utilitarianism's compelling idea, but see chapter 2 for why I think that it is.

All acts are either permissible or impermissible. All permissible acts are either optional or obligatory. And all optional acts are either merely permissible or supererogatory. These are the deontic statuses that an act can have. (As we will see in chapter 4, the idea that an act is supererogatory is, for me, solely a deontic notion and does not depend on whether its performance is, given the agent's motives and intentions, praiseworthy.)

[5] Like many philosophers these days, I believe that not only are there reasons to intend to perform certain actions and to believe certain propositions, but also reasons to desire certain outcomes. See, for instance, PARFIT 2011, SCANLON 1998, and SKORUPSKI 2010.

maximized.[6] In adopting a more plausible view about what agents ought to want, I hope to end up with a substantive moral theory that embodies utilitarianism's teleological conception of reasons while avoiding nearly all, if not all, of its counterintuitive implications. This substantive moral theory is what I call *commonsense consequentialism*, and it is the view that I will be defending. Unfortunately, though, there is a lot of ground that I must cover before I will be able to state the view with sufficient clarity and precision. In the meantime, I will settle for mapping out the course ahead.

§1.2 The plan for the rest of the book

In the next chapter, I will argue against *traditional act-consequentialism* (or "TAC" for short): the view that an act is morally permissible if and only if it maximizes the (impersonal) good. Utilitarianism is but one species of this view, but, as I show, the whole genus is susceptible to the same counterargument that I sketched above.[7] That is, all traditional versions of act-consequentialism, and not just utilitarianism, are guilty of requiring agents to act contrary to what they have most reason to do. We should, therefore, reject all traditional versions of act-consequentialism, for, as I will argue, we should accept *moral rationalism*: the view that an act's deontic status is determined by the agent's reasons for and against performing it, such that she can be morally required to do only what she has most reason to do, all things considered.

Interestingly, although moral rationalism leads us to reject all traditional versions of act-consequentialism, it also compels us to accept *act-consequentialism*, more generally—the view that an act's deontic status is determined by the agent's reasons for and against preferring its outcome to those of the available alternatives. Or at least it does so when conjoined with the *teleological conception of practical reasons*. Very briefly, it does so via the following argument:

1.1   An act's deontic status is determined by the agent's reasons for and against performing it, such that, if a subject, S, is morally required to perform an act, *x*, then S has most reason to perform *x*.[8] (Moral Rationalism).

---

   [6] At this point, one may object that although utilitarianism is committed to a certain view about what is good, it is not committed to any view about what agents ought to want. I address this worry in the next chapter.

   [7] Utilitarianism (i.e., maximizing act-utilitarianism) is a species of traditional act-consequentialism (cf. EYAL 2008). Accordingly, utilitarianism is the view that holds both that traditional act-consequentialism is true and that an act maximizes the good if and only if it maximizes aggregate utility.

   [8] At least one previous reader thought that it would be clearer if I substituted "in such a way that" for "such that." I am not clear on what the difference is myself, but if it would make things clearer for the reader, I would be happy to have the reader make this substitution here and throughout the rest of the book, as appropriate.

1.2 An agent's reasons for and against performing a given act are determined by her reasons for and against preferring its outcome to those of the available alternatives, such that, if S has most reason to perform x, then, of all the outcomes that S could bring about, S has most reason to desire that x's outcome obtains. (The Teleological Conception of Practical Reasons).

1.3 Therefore, an act's deontic status is determined by the agent's reasons for and against preferring its outcome to those of the available alternatives, such that, if S is morally required to perform x, then, of all the outcomes that S could bring about, S has most reason to desire that x's outcome obtains.[9] (Act-Consequentialism).[10]

Of course, it may seem strange to equate act-consequentialism with 1.3, but one of the things that I argue in chapter 2 is that act-consequentialism is best construed as a theory that ranks outcomes, not according to their impersonal value, but according to how much reason the agent has to desire that each outcome obtains.

In chapter 3, I explain and defend the teleological conception of practical reasons (i.e., 1.2 above). I begin by explaining why my statement of the teleological conception of practical reasons differs from that of some of its critics (e.g., T. M. Scanlon and Elizabeth Anderson) in eschewing talk of both value and desirability. I then proceed to clear up some common and potential misconceptions about the view. I also rebut Scanlon's putative counterexamples to the teleological conception of practical reasons, cases where putatively "many of the reasons bearing on an action concern not the desirability of outcomes but rather the eligibility or ineligibility of various other reasons" (SCANLON 1998, p. 84). I conclude the chapter by arguing that we should accept the teleological conception of practical reasons, because it has the unsurpassed ability to systematize our considered convictions about practical reasons.

In chapter 4, I try both to motivate and to undertake what is known as the consequentializing project: the project of accommodating, under an act-consequentialist framework, the sorts of intuitive deontic verdicts that are typically thought to be compatible with only nonconsequentialist theories. I argue that, when both "outcome" and "act-consequentialism" are broadly construed, it turns out that any remotely plausible nonconsequentialist theory can be consequentialized. The recipe for consequentializing a nonconsequentialist theory is simple: take whatever

---

[9] This is written so not to exclude satisficing versions of act-consequentialism, which deny that it is always obligatory to produce the highest ranked outcome.

[10] Traditional act-consequentialism is a species of act-consequentialism. Accordingly, traditional act-consequentialism is the view that holds both that act-consequentialism is true and that an act produces an outcome that the agent has optimal reason to want to obtain if and only if it maximizes the good, impersonally construed. (S has *optimal reason* to φ if and only if there is no alternative, ψ, such that S has more reason to ψ than to φ.)

considerations that the nonconsequentialist theory holds to be relevant to determining the deontic statuses of actions, and insist that those considerations are relevant to determining the proper ranking of outcomes. In this way, the consequentialist can produce a ranking of outcomes that when combined with her criterion of rightness yields the same set of deontic verdicts that the nonconsequentialist theory yields. The motive for consequentializing is, as I explain, to arrive at a moral theory that comports with our considered moral convictions without having to forfeit, as nonconsequentialist theories do, the compelling idea that an act's deontic status is determined by the agent's reasons for preferring its outcome to those of the available alternatives such that it can never be morally wrong for her to act so as to bring about the outcome that she has most reason to want to obtain.

In chapter 5, I continue with the consequentializing project by defending a rather peculiar version of act-consequentialism, which I call *dual-ranking act-consequentialism*:

> **DRAC** S's performing *x* is morally permissible if and only if, and because, there is no available act alternative that would produce an outcome that S has both more moral reason and more reason, all things considered, to want to obtain than to want *x*'s outcome to obtain.

Unlike more traditional versions of act-consequentialism, DRAC does not take the deontic status of an action to be a function of some *evaluative* ranking of outcomes.[11] Rather, it takes the deontic status of an action to be a function of a *non-evaluative* ranking that is in turn a function of two auxiliary, evaluative rankings: namely, (1) a ranking of outcomes in terms of how much moral reason the agent has to want each of them to obtain; and (2) a ranking of outcomes in terms of how much reason, all things considered, the agent has to want each of them to obtain. I argue that DRAC is promising in that it can accommodate certain features of commonsense morality that no single-ranking version of act-consequentialism can accommodate: namely, agent-centered options, supererogatory acts, and the self-other asymmetry.

I spend the bulk of the chapter defending DRAC against the charge that its dual-ranking structure is unmotivated. I argue that DRAC's dual-ranking structure is forced upon the act-consequentialist given that non-moral reasons can *successfully counter* moral reasons and thereby prevent them from giving rise to moral requirements.[12] For I argue that what an agent is morally obligated to do is not

---

[11] An evaluative ranking of outcomes is a ranking in terms of the agent's reasons (or some subset of her reasons) for preferring each outcome to the available alternatives.

[12] To say that the reasons to φ successfully counter the reasons to ψ (ψ ≠ φ) is to say that the reasons to φ prevent the reasons to ψ from being decisive by, say, equaling, outweighing, undermining, or silencing them. Another possibility is that the reasons to φ are incommensurable with the reasons to ψ such that there is sufficient reason both to φ and to ψ.

simply a function of what the balance of moral reasons supports her doing, nor is it a function of only what the balance of all reasons (moral and non-moral) supports her doing. It is, rather, a function of both. An act is morally obligatory if and only if it is what the agent has both most moral reason and most reason, all reasons considered, to do.

In chapter 6, I defend DRAC and its way of accommodating agent-centered options against Shelly Kagan's objection that if we defend the existence of agent-centered options by arguing that one's reasons for promoting one's own interests can successfully counter the moral reasons that one has for doing what is best for others, then what we end up with is a rational requirement to promote one's own interests, whereas what we wanted was both a moral, *and* a rational, option either to promote one's own interests or to do what is best for others (1991). Contrary to Kagan, I argue that we do not end up with a rational requirement to promote one's own interests—at least, we do not if we adopt, as I argue we should, a certain theory of objective rationality, namely, *rational securitism*. According to rational securitism, the objective rational status of an individual action is a function of the role that it plays in some larger plan of action that unfolds over time, and this plan of action, which may contain multiple actions performed at various times, is to be evaluated not with respect to whether the agent will be able to perform each part of the plan as the time for each arises, but with respect to whether, in embarking on the plan *now*, the agent will be able to ensure (*now*) that she will, in the future, perform all the corresponding parts of the plan.[13]

I argue that accepting rational securitism not only allows us to meet Kagan's objection, but also allows us to account for what Joseph Raz calls *the basic belief*: the belief that, in most typical choice situations, the relevant reasons do not require performing one particular act, but instead permit performing any of numerous act alternatives (1999, p. 100). What's more, I argue that moral securitism, which is the moral analogue of rational securitism, offers a better account of how agents morally ought to act when their future actions are not under their present deliberative control than either of its two main rivals—actualism and possibilism—do.[14]

In chapter 7 (the concluding chapter), I spell out what I take to be the most plausible version of consequentialism: namely, commonsense consequentialism. I state the argument for it and explain some of the advantages it has over traditional versions of consequentialism. In the process, I argue that the best version of consequentialism will: (1) evaluate sets of actions and not just individual actions; (2) presuppose (moral) securitism as opposed to actualism or possibilism; (3) index permissions and obligations to times; and (4) possess a dual-ranking structure on the model of dual-ranking act-consequentialism. As we will see, though, commonsense consequentialism, unlike dual-ranking act-consequentialism, is a version of

---

[13] I thank Mark Schroeder for this apt way of summarizing the view.

[14] The discussion of moral securitism actually does not appear until chapter 7.

indirect consequentialism, not act-consequentialism. Thus, on commonsense consequentialism, the moral permissibility of an individual action is determined not by how its outcome ranks relative to its alternatives, but by whether or not it is contained within some maximal set of actions whose outcome ranks at least as high as that of any alternative maximal set of actions. The resulting theory is one that can accommodate all the basic features of commonsense morality: imperfect duties, special obligations, supererogatory acts, agent-favoring options, agent-sacrificing options, agent-centered restrictions, and the self-other asymmetry. I then end the chapter by summarizing what has been shown and explaining what remains to be shown.

***

Before proceeding to chapter 2, I will, in the following three sections, address three preliminary matters. In the next section, §1.3, I will state my aims: that is, what it is that I aim to accomplish in these pages. Then, in §1.4, I will explain the sense of "ought" and "reason" with which I will be primarily concerned. And, in the last section, §1.5, I will describe the conventions that I will be following throughout the book—conventions regarding citations, symbolic notation, the numbering of propositions, and so on.

§1.3 My aims

Ultimately, I will be arguing for a certain moral theory: commonsense consequentialism. My aim, though, is not to convince anyone that commonsense consequentialism is the correct moral theory. That would be too ambitious, for the arguments that I will be presenting here are far from conclusive. In fact, I am not confident that commonsense consequentialism is the correct moral theory myself. I certainly would not wager any significant sum of money on its being the correct moral theory. There are at least two reasons why I and others should withhold their full endorsement of the view even after taking account of all the arguments in the book.

First, there will be some question about whether commonsense consequentialism can, as I hope, avoid the sorts of counterintuitive implications that plague more traditional versions of consequentialism. Let me explain. Roughly speaking, commonsense consequentialism holds that the deontic status of an action is a function of the agent's reasons for preferring its outcome to those of the available alternatives. If, for instance, an agent ought to prefer the outcome in which she has saved her lover to the outcome in which she has instead saved two strangers, then, according to commonsense consequentialism, it cannot be that she ought to save the two strangers rather than her lover. But how do we know which outcome the agent ought to prefer? Unfortunately, very little has been written on the topic, and there is, as far as I know, no fully worked out theory concerning what agents have reason to want and to prefer.[15] I certainly do not have such a theory. I will, then, have nothing more than our pre-theoretical intuitions to appeal to in trying to determine what it is that agents have reason to want and to prefer. I will argue that these pre-theoretical intuitions support the contention that commonsense consequentialism avoids the sorts of counterintuitive implications that plague more traditional versions of consequentialism. But, admittedly, this is all rather speculative since I do not have anything close to a fully developed theory about what agents have reason to want and to prefer. We should, therefore, withhold our full confidence in the view until these pre-theoretical intuitions have been vindicated by our best theory about what agents have reason to want and to prefer.

Second, since I will not, for lack of space, endeavor to conduct a thorough assessment of how commonsense consequentialism compares to its leading rivals, we cannot be confident that commonsense consequentialism is superior to its rivals. What I hope to do instead is to develop the theory as best I can and to present it as part of a coherent picture concerning our commonsense practical views—that is, as part of a coherent picture concerning our commonsense views about the nature and substance of both morality and rationality. Since I do not have space here to make the necessary comparative assessments, I cannot claim that commonsense consequentialism does the best job of explaining and systematizing our various moral intuitions, nor that it does the best job of cohering with our other intuitions concerning practical matters. I can claim only that it does an excellent job in each case.

My aim, then, is not to convince readers that commonsense consequentialism is the correct moral theory, but only to convince them that it is a promising moral theory—one that deserves to be taken seriously and one that is worthy of further consideration. If I succeed in achieving even this modest aim, I will be more than satisfied.

Although the primary aim of the book is to defend a particular consequentialist moral theory, the book will be of interest to more than just those concerned with consequentialist moral theory. Since I seek to defend commonsense consequentialism as part of a coherent whole concerning our commonsense views about the nature and substance of both morality and rationality, it should be of interest to anyone interested in metaethics and/or normative ethics. For beyond offering an account of morality, I offer accounts of practical reasons, practical rationality, and the objective/subjective obligation distinction. And beyond offering accounts of such ethical features as imperfect duties, supererogatory acts, and agent-centered options, I offer accounts of the relationships between

---

[15] This, no doubt, is due to the influence that David Hume has had. Nevertheless, it is an assumption of this book that, contrary to Hume, reason is the master of, not a slave to, desire (see, e.g., SCANLON 1998, chap. 1).

reasons and value, value and desire, reasons and desire, and, most importantly, between reasons and morality.

§1.4 Objective oughts and objective reasons

Throughout this book, I will be concerned with what agents *objectively* ought to do—that is, with what they ought to do given what the reason-constituting facts about their choice situation happen to be, and so irrespective both of what they take those facts to be and of what their evidence suggests that those facts might be. More precisely, an agent objectively ought to perform some particular alternative if and only if it is, in fact, the *best* alternative. The best alternative is not necessarily the one that would produce the best outcome. For to say that some alternative is the agent's best alternative is just to say that it is the alternative that she has most reason to perform, and, of course, it is an open question whether an agent has most reason to perform the alternative that would produce the best outcome.[16] Nevertheless, for the purposes of illustration, let us suppose that, in some particular instance, what an agent has most reason to do is to maximize the good. In that case, what she objectively ought to do is to perform the alternative that would, in fact, maximize the good, and this is so even if she believes that some other act would maximize the good, even if her evidence suggests that some other act would maximize the good, and even if she reasonably believes, contrary to fact, that she ought to refrain from maximizing the good.

When I talk about an agent's reasons, I am talking about her *objective reasons*. To understand what an objective reason is, consider the following example. Suppose that Ronnie and Bradley have both been invited to the same party. At the party, there will be good food, great company, excellent music, and even some dancing. But whereas Ronnie enjoys dancing, Bradley does not.[17] And let us suppose that neither Ronnie nor Bradley is aware of (or has any evidence for) the fact that there will be dancing at the party. Nevertheless, it seems that this fact counts as a reason (i.e., an objective reason) for Ronnie, but not for Bradley, to go to the party. As I would put it, Ronnie has an additional reason to go to the party—namely, that there will be dancing there.

Some philosophers would balk at my putting it in this way. Although they would accept that there *is* an additional reason for Ronnie to go to the party in virtue of the fact that there will be dancing there, they would deny that Ronnie *has* this reason to go. On their view, we must distinguish between (*i*) the existence

---

[16] For an excellent discussion of this issue, see HURLEY 2009, especially chapter 5.

[17] I borrow this example from SCHROEDER 2007b. See SCHROEDER 2009 for more on the distinction between objective and subjective reasons as well as for more on the distinction between objective and subjective oughts. See also J. ROSS 2006a (chaps. 7 and 8) for a useful discussion of this distinction.

of a reason for S to perform *x* and (*ii*) S's having a reason to perform *x*. On their view, S's *having* a reason to perform *x* is a matter of S's "possessing" that reason in virtue of bearing some epistemic relation to that reason, such as being aware of it or having sufficient evidence for it.[18] I, by contrast, think that we can appropriately talk of S's having a reason to perform *x* even if S is completely unaware of (and lacks any evidence for) any fact that counts in favor of S's performing *x*. Let me note, though, that even if I am wrong about this, I can say everything I want to say only using different words. So if I am wrong about this, then throughout the book I will need to replace all talk of S's having a reason, more reason, most reason, or decisive reason to φ with talk of there being a reason, more reason, most reason, or decisive reason for S to φ. And, thus, with regard to the objective sense of "ought," I would need to say "S objectively ought to perform *x* if and only if *there is* most reason for S to perform *x*" as opposed to "S objectively ought to perform *x* if and only if *S has* most reason to perform *x*." But since I think that it is perfectly fine to talk about S's having a reason to do *x* even in those instances in which S is unaware of (and lacks any evidence for) any fact that counts in favor of S's performing *x*, I will continue to talk and write in this way. If any readers object, they can make the appropriate substitutions throughout the book.

Returning now to "ought," we can better understand the objective sense of "ought" by noting that we use "ought" in this sense both when we wonder whether we ought to act as we believe that we should and when we assess, on the basis of twenty-twenty hindsight, whether we ought to have acted as we did. To illustrate, suppose that I am trying to defuse a bomb and that I am not sure whether it is the red or the green wire that I should cut. That is, I am not sure which one I must cut in order to deactivate it and which one, if cut, will detonate it. Even if the evidence that is available to me strongly supports my contention that cutting the green wire will deactivate the bomb, I may still wonder whether I ought to do so. Indeed, as I reach out to cut the green wire, I may wonder aloud: "Is this really what I ought to be doing?" Now let us suppose that after cutting the green wire I wake up in the hospital, for, as it turns out, I needed to cut the red wire to deactivate it. I may, then, say to myself: "I ought to have cut the red wire." In both of these two quoted sentences, I would be using "ought" in what I am calling the objective sense.[19]

---

[18] See SCHROEDER 2008a for a critique of this view—cf. LORD 2010. I agree with the proponents of this view that there can be decisive reason for S to φ, and yet, if S lacks sufficient evidence for believing that this is so, then it would be unreasonable to expect her to φ or to criticize her for failing to φ.

[19] This suggests another way of getting a grip on the notion of what an agent objectively ought to do: S objectively ought to perform *x* if and only if performing *x* is what a normatively conscientious person would do if she faced S's choice of alternatives and was aware of all the relevant reason-constituting facts. By contrast, S subjectively ought to perform *x* if and only if performing *x* is what a normatively conscientious person would do if she were in the exact same situation that S was in, facing S's choice of alternatives and all the normative and non-normative uncertainty that goes along with being in S's epistemic position.

We can talk not only about what an agent objectively ought to do, but also about what she is objectively required to do and about what she is objectively permitted (or not permitted) to do.[20] An agent is objectively required to perform an act if and only if she has decisive reason to perform that act. And she is objectively permitted to perform an act if and only if she has sufficient reason to perform that act—in other words, if and only if she does not have decisive reason to refrain from performing it.

Thus far, I have been talking about a particular objective "ought": the "ought" of objective rationality—that is, the "ought" that concerns what an agent has most reason to do, *all things considered*. There is also, however, an objective *moral* ought. An agent objectively morally ought to perform some particular alternative if and only if it is the morally best alternative—that is, the one that she has most *moral* reason to perform. Furthermore, an agent is objectively morally required to perform an alternative if and only if she has decisive moral reason to perform that alternative. And she is objectively morally permitted to perform an alternative if and only if she has sufficient moral reason to perform that alternative. The reader should assume that, throughout the book, I am talking either about what agents *objectively* morally ought to do or about what agents *objectively* ought to do, all things considered—unless, of course, I explicitly state otherwise.

Although my focus will be on the objective "ought," I do not claim that this is the only "ought."[21] Nor do I claim that it is the one that directly guides us in our first-person deliberations about what to do. Indeed, it is not, for we can base our first-person practical deliberations only on what we *think* is the case, not on what *is*, in fact, the case.[22] Furthermore, there is, at most, only a tenuous connection between an agent's being objectively morally required to perform an act and its being appropriate to advise her to perform it and/or to blame (or otherwise criticize) her for failing to perform it.[23] So I readily admit that the objective "ought" is neither the one that figures most prominently in our first-person practical delib-

---

[20] Here, I am using "ought to φ" in a sense that does not imply a requirement to φ. For instance, I may tell my dinner companion that she ought to try the duck, but, in so doing, I would not be claiming that she is in any sense required to try the duck. This sense of "ought" can be called the *advisory sense* of "ought." Another example of the advisory sense of "ought" comes from FERRY 2009: "You really ought to visit your mother on her birthday, but you have got to at least send a card." See also MCNAMARA 1996b.

[21] I should note that I am not committed to the view that, in ordinary English, the word "ought" is ambiguous between an objective sense and a subjective sense. My view is only that we need to draw the distinction between objective and subjective oughts in order to make sense of various normative facts regardless of whether there is such a distinction in natural language or not. See J. ROSS 2006a, p. 210.

[22] Derek Parfit (2011, p. 161) and Andrew Sepielli (2009) both make this point.

[23] There is, however, an essential connection between an agent's being objectively morally required to perform x and its being appropriate to blame her for *freely and knowledgeably* performing x—see §2.5.

erations nor the one that figures most prominently in to our everyday practices of blaming and advising. Nevertheless, objective oughts and reasons are of the utmost importance, for they are more fundamental than subjective oughts and reasons—or so I shall argue. But, first, let me explain why the objective "ought" is not the one that figures most prominently in our first-person practical deliberations or in our everyday practices of blaming and advising. To see this, it will be helpful to consider the following example, which I borrow, with minor revisions, from Derek Parfit (2011, pp. 159–160):

> *Mine Shafts:* A hundred miners are trapped underground in one of two mine shafts. Floodwaters are rising, and the miners are in danger of drowning. Sally can close one of three floodgates. Depending both on which floodgate she closes and on which shaft the miners are in, the results will be one of the following six possible outcomes, which are depicted in table 1.1.

Assume that Sally does not know which shaft the miners are in, but she knows all the above as well as the fact that, given the available evidence, there is a 50% (subjective) chance that the miners are in Shaft A as well as a 50% (subjective) chance that the miners are in Shaft B. As a matter of fact, though, the miners are in Shaft A.

It is clear that Sally objectively ought to close Gate 1, for Sally should, in this instance, do whatever would bring about the best available outcome, and o_1 is the best available outcome given that the miners are in Shaft A. Nevertheless, Sally, being a morally conscientious person, closes Gate 3. She closes Gate 3 even though she knows that closing Gate 3 is not what she objectively ought to do. She knows that there is a 50% chance that she objectively ought to close Gate 1 as well as a 50% chance that she objectively ought to close Gate 2, but absolutely no chance that she objectively ought to close Gate 3.

We may wonder, though, why a morally conscientious person would do what she knows that she objectively ought not to do. The answer lies with the fact that a morally conscientious person will be concerned not only with whether or not her acts are (objectively) morally permissible but also with how morally good/bad

Table 1.1

		The miners are in...	
		Shaft A	*Shaft B*
	Gate 1	o_1: Sally saves 100 lives	o_2: Sally saves no lives
Sally closes...	Gate 2	o_3: Sally saves no lives	o_4: Sally saves 100 lives
	Gate 3	o_5: Sally saves 90 lives	o_6: Sally saves 90 lives

her morally permissible/impermissible acts are.[24] Some morally permissible acts are much better than others. For instance, spending the afternoon volunteering for Oxfam is morally better than wasting the afternoon getting drunk, but both may be morally permissible. And some morally impermissible acts are much worse than others. For instance, committing genocide is much worse than telling a little lie, and killing someone with malice aforethought is morally worse than accidently, but negligently, hitting someone.

In light of the fact that permissible/impermissible acts come in varying degrees of moral goodness/badness, a morally conscientious person will do what she knows to be objectively wrong when she knows that trying to do what is objectively right risks committing a much graver wrong.[25] Thus, Sally closes Gate 3, knowing that this is objectively wrong. She does so because she knows that were she to try to do what is objectively right by closing either Gate 1 or Gate 2, she risks saving no one. And although saving only ninety miners is just as objectively wrong as saving no miners, the latter is a much graver wrong.[26] Thus, being a morally conscientious person, Sally saves ninety miners rather than risk saving none. So, as the above example illustrates, the objective "ought" is not the one that directly guides the first-person practical deliberations of morally conscientious persons.[27]

The above example also illustrates how it can be inappropriate to blame (or otherwise criticize) someone for doing what is objectively wrong as well as how it can be appropriate to blame someone for doing what is objectively right. Consider that we would not blame Sally for closing Gate 3 even if she did so knowing that this was objectively wrong. But we would blame her for closing Gate 1 even though this is objectively right. We would blame her, because, in closing Gate 1, she would be taking an unacceptable risk—a risk that no morally conscientious person would take. Since we think that it is *subjectively wrong* to take such risks, we would blame her for closing Gate 1.[28] The objective "ought," then, is not the one that is most directly relevant to our assessments of blame.[29]

---

[24] I borrow this point from BYKVIST 2009. See also GRAHAM 2010.

[25] I use "right" and "wrong" as synonyms for "permissible" and "impermissible," respectively.

[26] Impermissibility does not come in degrees; an act cannot be more (or less) impermissible than another—see, for instance, ALEXANDER 2008. By contrast, the moral goodness of an act does come in degrees. Some morally impermissible acts are morally worse than others. To say that one act is morally worse than another is just to say that there is more moral reason to refrain from performing the one than to refrain from performing the other. Alastair Norcross (2006a, 2006b) has argued that if the rightness (permissibility?) of actions is determined by the goodness of their outcomes, then, since goodness is gradable, then rightness must be gradable as well. For a reply to Norcross, see LAWLOR 2009a, LAWLOR 2009b, and §5.5.

[27] For a subtle and well-developed account of what does guide a morally conscientious person in her first-person practical deliberations, see ZIMMERMAN 2008.

[28] Roughly speaking, an act is subjectively wrong if and only if an agent in the normal frame of mind would be blameworthy for performing it—see GIBBARD 1990, pp. 44–45.

[29] Although the objective "ought" is not the one that is most salient to our *assessments* of blame, there is an essential connection between the objective "ought" and blameworthiness—see §2.5.

What about advice? Is there not some essential connection between what a fully informed and well-meaning advisor would advise an agent to do and what that agent objectively ought to do? This is what some philosophers claim, but they are, I believe, mistaken.[30] For one, whether a fully informed and well-meaning advisor should advise an agent to act as the agent objectively should depends on how the agent would react to the advice. If, for instance, the advisor knows that the agent would do the opposite of whatever she advises, she should, perhaps, advise the agent to do the opposite of what she objectively ought to do. And note that even here the connection is somewhat tenuous as the qualifier "perhaps" is meant to indicate, for whether a fully informed and well-meaning advisor should advise an agent to do *x* (even assuming that the advice will be taken) depends on whether advising that agent to do *x* is *the advisor's* best alternative, not on whether *x* is *the agent's* best alternative, and it is only the latter that determines what the agent objectively ought to do.

To illustrate, suppose that, in *Mine Shafts*, a fully informed and well-meaning advisor named Rick is in a position to advise Sally about which gate to close. Further suppose that the evil, but trustworthy, Boris has promised Rick that unless he advises Sally to close Gate 2, he is going to kill a thousand other innocent people. In this case, it seems that Rick should advise Sally to do what is objectively wrong, namely, to close Gate 2. So, from the fact that Rick, a fully informed and well-meaning advisor, ought (in every sense) to advise Sally to do *x*, it does not follow that Sally objectively ought to do *x*.

It may seem, though, that at least this much is true: if Sally objectively ought to do *x*, then Rick ought to advise Sally to do *x* if his doing so would have the direct effect of causing Sally to do *x* and no other direct effects, such as causing Boris to kill a thousand other innocent people.[31] But even this much is debatable, for we might think that whereas what Rick ought to do depends on what is his best alternative, what Sally ought to do depends on what is her best alternative. And it may be that, although the best alternative for Rick is to advise Sally to do *x*, *x* is not Sally's best alternative.

To illustrate, consider a different case—one that again involves Rick in the role of advisor and Sally in the role of advisee, but one that does not involve any

---

[30] At times, Derek Parfit (2011, p. 152) seems to make this mistake, equating what I objectively ought to do with what "any fully informed adviser ought to have told me that I ought to do." Joshua Gert (2004, p. 140) gives an account of the objective rational status of an action in terms of its having consequences that virtually everyone could see as allowing "someone sincerely to advise someone else to do it." Frank Jackson and Robert Pargetter (1986, p. 237) say, "If the *right* moral advice is to say no…, then what else can we conclude but that he [objectively] ought to say no?" And Jennie Louise (2009, p. 336) claims that it is my objective obligation that I φ in circumstances C "if and only if my fully informed and rational counterpart would advise me to φ in C."

[31] We should allow, though, that her advice may have other indirect effects—that is, the effects that Sally's doing *x* would have.

miners. Suppose that, in this new case, Rick must advise Sally either to hit or to refrain from hitting her daughter. Assume that this is the only issue on which Rick can advise Sally and that Sally will hit her daughter if and only if Rick advises her to do so. Further suppose that if Sally does not hit her daughter, she's going to kill her son. Assume that she *could* refrain both from hitting her daughter and from killing her son, as all she needs to do is to decide now to go straight to the gym and get her aggression out by hitting a punching bag. But since Sally has no intention of going to the gym, what she *would* do if she refrains from hitting her daughter is kill her son.[32]

Now, Rick's best alternative is to advise Sally to hit her daughter, for the only alternative available to him is to refrain from giving her this advice; in which case, Sally will do much worse, killing her son. In fact, no matter what Rick does, Sally is going to hurt one of her two children. Given this, the best alternative available to Rick is to advise Sally to hit her daughter—at least, this way no one will be killed. But, unlike Rick, Sally can ensure that she does not hurt anyone. All she has to do is to decide now to go the gym and get her aggression out by hitting a punching bag. So Sally's best alternative involves her venting her anger, not on her children, but on some punching bag. Here, then, is a case where the best alternative for Rick is to advise Sally to hit her daughter and yet Sally's hitting her daughter is not her best alternative. We might conclude, therefore, that some-times an advisor should advise an advisee to do something that the advisee objec-tively ought not to do (FELDMAN 1986, p. 56).[33]

We have seen, then, that whether an agent objectively ought to do x is not what is most important in determining whether it is appropriate to blame her for doing x or even in determining whether one should advise her to do x. We have also seen that the objective sense of "ought" is not the one that figures most prominently in our first-person deliberations about what to do. The reason that we cannot base our first-person practical deliberations on what we objectively ought to do is that we are always to some degree uncertain about what we objec-tively ought to do.[34] There are two sources of such uncertainty: non-normative uncertainty (i.e., uncertainty about matters of non-normative fact) and norma-tive uncertainty (i.e., uncertainty about matters of normative fact). Given uncer-tainty about such matters, we sometimes subjectively ought to do what we know to be objectively impermissible. This follows given the following plausible principle:

---

[32] I am using "could" and "would" in their ordinary senses. For instance, it seems perfectly natural for someone to say: "I could hit my child, but that is not something that I would ever do."

[33] I will have much more to say about this sort of case in chapter 7.

[34] For instructive and subtle accounts of what we ought (in some non-objective sense) to do when we do not know what we ought to do in the objective sense, see J. ROSS 2006b, SEPIELLI 2009, SEPIELLI 2010, and ZIMMERMAN 2008. And see BYKVIST 2009, GRAHAM 2010, and MOLLER 2009 for some poi-gnant criticisms of ZIMMERMAN 2008.

1.4 If an agent believes that her φ-ing has more expected *deontic value* than any other available alternative, then she subjectively ought to φ.[35]

The deontic value of an act is a measure of how much (objective) reason there is to perform it, and we get the expected deontic value of an action "by multiplying the subjective probability that some practical comparative is true by the objective [i.e., deontic] value of that action if it is true, doing the same for all of the other practical comparatives, and adding up the results"—*practical comparatives* are anything of the form: the balance of reasons favors S's doing *x* as opposed to *y* (SEPIELLI 2009, pp. 7 and 11).[36]

To illustrate the plausibility of 1.4, we need only look to examples such as *Mine Shafts*. Sally knows that closing Gate 3 is objectively impermissible. But she also knows that closing Gate 3 is the alternative with the highest expected deontic value, for Sally is, we will assume, certain that the balance of reasons favors her closing whichever gate would result in the most miners being saved. Given her certainty with regard to this normative fact, we can represent the expected deontic value of each of her alternatives simply as a function of the probability that the miners are in a particular shaft multiplied by the number of miners that would be saved by her closing a given gate on the assumption that they are in that shaft, which is what I have done in table 1.2. Since Sally knows that her closing Gate 3 has the highest expected deontic value, it is, given 1.4, subjectively wrong for Sally to do anything but close Gate 3.

Table 1.2

Alternative	Expected Deontic Value
Closing Gate 1	$(0.5 \times 100) + (0.5 \times 0) = 50$
Closing Gate 2	$(0.5 \times 0) + (0.5 \times 100) = 50$
Closing Gate 3	$(0.5 \times 90) + (0.5 \times 90) = 90$

[35] If the reader prefers, we could formulate this principle as well as the following principles in terms of what the agent ought to believe given her evidence as opposed to what she actually believes, as I have done here. In that case, the reader should just substitute "reasonably believes" for "believes" where appropriate. For why I have chosen to formulate these principles in terms of the agent's actual beliefs as opposed to her reasonable beliefs, see H. M. SMITH FORTHCOMING.

[36] For a more complete account, see SEPIELLI 2009. To avoid confusion, I have substituted Sepielli's term "objective value" with Zimmerman's less misleading term "deontic value" (ZIMMERMAN 1996, pp. 14–15). Regardless of which term we use, the notion to which it refers is meant to be a theory-neutral one. An act's objective/deontic value is just a measure of how much (objective) reason there is for the agent to perform it. Thus, we can hold that an agent subjectively ought to do what has the highest expected deontic value without committing ourselves to any substantive view about what she objectively ought to do. Also, along with the notion of an act's deontic value, there is the notion of an act's deontic moral value, which is a measure of how much moral reason there is for the agent to perform it. Thus, the moral analogue of 1.4 is: "If an agent believes that her φ-ing has more expected deontic moral value than any other available alternative, then she subjectively morally ought to φ."

Of course, 1.4 is not the only plausible principle concerning what agents subjectively ought to do. The following principles are also plausible:

1.5 If an agent believes (1) that her φ-ing is an atomic act (that is, a positive act that is not equivalent to the disjunction of two relevantly different positive acts), (2) that she is objectively required to φ, and (3) that there is no chance that she is objectively required to refrain from φ-ing, then she is subjectively required to φ.[37]

1.6 If an agent believes that there is a fair chance that her φ-ing is objectively wrong and that there is no chance that her refraining from φ-ing is objectively wrong, and if there is no chance that her refraining from φ-ing would, on balance, be worse for her or for others than her φ-ing, then she is subjectively required to refrain from φ-ing.

1.7 If an agent believes that she is likely to face the choice of whether or not to ψ, that whether or not she is objectively required to ψ depends on whether or not p is true, and that by φ-ing she could come to be in a better epistemic position with respect to p, then she is, other things being equal, subjectively required to φ.

Of course, this list is not meant to be exhaustive, and I do not have any systematic account of such principles. Nevertheless, it seems clear that any plausible, informative principle of this sort is going to need to appeal, as do 1.4–1.7, to some objective normative notion, such as the notion of what an agent has objective reason to do, the notion of what an agent objectively ought to do, or the notion of what an agent is objectively required to do. Those that do not appeal to any such objective normative notion will, I believe, turn out to be either implausible or uninformative.[38] To illustrate the vice of implausibility, take the following principle:

---

[37] This is based on a principle that comes from J. Ross 2006a, p. 218. If we let φ range over negative acts (i.e., acts of refraining from performing some positive act) as well as positive acts, we would get the counterintuitive result that Sally is subjectively required to refrain from closing Gate 3 given that she knows that she is objectively required to refrain from closing Gate 3. And if we let φ range over disjunctive acts, we would get the counterintuitive result that Sally is subjectively required to close either Gate 1 or Gate 2, because she is objectively required to close either Gate 1 or Gate 2.

Also, note that given this principle, there is a sense in which objective norms *are* action-guiding. After all, the belief that one is objectively required to φ and that φ is an atomic act will, given 1.5, lead the normatively conscientious agent to believe that she is subjectively required to φ. And this, presumably, will lead her to φ. So even if our first-person practical deliberations are not directly based on our judgments about what we are objectively required to do, it will sometimes be indirectly based on such judgments—see J. Ross 2006a, p. 217.

[38] I am concerned with only principles that are universally quantified over agents, for it seems to me that, qua moral philosopher, these are the sorts of principles that I should be providing. Thus, all the principles that I discuss here are implicitly universally quantified over agents. Nevertheless, I

1.8　It is subjectively permissible for an agent to φ if and only if her φ-ing would maximize expected utility.

This principle is implausible and not just because utilitarianism is implausible. Even if we were to grant utilitarianism (the view according to which it is [objectively] permissible for an agent to φ if and only if her φ-ing would maximize utility), 1.8 would still be implausible, precisely because it fails to appeal to the agent's (reasonable) beliefs about objective normative notions.

To illustrate, suppose that Peter is considering whether to murder Smith. Assume that Peter's murdering Smith would maximize both actual and expected utility, as Smith's organs could then be used to save Jones. But assume that Peter's refraining from murdering Smith would also maximize both actual and expected utility, for the actual and expected utility of saving Jones would only just offset the actual and expected disutility of murdering Smith. Assume, then, that the two options are tied for first place with regard to both actual and expected utility. Assume that Peter justifiably believes there is no chance that his refraining from murdering Smith is objectively wrong and that there is some subjective chance (whatever subjective chance there is that utilitarianism is false) that murdering Smith is objectively wrong. Assume that Peter's refraining from murdering Smith is, on balance, no worse for him or for others than his murdering Smith. Lastly, assume that Peter is in "the normal frame of mind" and thus is morally blameworthy (and/or rationally criticizable) for any subjectively impermissible acts that he performs.[39]

In this case, 1.8 implies that Peter's murdering Smith is subjectively permissible and, thus, not blameworthy. But, surely, given Peter's reasonable uncertainty with respect to utilitarianism's correctness, Peter would be blameworthy for murdering Smith. In murdering Smith, Peter would be taking a big subjective risk of doing what is objectively wrong. And there is no good reason for Peter to take this risk. After all, his refraining from murdering Smith carries no subjective risk of doing what is objectively wrong. And his refraining from murdering Smith is, on balance, no worse for him or for others than his murdering Smith. Thus, it seems that 1.6, not 1.8, gives the most plausible verdict in this case. Whereas 1.8 implausibly implies that Peter's murdering Smith is subjectively permissible, 1.6 rightly implies that Peter's murdering Smith is subjectively impermissible. So, given the

admit that one could come up with plausible and informative principles about what some particular agent who has certain specific credences regarding the relevant objective normative facts subjectively ought to do and that such a principle need not explicitly refer to any objective normative notion. But note that one would need to appeal to the agent's credences regarding the relevant objective normative facts when constructing such a principle.

[39]　Again, I am assuming that, roughly speaking, an act is subjectively wrong if and only if an agent in the normal frame of mind would be blameworthy for performing it—see GIBBARD 1990, pp. 44–45.

plausibility of principles such as 1.6, it seems that principles, such as 1.8, that seek to provide substantive answers about what agents subjectively ought to do without appealing to any objective normative notion are all going to turn out to be implausible.[40]

As I have just suggested, the point about the implausibility of 1.8 generalizes. To illustrate, suppose that F is some feature of actions that does not appeal to any objective normative notion. Suppose, for instance, that "F" stands for "an act that would cause the death of a serial pedophile." Any principle that holds that an agent subjectively ought to φ if φ is F (or if the agent believes that φ is F) is going to be implausible precisely because it does not appeal to the agent's beliefs about some objective normative notion. Unless the agent believes (or ought to believe) that she objectively ought to perform acts that are F, it cannot be that she subjectively ought to perform acts that are F (or acts that she believes that are F). For if she, instead, believes (and, perhaps, reasonably so) that she objectively ought to refrain from performing acts that are F, then she subjectively ought not to perform acts that are F (or acts that she believes that are F). So, again, we find that any plausible, informative principle about what an agent subjectively ought to do must appeal to the agent's beliefs about some objective normative notion.

Of course, I would admit that the following sorts of principles are plausible even though none of them appeal to any objective normative notion:

1.9   It is subjectively permissible for an agent to φ if and only if it is not subjectively impermissible for her to φ.

1.10 An agent subjectively ought to φ if and only if she has most subjective reason to φ.

1.11 An agent is subjectively required to φ if and only if she has decisive subjective reason to φ.

But although these principles are plausible (indeed, tautological), they are also completely uninformative. They do not provide any substantive answers regarding what agents subjectively ought to do. Thus, it seems that all principles about what agents subjectively ought to do that fail to appeal to some objective normative notion turn out to be either implausible in the way that 1.8 is or uninformative in the way that 1.9–1.11 are.

It seems, then, that objective normative notions are more fundamental than their subjective counterparts, for we can arrive at plausible, substantive answers

---

[40] This general line of argument comes from M. SMITH 2006. Smith argues that if we are concerned to give an account of subjectively right acts (i.e., the acts that we can legitimately expect agents to perform and to criticize them for failing to perform), then it is implausible to suppose that the subjectively right act is the one that maximizes expected value, for we do not hold agents responsible for failing to maximize expected *value*. At most, we hold them responsible for failing to maximize expected *"value-as-they-see-things"* (i.e., deontic value)—see pp. 142–145.

about subjective normative notions only by appealing to objective normative notions. What's more, it seems that, given 1.7, we have a prima facie obligation to do what we can to dispel as much of our normative uncertainty concerning objective normative notions as possible by theorizing both about what we have objective reason to do and about what we objectively ought to do. This is what I aim to do in this book, and it is, as I have just shown, a project of fundamental importance.

§1.5 Conventions that I will follow throughout the book

Sections, subsections, and tables will be numbered according to the chapter in which they appear. Thus, §3.2 is the second section of chapter 3, §§3.2.1 is the first subsection of §3.2, and table 4.1 is the first table in chapter 4. Major propositions will initially be set off from the rest of the text by additional line spacing above and below. These propositions will either be given an abbreviation, such as "TCR" for "the teleological conception of reasons," or be numbered according to the chapter in which they appear. Thus, 2.11 refers to the eleventh numbered proposition of chapter 2. These numbers and abbreviations will appear in boldface type in their first appearance. The use of lowercase letters will indicate specific instances of a more general proposition. Thus, 4.1a and 4.1b are both instances of 4.1. Where there are numerous versions of some significant abbreviated proposition, such as TCR, the various versions will be labeled as follows: TCR, TCR^1, TCR^2, ..., TCR^*. The lack of a superscript indicates that it is the initial formulation, a numbered superscript indicates which revision it is, and an asterisk indicates that it is the final formulation. Readers should consult the list of abbreviations whenever they need to be reminded of what a particular abbreviation stands for.

References in the text and footnotes are given by the author's last name, appearing in small capitals, and the year of publication. For instance, "SCANLON 1998" refers to Thomas Scanlon's *What We Owe to Each Other*, which was published in 1998. See the list of references in the back of the book for complete bibliographic information.

The act-tokens available to a given subject, S, will be labeled $a_1, a_2, ..., a_n$. Their corresponding outcomes will be labeled $o_1, o_2, ..., o_n$. Where there is no determinate fact as to which outcome would obtain were S to perform a given action, we must talk about the prospect, as opposed to the outcome, of that action. The *prospect* of an action is a probability distribution over the set of possible outcomes associated with that action. (I borrow the term "prospect" from J. ROSS FORTHCOMING.) The prospects of $a_1, a_2, ..., a_n$ will be labeled $p_1, p_2, ..., p_n$. Times will be labeled $t_0, t_1, ..., t_n$, where t_0 refers to the present. Since acts are rarely, if ever, performed in an instant, we should assume that, when I write, say, "S performed a_1 at t_3," "t_3" refers to the interval of time over which S performed a_1.

An agent's act alternatives consist in the set of mutually exclusive and jointly exhaustive act-tokens that are available to her at a given time.[41] This will always include the act of "doing nothing"—that is, the act of intentionally remaining motionless. The act of refraining from performing some act (type or token) is never itself an act-token but is always an act-type, which can be instantiated by numerous act-tokens.[42] I will refer to the "act" of refraining from performing a specific act using the tilde ($\sim$). Thus, "S performs $\sim a_1$" stands for "S refrains from performing a_1." I will use $A_1, A_2, \ldots, A_n$ to designate act-types, such as lying, cheating, stealing, and so on. These consist in sets of all and only those act-tokens that fall under the relevant descriptions. I will use $O_1, O_2, \ldots, O_n$ to designate the sets of outcomes corresponding to all and only those act-tokens in $A_1, A_2, \ldots, A_n$, respectively.

In addition to act-tokens and act-types, there are also *act-sets*. An act-set is a set of one or more acts (types or tokens) that are all jointly performable by a single agent. The acts in the set may be simple or compound, synchronous or asynchronous, consecutive or inconsecutive. I will use $\alpha_1, \alpha_2, \ldots, \alpha_n$ to designate act-sets. I will use $a_i, o_i, p_i, t_i, \alpha_i, A_i,$ and O_i as variables ranging over act-tokens, outcomes, prospects, times, act-sets, act-types, and sets of outcomes, respectively. Italicized letters, such as x, y, and z, will be used as variables that range over individual acts (be they types or tokens). I will sometimes use $x_1, x_2, \ldots, x_n$ to designate distinct acts. Greek letters, such as φ, χ, and ψ, range over everything for which agents can have reasons, including beliefs, desires, act-tokens, act-types, and act-sets.

Technical terms and phrases will be defined as they come up and will often be set off by italics in their initial appearance. Sometimes, though, these initial definitions do not match up exactly with those given in the glossary. This is because whereas the initial definitions often paper over certain complications that are not addressed until later on in the book, the glossary definitions represent my final formulations. Readers should consult the glossary if either they ever need to be reminded of a definition or they want to see what the final formulation will be.

I will typically use "she," "her," and "hers" as generic personal pronouns whenever the gender of the referent is unspecified, although I will occasionally use "he," "him," and "his" as generic personal pronouns, as when I must do so in order to remain consistent with some quoted passage. I realize that this is far from ideal, but all the alternatives seem to me to be just as bad if not worse.

---

[41] An act-token is a particular act performed by a particular agent at a particular time. Act-tokens are performable at most once and are not the sort of thing that can be instantiated.

[42] Act-types are universals that can, in general, be instantiated by a number of distinct act-tokens.

2

Consequentialism and Moral Rationalism

In this chapter, I make a presumptive case for moral rationalism: the view that agents can be morally required to do only what they have decisive reason to do, all things considered.[1] I argue that this view compels us to accept act-consequentialism, but at the same time leads us to reject all traditional versions of the theory. I begin by explaining how moral rationalism leads us to reject (maximizing act-) utilitarianism, the most traditional of all act-consequentialist theories.

§2.1 The too-demanding objection: How moral rationalism leads us to reject utilitarianism

As we saw in chapter 1, utilitarianism is too demanding. It implies that agents are morally required to sacrifice their projects, interests, and special relationships whenever doing so would produce more, even just slightly more, aggregate utility than not doing so would. Thus, according to utilitarianism, I am morally required to sacrifice my life, to neglect my relationship with my daughter, and to abandon my project of completing this book if I could thereby produce more, even just slightly more, aggregate utility. To demand that I make such sacrifices for the sake of such miniscule gains in aggregate utility is to demand more from me than can be rightfully or reasonably demanded of me.

To say that a given theory is *too* demanding is not merely, or even necessarily, to say that it demands quite a lot from agents in certain circumstances. Almost all moral theories demand quite a lot from agents in at least some circumstances.[2] What's more, a theory can be too demanding because some of its demands, though quite small, are more than can be rightfully or reasonably demanded of agents. Such is the case with utilitarianism.

---

[1] I assume, contrary to COPP 1997, that there is a normative standpoint from which we can judge what an agent has decisive reason to do, all things considered—in other words, that there is a normative standpoint from which we can judge what an agent just plain ought to do. For a reply to Copp, see McLEOD 2001 and note 15 of chapter 5.

[2] Paul Hurley (2006, p. 681) makes this point as well.

To illustrate, imagine that we live in a utopian world in which everyone is not only materially well-off but also extremely happy. And assume, as is in fact the case, that in addition to two other computers I own an ultra-portable laptop computer that I use only for travel. This computer is admittedly a luxury, which I use to pass the time on planes and in airports. To demand that I forfeit this luxury for the sake of promoting the greater good is not to impose any great demand on me. Yet a theory that required me to hand over my computer to some even more well-to-do person who already has *four* computers, including one ultra-portable laptop, would be too demanding. It is one thing to think that, in a non-utopian world, I would be required to give up such a luxury for the sake of saving some poor child's life, but it is quite another to think that, in a utopian world, I would be required to give up such a luxury for the sake of providing some well-to-do person with even more luxury than I have. Nevertheless, utilitarianism requires me to do just that if that is what would maximize utility, as where, for instance, this well-to-do person would get slightly more enjoyment out of my laptop than I would. And this is true even if the net gain to be had is but one measly utile, which is, as you will recall, equivalent to someone's experiencing the mildest of pleasures for the briefest of moments. To demand that I make such a sacrifice for the sake of benefiting someone who is even better off than me is to demand more from me than can rightfully or reasonably be demanded of me.

The foregoing suggests that a theory, such as utilitarianism, can be too demanding in virtue of requiring agents to make even rather small sacrifices, provided that those sacrifices, though small, are still more than can be rightfully or reasonably demanded of them. And the idea that utilitarianism can be too demanding either because it demands more from agents than can be *rightfully* demanded of them or because it demands more from agents than can be *reasonably* demanded of them suggests there are two possible senses in which utilitarianism might be too demanding: (1) it holds that agents are morally required to make sacrifices that they are not, in fact, morally required to make or (2) it holds that agents are morally required to make sacrifices that they do not have decisive reason to make, all things considered.[3] For now, let us call these sense$_1$ and sense$_2$, respectively. The claim that utilitarianism is too demanding in sense$_1$ is, perhaps, the more common of the two, but it is certainly not the only sense in which utilitarianism is claimed to be too demanding. To see this, consider that some utilitarians concede that their theory is too demanding but deny that this constitutes an objection to it.[4] If their claim was that utilitarianism is too demanding in sense$_1$, then this would make no sense, for if utilitarianism holds that we are morally required to make sacrifices that we are not, in fact, morally required to make, then

---

[3] In thinking about utilitarianism's being too demanding in sense$_2$, I have been greatly influenced by DORSEY FORTHCOMING.

[4] See, for instance, SIDGWICK 1966, SINGER 1999 (pp. 289 and 308–309), and D. SOBEL 2007b (p. 14). To be fair, I should note that Sobel never officially endorses consequentialism, let alone utilitarianism specifically. Nevertheless, we can glean from what he says that he thinks both that utilitarianism is too demanding in sense$_2$ and that this is no objection to the view.

it would indeed be false. One can, however, admit that utilitarianism is too demanding in sense$_2$ and yet deny that the theory is false. The thought would be that morality is itself too demanding, and so even if utilitarianism is too demanding, it could, nonetheless, be the correct moral theory.

Samuel Scheffler makes the point quite eloquently:

> Suppose that morality as represented by a certain philosophical theory strikes us as too demanding in what it requires of people. Does this, in principle, provide the basis for a legitimate objection, either to the theory or to morality itself? If so, is the problem that the theory has distorted the content of morality? Or is it that morality itself is excessively demanding, so that while the theory may be an accurate representation of the content of morality, people have reason to treat moral considerations as less weighty or authoritative than we may previously have supposed? (1992, p. 5)

But what does it mean to say that morality is itself too demanding? Here, the claim would seem to be that morality is too demanding in sense$_2$. As David Sobel puts it, "What morality asks, we could say, is too much to be the thing that the agent has most reason to do all things considered, but not too much to count as what morality asks" (2007b, p. 14). So, clearly, there are these two senses in which a moral theory might be thought to be too demanding. Let us call those theories that are too demanding in sense$_1$ *erroneously demanding* and call those theories that are too demanding in sense$_2$ *unreasonably demanding*.

I want to focus exclusively on the idea that utilitarianism is unreasonably demanding, for this is something about which most philosophers (utilitarians and non-utilitarians alike) can agree.[5] Given any plausible conception of practical reasons, utilitarianism is unreasonably demanding, for it is implausible to suppose that agents have decisive reason to make the sorts of sacrifices that utilitarianism requires them to make. For instance, utilitarianism requires me to sacrifice my life for sake of a one-utile net gain in aggregate utility. But it is implausible to suppose that I have decisive reason to do so. Of course, as I have noted above, one can admit that utilitarianism is unreasonably demanding and deny that this constitutes an objection to the theory. But some do consider the fact that utilitarianism is unreasonably demanding to be an objection to the theory.[6]

---

[5] Utilitarians who would agree with this include Henry Sidgwick (1966) and Peter Singer (1999, pp. 289 and 308–309). Non-utilitarians who would agree with this include Paul Hurley (2006) and Sarah Stroud (1998).

[6] For instance, Paul Hurley has, in a recent paper, argued against traditional forms of consequentialism, and these arguments proceed "within the widely held framing conviction that any plausible theory of moral standards must be such that rational agents typically have decisive reasons to avoid what these standards identify as cases of wrongdoing" (2006, p. 704). Sarah Stroud argues against consequentialism on the grounds that it conflicts with the following thesis: "If S is morally required to φ, then S has most reason to φ"—see STROUD 1998 (esp. pp. 171 and 182–184).

What, then, accounts for the disagreement? It seems to be this: unlike those who deny that a theory's being unreasonably demanding constitutes an objection to that theory, those who think that it does accept the following thesis, which I call *moral rationalism*:[7]

> **MR** If a subject, S, is morally required to perform an act, x, then S has most (indeed, decisive) reason to perform x, all things considered.[8]

If, on the one hand, moral rationalism is true, then the correct moral theory cannot be unreasonably demanding. And this explains why those who accept moral rationalism (e.g., Stroud) reject utilitarianism on account of its being unreasonably demanding, for moral rationalism and the fact that utilitarianism is unreasonably demanding implies that the theory is erroneously demanding and, thus, false. But if, on the other hand, moral rationalism is false, then the correct moral theory can be unreasonably demanding without being erroneously demanding. And this explains why those who reject moral rationalism (e.g., Singer) are content with the fact that utilitarianism is unreasonably demanding.[9]

So far, we have seen how the observation that utilitarianism is unreasonably demanding will lead those who accept moral rationalism to reject utilitarianism. Of course, I have not yet provided any reason to think that moral rationalism is true. In §2.5, I will rectify this by making a presumptive case for moral rationalism. But before proceeding with this case, I want to show how the objection that utilitarianism is unreasonably demanding is really just a species of a much more general objection.

---

[7] The thesis that I call *moral rationalism* (MR) sometimes goes by other names. David Brink calls moral rationalism "the supremacy thesis" (1997, p. 255), Stephen Darwall calls it "supremacy" (2006b, p. 286), Samuel Scheffler calls it "the claim of overridingness" (1992, pp. 52–54), John Skorupski calls it "the principle of moral categoricity" (1999, p. 170), Sarah Stroud calls it the "overridingness thesis" (1998, p. 171), and R. Jay Wallace calls it the "optimality thesis" (2006, p. 130).

[8] The essential idea is that agents can be morally required to do only what they are rationally required to do. Now, some philosophers (see, e.g., STROUD 1998) formulate this thesis using "most reason" in place of "decisive reason." This formulation is equivalent to mine unless either some reasons have no (rational) requiring strength (see GERT 2004 and DANCY 2004) or some reasons with requiring strength are silenced, undermined, or bracketed off by other factors or considerations (see, e.g., SCANLON 1998). If either is the case, then S's having most reason to perform x would not entail S's being rationally required to perform x. And, in that case, I assume that Stroud and the others would want to replace "most reason" with "decisive reason," where "S has decisive reason to perform x" just means "S's reasons are such as to make S (objectively) rationally required to perform x." In other words, S has decisive reason to perform x if and only if S lacks sufficient reason to perform any alternative to x.

[9] Interestingly, Paul Hurley has argued that Peter Singer is, despite his explicit denials of moral rationalism (see SINGER 1999, pp. 289 and 308–309), implicitly committed to the view or at least to something very close to it—see HURLEY 2009.

§2.2 The argument against utilitarianism from moral rationalism

The idea that utilitarianism is objectionable insofar as it is unreasonably demanding is really just a species of a much more general objection, for the objection proceeds on the assumption that moral rationalism is true, and once we accept moral rationalism, we should object to utilitarianism whenever it requires us to perform acts that we do not have decisive reason to perform, whether those acts be self-sacrificing acts or even self-benefiting acts. Thus, we should object to utilitarianism not only on the grounds that it sometimes requires agents to make sacrifices that they do not have decisive reason to make, but also on the grounds that it sometimes requires agents to perform self-benefiting acts that they do not have decisive reason to perform.

To illustrate, let us suppose that a woman named Anita would benefit from murdering her estranged uncle. Assume that she is crafty enough to get away with it and that, if she did, she would finally receive the heart transplant that she so desperately needs, for her uncle is an organ donor with the same rare blood group and tissue type that she has. Let us further suppose that murdering her uncle would produce the most aggregate utility, for let us assume that the gain in utility resulting from Anita's heart transplant would slightly more than offset the loss in utility resulting from her uncle's murder. Given this further stipulation, utilitarianism requires Anita to benefit herself by murdering her uncle. Arguably, though, she does not, in this instance, have decisive reason to commit murder. It seems that, in this instance, the moral reason that she has to refrain from committing murder outweighs the self-interested reason that she has to commit murder.

So, if we accept moral rationalism, we should object to utilitarianism because it sometimes requires agents to perform self-benefiting acts that they do not have decisive reason to perform. We can, then, offer the following general schema for constructing an argument against utilitarianism on the basis of moral rationalism (MR):

2.1 There exists an act, x_1, available to S that would produce the most aggregate utility but that S does not have decisive reason to perform, all things considered.

2.2 If utilitarianism is true, then S is morally required to perform any act that would produce the most aggregate utility. (From the definition of "utilitarianism").

2.3 So, if utilitarianism is true, then S is morally required to perform x_1. (From 2.1 and 2.2).

2.4 S is morally required to perform x_1 only if S has decisive reason to perform x_1, all things considered. (From MR).

2.5 So, S is not morally required to perform x_1. (From 2.1 and 2.4).

2.6 Therefore, utilitarianism is not true. (From 2.3 and 2.5).

The argument is deductively valid, and the only controversial premises are 2.1 and 2.4. Since 2.4 follows from moral rationalism and since I am interested in what follows if moral rationalism is true, I will focus on 2.1. To see just how plausible 2.1 is, consider the following two plausible candidates for x_1.

First, let x_1 be the act of your sacrificing the life of your partner (whose life, we will assume, is well worth living) for the sake of saving some stranger's life, where your doing so would produce the most aggregate utility, but where the net gain in aggregate utility would be quite small: one utile. Suppose, for instance, that both lives contain nearly the same amount of utility but that what accounts for there being more utility in saving the stranger's life is the fact that her life contains slightly more utility: an extra millisecond of mild pleasure. Assume that, but for this difference, the utility of your sacrificing the life of your partner would be the same as that of your refraining from doing so.

Clearly, in this case, you lack decisive reason to save the stranger's life, for the reason that you have to save your partner is at least as strong as, if not stronger than, the reason that you have to bring about an extra millisecond of mild pleasure. After all, let us assume that you have a very special relationship with your partner, involving years of personal history together and mutual love and respect for one another. Let us also assume that you care more about the welfare of your partner than you do about the welfare of this stranger, that you care more about the welfare of your partner than you do about producing small net gains in aggregate utility, and that saving your partner is what would best serve your own interests. On what plausible theory of practical reasons, then, would there not be at least sufficient reason for you to save your partner instead of this stranger? I cannot think of any.[10] Thus, this seems to be a clear case in which a subject, S (viz., you), could produce the most aggregate utility by performing an act, x_1 (specifically, the act of saving the stranger instead of your partner), but where x_1 is not something S has decisive reason to do.

Second, let x_1 be the act of murdering your partner so as to ensure that each of a billion and one people gets some minor benefit. Assume that, if you murder your partner, the loss in utility would be one billion utiles, and assume that the benefit to each of the billion and one people would be one utile. Thus, the net gain to be had in your murdering your partner is but one utile. To make 2.1 even more plausible, assume that your partner is undeservedly one of society's worst-off and that the billion and one people whom you could instead benefit are undeservedly soci-

---

[10] I can, of course, think of an implausible theory of practical reasons according to which you would not have even sufficient reason to save your partner: that is, the theory according to which S has sufficient reason to perform x if *and only if* S's performing x would maximize aggregate utility. But I know of no one who has argued for such a theory of practical reasons. Even utilitarians who think that there is always sufficient reason to maximize aggregate utility admit that there is also often sufficient reason to perform acts that would not maximize aggregate utility—see, for instance, SIDGWICK 1966.

ety's most well-to-do. In fact, let us assume that they are well-to-do only as a result of their exploiting society's worst-off, including your partner.

The idea that, in this situation, all the various reasons that you have to refrain from murdering your partner are, even when taken together, insufficient to successfully counter the fairly weak reason that you have to produce a net gain of one utile is quite implausible. Consider all the reasons that you have to refrain from murdering your partner: (*a*) the reason that you have to give priority both to your own welfare and to the welfare of those whom you love most, (*b*) the reason that you have to respect your partner's autonomy, (*c*) the reason that you have to give priority to society's worst off, and (*d*) the reason that you have to give priority to the deserving over the undeserving.[11] Given how much reason you have not to murder your partner and how little reason you have to produce a small net gain in aggregate utility, we should deny that you have decisive reason to murder your partner.

Given these two plausible candidates for x_1, we can be confident that there are at least two acts that have both the property of being what would produce the most aggregate utility and the property of not being what the agent has decisive reason to do, all things considered. So we should accept 2.1, and, therefore, acknowledge that utilitarianism cannot be the correct moral theory if moral rationalism is true. The problem for utilitarianism vis-à-vis moral rationalism is that utilitarianism forces us to ignore two important classes of rather weighty reasons—reasons that, in certain instances, have sufficient weight to successfully counter the reason that one has to maximize utility: (1) reasons that have nothing to do with promoting utility, such as the reason one has to ensure that utility is fairly distributed and (2) reasons that stem from the special relations that we bear to ourselves and our loved ones, such as the reason that we have to favor ourselves and our loved ones when deciding whose utility to promote.[12] If a moral theory, such as utilitarianism, ignores such reasons, it will conflict with moral rationalism.[13]

And it is not just utilitarianism that ignores whole classes of reasons. All forms of traditional act-consequentialism do so as well. According to all forms of *traditional act-consequentialism* (TAC), we should accept the following *criterion of rightness* (cr):

TAC$_{cr}$ S's performing x is morally permissible if and only if S's performing x would maximize the good (impersonally construed).

---

[11] Some utilitarians might deny that *b–d* are in fact reasons, but most utilitarians admit that *a* is indeed a reason and, moreover, that it is a reason that often successfully counters the reason that one has to produce small net gains in aggregate utility.

[12] Recall that to say that the reasons to φ successfully counter the reasons to ψ is to say that the reasons to φ prevent the reasons to ψ from being decisive by, say, equaling, outweighing, undermining, or silencing them. Another possibility is that the reasons to φ are incommensurable with the reasons to ψ such that there is sufficient reason both to φ and to ψ.

[13] This sort of argument comes from STROUD 1998.

This criterion of rightness would have us ignore two important classes of rather weighty reasons—reasons that, in certain instances, have sufficient weight to successfully counter the reason that one has to maximize the good: (1) reasons that have nothing to do with promoting the good, such as the reason one has to refrain from violating someone's autonomy even when doing so is a means to promoting the good, and (2) reasons that stem from the special relations that we bear to ourselves and our loved ones, such as the reason one has to promote the good by saving one's own loved one as opposed to by helping some stranger save her loved one.[14]

Insofar as we think either that we have reasons to do things besides promote the good or that the weight of our reasons to perform various good-promoting acts depends on our relationship to those whose good would thereby be promoted, we should also think that TAC_{cr} ignores certain reasons and/or their proper weights.[15] And if this is right, then TAC_{cr} will conflict with moral rationalism. Indeed, we could easily revise the argument that I gave against utilitarianism above so as to constitute an argument against traditional act-consequentialism. We need only substitute "traditional act-consequentialism" for "utilitarianism" and "the good" for "aggregate utility" in the above argument.

§2.3 How moral rationalism compels us to accept consequentialism

We have seen how moral rationalism leads us to reject traditional versions of act-consequentialism, such as utilitarianism.[16] Interestingly, moral rationalism also compels us to accept act-consequentialism (hereafter simply "consequentialism"). Or so I will argue. I will show that at the heart of utilitarianism lies a certain conception of practical reasons that when conjoined with moral rationalism compels us to accept consequentialism.

Many utilitarians and non-utilitarians agree that there is something compelling, perhaps even "spellbinding," about utilitarianism and that this is what

---

[14] Even if the traditional act-consequentialist holds, say, that there is more value in a person's life being saved by a loved one than there is in a person's life being saved by some stranger, she must deny that there is, other things being equal, any gain in value to be had by saving one's own loved one as opposed to helping someone else to save her loved one.

[15] I borrow this point from STROUD 1998. Paul Hurley (2009) makes a similar point, although he focuses on the fact that TAC_{cr} ignores "nonimpersonal reasons." I think, though, that the challenge is broader than that, for it seems that a person could consistently hold that there are impersonal reasons that have nothing to do with promoting the good.

[16] The reader should assume that, unless otherwise indicated, "consequentialism" is short for "act-consequentialism" and that "nonconsequentialism" is short for "non–act-consequentialism." On my usage, then, rule-consequentialism is a version of nonconsequentialism.

explains: (1) why utilitarianism has persevered despite its implications being so wildly at odds with our most firmly held moral convictions; (2) why it tends "to haunt even those of us who will not believe in it" (FOOT 1985, p. 196); and (3) why the move to rule utilitarianism seems to be "an unsatisfactory answer to the problem of reconciling utilitarianism with common moral opinion" (FOOT 1985, p. 198).

But what is utilitarianism's compelling idea? As many philosophers see it, it is consequentialism itself (e.g., FOOT 1985, p. 196). And, as I see it, what compels us to accept consequentialism is the fact that it embodies a certain conception of practical reasons: what is sometimes called the "teleological conception of reasons" (SCANLON 1998, p. 84). On this view, an agent's reasons for performing an action are determined by her reasons for preferring its outcome to those of the available alternatives, such that, if S has most reason to perform x, then, of all the outcomes that S could bring about, S has most reason to desire that x's outcome obtains.[17] The intuitive idea is that since our actions are the means by which we affect the way the world goes, and since our intentional actions necessarily aim at making the world go a certain way, it is only natural to suppose that our reasons for action are a function of our reasons for preferring some of these possible worlds to others, such that what each agent has most reason to do is to bring about the possible world, which of all those that she can actualize through her actions, is the one that *she* has most reason to want to be actual.

Of course, we must acknowledge that no conception of reasons could ever compel us to accept consequentialism unless moral rationalism is true. If moral rationalism is false, then moral requirements are not a species of the requirements of reason. And if moral requirements are not a species of the requirements of reason, then it is hard to see why we should think that any conception of reasons could compel us to accept consequentialism. It seems, then, that it is actually not a single idea, but the following argument, that compels us to accept consequentialism:[18]

2.7　An act's deontic status is determined by the agent's reasons for and against performing it, such that, if a subject, S, is morally required to perform an act, x, then S has most reason to perform x.[19] (Moral Rationalism).

2.8　An agent's reasons for and against performing a given act are determined by her reasons for and against preferring its outcome to those of the available

---

[17] Although this view is one that many find intuitively compelling, it is not without its critics—see, for instance, SCANLON 1998 (pp. 50–64 and chap. 2). But see chapter 3 and PORTMORE FORTHCOMINGc for a defense of this view.

[18] In earlier works, I had misidentified consequentialism's compelling idea first as the "idea that it is always permissible to bring about the best available state of affairs" (PORTMORE 2005, p. 95) and then subsequently as the idea that it is always permissible to act so as to bring about the outcome that one has reason to prefer above all other available alternatives (PORTMORE 2007, p. 50). Both are problematic—see SCHROEDER 2007a and SACHS 2010, respectively.

[19] As mentioned in note 8 above, the second clause in 2.7 is equivalent to moral rationalism assuming both that all reasons have (rational) requiring strength and that no reason with requiring

alternatives, such that, if S has most reason to perform x, then, of all the outcomes that S could bring about, S has most reason to desire that x's outcome obtains.[20] (The Teleological Conception of Practical Reasons).

2.9 Therefore, an act's deontic status is determined by the agent's reasons for and against preferring its outcome to those of the available alternatives, such that, if S is morally required to perform x, then, of all the outcomes that S could bring about, S has most reason to desire that x's outcome obtains.[21] (Act-Consequentialism).

§2.4 What is consequentialism?

I have been assuming that "outcome" and "consequentialism" are to be construed broadly. Broadly construed, an act's outcome is the possible world that would be actual if it were performed.[22] And, broadly construed, consequentialism is the view that an act's deontic status is determined by how its outcome ranks relative to those of the available alternatives on some evaluative ranking, such that an act is morally obligatory only if its outcome outranks those of the available alternatives.[23] But even so, 2.9 is not obviously equivalent to this definition. According to this definition, consequentialist theories hold that acts are permissible or imper-

strength is ever silenced, undermined, or bracketed off by other factors or considerations. If either assumption is false, I will need to revise this argument so as to replace "most reason" with "decisive reason" throughout, which is something I could do with no ill effect for my argument. I choose, here, to talk about what there is most reason to want and to do only because this talk seems more natural when making comparative judgments.

The first clause in 2.7 goes beyond MR itself in positing an explanatory relation between an act's deontic status and the reasons there are to perform it. I am assuming, then, that moral rationalists would be happy to endorse this. Lastly, note that even 2.7 is not the version of moral rationalism that I ultimately endorse. For that version, see MR* in §7.4.

[20] Michael Smith (2005, p. 17) seems to endorse the teleological conception of reasons, although he formulates it a bit differently: "(x)(t)(x at t has all things considered reason to φ in circumstances C iff φ-ing is the unique action of those x can perform at t that brings about what x would desire most happens in C if his psychology met all rational requirements and ideals of reason."

[21] It may be that some outcomes are incommensurable such that, in some instances, there is an alternative to x's outcome that S has neither more nor less, nor equal, reason to desire. In such instances, S will not have most reason to desire that x's outcome obtains and, consequently, will not be morally required to perform x.

[22] On why consequentialists should construe an act's outcome to include not merely its causal consequences but everything that would be the case were it to be performed, see BROOME 1991 (pp. 3–4), SCHEFFLER 1994 (pp. 1–2), SOSA 1993 (pp. 101–102), WILLIAMS 1973 (pp. 86–87), and especially CARLSON 1995 (p. 10 and chap. 4).

[23] I write "only if" as opposed to "if and only if" so as not to exclude satisficing versions of consequentialism, which deny that it is always obligatory to produce the highest ranked outcome. And I

missible in virtue of how their outcomes rank relative to those of the available alternatives on some evaluative ranking. According to 2.9, by contrast, consequentialist theories hold that acts are permissible or impermissible in virtue of the agent's reasons for and against preferring its outcome to those of the available alternatives. What, then, is the connection between an evaluative ranking of outcomes and a ranking of outcomes in terms how much reason the agent has to want each of them to obtain? The answer lies in understanding what an evaluative ranking of outcomes is. It is a ranking of outcomes in terms of the agent's reasons (or some subset of her reasons) for preferring each outcome to the available alternatives, for it seems that what ties all the different varieties of goodness—such as *goodness for* or *goodness that*—together is that they are all to be understood in terms of reasons for desiring (or for preferring).

For instance, we can understand *better that* and *better for* as follows: [24]

Better that: For all states of affairs p and q, it is better that p is the case than that q is the case if and only if the set of all the right kind of reasons to prefer its being the case that p to its being the case that q is weightier than the set of all the right kind of reasons to prefer its being the case that q to its being the case that p.[25]

Better for: For all subjects S and all states of affairs p and q, it is better for S that p is the case than that q is the case if and only if the set of all the right kind of reasons to prefer, for S's sake, its being the case that p to its being the case that q is weightier than the set of all the right kind of reasons to prefer, for S's sake, its being the case that q to its being the case that p.[26]

---

define "consequentialism" in terms of "some evaluative ranking" as opposed to a ranking of outcomes with respect to their goodness so as not to exclude egoism, which ranks outcomes not with respect to how good they are, but with respect to how good they are *for the agent*. And, strictly speaking, consequentialism need not make the deontic statuses of actions a function of some single evaluative ranking; it could instead make it a function of some set of evaluative rankings, as is the case with dual-ranking act-consequentialism—see chapter 1 and especially chapter 5.

[24] These are adapted from SCHROEDER 2010 and SCHROEDER 2008b.

[25] If facts such as the fact that an evil demon will torture me unless I prefer its being the case that p to its being the case that q are genuine reasons for me to have this preference and not just reasons for me to desire, and to act so as to ensure, that I have this preference, then the right kind of reasons must exclude such reasons, for even if such a fact did constitute a genuine reason for me to prefer its being the case that p to its being the case that q, it would have no bearing on whether or not it is better that p is the case than that q is the case. See PARFIT 2011 (Appendix A), RABINOWICZ & RØNNOW-RASMUSSEN 2004, SCHROEDER 2010, and ZIMMERMAN FORTHCOMING for more on this problem, which is known as *the wrong-kind-of-reasons problem*.

[26] To avoid circularity, we will need to find some way of explicating "for S's sake" in terms other than "for S's own good." Chris Heathwood (2008) presents an interesting argument against this sort of account, but see JOHANSSON 2009 for a possible reply. See also RØNNOW-RASMUSSEN 2007 and RØNNOW-RASMUSSEN 2009.

Different consequentialist theories employ different evaluative rankings, which, in some instances, appeal to different varieties of goodness. For instance, on egoism, outcomes are ranked in terms of how *good* they are *for* the agent, whereas, on traditional act-consequentialism, outcomes are ranked in terms of how *good* it would be *that* they obtain.[27] And since all these varieties of goodness are ultimately to be understood in terms of reasons for preferring, we should understand consequentialism to be the view according to which an act's deontic status is determined by the agent's reasons for and against preferring its outcome to those of its alternatives. We should, therefore, take 2.9 to be equivalent to the view that an act's deontic status is determined by how its outcome ranks relative to those of the available alternatives on some evaluative ranking, such that an act is morally obligatory only if its outcome outranks those of all other available alternatives.

If this is right, then what differentiates one consequentialist view from another are their differing commitments concerning what agents have most reason to desire, all things considered. Whereas, say, the utilitarian is committed to the view that each agent has most reason, all things considered, to desire the outcome that she has most impartial reason to desire, the egoist is committed to the view that each agent has most reason, all things considered, to desire the outcome that she has most self-interested reason to desire. Thus, the utilitarian is committed to the view that there are no partial reasons for preferring one outcome to another, or, if there are, that these are always overridden by whatever impartial reasons there are for preferring the one to the other. And the egoist, by contrast, is committed to the view that there are no altruistic reasons for preferring one outcome to another, or, if there are, that these are always overridden by whatever self-interested reasons the agent has for preferring the one to the other.

The idea that egoists and utilitarians are committed to certain views about what agents have most reason, all things considered, to desire may seem a bit strange. In particular, it may seem strange to suggest that someone who holds that an act is morally permissible if and only if it maximizes the good could fail to be a consequentialist just because she thinks that partial reasons can provide an agent with decisive reason for preferring a worse outcome to a better outcome. She might, for instance, hold that although it would be better if some child more gifted than her own survives, she ought, all things considered, to prefer that her less gifted child survives. In this case, she will hold that she ought to act so as to ensure that the more gifted child survives even though she ought to prefer the possible world in which she acts instead to ensure that her less gifted child survives. Since she thinks that she is morally required to act so as to produce an out-

---

[27] As I understand it, *egoism* is the view that holds both that act-consequentialism is true and that an act produces an outcome that S has optimal reason to want to obtain if and only if it maximizes S's utility.

come that she does not have most reason to desire, she will, if 2.9 is definitive of consequentialism, count as a nonconsequentialist.[28]

So if we take 2.9 to be definitive of consequentialism, then this would seem to imply that many philosophers misuse the term "consequentialism to refer to all and only those theories that direct each agent to bring about the best outcome rather than to all and only those theories that direct each agent to bring about the outcome that, of all those available to her, is the one that she has most reason to desire. This is a fairly radical conclusion. I suspect, therefore, that many readers will reach the opposite conclusion: that I am the one who is misusing the term "consequentialism."

In fact, none of us are misusing the term, for "consequentialism" is a term of art. More specifically, as Walter Sinnott-Armstrong (2003) points out, "consequentialism" tends to be used as a family resemblance term. He says:

> In actual usage, the term "consequentialism" seems to be used as a family resemblance term to refer to any descendant of classic utilitarianism that remains close enough to its ancestor in the important respects. Of course, different philosophers see different respects as the important ones. Hence, there is no agreement on which theories count as consequentialist.

Now, my own view is that what is most important and compelling about utilitarianism is that it can be seen as deriving from 2.9 and the further assumption that what agents always have most reason to desire, all things considered, is the outcome with the most aggregate utility. Thus, it is not surprising that I take 2.9 to be definitive of the broader notion: namely, consequentialism. But since others may find different aspects of utilitarianism compelling, they will reject my definition. We should not quibble, though, over such unimportant terminological issues. If readers find my definition of "consequentialism" too revisionary, then they should label 2.9 something besides "consequentialism": "rational-desire teleology," perhaps.[29] What is important is not what we call 2.9-type theories, but

---

[28] To say that 2.9 is definitive of act-consequentialism is not to say that 2.7 (i.e., moral rationalism) is definitive of act-consequentialism. It is not. One can accept 2.9 and reject moral rationalism, as many traditional act-consequentialists do. This is why moral rationalism can lead us to reject all traditional versions of act-consequentialism while at the same time compelling us to accept some version of act-consequentialism.

[29] Rational-desire teleology would contrast, then, with both *impersonal-value teleology* (the view that an act's deontic status is determined by the impersonal value of its outcome, such that, if S is morally required to perform x, then S's performing x would produce the most good, impersonally construed) and *personal-value teleology* or egoism (the view that an act's deontic status is determined by the personal value of its outcome, such that, if S is morally required to perform x, then S's performing x would produce the most good for S). Some might prefer, then, to reserve the term "consequentialism" for only impersonal-value teleology.

whether such theories are interesting and plausible, as I hope to establish. Of course, I have to call these theories something, and given my views about what is most compelling about a theory like utilitarianism, it makes most sense for me to call them consequentialist theories. Let me just stipulate, then, that, as I will use the term "consequentialism," a theory is (act-) consequentialist if and only if it entails 2.9. We can, then, put aside the rather uninteresting question of whether this is in fact the definition that best comports with common philosophical usage and focus instead on my arguments that consequentialism, so defined, is both interesting and plausible.[30]

§2.5   The presumptive case for moral rationalism

So far, we have seen how moral rationalism compels us to accept consequentialism while at the same time leading us to reject all traditional versions of the theory. Of course, these observations are of little interest unless moral rationalism is true, and I have yet to provide any reason for thinking that it is. Below, I attempt to rectify this. Let me forewarn the reader, though, that the case that I will be making in this chapter is, at best, a presumptive one.[31] My arguments will establish only that those who reject moral rationalism must also reject an intuitively plausible premise. Thus, there is a price to be paid in rejecting moral rationalism. Of course, there is often a price to be paid in rejecting a philosophical thesis. And, perhaps, some will think that, in this instance, the price is worth paying.

But even if the arguments in this chapter lack definitiveness, my case for moral rationalism does not rest with them alone. Part of my case for moral rationalism is that it coheres well with the other theses that I will be arguing for in the book. Ultimately, then, my case for moral rationalism depends on how plausible this picture of morality, rationality, and the relationship between the two is on the whole. It will not, however, be until the very last chapter that the whole picture will come fully into view. So, in the meantime, I will settle for presenting a presumptive argument in favor of moral rationalism. But, first, I will need to explain how moral rationalism differs from three related theses about the over-

---

[30] I find the issue of how "consequentialism" is to be defined so as to accurately reflect common philosophical usage rather uninteresting. What's more, I think that it may even be pointless to try to resolve the issue, as there does not seem to be any set of individually necessary and jointly sufficient conditions that captures all the various uses of the term that are to be found in the literature.

[31] One reason that the case that I will be making is, at best, a presumptive one is that I do not, for reasons of space, attempt to address all the various objections and counterarguments that have been leveled against moral rationalism. For instance, Shaun Nichols (2002) has argued that a recent empirical study, which he himself conducted and which probes people's intuitions about psychopaths, undermines moral rationalism. Although I do not have space here to address Nichols's interesting argument, I think that others have adequately defended moral rationalism against his argument. See, for instance, KENNETT 2006. For more on this issue, see also JOYCE 2008a, NICHOLS 2008, and JOYCE 2008b.

ridingness of morality and moral reasons. There is potential for confusion here since some philosophers equate moral rationalism with the view that morality is overriding, and some even refer to moral rationalism as the "overridingness thesis" (e.g., STROUD 1998, p. 171).[32]

Recall that, according to moral rationalism, an agent can be morally required to perform an act only if she has decisive reason to perform that act, all things (and, thus, all reasons) considered. It is important not to confuse this thesis about moral requirements and *reasons generally* with the following thesis about moral requirements and *moral reasons specifically*:

> **MO** If S has more moral reason to perform x than to perform y ($y \neq x$), then S is not morally permitted to perform y. And, thus, if S has most moral reason to perform x, then S is morally required to perform x.[33]

According to MO, moral reasons are *morally overriding* (hence, the abbreviation "MO"). To say that one type of reason, say, m-reasons, overrides another, say, n-reasons, with respect to a certain kind of normative status, N, is to say that, in any situation in which both types of reasons are present and an act, x, has a certain N-status, no modification of that situation that involves affecting only what n-reasons there are will change x's N-status. That is, if m-reasons override n-reasons with respect to an act's N-status, then even the weakest m-reason trumps the strongest n-reason in the determination of that act's N-status.

To illustrate, suppose that I am morally required to keep my promise to meet with a student to discuss his exam grade, that the reason that I have to keep this

---

[32] The question of whether or not moral requirements override, say, prudential requirements (i.e., requirements of self-interest) is not the same question as whether or not moral rationalism is true. Moral requirements override prudential requirements if and only if both (1) there are cases in which moral requirements conflict with prudential requirements, and (2) in all these cases of conflict, agents have decisive reason, all things considered, to act as they are morally required to act. Now, consider the following three views: (*a*) S's performing x is morally required if and only if S's performing x would be optimific in terms of its production of S's utility (i.e., ethical egoism); (*b*) S's performing x is prudentially required if and only if S's performing x would be optimific in terms of its production of S's utility (i.e., *consequentialist prudence*); and (*c*) S has decisive reason to perform x if and only if S's performing x would be optimific in terms of its production of S's utility (i.e., *rational egoism*). If all three of these views were true, then moral rationalism would be true even though moral requirements would not override prudential requirements. In this case, moral requirements would not override prudential requirements for the simple fact that they would never conflict.

[33] I call any reason that is relevant to determining an act's deontic status a *morally relevant reason*, but I reserve the label *moral reason* for only those reasons that, morally speaking, count for or against performing some action. This is an important distinction to make, because it may be that not all morally relevant reasons are moral reasons. That is, it may be that some reasons can justify performing acts that it would otherwise be morally impermissible to perform without themselves, morally speaking, counting in favor of (or against) those acts. For more on this issue, see chapter 5.

promise is a moral reason, that the reason I have to break this promise is a rather weak self-interested reason (e.g., the reason that I have to avoid making an extra trip to campus), and that the reason that I have to further my own self-interest is a non-moral reason. If moral reasons override non-moral reasons with respect to an act's moral status (that is, if moral reasons are morally overriding), then no modification of this case in which only the strength and/or number of the relevant non-moral reasons are altered will change the fact that I am morally required to meet with the student. Thus, even if someone were to offer me a million dollars to give a lecture during the time at which I had promised to meet with the student, I would still be morally required to meet with the student, foregoing this unique opportunity to make a million dollars. If moral reasons are morally overriding, then the non-moral reason that I have to make a million dollars is, no matter how strong, powerless to prevent the moral reason that I have to keep my promise from generating a moral requirement to do so, no matter how trivial this promise, and no matter how weak the moral reason stemming from it.[34]

We should reject MO, as I hope the above example makes clear. In any case, I will be arguing against MO in chapter 5. And it is important to keep in mind that I am presuming that MO is false, for I readily admit that, were MO true, moral rationalism would be untenable. To see why, we need only note that MO and moral rationalism together entail the following implausible view:

RO If S has more moral reason to perform x than to perform y ($y \neq x$), then S is not rationally permitted to perform y. And, thus, if S has most moral reason to perform x, then S is rationally required (i.e., has decisive reason, all things considered) to perform x.[35]

According to RO, moral reasons are *rationally overriding* (hence, the abbreviation "RO"). If this thesis were true, then it would always be *objectively irrational* (i.e., contrary to reason) to refrain from doing what one has most *moral* reason to do, even when what one has most moral reason to do is supported by only the most trivial of moral reasons and opposed by the weightiest of non-moral reasons.[36] This is implausible, for it seems that, in many instances, we have sufficient reason, all things con-

---

[34] Since I want the reason that I have to make the million dollars to be a non-moral reason, let us assume that I must spend all the money on luxuries for myself and, thus, that only I will benefit.

[35] Actually, the first sentence in RO follows straightforwardly from MO and moral rationalism only if we assume that the following claim is implicit in my original formulation of moral rationalism (i.e., MR): if S is not morally permitted to perform y, then S is not rationally permitted to perform y. But since this claim is equivalent to "If S is morally required to perform $\sim y$, then S is rationally required (i.e., has decisive reason, all things considered) to perform $\sim y$," which is just an instance of the claim that is explicit in my original formulation of moral rationalism, it is safe to say that RO is entailed by MO and moral rationalism.

[36] An act is *objectively irrational* if and only if the agent has decisive reasons not to perform it. Whenever I use the words "rational" and "irrational" without qualification, I mean to be talking about what is *objectively* rational or irrational.

sidered, to act contrary to what we have most moral reason to do. It seems, for instance, that I would have sufficient, if not decisive, reason to break my promise to meet with a student to discuss his exam grade if this is the only way for me to take advantage of some unique opportunity to make a million dollars. So, given that RO is implausible, we had better not accept both MO and moral rationalism, which together entail RO. Thus, my case in favor of moral rationalism is contingent upon our finding MO implausible. If what I have said so far is not enough to convince you of the implausibility of MO, then, for now, you will just have to accept my promise to provide more compelling reasons for rejecting MO in chapter 5.

Some philosophers do not conflate moral rationalism with MO, but they do something that is nearly as bad: they suggest that moral rationalism is inextricably linked to the view that moral requirements are themselves *reason-providing*—that is, to:

> **RP** The fact that S is morally required to perform *x* constitutes (and, thus, provides) an overriding (and, hence, decisive) reason for S to perform *x*.

Stephen Darwall, for instance, links moral rationalism to the view that "moral obligations always give agents conclusive reasons for acting that outweigh or take priority over any potentially competing considerations" (2006a, p. 26). And David Brink does the same in writing: "Moral requirements provide agents with overriding reasons for action; necessarily, it is on balance irrational to act contrary to moral requirements" (1997, p. 256).[37] But the two are not inextricably linked; one can accept that there is always decisive reason to do what one is morally required to do (that is, moral rationalism) while denying that moral requirements provide agents with overriding reasons to abide by them (that is, RP). The fact that S is morally required to perform *x* may indicate that there are certain sorts of reasons for S to perform *x* that are indeed decisive, but the fact the S is morally required to perform *x* does not *itself* constitute an additional reason (let alone a decisive one) for S to perform *x*—at least, not in my opinion.[38]

So although some may be compelled to accept moral rationalism because they think that moral requirements generate overriding reasons to abide by them, others, like myself, may be driven to accept moral rationalism because they think that morality is limited in what it can require of us—that morality can require us to do only that which we have decisive reason to do, all things considered. The

---

[37] Thomas Scanlon endorses RP. He says, "the fact that a certain action would be morally wrong seems to provide a powerful reason not to do it, one that is, at least normally, decisive against any competing considerations" (1998, p. 1).

[38] Of course, I would allow for the possibility that the fact that S is morally required to perform *x* could in conjunction with certain other facts constitute a reason for S to perform *x*, as where, say, S desires to do what she is morally required to do and the fact that her performing *x* would fulfill one of her desires constitutes a reason for her to perform *x*.

thought would be that although moral requirements do not generate overriding reasons to abide by them, moral rationalism is, nevertheless, true, for non-moral reasons serve to constrain what morality can require of us in that they sometimes successfully counter our moral reasons, preventing them from generating moral requirements. But although non-moral reasons, such as self-interested reasons, serve to constrain what morality can require of us, it does not follow that self-interest reigns supreme. It is plausible to suppose that although self-interested reasons sometimes successfully counter moral reasons, thereby making it permissible for us to act contrary to what we have most moral reason to do, other times moral reasons prove decisive (all things considered), thereby making it obligatory for us to act contrary to our self-interest, as is the case from above in which Anita has decisive moral reason to refrain from murdering her uncle.

Interestingly, if we deny both MO and RO, then moral rationalism becomes not only tenable, but nearly unassailable, for if we admit that non-moral reasons can prevent moral reasons from generating moral requirements (and this is, as I argue in chapter 5, what we should say if we deny both MO and RO), then what besides moral rationalism offers a more plausible account of when they do so? If moral rationalism is true, then non-moral reasons will prevent moral reasons from generating moral requirements when they successfully counter them. And if the non-moral reasons in favor of performing a given act do not justify performing that act—thereby making it morally permissible to perform that act—when they successfully counter all other reasons (moral and non-moral) for doing otherwise, then when?

So, as I noted earlier, part of my case for moral rationalism is that it coheres well with other claims that I defend in the book, such as the claim that both RO and MO are false. But, as I also mentioned, there are other independent grounds for accepting moral rationalism. Below, I offer an independent argument for moral rationalism. The argument is not original to me, but I hope to state it more precisely than it has heretofore been stated. Moreover, I hope to buttress the argument by providing an original argument for its most controversial premise. Before I can state either argument, though, I need to explain some terminology.

First, to say that S performs ~x is to say that S performs the "act" of refraining from performing x. So if x is, for instance, the act of pushing some specific button at some particular time, then ~x is the "act" of refraining from pushing that button at that time.

Second, to say that S has *decisive reason* to φ is to say that S's reasons are such as to make S objectively rationally required to φ, and to say that S has *sufficient reason* to φ is to say that S's reasons to φ are such as to make S objectively rationally permitted to φ. Thus, S has decisive reason to φ if and only if S does not have sufficient reason to ~φ. I will use "S has decisive reason to φ" and "S has sufficient reason to φ" as shorthand for "S has decisive reason to φ, all things considered" and "S has sufficient reason to φ, all things considered," respectively.

Third, to say that S has sufficient reason to perform ~x is to say that there is at least one act-token that is an instance of S's refraining from performing x that S has sufficient reason to perform. Likewise, to say that S has decisive reason to perform ~x is to say that there is at least one act-token that is an instance of S's refraining from performing x that S has decisive reason to perform.

Fourth, to say that S *freely performs* x (or ~x)[39] is to say that S performs x having the relevant sort of control over whether or not she performs x—that is, the sort of control that is necessary for her being an appropriate candidate for praise or blame with respect to her having performed x. More specifically, to say that S freely performs x is to say that S satisfies whatever other conditions in addition to having the relevant sort of knowledge (such as knowledge about what she is doing and about what she is bringing about) that is necessary for her to be morally responsible for having performed x.

Fifth, to say that S *knowledgeably performs* x is to say that S performs x knowing all the relevant facts—the relevant facts being those facts the ignorance of which would either inculpate or exculpate her for performing x.

Sixth, to say that S is *morally blameworthy* (hereafter, simply "blameworthy") for performing x is to say both that it is appropriate for S to feel guilt about having performed x and that it is appropriate for others to feel indignation—and, perhaps, also resentment—in response to S's having performed x. And, here, I use "appropriate" in the sense of being apt, fitting, or correct and, thus, in the same sense that fear is the appropriate response to the perception of danger. In this sense, it can be appropriate to blame oneself or someone else even though having this attitude (and/or expressing it) would not be instrumental in bringing about any good.[40]

Seventh and last, when I say that S is morally required to perform x, I mean this in the objective sense—that is, I mean that S is *objectively* morally required to perform x.

With these terms defined, I can now state the argument as follows:

2.10 If S is morally required to perform x, then S would be blameworthy for freely and knowledgeably performing ~x.[41]

2.11 S would be blameworthy for freely and knowledgeably φ-ing only if S does not have sufficient reason to φ.[42]

---

[39] Hereafter, I will leave the "(or ~x)" implicit.

[40] It is important to keep distinct the issue of whether it is appropriate to blame someone for doing x and the issue of whether it is appropriate to intend to perform an act that constitutes the outward expression of this attitude. One can be appropriate without the other being appropriate. See §§3.2.3 for more on this matter. And see BENNETT 1980, STRAWSON 1962, and WALLACE 1994 for criticisms of the view that blame is appropriate if and only if the outward expression of this attitude would lead to a desired change in the agent and/or her behavior.

[41] "S would be blameworthy for freely and knowledgeably performing ~x" should be read as shorthand for "S is blameworthy if S freely and knowledgeably performs ~x."

[42] Note that 2.11 entails: "S would be blameworthy for freely and knowledgeably performing ~x only if S does not have sufficient reason to perform ~x, all things considered." One need only substitute "~x" for "φ."

2.12 So, if S is morally required to perform x, then S does not have sufficient reason to perform ~x. (From 2.10 and 2.11).

2.13 If S does not have sufficient reason to perform ~x, then S has decisive reason to perform x. (From the definitions of "sufficient reason" and "decisive reason" above).

2.14 Therefore, if S is morally required to perform x, then S has decisive reason to perform x—and this is just moral rationalism (MR). (From 2.12 and 2.13).[43]

The argument is deductively valid, and it seems that 2.11 is the only assumption that is not a conceptual truth. Premise 2.13 is clearly a conceptual truth. And 2.10 expresses the common assumption that there is a conceptual connection between wrongdoing and blameworthiness.[44] Although there may not be an essential connection between wrongdoing and blameworthiness per se, there is, it seems, an essential connection between blameworthiness and *freely and knowledgeably* doing what is wrong. And if this is right, then anyone who denies moral rationalism is committed to denying 2.11. Yet 2.11 is intuitively plausible—even those who deny moral rationalism admit as much.[45] Besides, there is, I think, a sound argument for 2.11, which is based on assumptions that are even more intuitively plausible than 2.11 itself. But before I present that argument, let me rebuff some putative counterexamples to 2.11.[46]

---

[43] This sort of argument for moral rationalism is not original to me. Darwall (2006a and 2006b, p. 292) and Skorupski (1999, pp. 170–171) make similar arguments for moral rationalism. And Shafer-Landau (2003, pp. 192–193) presents the same kind of argument but for a considerably weaker thesis: namely, if S is morally required to perform x, then S has a (not necessarily decisive or even sufficient) reason to perform x.

[44] See, for instance, DARWALL 2006a, GIBBARD 1990, MILL 1991, and SKORUPSKI 1999.

[45] For instance, David Sobel, who explicitly denies moral rationalism in D. SOBEL 2007a, claims in D. SOBEL 2007b that it "seems quite intuitive that earnestly blaming a person for O-ing entails the view that the agent all things considered ought not to have O-ed" (p. 155). And he says, "It also seems quite intuitive to say that if one is acting as one has most reason to act, then one is acting as one ought and therefore one's action is not worthy of blame" (p. 156).

[46] Jussi Suikkanen and Paul McNamara have both suggested that 2.11 might have problematic implications in the following sort of case. Suppose that I accidentally (and, perhaps, also non-negligently) make two incompatible appointments: A and B. They are incompatible, because they are for the same time but in different locations. Assume, though, that A and B are equally important. Given their equal importance, it may seem that I have sufficient reason to break A as well as sufficient reason to break B. And, thus, according to 2.11, neither would be blameworthy. Yet, surely, this is a moral dilemma if ever there was one, and so I would be blameworthy no matter which appointment I break. So 2.11 seems to rule out moral dilemmas. But, in fact, as Howard Nye has pointed out to me, 2.11 rules out moral dilemmas only if there are no rational dilemmas, and it is unclear why anyone would want to claim that there can be moral dilemmas but no rational dilemmas. So if someone wants to claim that I would be blameworthy no matter which appointment I break, then that someone should also claim that I lack sufficient reason to break either appointment and so would be doing something contrary to reason no matter which appointment I break.

Consider the following example. Suppose that Arthur, a white supremacist, sneaks up behind an unsuspecting black man, named Bert, and clubs him over the head, knocking him unconscious. He does so out of hatred for blacks. However, unbeknownst to Arthur, Bert was just about to shoot and kill his ex-girlfriend Carla, who, we will suppose, is completely innocent. As it turns out, then, Arthur's act saves Carla's life. Arthur had, then, sufficient reason to club Bert over the head, for assume that any less violent or injurious act would have been insufficient to save Carla's life. Nevertheless, Arthur is clearly blameworthy. So this may seem to be a counterexample to 2.11. But note that Arthur does not *knowledgeably* club Bert over the head. Arthur is ignorant of the fact that his clubbing Bert over the head is necessary to save Carla's life, and it is his ignorance of this fact that inculpates him. The antecedent in 2.11 is, therefore, false, and so this is no counterexample to 2.11.

Of course, a better putative counterexample is certainly in the neighborhood. Imagine, for instance, a slightly different version of the above case. In this version, Arthur knows all the relevant facts and, thus, freely *and knowledgeably* clubs Bert over the head. Nevertheless, what motivates him is not the thought that doing so will save Carla but only the desire to hurt a black person. Here, too, it seems that Arthur had sufficient reason to club Bert over the head, and yet clearly he is blameworthy.[47] But although it is clear that Arthur is blameworthy, it is far from clear that Arthur is blameworthy for clubbing Bert over the head. I think that we can rightly blame Arthur for his vicious motive, for his malevolent intent, and for his racist attitudes.[48] We can even rightly blame him both for acting out of hatred and malice and for being willing to club Bert over the head even if there is no good reason to do so.[49] But I do not think that we can rightly blame him for clubbing Bert over the head, as this is exactly what he should have done. Later in life, when Arthur finally comes to realize the error of his ways, what he should come to regret and feel guilty about is the fact that he was a racist who acted out

---

[47] I thank Mike Almeida, Richard Yetter Chappell, and Clayton Littlejohn for proposing these sorts of putative counterexamples. Another type of putative counterexample, suggested to me by Peter de Marneffe, is Sophie's choice. It may seem both that Sophie had sufficient reason to choose to save her son and that it was, nevertheless, appropriate for her to have felt guilty for having made this choice. This, however, is a tricky case. My suspicion is that although we may think her guilt appropriate insofar as we question whether she truly had sufficient reason to sacrifice her daughter, we should not think it *appropriate* for her to have felt guilty (in the sense of this feeling being apt as opposed to psychologically normal) insofar as we think that she did have sufficient reason to make the choice that she made. But it does seem reasonable to question whether she in fact had sufficient reason to make the choice that she made. We might think, for instance, that she had decisive reason to give each child an equal chance at being saved and that it was, therefore, appropriate for her to have felt guilty insofar as she failed to do so—perhaps, she chose to save her son because he was her favorite. Or we might think that a mother never has sufficient reason to sacrifice her child, not even for the sake of ensuring that at least one of her two children survives.

[48] For how we can be held morally responsible for our attitudes, see SCANLON 1998, A. M. SMITH 2005, and A. M. SMITH 2008.

[49] I rely here upon what David Copp calls a "finely nuanced view about the object of blame." See COPP 2003, pp. 285–289, for an excellent discussion.

of hatred and malice. Arthur should not, however, regret having clubbed Bert over the head, nor should he feel guilty for having done so, for this is what he had sufficient (indeed, decisive) reason to do. To accept blame for having φ-ed, one must judge that one should not have φ-ed. But although he should neither have wished Bert harm nor acted out of hatred or malice, he should have clubbed him over the head, as this was necessary to save Carla's life.

In arguing that Arthur should be blamed, not for clubbing Bert over his head, but for his malicious intent, for his racist attitudes, and for his acting out of malice, I have appealed to 2.11. This may seem illegitimate, but I am trying to establish only that if one finds 2.11 intuitively plausible, the above examples should not dissuade one from accepting 2.11. Although it is clear that Arthur is blameworthy for something, it is not clear that he is blameworthy for freely and knowledgeably doing anything that he had sufficient reason to do. Thus, the proponent of 2.11 can reasonably claim that there is no φ such that Arthur had sufficient reason to φ and yet is blameworthy for freely and knowledgeably φ-ing. If, on the one hand, we let "φ" stand for "clubbing Bert over the head," then although it is clear that Arthur had sufficient reason to φ, it is not so clear that he is blameworthy for freely and knowledgeably φ-ing. And if, on the other hand, we let "φ" stand for, say, "acting out of malice," then although it is clear that Arthur is blameworthy for freely and knowledgeably φ-ing, it is not so clear that he had sufficient reason to φ.[50] So I do not see any definitive counterexample to 2.11. Having cleared that up, let me now explain why we should accept 2.11.

The thought underlying 2.11 is that agents are blameworthy only for freely and knowledgeably doing what they lack sufficient reason to do. One way to bring out the intuitive plausibility of this claim is to point to the tension there is in blaming someone for acting in a certain way while acknowledging that she had sufficient reason to act in that way. Stephen Darwall puts the point thusly:

> It seems incoherent...to blame while allowing that the wrong action, although recommended against by some reasons, was nonetheless the sensible thing to do, all things considered.... Part of what one does in blaming is simply to say that the person shouldn't have done what he did, other reasons to the contrary notwithstanding. After all, if someone can show that he had good and sufficient reasons for acting as he did, it would seem that he *has* accounted for himself and defeated any claim that he is to blame for anything. Accepting blame involves an acknowledgment of this proposition also. To feel guilt is, in part, to feel that one shouldn't have done what one did. (2006b, p. 292)[51]

---

[50] Note that saying that Arthur acted out of malice is not equivalent to saying that Arthur clubbed Bert over the head. These are not two equivalent descriptions of the same act, for Arthur can club Bert over the head without acting out of malice.

[51] See also DARWALL 2006a, especially p. 98.

Another way to bring out the intuitive plausibility of 2.11 is to point to the tension that there is in holding someone morally responsible for her actions on account of her having the capacity to respond appropriately to the relevant reasons and then blaming her for responding appropriately to the relevant reasons by doing what she had sufficient reason to do. Let me explain. It seems that an agent can be blameworthy for her actions only if she is morally responsible for them and that she can be morally responsible for them only if she has the relevant sort of control over her actions.[52] What's more, it is plausible to suppose that she has the relevant sort of control over her actions only if she has the capacity to respond appropriately to the relevant reasons—that is, the capacity both to recognize what the relevant reasons are and to react appropriately to them, being moved by them in accordance with their associated strengths.[53] Indeed, it is this capacity for responding appropriately to the relevant reasons, which sane adult humans typically possess and which children, animals, and the criminally insane typically lack, that distinguishes those who can be blameworthy for their actions from those who cannot.

Given that an agent can be blameworthy only if she has the capacity to respond appropriately to the relevant reasons, it is important to note that, in flawlessly exercising this capacity, she could be led to perform any act that she has sufficient reason to perform. Indeed, if there is but one act that she has sufficient reason to perform, then this capacity will, if exercised flawlessly, lead her both to recognize that this is the only act that she has sufficient reason to perform and to react by

---

[52] Some deny that *volitional control* is a necessary condition for moral responsibility, where, roughly, S has volitional control over whether or not she φs only if both (1) she has the capacity to intend to φ and (2) whether or not she φs depends on whether or not she intends to φ. More specifically, some argue that we can appropriately be held responsible for our judgment-sensitive attitudes even if we do not have volitional control over them—see, for instance, SCANLON 1998, A. M. SMITH 2005, and A. M. SMITH 2008. The thought is that an agent is morally responsible for something if and only if it is rightly attributable to her in that it expresses her judgments, values, or normative commitments. This view is known as attributionism, and it contrasts with volitionalism (see, e.g., LEVY 2005). But even attributionists allow that volitional control can be relevant in determining moral responsibility for bodily movements. Angela M. Smith, for instance, says: "In some cases (e.g., in determining a person's responsibility for a bodily movement), it may make sense to ask whether the agent has *voluntarily chosen* the thing in question, because that will determine whether that thing can reasonably be taken to express her judgments" (2008, p. 368). In any case, what matters to attributionists is whether the action is connected to the agent's underlying normative judgments such that she can, in principle, be called upon to defend it with reasons and be blamed if no adequate defense can be provided (A. M. SMITH 2008, p. 370). Given that citing sufficient reason for performing an action is presumably an adequate defense of one's performing that action, attributionists seem committed to my claim that S would be blameworthy for freely and knowledgeably φ-ing only if S does not have sufficient reason to φ—that is, to 2.11.

[53] We may need to talk about the capacities of mechanisms rather than the capacities of agents— see FISCHER & RAVIZZA 1998, especially p. 38. If so, my argument could easily be revised so as to replace all talk of the agent's capacity to respond appropriately to the relevant reasons with talk of the reasons-responsiveness of the mechanism that issued in the agent's action.

performing it. But if an agent is morally responsible and, thus, potentially blameworthy in virtue of having the capacity to respond appropriately to the relevant reasons, then how can we rightly blame her for doing something that she has sufficient reason to do when, in flawlessly exercising this very capacity, this is what she is led to do? Surely, it cannot be that the very capacity that opens the door to an agent's being blameworthy is the one that leads her to perform blameworthy acts. And yet this is exactly what we would be allowing if we held that agents can be blameworthy for performing acts that they have sufficient reason to perform, for it is their capacity to respond appropriately to the relevant reasons that opens the door to their being blameworthy in the first place—a capacity that, when exercised flawlessly, leads them to perform acts that they have sufficient reason to perform.

To put the point in slightly different terms, it seems inappropriate to hold an agent responsible on the condition that she has the capacity to be guided by sound practical reasoning and then blame her for acting as she might very well be led to act if she is guided by sound practical reasoning. And since an agent can be led to perform any act that she has sufficient reason to perform when guided by sound practical reasoning, it seems inappropriate to blame her for freely and knowledgeably doing what she has sufficient reason to do.

More formally, the argument for 2.11 is this:

2.15 S is morally responsible for whether or not she φs and, thus, potentially blameworthy for φ-ing or failing to φ only if S has the relevant sort of control over whether or not she φs.

2.16 S has the relevant sort of control over whether or not she φs only if S has the capacity to respond appropriately to the relevant reasons (both moral and non-moral).[54]

2.17 So, S is potentially blameworthy for whether or not she φs only if S has the capacity to respond appropriately to the relevant reasons. (From 2.15 and 2.16).

2.18 If S has sufficient reason to φ, then, in flawlessly exercising her capacity to respond appropriately to the relevant reasons, S could be led to freely and knowledgeably φ.[55]

---

[54] For a further defense of 2.15 and 2.16, see FISCHER & RAVIZZA 1998. Note that it is not enough for an agent to have the capacity to respond appropriately to non-moral reasons. To be morally responsible, an agent must have the capacity to respond, and respond appropriately, to moral reasons as well. Certain psychopaths have the capacity to respond appropriately to non-moral reasons but are incapable of recognizing the fact that the rights and interests of others provide them with reasons (specifically, moral reasons) for acting in ways that respect their rights and promote their interests. Such psychopaths are not morally responsible for their actions—see FISCHER & RAVIZZA 1998, pp. 76–81.

[55] Whether she would or not depends on whether she also has sufficient reason to φ. It could be, after all, that she has sufficient reason both to φ and to refrain from φ-ing.

2.19 If S is potentially blameworthy for whether or not she φs only if she has the capacity to respond appropriately to the relevant reasons, then S cannot be blameworthy for freely and knowledgeably φ-ing when, in flawlessly exercising this capacity, S could be led to freely and knowledgeably φ.

2.20 So, S would not be blameworthy for freely and knowledgeably φ-ing if S has sufficient reason to φ. (From 2.17, 2.18, and 2.19).[56]

2.21 Therefore, S would be blameworthy for freely and knowledgeably φ-ing only if S does not have sufficient reason to φ—and this is just 2.11. (From 2.20 by contraposition).

In considering this argument, it will be helpful to have a specific example in mind. So consider a revised version of the example in which I have promised to meet with a student to discuss his exam grade but have the unique opportunity to make some extra money by giving a lecture instead. Assume that I am offered just enough money so that I have just as much reason, all things considered, to give the lecture as to show up for my meeting with the student as promised. And assume that I have considerably less reason to do anything else. That is, assume that I have both sufficient reason to keep my promise and sufficient reason to give the lecture and insufficient reason to do anything else. Furthermore, assume that I am strongly responsive to reasons, meaning both that I always recognize what the relevant reasons are and that I am always moved to act in accordance with their associated strengths, such that I always do what I have decisive reason to do, only do what I have sufficient reason to do, and choose arbitrarily which of two acts to perform (by, say, tossing a coin) if and only if I have sufficient and equivalent reason to do either. Thus, being strongly reasons-responsive and having sufficient and equivalent reason to do either, I choose arbitrarily to give the lecture. Suppose, for instance, that I first designate heads to giving the lecture and designate tails to keeping my promise and then toss a coin, which lands heads. As a result, I decide to give the lecture.

Of course, being strongly reasons-responsive, I would have kept my promise and met with the student had there been decisive reason to do so. For instance, I would have kept my promise had my moral reason for doing so been a bit stronger, as where, say, the student's scholarship was at stake. Likewise, I would have kept my promise had my self-interested reason for giving the lecture been a bit weaker, as where, say, the monetary offer had been a bit less. And had there been a third option that I had decisive reason to do (e.g., saving some drowning child), I would have done that instead. But, as it was, none of these were the case. As it was, I had sufficient reason to give the lecture and thereby break my promise to meet with the student. And that is what I did, having flawlessly exercised my capacity for sound practical reasoning.

---

[56] Roughly, the structure of the argument from 2.15–2.19 to 2.20 goes something like this: B → R, R → C, S → L, (B → C) → (L → ~B) ∴ S → ~B.

Given my flawless execution of my capacity for sound practical reasoning, how can I be faulted for breaking my promise? Is it not inappropriate to hold me morally responsible and, thus, potentially blameworthy in virtue of my capacity for being guided by sound practical reasoning and then blame me for acting as sound practical reasoning leads me to act? Should not even the student admit that, had he been in my situation and perfectly rational, he might also have been led to act as I did? And if so, how can he rightly resent me for acting as he would have acted?

Of course, things would have been different had there been decisive reason for me to have kept my promise. In that case, it would have been appropriate for the student to resent me for breaking my promise to him. If I had decisive reason to keep my promise as well as the capacity to respond appropriately by recognizing this fact and reacting appropriately to it, then I must have failed to have done something that I could, and should, have done. Perhaps, I failed to recognize the fact that I had decisive reason to keep my promise even though I was capable of doing so. Or, perhaps, I recognized that I had decisive reason to do so, but failed to react appropriately even though I had the capacity to do so—perhaps, I was weak-willed and gave into the temptation to earn some easy money. In either case, I would have failed in some way and could, then, rightly be blamed for this failure. So I see how it can be appropriate to blame someone for failing to do what she had decisive reason to do, but I do not see how we can rightly blame someone for freely and knowledgeably doing what she had sufficient reason to do.

Admittedly, lots of people perform acts that they have sufficient reason to perform and are, nonetheless, blameworthy, because they were motivated by some consideration that should not have motivated them. Such is the case in the example from above where Arthur does what he has sufficient reason to do out of a desire to see people of a certain race harmed. But, as I noted above, I think that in this case we should not blame Arthur for doing anything that he had sufficient reason to do (such as, clubbing Bert over the head). The alternative would be to allow that people can be blameworthy for freely and knowledgeably doing what they had sufficient reason to do, and that, I have argued, is inappropriate insofar as the very capacity that makes them subject to blame can lead them, when exercised flawlessly, to do what they have sufficient reason to do. The only way to forestall such a possibility is to insist upon moral rationalism, which, I have argued, we should.

Still, the person who wishes to deny moral rationalism might balk at 2.16, arguing that when it comes to being morally responsible, what is relevant is not the capacity to respond in a *rationally* appropriate manner, but rather only the capacity to respond in a *morally* appropriate manner.[57] Of course, this person must insist that the two can come apart and that, although doing what one recognizes as having sufficient reason to do is always a rationally appropriate

---

[57] To be clear, "to respond appropriately" should be taken as shorthand for "to respond in a rationally appropriate manner" both in 2.16 and throughout the rest of the argument.

response, it is sometimes a morally inappropriate response.[58] But why think this? Why think that it is morally inappropriate to respond to moral reasons as it is rationally appropriate to respond to them? A moral reason is just a certain type of reason, and, as a reason, it has a certain weight. So why think that it is morally inappropriate to give moral reasons only as much weight as they in fact have?

In any case, when we talk of an agent's needing control over her actions in order to be held morally responsible for them, the relevant sort of control seems to be *rational* self-control—that is, the capacity to respond in a rationally appropriate manner to the relevant reasons. If it were anything else, then someone could be strongly reasons-responsive and, for that reason, lack the sort of control that is essential for moral responsibility. But the idea that an agent could fail to be morally responsible on account of her being strongly reasons-responsive is quite counterintuitive.

§2.6 Some concluding remarks

I have claimed that there is an essential connection between blameworthiness and freely and knowledgeably violating a moral requirement (see 2.10). And I have argued that given this essential connection and the fact that it is inappropriate to blame agents for freely and knowledgeably doing what they have sufficient reason to do (see 2.11), we should accept moral rationalism. In closing, I want to do three things. First, I want to explain why we cannot similarly argue for the legal analogue of moral rationalism. Second, I want to show how the truth of moral rationalism and the falsity of this legal analogue allow us to explain why moral requirements,

---

[58] I thank Pat Greenspan for raising this possible objection to 2.16. As far as I know, however, no one has defended such a position in print. Even those who think that being morally (or normatively) competent is a necessary condition for being morally responsible stop well short of suggesting that this competency requires the capacity to respond by giving moral reasons *more* than their due rational weight. Rather, they suggest, to the contrary, that agents must have the ability to grasp and respond to both moral *and* non-moral reasons—see, for instance, FISCHER & RAVIZZA 1998 (chap. 3) and WOLF 1990 (chap. 6). Indeed, at least one author (viz., Susan Wolf) explicitly claims that responsibility entails the ability to appreciate and act in accordance with *all* the reasons there are, including both moral and non-moral reasons—see WOLF 1990, p. 141. On Wolf's Reason View of responsibility, "*full* freedom and responsibility will involve the ability to appreciate reasons that come from a variety of sources" (1990, p. 141), and she explicitly notes that "our image of the agent who is most able to see and understand what reasons there are need not coincide with that of the agent who is most acutely sensitive particularly to *moral* reasons" (1990, p. 137). And although she claims that freedom and responsibility involve the ability to appreciate and act in accordance with what she calls the "True and the Good," she makes clear that "appreciation of the Good need not be confined to appreciation of the *moral* good. Indeed, in certain contexts, appreciation of the moral good may interfere with one's ability to appreciate the nonmoral good or with one's ability to recognize reasons for preferring a morally inferior course of action" (1990, p. 137). Thus, being overly sensitive to moral reasons can diminish one's freedom and responsibility by diminishing one's rational self-control.

but not legal requirements, can be defeated by the presence of sufficient reasons for the agent's doing otherwise. And, third, I want to explain why all would not be lost even if moral rationalism turns out to be false. I will take each in turn.

The legal analogue of moral rationalism is *legal rationalism*:

> **LR** If S is legally required to perform x, then S has decisive reason to perform x, all things considered.

The reason why moral rationalism is plausible, whereas legal rationalism is implausible, is that whereas there is an essential connection between freely and knowledgeably violating a moral requirement and the appropriateness of emotions such as guilt, resentment, and indignation, there is no essential connection between freely and knowledgeably violating a legal requirement and the appropriateness of such reactive attitudes.

An agent can freely and knowledgeably violate a legal requirement without its being appropriate either for her to feel guilt or for others to feel indignation. To illustrate, consider that if in my rush to get my critically injured daughter to the emergency room I proceed through an intersection against the red light after looking carefully to ensure that I can do so safely, I will have freely and knowledgeably broken the law. But I should not feel guilty for having done so. Nor should others be indignant for my having done so. After all, I did not put anyone at risk, as I did slow down and look carefully before proceeding against the red light. And although I did break the law, it cannot be claimed that in doing so I failed to show adequate respect for the law, for we are assuming that I had decisive reason to break the law in this instance.

So, it should come as no surprise that we can argue for moral rationalism on the assumption that we cannot rightly be blamed for freely and knowledgeably doing what we have sufficient reason to do, but that we cannot similarly argue for legal rationalism given the lack of any essential connection between the violation of a legal requirement and the appropriateness of such reactive attitudes.

Interestingly, the truth of moral rationalism along with the falsity of legal rationalism allows us to explain why moral requirements, but not legal requirements, can be defeated by the presence of sufficient reasons for the agent's doing otherwise. To illustrate how moral requirements can be defeated in this way, consider the following example. It is Tuesday morning and Professor Collins is lamenting the fact that he has to drive to campus this afternoon to hold office hours when he gets a call from a friend informing him of a rare opportunity to meet Hall-of-Famer Reggie Jackson. Now Collins is a huge fan who has for many years wanted to meet Jackson. Meeting him would be one of the highlights of his life. Unfortunately, it is too late to cancel his office hours. So, if he does not hold them, some students may show up and wait in vain.[59]

---

[59] This case comes from PORTMORE 2003 and is adapted from WOLF 1986, p. 142.

So what should he do? Should he go and meet his childhood hero, or should he instead go to his office just in case some of his students want to complain about their grades? Intuitively, it seems that, in light of how important it is to him, he has sufficient reason, all things considered, to take advantage of this once-in-a-lifetime opportunity to meet his childhood hero. What's more, it seems morally permissible for him to do so as well, and this seems true even if we suppose that his going to meet his childhood hero will benefit no one besides himself. Interestingly, though, we think that, if he did not have sufficient reason to be somewhere else, he would be morally required to hold his office hours. After all, he has at least a prima facie obligation to fulfill his commitments and agreeing to hold office hours is a kind of commitment. So why is it, in this case, that the moral reason that he has to fulfill his commitment to hold office hours fails to generate a moral requirement for him to do so?

The explanation cannot be that Collins has as much moral reason to meet Jackson as to fulfill his commitment to hold office hours, for it seems that the self-interested reason that he has to meet Jackson is a non-moral reason. Consider that if he were choosing between meeting Jackson and staying home and staring at the ceiling, he would not be morally obligated to meet Jackson. Nor would his meeting Jackson be morally supererogatory. Indeed, it seems that the fact that he would personally benefit from meeting Jackson counts not at all in favor of his meeting Jackson—not morally speaking, that is. Thus, it seems that his reason to meet Jackson is a non-moral reason.

The explanation, then, for why Collins is not morally required to hold office hours seems to be that the self-interested and non-moral reason that he has to meet Jackson, being sufficiently strong, morally justifies his failing to fulfill his commitment to hold office hours. Thus, we seem to be implicitly committed to moral rationalism—that is, to the idea that an agent cannot be morally required to do what she has sufficient reason not to do. If instead moral rationalism were false, we would expect that if we were to take a case in which an agent has decisive reason to fulfill a moral requirement and then imagine a series of variants on that case in which the agent has ever stronger non-moral reasons to do something else, we would eventually arrive at a case in which the agent had sufficient reason to violate that moral requirement. But we never do arrive at such a case. For as soon as we are willing to say that the agent has sufficient reason to do that something else, we are no longer willing to say that she is morally required to refrain from doing that something else.

To illustrate, consider the case in which I have promised to hold office hours and have nothing better to do. Clearly, in this case, what I should do, all things considered, is hold my office hours as promised, and it seems that I am morally required to do so as well. But now imagine a series of variants on this case in which I have an ever stronger self-interested reason to do something else. At some point, we are willing to say that I now have sufficient reason to violate my commitment to hold office hours. Yet once we get to this point, we are no longer willing to say that I am morally required to hold these office hours. The Reggie Jackson example is a case in point. The self-interested and non-moral reason that Collins has to take advantage of this once-in-a-lifetime opportunity to meet his childhood hero successfully counters the moral reason that he has to hold office hours, the result being that he is neither rationally nor morally required to hold office hours. (Of course, this is not to deny that he would be morally required to make it up to those students who showed up and waited in vain.) It seems, then, that an agent's having sufficient reason to refrain from performing some act defeats what would otherwise be a moral requirement for her to perform that act.

Compare this to what effect an agent's having sufficient reason to do otherwise has on legal requirements. As we did above, let us start with a case in which I have decisive reason to obey the requirement—in this case, a legal requirement. Imagine, then, a case in which I come upon a red light while not in any hurry and know that, if I were to proceed against the red light, I would certainly get a ticket, as there are red-light cameras installed at the intersection. Now, imagine a series of variants on this case in which I have ever stronger and eventually sufficient reason to proceed against the red light. At the point at which we think there is sufficient reason for me to proceed against the red light, we do not conclude that there is no longer any legal requirement for me to wait for the green to proceed. In this respect, legal requirements differ from moral requirements. Legal requirements are not defeated by the agent's having sufficient reason to do otherwise. But what accounts for the difference? It seems to be the fact that whereas moral rationalism is true, legal rationalism is false. So besides the fact that moral rationalism is supported by the argument from blameworthiness, we should accept moral rationalism because it helps us to explain why non-moral reasons can, when sufficiently strong, prevent moral reasons from generating moral requirements.[60]

But what if I am wrong about all this? What if in spite of all my arguments to the contrary moral rationalism turns out to be false? If moral rationalism is false, then we do not have decisive reason to abide by all of morality's requirements. And, in that case, it seems to me that what we need to know is which moral requirements are the ones that we have decisive reason to obey, for it is only those that we just plain ought to obey. In that case, let us call the moral requirements that agents have decisive reason to obey *schmoral requirements*. I think that if I were convinced that moral rationalism was false, I would be more interested in giving an account of *schmorality* than in giving an account of morality. After all, it would seem, then, that providing a theory of schmorality is of much greater practical importance than providing an account of morality. And, in giving an account of schmorality, I could certainly appeal to *schmoral rationalism*, which would be analytically true:

SR If S is schmorally required to perform *x*, then S has decisive reason to perform *x*, all things considered.

---

[60] I will have more to say on this topic in chapter 5.

So if moral rationalism is false, then I suggest replacing "schmoral" for "moral" and "schmoral rationalism (or SR)" for "moral rationalism (or MR)" throughout the book. I do not think that anything of practical significance would be lost in doing so.

At this point, though, one might wonder why we should not just focus on what we have decisive reason to do and pay no mind to whether or not it would be morally wrong to refrain from doing what we have decisive to do. In response, I would argue that, as rational beings, we are not only interested in what we ought to *do*, but also in how we ought to *feel* and, in particular, whether we ought to feel guilt, indignation, and/or resentment in response to someone's failing to do what she had decisive reason to do. If we were interested only in what we ought to do, then we could just ignore moral requirements and focus solely on what we have decisive reason to do. But even if not particularly relevant to whether we ought to do something, the fact that an act is morally (or schmorally) required is highly relevant to the appropriateness of feeling various blaming emotions, such as guilt, indignation, and resentment. Someone can freely and knowledgeably do something contrary to what she has decisive reason to do, but unless that act is also morally (or schmorally) wrong it would be inappropriate to blame her for acting as she did.[61] After all, not every act that is contrary to reason is also wrong. For instance, many imprudent acts are, it seems, contrary to what there is decisive reason to do but are not wrong. So even if in wondering what we ought to do we can just ignore moral requirements (or schmoral requirements), we cannot ignore moral requirements (or schmoral requirements) if we want to know when it is appropriate to feel various blaming emotions, such as guilt, indignation, and resentment.

***

In this chapter, I have argued both that we should accept moral rationalism and that all traditional versions of consequentialism require us to perform acts that we lack decisive reason to perform. Therefore, we should reject all traditional versions of consequentialism. But I have also argued that moral rationalism compels us to accept consequentialism—at least, it does if we accept a certain plausible conception of practical reasons. In the next chapter, I will examine this conception of practical reasons more closely, explaining why it is attractive, why recent attacks on it have failed, and why we should think that it is uniquely positioned to offer the most unified and systemic account of our considered convictions about practical reasons.

---

[61] I think that if we were to reject moral rationalism, we would have to reject 2.10 as well and hold that when someone freely and knowledgeably acts wrongly, we can blame them only if they did not do so in virtue of having sufficient reason to do so. Thus, if we reject moral rationalism, it is not moral requirements but schmoral requirements that would be conceptually tied to blame.

3

The Teleological Conception
of Practical Reasons

It is through our actions that we affect the way the world goes. Indeed, whenever we face a choice of what to do, we also face a choice of which of various possible worlds to actualize.[1] Moreover, whenever we act *intentionally*, we act with the aim of making the world go a certain way. The aim need not be anything having to do with the causal consequences of the act. The aim could be nothing more than to bring it about that one performs the act. For instance, one could intend to run merely for the sake of bringing it about that one runs. The fact remains, though, that for every intentional action there is some end at which the agent aims.

If our actions are the means by which we affect the way the world goes, and if our intentional actions necessarily aim at making the world go a certain way, then it is only natural to suppose that what we have most reason to do is determined by which way we have most reason to want the world to go. To put things more precisely, an agent's reasons for action are a function of her reasons for preferring certain possible worlds to others, such that what she has most reason to do is to bring about the possible world, which of all those that she can actualize, is the one that she has most reason to want to be actual. This is what is known as the *teleological conception of practical reasons*.[2]

Whether this is the correct conception of practical reasons is important not only in its own right, but also in virtue of its potential implications for moral

---

[1] I will assume that for each act available to the agent there is some determinate fact as to what the world would be like if she were to perform that act. This assumption is sometimes called *counterfactual determinism*—see, e.g., BYKVIST 2003, p. 30. Although this assumption is controversial, nothing that I will say here hangs on it. I make the assumption only for the sake of simplifying the discussion. If counterfactual determinism is false, then instead of correlating each act with a unique possible world, we will need to correlate each act with a probability distribution over the set of possible worlds that might be actualized if the agent were to perform the act.

[2] Whenever I speak of practical reasons or reasons for action, I am referring to normative reasons for action. A normative reason for action is some fact that counts in favor of the agent's performing that action. Normative reasons contrast with explanatory reasons (i.e., facts that explain why the agent performed the action). One particularly important subclass of explanatory reasons is the set of motivating reasons, the facts that motivated the agent to perform the action—that is, the facts that the agent took to be her reasons for performing the action. See DARWALL 2006b, p. 285.

theorizing. As I argued in the previous chapter, this conception of practical reasons in conjunction with moral rationalism (MR) compels us to accept consequentialism. In this chapter, I will argue that we should accept the teleological conception of (practical) reasons—or "TCR" for short. These arguments for TCR in conjunction with my arguments for moral rationalism in the previous chapter jointly constitute my argument for consequentialism.

The teleological conception of reasons (i.e., TCR) is, on its face, quite plausible. Even its critics admit as much.[3] Since TCR is prima facie plausible, my main task will be to show that it is not subject to the sorts of objections that critics have leveled against it. Thus, I will spend most of this chapter rebutting objections and clearing up misconceptions. Nevertheless, I will, in the second half of the chapter, try to offer some positive arguments for it.

The chapter has the following structure. In §3.1, I offer a more precise statement of TCR, showing that the view consists in three distinct claims. And I explain why my statement of the view differs from those of some of its critics in eschewing talk of both value and desirability. Then, in §3.2, I clear up some common and potential misconceptions about the view. In §3.3, I rebut Scanlon's putative counterexamples to TCR, cases where putatively "many of the reasons bearing on an action concern not the desirability of outcomes but rather the eligibility or ineligibility of various other reasons" (SCANLON 1998, p. 84). And, finally, in §3.4, I provide arguments for each of TCR's three claims and for TCR as a whole.

§3.1 Getting clear on what the view is

Let me start by stating the view as precisely as I can. Let $a_1, a_2, \ldots, a_n$ be the set of mutually exclusive and jointly exhaustive act alternatives available to a subject, S. Let $o_1, o_2, \ldots, o_n$ be their corresponding outcomes, where an act's outcome is construed broadly as the possible world that would be actual were the act to be performed.[4] More precisely, then, the teleological conception of reasons can be stated as follows:

> **TCR** (1) S has more reason to perform a_i than to perform a_j if S has more reason to desire that o_i obtains than to desire that o_j obtains; (2) S has more reason to perform a_i than to perform a_j only if S has more reason to desire that o_i obtains than to desire that o_j obtains; and (3) if S has more reason to perform a_i than to perform a_j, then this is so in virtue of the fact that S has more reason to desire that o_i obtains than to desire that o_j obtains.[5]

---

[3] Scanlon, for instance, admits that this view "sounds plausible" (1998, p. 84).

[4] Again, I am assuming counterfactual determinism—see note 1 above.

[5] Of course, I have been assuming, for the sake of simplifying the discussion, that the laws of nature are deterministic and that, therefore, counterfactual determinism is true. Nevertheless,

More concisely, then, TCR is the view that S has more reason to perform a_i than to perform a_j if and only if, and because, S has more reason to desire that o_i obtains than to desire that o_j obtains.[6] For my purposes, though, it will be useful to keep the three claims separate; I will refer to them as TCR-1, TCR-2, and TCR-3, respectively. And although not stated above, I take TCR to include the claim that S has a reason to perform a_i if and only if, and because, S has a reason to desire that o_i obtains.

Having stated the view as precisely as I can, I will now proceed to clarify it, explaining in the process how and why it differs from T. M. Scanlon's statement of the view, which goes as follows: "the purely teleological conception of reasons [is the view] according to which, since any rational action must aim at some result, reasons that bear on whether to perform an action must appeal to the desirability or undesirability of having that result occur, taking into account also the intrinsic value of the act itself" (SCANLON 1998, p. 84). Although my statement of TCR

I should allow for the possibility that counterfactual determinism is false. Thus, strictly speaking, TCR needs to be reformulated so as to take reasons for action to be a function of how much reason the agent has to desire the *prospect* of each alternative action as opposed to the *outcome* of each alternative action. For if counterfactual determinism is false, there may be more than one possible outcome associated with a given action. Now, the *prospect* of an action is a probability distribution over the set of possible outcomes associated with that action. (I borrow the term "prospect" from J. ROSS FORTHCOMING.) So let $p_1, p_2, \ldots, p_n$ be the prospects of $a_1, a_2, \ldots, a_n$, respectively. And let $p_i, p_j,$ and p_k be variables that range over such prospects. We should, then, replace TCR with the following:

TCR^1 (1) S has more reason to perform a_i than to perform a_j if S has more reason to desire p_i than to desire p_j; (2) S has more reason to perform a_i than to perform a_j only if S has more reason to desire p_i than to desire p_j; and (3) if S has more reason to perform a_i than to perform a_j, then this is so in virtue of the fact that S has more reason to desire p_i than to desire p_j.

Again, to simplify the discussion within the body of the book, I will stick with TCR even though, strictly speaking, TCR is not what I am advocating.

As I see it, how much reason S has to desire p_j is a function of $\Sigma_i[Pr(o_i/a_j) \times D_s(o_i)]$, where a_j is the given action, $Pr(o_i/a_j)$ is the objective probability of o_i's obtaining given S's performance of a_j, and $D_s(o_i)$ is the S-relative desirability value of o_i, which is just a measure of how much reason S has to desire that o_i obtains. Thus, as I see it, S has more reason to desire p_j than to desire p_k if and only if $\Sigma_i[Pr(o_i/a_j) \times D_s(o_i)]$ is greater than $\Sigma_i[Pr(o_i/a_k) \times D_s(o_i)]$.

[6] It may be objected that complete possible worlds—or, in other words, total outcomes, such as o_i—are far too complex to be the objects of one's conscious desires. And, as the objection might run, if o_i is not the sort of thing that one can desire, then it is not the sort of thing that one can have reason to desire. But I do not see why one must have every aspect of o_i conscious before one's mind in order to desire it or to have reason to desire it. It seems clear to me that there are reasons for individuals to desire certain total outcomes and to prefer them to others. For instance, the fact that Smith's child as opposed to some stranger's child would be saved if she performs a_1 as opposed to a_2 is clearly a reason for her to prefer o_1 to o_2. And although Smith may be incapable of appreciating in total all the various reasons that she has for preferring o_1 to o_2, this does not mean that she cannot have most reason to prefer o_1 to o_2. After all, which total outcome Smith has most reason to prefer is simply a function of whatever the various specific reasons, on balance, support her preferring. I do not see, then, why Smith must be capable of having every aspect of o_1 before her mind in order to have most reason to desire it or to prefer it.

differs from Scanlon's in how it is worded, I do not believe that it differs in substance from the view that he intended to describe—or so I shall argue. I take my statement of TCR to differ from Scanlon's only in its degree of clarity and precision. There are, in fact, five separate points that need clarifying.

§§3.1.1 Reasons for desiring as opposed to desirability

Unlike Scanlon, I state TCR in terms of the agent's reasons for desiring various possible outcomes as opposed to the desirability of those outcomes. To see why, we must first get clear on what the difference is. Let us start with what it means to say that an outcome is desirable. To say that that an outcome, o_i, is desirable is to say that it is fitting to desire that o_i obtains. And to say that it is fitting to desire that o_i obtains is just to say that there are sufficiently weighty reasons of the right kind to desire that o_i obtains.[7] What are the right kinds of reasons? They are all and only those reasons that are relevant to determining whether, and to what extent, o_i is desirable. Let us call these *fittingness reasons.*

I will not attempt to give a complete account of what sorts of reasons are, and what sorts of reasons are not, fittingness reasons. These are controversial issues, and I have nothing new to add to the growing debate. Even so, I can plausibly claim that there are some clear cases of what would not count as fittingness reasons. First, if facts such as the fact that an evil demon will torture me unless I desire that o_i obtains constitute genuine reasons for me to desire that o_i obtains, then these are clearly not fittingness reasons, for such pragmatic "reasons" for desiring that o_i obtains clearly have no bearing on whether, or to what extent, o_i's obtaining is desirable.[8] Now, as a matter of fact, I do not think that such pragmatic "reasons" do constitute genuine reasons for desiring that o_i obtains. I think instead that they constitute reasons only to want, and to act so as to cause oneself, to desire that o_i obtains. If, however, I am wrong about this, then admittedly I will need to revise TCR so as to exclude such pragmatic "reasons," for such reasons are no more relevant to whether one should act so as to bring it about that o_i obtains than they are to whether o_i's obtaining is desirable.[9]

---

[7] More precisely, we should first say that, for all states of affairs p and q, it is better (i.e., preferable) that p is the case than that q is the case if and only if the set of all the *fittingness reasons* for preferring its being the case that p to its being the case that q is weightier than the set of all the *fittingness reasons* for preferring its being the case that q to its being the case that p. Then we can say that it is good (i.e., desirable) that p is the case if and only if the state of affairs in which it is the case that p is better than (i.e., preferable to) most of the states of affairs in the relevant contextually supplied comparison class. For more on this, see SCHROEDER 2010 and SCHROEDER 2008b.

[8] This is known as the *wrong-kind-of-reasons problem* for the fitting-attitude or buck-passing account of value (or desirability). For more on this problem and for some potential solutions to it, see RABINOWICZ & RØNNOW-RASMUSSEN 2004 and SCHROEDER 2010.

[9] The revised version of TCR would, then, read as follows: (TCR²) S has more reason to perform a_i than to perform a_j if and only if, and because, the set of all the *non-pragmatic reasons* that S has for

Second, it seems clear that agent-relative reasons are not fittingness reasons. To see why, consider that, in contrast to some stranger, I might have weightier (agent-relative) reasons to prefer the outcome in which my child lives to the outcome in which her child lives. But it would be odd to say that this is because the outcome in which my child goes on living is, other things being equal, better or more desirable than the outcome in which her child goes on living. Other things being equal, the outcome in which my child lives is neither more nor less desirable than the outcome in which her child lives. So although one can have agent-relative reasons for preferring one outcome to another, this does not entail that the one is better than, or preferable to, the other.[10] And, thus, agent-relative reasons for preferring one outcome to another are not fittingness reasons for preferring the one to the other.[11]

---

desiring that o_i obtains is weightier than the set of all the *non-pragmatic reasons* that S has for desiring that o_j obtains. Pragmatic reasons for S to desire that o_i obtains are reasons that are provided by facts about the consequences of S's desiring that o_i obtains, and non-pragmatic reasons are just reasons that are not pragmatic—for a more careful account of the relevant distinction, see STRATTON-LAKE 2005. The distinction that I am drawing between pragmatic and non-pragmatic reasons is closely related to Derek Parfit's (2001) distinction between state-given and object-given reasons as well as to Christian Piller's (2006) distinction between attitude-related and content-related reasons; it is not clear to me, though, that either is extensionally equivalent to mine.

As will be evident shortly, it is important to note that many agent-relative reasons for S to desire that o_i obtains, such as the fact that S's child will live if and only if o_i obtains, are non-pragmatic reasons and thus will not be excluded by the restriction to non-pragmatic reasons in TCR².

[10] This is known as the *partiality challenge* to the fitting-attitude or buck-passing account of value. See OLSON 2009, SUIKKANEN 2009b, and ZIMMERMAN FORTHCOMING for some potential solutions to this particular problem.

[11] There are also time-relative reasons for preferring one outcome to another (and these too are not fittingness reasons). Sometimes, for instance, the preference that an agent should have before choosing to perform some action is the opposite of what it should be at some point after performing that action. Suppose, for instance, that Ana decided not to have an abortion even after learning that her fetus might have Down syndrome. Consequently, she gave birth to a boy, named Bill, with Down syndrome, who is now eight. She ought, at this point, be glad that she did not have an abortion. After all, she does, at this point, have a very special bond with her son Bill, whom she has come to love for exactly who he is, which includes the fact that he has Down syndrome. If she could somehow take it all back and make the decision over, she should not wish/prefer (at this point) that she had had the abortion and then later given birth to a child without Down syndrome. Interestingly, though, this is compatible with our thinking that at the time of her initial decision, a time before she had formed any special relationship with what was then just an early-stage fetus, she should have preferred the outcome in which she had had the abortion and then later given birth to a child without Down syndrome. That would have been the better outcome, and, at the time of her initial decision, she had no reason to prefer the worse outcome in which she has a child with Down syndrome.

Given that what it is reasonable to prefer can change over time, TCR should actually be time-indexed. Consequently, TCR should be revised as follows: (TCR³) S has at t_i more reason to perform a_i than to perform a_j just when, and because, S has at t_i more reason to desire that o_i obtains than to desire that o_j obtains. Even this is not the version of the teleological conception of reasons that I ultimately endorse. For that version, see TCR* in §7.4. For more on the issue of how it can be reasonable to prefer that a loved one exists even though one recognizes that there is a preferable state of affairs in which that loved one does not exist, see E. HARMAN 2009.

It is this last exclusion that makes trouble for stating TCR in terms of the value or the desirability of outcomes. If TCR is to be stated in terms of value/desirability and value/desirability is to be understood exclusively in terms of agent-neutral reasons for desiring, then TCR will automatically disallow agent-relative reasons for action, such as the agent-relative reason that I have to save my own child as opposed to some stranger's child. Yet there is no reason why the teleologist should exclude the possibility of agent-relative reasons for action, as even the critics of TCR admit. Scanlon, for instance, says, "The teleological structure I have described is often taken to characterize not only 'the good' impartially understood, but also the good from a particular individual's point of view (the way she has reason to want things to go)" (1998, p. 81). So if we are to allow that one agent might have a reason to bring about a state of affairs that another has no reason to bring about or that one agent might have more reason to bring about some state of affairs than another agent does, then we must state TCR not in terms of the value/desirability of states of affairs, but in terms of the reasons that the various agents have to desire that these states of affairs obtain.

Interestingly, Scanlon is aware that agent-relative reasons for valuing/desiring are not fittingness reasons. He says, "To claim that something is valu*able* (or that it is 'of value') is to claim that others also have reason to value it, as you do" (1998, p. 95). Furthermore, he claims that "we can, quite properly, value some things more than others without claiming that they are more valuable" (1998, p. 95). That is, we can properly value/desire some outcomes more than others without claiming that they are better than, or preferable to, those others. This is because which outcome is most preferable (or best) is a function of only our agent-neutral reasons for preferring them to the others, whereas which outcome we have most reason to prefer is a function of both our agent-relative and our agent-neutral reasons for preferring them to the others.

Jussi Suikkanen (2009b, p. 6) makes a similar point. He argues that it is better (impersonally speaking) that o_i obtains than that o_j obtains if and only if it would be fitting for an impartial spectator to prefer o_i to o_j. An impartial spectator must be both impartial and a mere spectator. To ensure that she is impartial, we must assume that she has no personal relations with anyone involved. And to ensure that she is a mere spectator, we must assume that she is not involved either in bringing it about that o_i obtains or in bringing about that o_j obtains. Thus, the impartial spectator can have nothing but agent-neutral reasons for preferring one outcome to the other. But, unlike the impartial spectator, situated agents can have agent-relative reasons for preferring one outcome to another given both their agential relations to those outcomes and their personal relations with those who would be better or worse off were those outcomes to obtain. So whereas it can, for instance, be fitting for me to prefer the outcome in which my child lives to the one in which some stranger's child lives given my personal relations with my child, it would not be fitting—at least, not if other things are equal—for an impartial spectator to have the same preference. And thus it can be appropriate for me to prefer the outcome in which my child lives even if this outcome is not better than (or preferable to) the one in which the stranger's child lives.

Now, if we can properly value/desire some outcomes more than others without claiming that they are better than, or preferable to, those others, then we should ask: Why does Scanlon state the teleological conception of reasons in terms of value/desirability when he clearly wants to allow that the teleologist can accommodate agent-relative reasons for valuing/desiring and, consequently, agent-relative reasons for action? The answer is that when Scanlon talks about value/desirability in the context of TCR, he means for this to include agent-relative value or what he refers to as "the good from a particular individual's point of view." Indeed, he brings up the teleological conception of reasons to explain why some think that we must assign agent-relative disvalue to an agent's killing in order to make sense of agent-centered restrictions against killing (1998, pp. 94–95). But since Scanlon equates what is "good [or desirable] from a particular individual's point of view" with "the way she has reason to want things to go" (1998, p. 81), he should have no objection to my stating TCR in terms of the agent's reasons for desiring. Indeed, given what he says, we should think that my statement of TCR in terms of the agent's reasons for desiring various outcomes is equivalent to his statement of TCR in terms of the value/desirability of outcomes, for, in his statement of TCR, he just means for his talk of the value/desirability of an outcome to stand for the agent's reasons for wanting that outcome to obtain.

So it is important to note that TCR is to be understood in terms of reasons to desire and not necessarily in terms of (impersonal) value or desirability. With that said, I will occasionally revert back to talking about the value/desirability of states of affairs, since this is the language that TCR's critics so often employ. Keep in mind, though, that these critics mean for value/desirability to somehow include what is "good from a particular individual's point of view," which they equate with "the way she has reason to want things to go" (SCANLON 1998, p. 81). So they are not using words such as "valuable" and "desirable" in their ordinary, impersonal senses.[12] The reader should, then, assume that when I revert back to talk of desirability so as to engage TCR's critics on their own terms, I am using the word "desirable" as they do, as a kind of shorthand for "that which the agent has sufficiently weighty reasons to desire."

§§3.1.2 Total outcomes as opposed to intended effects

Another way that my statement of TCR differs from Scanlon's is that I formulate TCR broadly in terms of reasons to desire total outcomes, and not narrowly in terms of reasons to desire the results that the agent aims to produce. It seems that Scanlon meant to formulate TCR in terms of total outcomes, since, as he points out, the "result" of the action must take into account "the action itself" (1998, p. 84). The problem is that his statement of TCR, as quoted at the beginning of

---

[12] See SCHROEDER 2007a for more on this point.

this section, is somewhat unclear on this point in that it refers to "*that* result [emphasis added]," which in this case refers back to the result at which the action was aimed. The problem, then, is that the reasons for performing an action may lie, in part, with the results at which the agent did not aim. I assume that Scanlon would agree, and, thus, I have formulated TCR in terms of total outcomes as opposed to the intended effects.

Note, then, that, as I have stated TCR, it is not restricted to only the causal consequences of actions.[13] Indeed, it would be odd for the teleologist (which is what I call the proponent of TCR) to exclude in advance from consideration any of the ways that the world might change as a result of an agent's performing an act. For instance, one way the world changes when a subject, S, performs an act, a_1, is that the world becomes one in which S has performed a_1. And, as a result of S's having performed a_1, it may also thereby be true that S has fulfilled her past promise to perform an act of that type.[14] Since all these ways in which the world might change could potentially make a difference as to whether or not S has a reason to desire that o_1 obtains and, if so, how much reason, we should formulate TCR, as I have, so that it does not exclude from consideration such possibly relevant non-causal consequences.

§§3.1.3 Reasons (to intend) to act

Following Scanlon, when I talk about reasons to perform an action, I am, strictly speaking, referring to reasons to intend to perform that action. Most immediately, practical reasoning gives rise not to bodily movements, but to intentions. Of course, when all goes well, these intentions result in some bodily movement, and the end-product is, then, an intentional action. Nevertheless, the most immediate product of practical reasoning is an intention to perform some act, not the act itself (SCANLON 1998, pp. 18–22). Having clarified this, I will, however, sometimes (when it seems not to matter) slip into the more customary way of speaking in terms of reasons for action.[15]

Note, though, that I do not consider facts such as the fact that I will receive some reward or punishment if I intend to φ to constitute genuine reasons for or against

---

[13] Even critics of TCR admit that teleologists can be concerned with more than just the causal consequences of acts. See, for instance, SCANLON 1998 (pp. 80 and 84) and WALLACE 2010 (p. 520).

[14] Thus TCR will not be exclusively forward-looking. The teleologist can hold that S has a reason to desire that o_1 obtains in virtue of the fact that, in performing a_1, she thereby fulfills her past promise to perform an act of that type. For more on this point, see STURGEON 1996, pp. 511–514, and ANDERSON 1996, p. 541. Of course, the teleologist must deny that S has a reason to desire the outcome in which her promise is fulfilled in virtue of the fact that she has a reason to fulfill her promise. For the teleologist, it is the other way around: she has a reason to fulfill her promise in virtue of the fact that she has a reason to desire that her promise is fulfilled.

[15] As I see it, all talk of reasons for action is really just a somewhat sloppy but more idiomatic way of talking about reasons for intending to act. That is, I do not think that there is any distinction

my intending to φ. The judgment that the intentional content of one's intention to φ, namely, φ, has certain consequences that one has reason to desire (call this a *content-directed judgment*) is the sort of judgment that can give rise to an intention to φ and that, if true, constitutes a reason to φ. But the judgment that one's having the attitude of intending to φ would have consequences that one has reason to desire (call this an *attitude-directed judgment*) is not the sort of judgment that can give rise to an intention to φ, nor is it, to my mind, the sort of judgment that, if true, constitutes a reason to intend to φ.[16] If I am wrong about this, if the truth of such an attitude-directed judgment does constitute a reason to intend to φ, then I will need to rethink my view that a reason to intend to φ is just a reason to φ, for the fact that I will be rewarded if I intend now to drink some toxin tomorrow is certainly no reason to drink that toxin when tomorrow comes around.[17]

§§3.1.4 The narrow as opposed to the broad construal of desire

Although some philosophers (e.g., HEUER 2004, p. 48) take a desire to be nothing more than a disposition to act, where one desires that o_i obtains if and only if one is disposed to act so as to bring it about that o_i obtains (that is, to perform a_j), I will, following Scanlon, use "desire" in the more narrow, ordinary sense, such that one desires that o_i obtains only if one finds the prospect of o_i's obtaining in some way attractive or appealing.[18]

On this more narrow interpretation, desiring that o_i obtains is sufficient for being motivated (to some extent) to perform a_j, but being motivated to perform a_j is not sufficient for desiring that o_i obtains.[19] Thus, in Warren Quinn's famous example of a man who has a compulsive urge that disposes him to turn on every radio he sees despite his failing to see anything appealing about either these acts themselves or their effects (1993, p. 236), we do not have a genuine case of desire—at least, not in the sense that I will be using the term "desire." As I see it, then, having a desire involves a complicated set of dispositions to think, feel, and react in various ways (SCANLON 1998, p. 21). A person who desires that o_i obtains will find the prospect of its obtaining appealing, will to some extent be motivated

---

between what we ought, or have reason, to do and what we ought, or have reason, to intend to do. The latter is just a precisification of the former. If I am wrong about this, then TCR should be taken to be a view about reasons for action.

[16] See SCANLON 2007, especially pp. 90–91.

[17] This example comes from KAVKA 1983.

[18] To find o_i's obtaining in *some way* attractive or appealing, one need not have all that o_i's obtaining entails conscious before the mind. Ana might know that the only way to ensure that her daughter excels in school is to hire Bill (a tutor) and, consequently, find the outcome resulting from her hiring Bill in this respect appealing.

[19] Because one can be motivated (to some extent) to perform a_i without being sufficiently motivated to perform a_j, desiring that o_i obtains does not necessarily result in an intention to perform a_i. After all, one can have conflicting motives.

to perform a_i, and will, perhaps, have her attention directed insistently toward considerations that present themselves as counting in favor of o_i's obtaining (SCANLON 1998, p. 39).[20]

Unlike Scanlon, though, I do not think that "desiring something involves having a tendency to see something good or desirable about it" (1998, p. 38). This suggests that preferring o_i to o_j involves having a tendency to see o_i as better than (or preferable to) o_j. But I do not think that can be right, as I can, even other things being equal, prefer the outcome in which I am saved to the outcome in which five others are saved without having any tendency to see the former as better than the latter. Of course, I might rightly think that the former is better *for* me, but that is not the same as thinking that it would better if I was the one who was saved. I think, then, it is more accurate to say that desiring something typically involves having a tendency to see something about it as providing one with a reason to desire it—likewise, for preferring.

§§3.1.5 The teleological conception of reasons (i.e., TCR) as opposed to just the bi-conditional that it entails

To be a teleologist, it is not enough to accept the bi-conditional that is entailed by the conjunction of TCR-1 and TCR-2 (call this bi-conditional "TCR-1+2"); the teleologist must accept TCR-3 as well. Of course, TCR-3 is but one of three possible explanations for the truth of the bi-conditional stated by TCR-1+2. To illustrate, let "PER" stand for "S has more reason to *per*form a_i than to perform a_j" and let "DES" stand for "S has more reason to *des*ire that o_i obtains than to desire that o_j obtains." The three possible explanations for TCR-1+2—that is, for "PER if and only if DES"—are: (*i*) "PER, because DES"; (*ii*) "DES, because PER"; or (*iii*) both "PER, because BET" and "DES, because BET"—where, for instance, "BET" might stand for "o_i is *bet*ter than o_j."[21] In defending TCR, I must not only defend TCR-1+2, but also argue that it is explanation *i* as opposed to either explanation *ii* or explanation *iii* that explains TCR-1+2; that is, I must defend TCR-3 in addition to both TCR-1 and TCR-2. But before I proceed to defend TCR, I will first try to clear up some actual and potential misconceptions about the view.

---

[20] I am not sure whether the last of these three is essential to desiring, as the qualifier "perhaps" is meant to indicate. For reasons to doubt that it is essential to desiring in the ordinary sense, see CHANG 2004b, especially pp. 65–66.

[21] These three explanations are analogues of the three possible causal explanations for a correlation between events a and b: (1) a causes b, (2) b causes a, or (3) a and b have a common cause. I thank Mark Schroeder and G. Shyam Nair for pointing out the need to consider such common "cause" explanations. And I thank Schroeder for suggesting that someone might take "o_i is *bet*ter than o_j" to be the common "cause."

§3.2 Clearing up some misconceptions about the view

There are a number of misconceptions about TCR that have led philosophers to reject it for mistaken reasons. Below, I try to clear up some of these misconceptions.

§§3.2.1 The teleological conception of reasons (i.e., TCR) is compatible with value concretism

Although Scanlon (1998, pp. 79–81) lumps the two together, TCR is distinct from, and independent of, *value abstractism:* the view that the sole or primary bearers of intrinsic value are certain abstracta—facts, outcomes, states of affairs, or possible worlds.[22] On value abstractism, there is only one kind of value, the kind that is to be promoted, and so the only proper response to value is to desire and promote it, ensuring that there is as much of it as possible. The contrary view—the view that the fundamental bearers of intrinsic value are concrete entities (e.g., persons, animals, and things)—is called *value concretism.*[23]

Contrary to what Scanlon and others (e.g., ANDERSON 1993) have claimed, there is no reason why the teleologist cannot accept value concretism.[24] Indeed, the teleologist can accept all of the following claims: (*a*) that concrete entities— persons, animals, and things—are the primary bearers of intrinsic value; (*b*) that states of affairs generally have only extrinsic value in that they generally have no value apart from our valuing concrete entities;[25] (*c*) that "our basic evaluative attitudes—love, respect, consideration, affection, honor, and so forth—are nonpropositional...attitudes we take up immediately toward persons, animals, and

---

[22] This is true whether TCR is to be formulated in terms of how much reason the agent has to desire the available outcomes or in terms of how valuable/desirable (in the ordinary, agent-neutral sense) the available outcomes are.

[23] I borrow the terms *concretism* and *abstractism* from TÄNNSJÖ 1999.

[24] Elizabeth Anderson is, as I see it, another leading critic of TCR. Although she uses the term "consequentialism" as opposed to "teleology," she defines "consequentialism" so broadly (see 1993, pp. 30–31) that it is, in spirit, equivalent to TCR. She says, for instance, "consequentialism specifies our rational aims, and then tells us to adopt whatever intentions will best bring about those aims" (ANDERSON 1996, p. 539), which is exactly what TCR tells us to do. Thus, as Anderson uses the term, "consequentialism" refers not to a moral theory but to a conception of practical reasons that is roughly equivalent to TCR. In certain passages, Anderson, like Scanlon, defines "consequentialism" in terms of value as opposed to reasons to desire. But, as with Scanlon, this is only because she talks as if intrinsic goods include both what is good for an individual and what is good relative to an individual (ANDERSON 1993, pp. 30–31).

[25] The reason for the qualifier "generally" in claim *b* is that Anderson does allow for the possibility that a state of affairs can have intrinsic value if it is one that is intrinsically interesting. Anderson says, "Interest does seem to be an evaluative attitude that can take a state of affairs as its immediate and independent object. This is an exception to the general rule that states of affairs have no intrinsic value" (1993, p. 27).

things, not toward facts" (ANDERSON 1993, p. 20); and (*d*) that both value itself and our valuations are deeply pluralistic, that there are many ways that we experience things as valuable (e.g., as interesting, admirable, beautiful, etc.) and that there are many different kinds of value as well as different modes of valuing that are appropriate to each (e.g., "beautiful things are worthy of appreciation, rational beings of respect, sentient beings of consideration, virtuous ones of admiration, convenient things of use"—ANDERSON 1993, p. 11). As I will now explain, TCR is compatible with all of claims *a* through *d*.

As rational *beings*, we appropriately respond to different sorts of things with different sorts of attitudes. We appropriately respond to beautiful objects by appreciating them, we appropriately respond to rational persons by respecting them, and we appropriately respond to desirable states of affairs (desirable in the ordinary, agent-neutral sense) by desiring their actualizations—at least, that is how we appropriately respond to them when we do not have weightier agent-relative or time-relative reasons to desire that they not be actualized. As rational *agents*, though, it is only the last of these three that is pertinent, for, as agents, we can effect only outcomes. We cannot bring about concrete entities; a concrete entity is not the sort of thing that we can bring about or actualize through our actions. Of course, we can act so as to bring it about that a certain concrete entity exists or that our actions express our respect for rational persons, but these are states of affairs, not concrete entities.

As agents, then, we have the ability to actualize only certain possible worlds or states of affairs. Indeed, purposive action must aim at the realization of some state of affairs. So the teleologist can admit that we have reasons to have all sorts of different attitudes, including reasons to have certain non-propositional attitudes (such as, respect) toward various concrete entities (such as, rational persons). But the teleologist will insist that when it comes to the particular attitude of intending to act in some way, the reasons for having this attitude must always be grounded in the reasons that the agent has to desire that certain possible worlds or states of affairs be actualized. It is a mistake, however, to think that the teleologist is, in addition, committed to the denial of any of claims *a* through *d* above.[26]

§§3.2.2 The teleological conception of reasons (i.e., TCR) is compatible with appropriately valuing goods such as friendship

Another common misconception concerning TCR is that it is incompatible with the thought that, with respect to goods such as science and friendship, taking them to be valuable is not simply, or even primarily, a matter of promoting certain states of affairs (cf. SCANLON 1998, p. 88). Take friendship, for instance. The teleological

---

[26] This point is not particularly new, although it bears repeating given the stubborn persistence of this misconception. Others who have made essentially the same point include ARNESON 2002 and STURGEON 1996.

conception of reasons (i.e., TCR) does not imply that the only reasons provided by my friend and our friendship are reasons to promote certain states of affairs. The teleologist can accept that I have reasons to care about my friend, to empathize with her pain, to take joy in her successes, and so on, and that these are not reasons to promote certain states of affairs, but rather reasons to have certain non-propositional attitudes and feelings. The teleological conception of reasons (i.e., TCR) is, then, compatible with the thought that what lovers, friends, and family members value, fundamentally, is *each other* as opposed to certain states of affairs.

The teleological conception of reasons (i.e., TCR) is also compatible with the thought that a person who values friendship will see that what she has reason to do, first and foremost, is to be a good friend to her current friends and that these reasons are weightier than whatever reasons she has to cultivate new friendships or to foster good friendship relations among others (cf. SCANLON 1998, pp. 88–89). The teleologist can even hold that my friendships generate agent-centered restrictions on my actions (cf. ANDERSON 1993, pp. 73–74), such that I have more reason to refrain from betraying one of my own friends than to prevent more numerous others from betraying theirs.

This is all possible given that TCR allows for agent-relative reasons. If there were only agent-neutral reasons, (e.g., agent-neutral reasons to promote friendships and to prevent friends from betraying one another), then I would often have sufficient reason to neglect one of my current friendships if I could thereby cultivate two or more new ones, and I would often have sufficient reason to betray one of my own friends if I could thereby prevent more numerous others from betraying their friends. But, as even critics of TCR admit (e.g., SCANLON 1998, p. 81), TCR is compatible with the existence of agent-relative reasons and thus with the idea that whereas *you* will have more reason to prefer that *your* friends are not betrayed, *I* will have more reason to prefer that *my* friends are not betrayed.[27] And such agent-relative reasons to prefer the possible world in which your friends as opposed to my friends are betrayed will, given TCR, generate agent-relative reasons for me to refrain from betraying one of my own friends even for the sake of preventing you from betraying two of yours.[28] And TCR certainly allows for the possibility that such reasons will be decisive and thereby generate an agent-centered restriction against betraying one's own friends even for the sake of preventing more numerous others from betraying theirs.

---

[27] The teleological conception of reasons (i.e., TCR) would be incompatible with the existence of agent-relative reasons only if it were to be formulated in terms of how valuable/desirable (in the ordinary, agent-neutral sense) the available outcomes are. But, as I have shown, neither Scanlon nor Anderson thinks that this is the way to formulate TCR.

[28] Similarly, the teleologist can even hold that I have an agent-relative reason to prefer *your* betraying my friends to *my* betraying my friends and that this agent-relative reason will, given TCR, generate an agent-relative reason for me to refrain from betraying one of my friends even for the sake of preventing you from betraying two of my friends.

What's more, TCR is compatible with the claim that I should not abandon my current friends even for the sake of cultivating more numerous new friendships, for the teleologist can hold that I currently have good time-relative reasons for preferring the preservation of my current friendships to the creation of otherwise similar new friendships given the shared history that I have with my current friends and the lack of any shared history (at present) with those possible future friends (HURKA 2006, p. 238).[29] And the teleologist can accept not only that one should not destroy one's own current friendships for the sake of creating more numerous future friendships for oneself or for others, but also that, out of respect for friendships generally, one should not destroy someone else's friendship for the sake of preventing numerous others from doing the same. Again, because the teleologist can hold that there are agent-relative reasons for preferring one possible world to another, the teleologist can hold that I should prefer the state of affairs in which, say, five others each destroy someone else's friendship to the state of affairs in which I myself destroy someone else's friendship.

§§3.2.3 The teleological conception of reasons (i.e., TCR) is compatible with the view that attitudes such as belief and blame are rationally justified on non-pragmatic grounds

Elizabeth Anderson has claimed that the teleologist is committed to the implausible view that all attitudes (blaming, believing, intending, etc.) are rationally justified on pragmatic grounds—that is, on the grounds that the agent's having the given attitude would have desirable consequences. For instance, she claims that the teleologist (or what she calls the "consequentialist") must hold that beliefs "are justified to the degree that they bring better states of affairs into existence" (ANDERSON 1993, p. 39). This is mistaken for at least three reasons.

First, note that the teleologist does not even hold that whether one is rationally justified in having the intention to perform a_i is a function of the desirability of the consequences of one's having this attitude. The teleological conception of reasons (i.e., TCR) does not imply, for instance, that the fact that an evil demon has threatened to produce undesirable consequences unless you intend to perform a_i gives you a reason to intend to perform a_i. On TCR, it is the fact that your *performing* a_i will have desirable consequences (or, as I would prefer to say, consequences that you have sufficiently weighty reasons to desire), not the fact that your *intending to perform* a_i will have desirable consequences, that provides you with a reason to intend to perform a_i.[30] Thus, it

---

[29] As mentioned in note 11, TCR should, then, be revised as follows: (TCR³) S has at t_i more reason to perform a_i than to perform a_j just when, and because, S has at t_i more reason to desire that o_i obtains than to desire that o_j obtains.

[30] To see that these can come apart, consider that one can, say, knock over a bucket without forming the intention to do so and that one can form the intention to do so without succeeding. On TCR, the reasons that one has to intend to knock over a bucket depend on what the world would be like if one were to knock over the bucket (whether or not one would do so intentionally), not on what the world would be like if one were to form the intention to do so (whether or not one would succeed).

is the consequences of *the act*, not of *the intention*, that are relevant on TCR. And so there is no way to generalize from the claim that intending to do a_i is justified on the grounds that *performing* a_i is instrumental in bringing about certain desirable consequences to the claim that attitudes, such as the belief that p, are justified on the grounds that *having these attitudes* is instrumental in bringing about certain desirable consequences. It is just not analogous.

Second, even if it were true that the teleologist thought that the rationality of intending to perform a_i depends on the desirability of the consequences of having this attitude, it is not clear why the teleologist would be committed to the more general claim that this is true of *all* attitudes. Why could the teleologist not hold that what is true of intending to act is not true of other attitudes?[31]

Third, it seems that Anderson must be mistakenly assuming that mental attitudes such as blaming and believing are actions in the relevant sense, as this seems to be the only possible explanation for why she thinks that the teleologist is committed to the view that blaming and believing are rationally justified on the grounds that "performing" these "actions" would have desirable consequences. But, unlike intentional actions, we do not "perform" the "act" of blaming (or believing) at will—that is, by intending to blame (or to believe). Take belief, for instance. We often form beliefs involuntarily in response to our perceptual experiences. These belief formations are not intentional actions, for we do not form these beliefs as the result of our intending to form them. Since blaming and believing are not intentional actions, they are not the sorts of things to which TCR applies.

So the teleologist can accept, contrary to what Anderson claims, that whether a person has sufficient reason to believe that p depends only on what her evidence is for the truth of p and not on the desirability of the consequences of her believing that p. And the teleologist can accept that whether blaming someone is rationally justified depends only on whether there is sufficient reason to blame that someone. Of course, the teleologist is committed to the view that whether one is rationally justified in intending to act so as to criticize, punish, or otherwise censure someone does depend on the consequences of such an act. But this is distinct from the attitude of blaming someone for her actions—that is, the attitude of feeling guilt, resentment, or indignation in response to her actions (LEVY 2005, p. 2). One can blame a person for her wrongdoing without intending to act so as to criticize, punish, or otherwise censure her.

§§3.2.4 The teleological conception of reasons (i.e., TCR) is compatible with passing the normative buck from value to reasons

Lastly, it should be noted that TCR is compatible with a buck-passing account of value, where the domain of reasons is taken to be explanatorily prior to the

---

[31] Or if one prefers to talk about reasons for action as opposed to reasons for intending to act, why can't the teleologist hold that although reasons for action are a function of our reasons for desiring its consequences, neither reasons for believing nor reasons for blaming are a function of our reasons for desiring the consequences that stem from our having these attitudes?

domain of value—thus the normative buck is passed from value to reasons. There is potential for confusion here, for Scanlon sometimes formulates the buck-passing account of value specifically in terms of reasons for *action*, and TCR does treat evaluative reasons (e.g., reasons to desire) as explanatorily prior to practical reasons (i.e., reasons for action).[32] Nevertheless, TCR is compatible with the following more general formulation of the buck-passing account of value: *x*'s being good or valuable is just the purely formal, higher order property of having other properties that provide sufficiently weighty reasons of the right kind to respond favorably toward *x*. This leaves open what the relevant favorable response will be, and, arguably, it will vary depending on the kind of thing that is being evaluated. In the case of a rational person, the relevant response might be to have respect for that person. In the case of a valuable state of affairs, the relevant response might be to desire that it obtains.

If this is right, then TCR is perfectly compatible with the buck-passing account of value. An agent-neutral teleologist could, for instance, hold that reasons for actions are a function of the value (or the desirability) of the states of affairs that those actions produce, but still ultimately pass the normative buck back to reasons by claiming that what it is for a state of affairs to be valuable/desirable (in the ordinary, agent-neutral sense) is for it to have the purely formal, higher order property of having other properties that provide sufficiently weighty reasons (of the right kind) to desire it.[33]

§3.3 Scanlon's putative counterexamples to the view

Besides these misconceptions, some philosophers are led to reject TCR on the basis of putative counterexamples. Scanlon, for instance, uses examples to argue that "many of the reasons bearing on an action concern not the desirability of outcomes but rather the eligibility or ineligibility of various other reasons..., [and] judging that a certain consideration does not count as a reason for action is not equivalent to assigning negative intrinsic value to the occurrence of actions based on this reason" (1998, p. 84). Unfortunately, it is not clear what he is trying to establish by this. One possibility is that he is pointing out that there are sometimes reasons for *believing* (he says "judging") that a certain fact does not count as a reason to perform a given act and that these *epistemic* reasons (i.e., reasons for belief) do not concern the desirability of outcomes. But, then, this is no

---

[32] Scanlon says, for instance, that "to call something valuable is to say that it has other properties that provide reasons for behaving in certain ways with regard to it" (1998, p. 96).

[33] The agent-neutral teleologist holds that the best outcome (in the ordinary, agent-neutral sense) available to a given agent is necessarily the one she ought to prefer to all other available alternatives, either because fittingness reasons for preferring one outcome to another are the only reasons for preferring one outcome to another or because fittingness reasons always override non-fittingness reasons.

counterexample to TCR. To provide a counterexample to TCR, Scanlon must provide an example in which we are compelled to think that there are *practical* reasons (reasons for action) that do not concern the desirability of outcomes, not an example in which we are compelled to think that there are epistemic reasons that do not concern the desirability of outcomes. As we saw in §§3.2.3, the teleologist can accept that reasons for belief do not concern the desirability of outcomes. This, then, is clearly not the most charitable way to interpret Scanlon.

So let us consider his actual examples. In chapter 1, section 10, of *What We Owe to Each Other*, he provides examples in which an agent "judge[s] one consideration, C, to be a reason for taking another consideration, D, not to be relevant to ... [his or her] decision whether or not to pursue a certain line of action" (1998, p. 51). What he gives us, then, are not reasons that concern the eligibility or ineligibility of various other reasons, but rather reasons that concern whether or not one ought to *take* various other reasons into account in one's deliberations, and taking other reasons into account in one's deliberation is itself an action.[34] Moreover, the reasons for or against taking other reasons into account in one's deliberations do seem to concern the comparative desirability of the outcomes associated with doing so versus not doing so. Indeed, in the sorts of examples that Scanlon provides, the reason not to take a certain consideration into account in one's deliberations is that doing so would have an undesirable effect (or, at least, an effect that one has good reason to want to avoid). And so Scanlon's putative counterexamples are not counterexamples after all.

It seems, then, that Scanlon may be conflating reasons for and against performing an act with reasons for and against taking into account various considerations when deciding whether or not to perform that act. But the act of taking into account (or ignoring) various considerations when deciding whether or not to perform, say, a_1 is not the act of performing a_1; it is, rather, an entirely different act. So let a_2 be the act of taking into account certain considerations when deciding whether to perform a_1.[35] It seems that when we consider whether or not

---

[34] The verb "to take" has many senses. In one sense, to take something to be irrelevant is to regard or treat it as irrelevant with the implication that this may be contrary to fact. This is how I am interpreting Scanlon here. Thus, I am assuming that, by the phrase "taking another consideration, D, not to be relevant," he means "treating another consideration, D, as being irrelevant (whether or not it is, or is believed to be, relevant)." If instead Scanlon is using his phrase to mean "believing D not to be relevant," then he is not talking about reasons for action (or, as he says, "reasons bearing on an action"), but is instead talking about reasons for belief. If he is talking about such epistemic reasons, then, as I explain above, this poses no problem for TCR, which instead concerns practical reasons.

[35] I am, perhaps, speaking a bit loosely when I treat taking into account (or ignoring) some consideration as itself a voluntary act, for, admittedly, whether one takes into account (or ignores) some consideration is not always directly under one's volitional control. In those cases in which it is not directly under one's volitional control, though, one can still intend to do that which will cause oneself to take into account (or ignore) that consideration. For instance, if I want to take into account certain considerations, I will intentionally focus my attention on considerations of that sort. And if,

to perform a_2, we should, as TCR implies, consider the agent's reasons for and against desiring that o_2 obtains. Thus TCR does not deny that the reasons for and against performing a_2 (i.e., taking into account certain considerations when deciding whether to perform a_1) may have nothing to do with the reasons for and against desiring that o_1 obtains. What it denies is only that the reasons for and against performing a_2 may have nothing to do with the reasons for and against desiring that o_2 obtains. And none of Scanlon's examples repudiate this, as I will now show.

Consider one of Scanlon's main examples, one in which I have met someone for a game of tennis. Assume that I have determined that there are no strong reasons for or against my playing to win so that whether I have reason to play to win just depends on what I would enjoy doing at the moment. And assume that what I would enjoy most at this moment is playing to win, and so this is what I have decided to do. Given all this, Scanlon claims, contrary to TCR, that the fact that my succeeding in making a certain strategic shot might make my opponent feel crushed or disappointed just is not relevant to whether or not I should make the shot.

I do not think that we should accept this claim. Now, Scanlon never says what consideration is the reason for me to ignore this other consideration (i.e., that my opponent might feel crushed) when deciding whether or not to make this strategic shot, but clearly it is some pragmatic consideration such as the fact that it is very difficult, if not impossible, to play to win while taking these sorts of considerations into account. Or maybe it is the fact that one cannot enjoy a good competitive game if one is constantly worrying about whether one's opponent's feelings might get hurt. But notice that we are now appealing to the desirability of taking my opponent's feelings into account, which is precisely what the teleologist holds to be relevant. The fact that we are not appealing to the desirability of my making the strategic shot and weighing the desirability of the outcome in which I make the shot against the desirability of the outcome in which I do not make the shot is neither here nor there. So it seems that this example shows only that the desirability or undesirability of embarrassing my opponent is not relevant to whether or not I should ignore his potential embarrassment when deciding whether to make a certain shot. It does not, however, show that the desirability or undesirability of embarrassing my opponent by making a certain strategic shot is irrelevant to whether or not I should make that shot.

Perhaps, even this is not the most charitable way of interpreting Scanlon. Perhaps, we should interpret Scanlon to be offering this not as a counterexample,

---

instead, I want to ignore those considerations, I will intentionally focus my attention elsewhere, purposely and immediately diverting my attention to something else whenever a consideration of that sort creeps into my consciousness. So the expression "taking into account (or ignoring) certain considerations" should, perhaps, be taken as a convenient shorthand for "doing that which will cause oneself to take into account (or ignore) certain considerations."

but rather as the first step in an argument against TCR. That is, Scanlon could be arguing as follows:

3.1 In many cases, we do not, when deliberating about what to do, treat the fact that an act would have certain desirable/undesirable consequences as a reason for/against performing it. For instance, when playing to win, we do not treat the fact that taking a certain shot would embarrass one's opponent (an admittedly undesirable consequence) as a reason against taking the shot.

3.2 Our deliberative experience in such cases fits better with (*a*) the contention that these are cases in which the agent treats as non-reasons facts that are actually non-reasons than it does with (*b*) the contention that these are cases in which, on pragmatic grounds, the agent acts so as to cause herself to treat as non-reasons facts that are, in fact, reasons (reasons with actual weight).[36]

3.3 Therefore, absent some other reason for accepting *b*, we should accept *a*, which supports the contention that TCR is false.[37]

Unfortunately, though, Scanlon never even considers *b* and so never explains why he thinks that the phenomenology of our actual deliberations supports *a* as opposed to *b*. Perhaps, he just thinks it is obvious. If so, then all I can do is cite my dissent. When I reflect on my first-person deliberations in such cases, it feels to me like I am deciding on pragmatic grounds to ignore certain relevant reasons. To borrow another one of Scanlon examples: when I serve on a search committee and ignore how I would personally benefit from our hiring the candidate who specializes in moral philosophy, this feels like a case in which I am choosing to ignore a genuine, self-interested reason that I have to recommend to the department the candidate who specializes in moral philosophy. I choose to ignore this self-interested reason, because I recognize that I have better reason to want to live up to the standards associated with the role of being a good search committee member, and those standards require me to make my recommendation on the basis of what would be best for our program as a whole, and not on the basis of what would be best for me.

So when I consider the phenomenology of these cases, they seem to me to support *b*, and Scanlon gives me no reason to think that I am mistaken in this, as he fails to even consider *b*, let alone explain why he thinks that the phenomenology supports *a* instead. And, even if I am wrong about the phenomenology, Scanlon's argument fails to establish that TCR is false, for, as we will see presently, there are reasons to accept TCR and thus *b* even if the phenomenology supports *a*

---

[36] In calling these considerations "non-reasons," I mean to allow that these considerations may count as genuine reasons in other contexts. The assumption, here, is only that due to their being silenced, undermined, or bracketed off, these considerations have ceased to be reasons in the context at hand.

[37] Something along these lines was suggested to me by Peter de Marneffe.

instead. After all, things are not always as they seem to be. Thus, even if I am wrong and the phenomenology fits better with a, we should accept a only if there are no better reasons for accepting b instead.

§3.4 Arguments for the view

Having argued that many of the reasons that philosophers have given for reject-ing TCR are not in fact good reasons, I will now argue that there are good reasons to accept each of TCR's three claims. Furthermore, I will argue that there are good reasons for accepting TCR that go beyond the reasons for accepting each of its three claims.

§§3.4.1 In defense of TCR-1

According to TCR-1, if S has more reason to desire that o_i obtains than to desire that o_j obtains, then S has more reason to perform a_i than to perform a_j. To deny TCR-1 is to hold that the following is possible for an agent who must perform either a_i or a_j: she ought to prefer the outcome in which she has performed a_i (viz., o_i) even though a_i is not the alternative that she ought to perform. Given such a possibility, the agent ought to hope that she performs the alternative (viz., a_j) that she ought not to perform.[38] And if, in spite of hoping that she will perform a_j, she performs a_j, she ought to wish that she had performed a_i instead. I find this coun-terintuitive. Surely, agents should not hope that they will act as they should not act. Nor should they wish that they had acted as they should not have acted. To avoid such counterintuitive implications, we should accept TCR-1.

To illustrate how the denial of TCR-1 can lead to such counterintuitive implica-tions, imagine that I am on a hill beside a lake and that I must decide whether or not to run as fast as I can down the hill to the lake's only boat dock. Suppose that Richard and his two daughters are complete strangers to me, that my daughter and Richard's two daughters are all drowning, that there is only enough time to rescue either my daughter or Richard's two daughters (as they are at separate ends of the lake), that there is only one boat tied to the boat dock, and that there is no other way to rescue the children. Further suppose that if I run as fast as I can down to the boat dock, I will get there first and rescue my daughter. If, however, I do not run as fast as I can, Richard will get there first and rescue his two daugh-ters. Assume that everything else is equal.

Let us stipulate that o_1 (i.e., the possible world in which I run as fast as I can and rescue my daughter) will obtain if and only if I perform a_1 (i.e., the act of

---

[38] I am assuming that if S ought to prefer o_i to o_j, and if o_i's obtaining as opposed to o_j's obtaining depends on S's performing a_i instead of a_j, then S ought to hope that she performs a_i instead of a_j.

running as fast as I can down to the boat dock). And let us stipulate that o_2 (i.e., the possible world in which I refrain from running as fast as I can and thereby allow Richard to rescue his two daughters) will obtain if and only if I perform a_2 (i.e., the "act" of refraining from running as fast as I can down to the boat dock).[39] Lastly, let us assume, for the sake of argument, that o_2 is, impersonally speaking, better than o_1, but that, in this instance, I ought not to do what would bring about the impersonally best outcome (viz., a_2). That is, let us assume that I should perform a_1, thereby rescuing my daughter.

Interestingly, if we deny TCR-1, the following is possible: I ought, all things considered (that is, have most reason, all things considered), to prefer o_2 to o_1 even though I ought, as stipulated, to perform a_1 as opposed to a_2. Given such a possibility, I ought to hope that I perform the act that I ought not to perform. After all, it seems that if I ought, all things considered, to prefer the outcome in which I have performed a_2 (viz., o_2), an outcome that will obtain only if I perform a_2, then I ought to hope that I will perform a_2. Yet a_2 is the alternative that I ought not to perform. Thus, on this possibility, I ought to hope that I will act as I ought not to act. Again, I find this counterintuitive. It seems much more plausible to accept TCR-1 and thereby deny such possibilities. We can deny such possibilities by accepting TCR-1 and claiming that given that I ought to perform a_1 as opposed to a_2, it cannot be that I ought to prefer o_2 to o_1.

Of course, I have stipulated that o_2 is, impersonally speaking, better than o_1. And, given this, an impartial spectator ought to prefer o_2 to o_1. But just because an impartial spectator ought to prefer o_2 to o_1, we should not think that I ought to prefer o_2 to o_1. After all, I differ from an impartial spectator in that I am neither impartial nor a mere spectator. Unlike an impartial spectator, I bear certain agential relations to these two outcomes (i.e., I am the agent whose actions determine which outcome will obtain), and I bear a special relation to my daughter, who will be better off if o_1 obtains. Given these relations and, in particular, the special relationship that I have with my daughter, I ought to prefer o_1 to o_2 despite the fact that o_2 is, impersonally speaking, better than o_1.

So, although I have good agent-neutral reasons for preferring o_2 to o_1, it seems that I have even better agent-relative reasons for preferring that my daughter is saved. To deny this is to allow that I can have decisive reason to act so as to save my own daughter even though I have decisive reason to prefer the outcome in which I have instead acted so as to allow Richard to save his two daughters. Such a claim is, I have suggested, counterintuitive. And if we want to avoid such counterintuitive implications, then we should hold that an agent's reasons for performing an act

[39] For the sake of simplifying the discussion, I am assuming that there are only two act-tokens available to me: one that falls under the description of my running as fast as I can down to the boat dock and another that falls under the description of my refraining from running as fast as I can down to the boat dock. If it is necessary, the reader can assume that these are the only two alternative act-tokens available to me, because God will immediately cause me to cease to exist should I attempt to perform any other act-token.

must always track her reasons for preferring the outcome in which she has performed that act to the outcome in which she has refrained from performing that act. And, thus, we should think that it will never be the case that an agent has more reason to desire that o_i obtains than to desire that o_j obtains but more reason to perform a_j than to perform a_i. That is, we should accept TCR-1.

§§3.4.2 In defense of TCR-2

Similar considerations count in favor of TCR-2. According to TCR-2, if S has more reason to perform a_i than to perform a_j, then S has more reason to desire that o_i obtains than to desire that o_j obtains. To deny TCR-2 is to hold that the following is possible for an agent who must perform either a_i or a_j: she ought to perform a_i even though the outcome in which she has performed a_i (viz., o_i) is not the outcome that she ought to prefer. Given such a possibility, the agent ought to perform a_i even though she ought not to hope that she will perform a_i. And if she fails to perform the act that she ought to perform (viz., a_i), she ought not to wish that she had. I find this counterintuitive as well. Surely, agents should hope that they will act as they ought to act and should wish that they had acted as they should have acted. To avoid such counterintuitive implications, we should accept TCR-2.

To illustrate how the denial of TCR-2 can lead to such counterintuitive implications, imagine that I must decide whether or not to lie to Henri about Ida's whereabouts. Assume that Henri is looking to kill Ida, that Ida is completely innocent, that Henri will fail to kill Ida only if I lie to him, and that I know all of this. Let us stipulate that o_3 (i.e., the possible world in which I lie to Henri and thereby prevent him from killing Ida) will obtain if and only if I perform a_3 (i.e., the act of lying to Henri). And let us stipulate that o_4 (i.e., the possible world in which I refrain from lying to Henri and thereby allow him to kill Ida) will obtain if and only if I perform a_4 (i.e., the "act" of refraining from lying to Henri).[40] Assume that everything else is equal. Lastly, assume, for the sake of argument, that I ought to prefer o_3 to o_4, for the agent-neutral reasons that I have for preferring the outcome that is least bad (in this case, the one in which I have lied to Henri, thereby preventing him from killing Ida) decisively oppose the agent-relative reasons that I have for preferring the outcome in which I have refrained from treating anyone as a mere means (in this case, the one in which I have refrained from lying to Henri as a means to preventing him from killing Ida).

Interestingly, the one who denies TCR-2 can say that although I ought to prefer the outcome in which I have lied to Henri, I ought, as Kant claimed, to refrain from lying to Henri. But if we really believe that I ought to prefer o_3 to o_4, why would we insist that I ought to perform a_4 as opposed to a_3? If we insist that such

---

[40] Here, too, I am assuming, merely for sake of simplifying the discussion, that there are only two act-tokens available to me: one that falls under the description of my lying to Henri and another that falls under the description of my refraining from lying to Henri.

is the case, then we must hold that I ought to perform the alternative that I ought to hope that I do not perform. It seems much more plausible to accept TCR-2 and accept that if I ought to prefer the outcome in which I have lied to Henri, then I ought, contrary to Kant, to lie to Henri.

So to preserve both the intuition that an agent ought to hope that she will perform an act if and only if she ought to perform that act and the intuition that an agent ought to wish that she had acted differently if and only if she did not act as she should have, we should accept both TCR-1 and TCR-2. That is, we should accept TCR-1+2: S has more reason to desire that o_i obtains than to desire that o_j obtains if and only if S has more reason to perform a_i than to perform a_j.

§§3.4.3   In defense of TCR-3

As I noted in §§3.1.5, the teleologist is committed not only to TCR-1+2, but also to the right-hand side of that bi-conditional having explanatory priority. Thus, the teleologist must defend TCR-3: if S has more reason to perform a_i than to perform a_j, then this is so in virtue of the fact that S has more reason to desire that o_i obtains than to desire that o_j obtains.

In defense of TCR-3, I will argue that it is more plausible than its alternatives. If we let "PER" stand for "S has more reason to *perform* a_i than to perform a_j" and let "DES" stand for "S has more reason to *desire* that o_i obtains than to desire that o_j obtains," then TCR-3 is the view that, in every instance, "PER, because DES." And the three possible alternatives to this view are: (1) in every instance, "DES, because PER"; (2) in some but not all instances, "PER, because DES," and, in every other instance, "DES, because PER"; and (3) in every instance, both "PER, because BET" and "DES, because BET"—where, for instance, "BET" might stand for "o_i is *better* than o_j."

The First Alternative: The first alternative to TCR-3 is to hold that what explains the truth of the bi-conditional "PER if and only if DES" is that, in every instance, "DES, because PER," not "PER, because DES," as TCR-3 supposes. This is to hold that when S has more reason to desire that o_i obtains than to desire that o_j obtains, this is *always* because S has more reason to perform a_i than to perform a_j. But this is clearly false, as one simple example is sufficed to show. Suppose that a_5 is the act of putting my money into a savings account that yields 2% annually and that a_6 is the act of putting my money into a savings account that yields 1% annually. Assume that both savings accounts are otherwise equal and that, other things being equal, I am better off putting my money in a higher yielding savings account. In this case, it is clear that what explains the fact that I have more reason to perform a_5 than to perform a_6 is the fact that I have more reason to desire that o_5 obtains than to desire that o_6 obtains. The same would seem to hold for any other purely prudential choice, for surely no one would argue that the reason I have for preferring the outcome in which I am prudentially better off is that this is the outcome in which I have done what was prudent (i.e., what I had most prudential reason to do). We should, then, reject the first alternative

Perhaps this is too quick. After all, Elizabeth Anderson has argued that an action is rational only if it adequately expresses one's rational evaluative attitudes (e.g., respect, consideration, and appreciation) toward persons, animals, and things. And, on her view, it is rational to adopt the aim (or the end) of bringing about some state of affairs only if the act that would bring it about is itself rational. For instance, on her view, I have reason to want, and to aim to bring about, the state of affairs in which I spend time alone with my wife only because it is rational for me to act in ways that express my love for my wife. On Anderson's view, then, whether I have reason to want, and to adopt as my end, the state of affairs in which I spend time alone with my wife depends on whether it is rational for me to act so as to adequately express my love for her. And, perhaps, Anderson would similarly argue that whether I have reason to want, and to adopt as my end, the state of affairs in which I am better off depends on whether it is rational for me to act so as to make myself better off.

Anderson's view, then, seems contrary to TCR-3 in that it holds that the rationality of desiring and pursuing some end, e_1, can depend on the rationality of performing the act that brings it about, not vice versa. Despite appearances, though, Anderson's view need not be contrary to TCR-3. Whether it is or not depends on whether there is some further end, e_2, in virtue of which it is rational to perform the act that brings about e_1. For instance, it may be that my wanting and pursuing the state of affairs in which my wife and I spend time alone together is rational only because it is rational for me to want and pursue the state of affairs in which my actions adequately express my rational evaluative attitudes toward her. If this is right, then there is no conflict between Anderson's view and TCR-3, for if this is right, then what ultimately accounts for the rationality of performing a given act is the rationality of wanting some end to obtain, not vice versa. The issue, then, is whether or not Anderson's injunction to act only in ways that express one's rational attitudes toward persons, animals, and things is extensionally equivalent to the injunction to act so as to promote some end—that is, some state of affairs.

In fact, Anderson argues that her injunction, which she calls "E," to act only in ways that *express* one's rational attitudes toward persons is not extensionally equivalent to the injunction, which she calls "P," to act so as to *promote* the state of affairs in which one's actions adequately express one's rational attitudes. She argues that E is no more extensionally equivalent to P than the injunction, E' (i.e., E prime), to make only logically valid inferences is extensionally equivalent to the injunction, P', to act so as to promote the state of affairs in which one makes logically valid inferences. In both cases, the latter (P or P') tells one to do something that the former (E or E') does not: in the case of P, to perform more acts that adequately express one's rational attitudes toward persons and, in the case of P', to make more valid inferences. Moreover, unlike E, "P tells me to violate E, if by doing so I can bring about more events containing E than if I never violated E" (ANDERSON 1996, p. 544). Thus, unlike E, P tells me to betray my wife by committing adultery if my doing so will create an opportunity for me to more fully express my love for her than I otherwise would have, as where this betrayal will enable a reconciliation that allows me to express my love for her more fully than before (ANDERSON 1996, p. 545). Anderson shows, therefore, that E and P yield different prescriptions.

But these differences in what E and P prescribe do not demonstrate that E is not equivalent to *some* injunction to promote a state of affairs; they only demonstrate that E is not extensionally equivalent to P. So consider P*: act so as to *promote* the state of affairs in which as few of one's actions as possible fail to adequately express one's rational attitudes. Unlike P, P* does not tell one to act so as to promote more instances of acting in ways that express one's rational attitudes toward persons. And, like E, it functions as a constraint, telling one to refrain from violating E (i.e., to refrain from acting in a way that fails to adequately express one's rational attitudes toward persons) even in order to bring about more events containing E (i.e., more events in which one adequately expresses one's rational attitudes toward persons). Of course, P* directs an agent to violate E if her doing so will minimize her own violations of E. But, as Nicholas Sturgeon (1996, p. 521) has pointed out, it is hard to imagine any but the most fanciful of cases in which an agent's violating E now will prevent her from committing more numerous, comparable violations of E in the future. Nor is it obvious that, in such fanciful cases, it is E rather than P* that gets the more intuitively plausible results.[41] But rather than debate the issue as to whether E or P* is more plausible, it is clear that E is extensionally equivalent to P**: act so as to *promote* the state of affairs in which one's current actions do not fail to adequately express one's rational attitudes toward persons.[42] P** and E yield the exact same prescriptions, and so we see that there is nothing that E can account for that P** cannot account for. And since the proponent of TCR-3 can adopt P** and thereby account for all the intuitive judgments that Anderson appeals to, there is no reason for us to think that Anderson's view, even if correct, is incompatible with TCR-3.

I have argued, then, that in many instances what an agent has reason to do depends on what she has reason to desire, not vice versa. For instance, it seems that I have reason to put my money in a higher yielding savings account, because I have reason to prefer the state of affairs in which I earn more interest on my savings. And I have shown that, contrary to initial appearances, Anderson's view, even if correct, gives us no reason to deny this.

The Second Alternative: This brings us to the second alternative to TCR-3, which is to claim that what explains the truth of the bi-conditional "PER if and only if

[41] For more on this issue, see PORTMORE 1998 and §4.3.

[42] For any deontological injunction prohibiting agents from performing a certain type of action, there is, as I and others have argued, an equivalent consequentialist injunction requiring agents to bring about a certain state of affairs. See, for instance, chapter 4, PORTMORE 2007, PORTMORE 2009, and LOUISE 2004.

DES" is that, in some instances, "PER, because DES," in other instances, "DES, because PER," but, in every instance, one or the other. The problem with this view is that it is fragmented, and thus its proponents owe us some explanation as to why sometimes reasons for acting are explanatorily prior and other times reasons for desiring are explanatorily prior. Until such an explanation is forthcoming, we should, I believe, accept the more unified and systematic TCR-3 instead.

The Third Alternative: The third and final alternative to TCR-3 is the view that what explains the truth of the bi-conditional "PER if and only if DES" is that, in every instance, both "PER, because BET" and "DES, because BET." We should, I think, reject this third alternative. Consider what BET might be. That is, consider what might possibly explain both PER and DES. The most obvious candidate is that "BET" stands for "o_i is *better* than o_j." However, if "BET" stands for "o_i is *better* than o_j," then we should reject the claim that "DES, because BET," for it seems that sometimes agents have more reason to desire that o_i obtains than to desire that o_j obtains even though o_i is *not* better than o_j. And so it cannot be that, in every instance, what explains DES is BET.

To illustrate, consider the case from §§3.4.1. In this case, I have more reason to desire o_1 (the possible world in which I run as fast as I can and rescue my daughter) than I have to desire o_2 (the possible world in which I refrain from running as fast as I can and thereby allow Richard to rescue his two daughters) even though o_2 is, impersonally speaking, better than o_1. In this case, it seems that my agent-relative reasons for preferring that my own daughter is saved outweigh my agent-neutral reasons for preferring the better outcome. Since, in this case, I have reason to prefer the worse outcome (viz., o_1), it cannot be that what explains why I have more reason to desire that o_1 obtains than to desire that o_2 obtains is that o_1 is better than o_2, for this is simply false.

So, if the only likely candidate for "BET" is "o_i is *better* than o_j," and if, on this interpretation of "BET," we should reject "DES, because BET," as I have argued, then we should reject this third alternative to TCR-3. Of course, these might seem like two big *if*s. So the argument here is only presumptive. Given the prima facie plausibility of these antecedents, there is a presumptive case to be made against this third alternative to TCR-3. But even if the case is only a presumptive one, it is important to note that the burden is on the critic of TCR to supply some more plausible interpretation of "BET."

§§3.4.4 In defense of TCR on the whole

Admittedly, the arguments for TCR-1, TCR-2, and TCR-3 are not decisive. For one thing, the arguments for TCR-1 and TCR-2 relied on certain intuitions that perhaps not everyone will share. For another, I have not canvassed every possible interpretation of "BET," but have considered only the one that has seemed most obvious to me. So let me explain why even those who do not find my arguments for each of TCR's individual three claims decisive, nevertheless, have good reason to accept TCR on the whole.

Compared to its alternatives, TCR does a far superior job of systematizing our various substantive convictions about what we have reason to do. Everyone seems to admit that in at least some instances an agent's reasons for performing a given action derive from her reasons for desiring its outcome. For instance, we think that, other things being equal, you have more reason to choose the more pleasure-inducing meal option to the less pleasure-inducing meal option if and only if, and because, you have more reason to desire the outcome in which you experience more pleasure than to desire the outcome in which you experience less pleasure. No one thinks that it is the other way around: that you have more reason to want the outcome in which you experience more pleasure because you have more reason to choose the more pleasure-inducing meal option. The only point in contention, then, is whether reasons for action always derive from reasons for desiring. Some have thought not, for they have thought that there are certain substantive views about value and practical reasons that TCR cannot accommodate—for example, the view that it is certain concrete entities, and not states of affairs, that are the primary bearers of intrinsic value and that, when playing to win at a game of tennis, there are reasons not to take certain other considerations into account when deciding whether to make a particular strategic shot. But, as I have shown, this is a misconception: there are no substantive views about values and reasons that TCR cannot accommodate. The teleological conception of reasons (i.e., TCR) is an extremely ecumenical and accommodating view. Thus, another reason to accept TCR, apart from both its prima facie plausibility and the reasons there are to accept each of its three constitutive claims, is that TCR provides a systematic account of our various substantive views about reasons for action.

***

In this chapter, I have defended TCR against putative counterexamples, and I have tried to ward off many actual and potential misconceptions about the view. I have shown that TCR is quite ecumenical and that, consequently, we do not have to give up any of our substantive views about values or reasons to accept it.[43] I have also offered positive arguments in favor of each of TCR's three claims. Moreover,

---

[43] Perhaps, some will think that I have been too successful in defending TCR. That is, some might think that if TCR is really as ecumenical as I have claimed, then it rules nothing out and is, therefore, trivial. This is not so. Although TCR is compatible with any substantive view about what we have most reason to do as well as with any substantive view about what we have most reason to desire, it does rule out certain views. For one, it rules out the view that S has most reason to do a_j, but does not have most reason to desire that o_j obtains. For, according to TCR, S has most reason to do a_j if and only if S has most reason to desire that o_j obtains. For another, it rules out the view that S has most reason to desire that o_j obtains in virtue of the fact that S has most reason to do a_j. For, according to TCR, it is the other way around.

I have argued that TCR is unsurpassed in its ability to systematize our considered convictions about practical reasons.

If the arguments in this and the preceding chapter succeed, we should, then, accept both moral rationalism and the teleological conception of practical reasons. And these two theses entail a third: namely, act-consequentialism. The argument, you will recall, goes as follows:

3.4 An act's deontic status is determined by the agent's reasons for and against performing it, such that, if a subject, S, is morally required to perform an act, x, then S has most reason to perform x. (Moral Rationalism).

3.5 An agent's reasons for and against performing a given act are determined by her reasons for and against preferring its outcome to those of the available alternatives, such that, if S has most reason to perform x, then, of all the outcomes that S could bring about, S has most reason to desire that x's outcome obtains. (The Teleological Conception of Practical Reasons).

3.6 Therefore, an act's deontic status is determined by the agent's reasons for and against preferring its outcome to those of the available alternatives, such that, if S is morally required to perform x, then, of all the outcomes that S could bring about, S has most reason to desire that x's outcome obtains. (Act-Consequentialism).[44]

But although we should accept act-consequentialism, we should, as I argued in the preceding chapter, reject all traditional versions of act-consequentialism, for all traditional versions of act-consequentialism conflict with moral rationalism. So, in the remaining chapters, I will show how we might go about constructing a version of consequentialism that does not conflict with moral rationalism—one that comports with our considered convictions both about what we are morally required to do and about what we are rationally required to do. I will start, in the next chapter, by showing how any plausible nonconsequentialist theory can be consequentialized, which is to say that, for any plausible nonconsequentialist theory, we can construct a consequentialist theory that yields the exact same set of deontic verdicts that it yields. This will establish that we can consequentialize a nonconsequentialist theory whose deontic verdicts comport with both moral rationalism and our considered convictions about what we have decisive reason to do.

---

[44] As I noted in the previous chapter, some might prefer to call this *rational-desire teleology*, since, unlike traditional act-consequentialism, it takes the deontic statuses of actions to be a function of the agent's reasons for desiring their outcomes as opposed to the value of their outcomes. Nevertheless, "'act-consequentialism'" is a term of art, and I will use it to refer to 3.6. The reader should keep in mind, though, that it does not matter what we call it. What matters is only whether 3.6 is a plausible view.

4

Consequentializing Commonsense
Morality

Unlike utilitarianism, nonconsequentialist theories—at least, the plausible ones[1]—tend to comport with our considered moral convictions. In so doing, plausible nonconsequentialist theories avoid the sorts of deontic verdicts that got utilitarianism in so much hot water vis-à-vis moral rationalism. Recall from chapter 2 that utilitarianism conflicts with moral rationalism, for it requires agents to maximize aggregate utility even when they have sufficient reason to do otherwise. Unlike utilitarianism, though, plausible versions of nonconsequentialism comport with moral rationalism—at least, they do given certain plausible assumptions about what agents have decisive reason to do.

In this chapter, I hope to demonstrate that any plausible nonconsequentialist theory can be consequentialized, which is to say that, for any plausible nonconsequentialist theory, we can construct a consequentialist theory that yields, in every possible world, the exact same set of deontic verdicts that it yields. Since plausible nonconsequentialist theories tend to yield deontic verdicts that comport with moral rationalism, this will establish that some consequentialist theories (specifically, those that are extensionally equivalent to their plausible nonconsequentialist counterparts) comport with moral rationalism—again, given certain plausible assumptions about what agents have decisive reason to do. What's more, these consequentialist theories will retain what we found most compelling about utilitarianism in the first place: its consequentialism, which we were driven to accept given the attractiveness of both moral rationalism and the teleological conception of reasons—or so I argued in the last two chapters. Thus, by consequentializing a

---

[1] Here, I have in mind those nonconsequentialist theories that have attained some prominence in the literature, theories such as Kantianism, Rossian pluralism (W. D. Ross 1930), Scanlonian contractualism (SCANLON 1998), Hooker's rule-consequentialism (HOOKER 2000), neo-Aristotelian virtue ethics (FOOT 2001 and HURSTHOUSE 1999), Slote's agent-based virtue ethics (SLOTE 2001), Kamm's rights-based deontology (KAMM 2007), and so on. (Recall that I use the term "nonconsequentialism" as shorthand for "*non*–act-consequentialism." Thus, Hooker's rule-consequentialism counts as a nonconsequentialist theory on my terminology.)

plausible nonconsequentialist theory, we can construct a substantive version of consequentialism that takes what is best from both utilitarianism and nonconsequentialism. From utilitarianism, this newly constructed version of consequentialism takes utilitarian's compelling idea—namely, the idea that an act's deontic status is determined by the agent's reasons for preferring its outcome to those of the available alternatives such that it can never be morally wrong for her to act so as to bring about the outcome that she has most reason to want to obtain. And, from nonconsequentialism, it takes nonconsequentialism's intuitively plausible deontic verdicts and their compatibility with moral rationalism.

The chapter has the following structure. In §4.1, I show how to consequentialize a nonconsequentialist theory. In §4.2, I demonstrate that, for any remotely plausible nonconsequentialist theory, there is a consequentialist counterpart theory that is deontically equivalent to it such that the two theories are extensionally equivalent with respect to their deontic verdicts. I call this the *deontic equivalence thesis* or "DET" for short. I go beyond previous attempts to demonstrate DET by showing that, for any remotely plausible nonconsequentialist theory, we can construct a consequentialist counterpart theory that mimics its verdicts not only about what is permissible but also about what is supererogatory. What's more, I show that consequentialism can accommodate moral dilemmas, agent-centered options, agent-centered restrictions, and the self-other asymmetry.

In §4.3, I show that whereas consequentialism can accommodate any deontic verdict that nonconsequentialism can accommodate, some prominent nonconsequentialist theories are unable to accommodate certain plausible deontic verdicts that consequentialism can accommodate. Thus, even just in terms of accommodating our considered moral convictions, consequentialism actually has a leg up on some of its nonconsequentialist rivals. In §4.4, I take issue with those who have claimed that one implication of DET is that every nonconsequentialist theory can be fairly regarded as a form of consequentialism, and that, therefore, we are all consequentialists. Lastly, in §4.5, I argue that although the consequentializer will need to appeal to our considered moral convictions in determining how outcomes rank, this in no way renders the resulting consequentialist position circular or uninformative.

§4.1 How to consequentialize

The recipe for consequentializing a nonconsequentialist theory is quite simple: take whatever considerations that, on the nonconsequentialist theory, determine the deontic statuses of actions and insist that those considerations determine how their outcomes rank. In this way, the consequentialist can produce a ranking of outcomes that when combined with her criterion of rightness yields, in every possible world, the same set of deontic verdicts that the nonconsequentialist theory yields, such that, for any deontic predicate (e.g., "optional," "obligatory," "impermissible," etc.), the resulting consequentialist counterpart theory and the original nonconsequentialist theory will be in perfect agreement as to the set of actions that are in the extension of that predicate. Such theories are *deontically equivalent*.

To illustrate, suppose that we want to consequentialize some nonconsequentialist theory, turning it into a version of maximizing act-consequentialism, according to which an act is morally permissible if and only if its outcome is not outranked by that of any other available act alternative. The procedure for doing so is as follows. For any act that the nonconsequentialist theory takes to be morally permissible, deny that its outcome is outranked by that of any other available act alternative.[2] For any act that the nonconsequentialist theory takes to be morally impermissible, hold that its outcome is outranked by that of each permissible act alternative. And, for any act that the nonconsequentialist theory takes to be morally obligatory, hold that its outcome outranks that of every other available act alternative.[3] This procedure produces a ranking of outcomes that when combined with maximizing act-consequentialism's criterion of rightness yields a deontically equivalent version of maximizing act-consequentialism.

Of course, the rankings of outcomes will need to be agent-relative (and, perhaps, also time-relative) in order to consequentialize certain nonconsequentialist theories, such as those that incorporate agent-centered restrictions. To see this, suppose that I have the choice of performing either A_1 or A_2 (with corresponding outcomes O_1 and O_2) and that you have the choice of performing either A_3 or A_4 (with corresponding outcomes O_3 and O_4).[4] Assume both that you will perform A_3 if and only if I perform A_1 and that you will perform A_4 if and only if I perform A_2.[5] Assume that A_1 involves my staying still, which will cause no one's death, and that A_2 involves my moving about, which will cause the death of Alex. Assume that A_3 involves your moving about, which will cause the death of both Alex and Bonnie, and that A_4 involves your staying still, which will cause no one's death. So O_1 is the possible world in which I stay still and you move about, thereby causing the death of both Alex and Bonnie. And O_2 is the possible world in which I move about— thereby causing the death of Alex—and you stay still. And given both that you will

---

[2] An act alternative is any of the mutually exclusive and jointly exhaustive act-tokens that are available to a given agent at a given time.

[3] I am assuming that an act is morally obligatory if and only if it is the only morally permissible alternative available to the agent. See VALLENTYNE 1989, section 3.

[4] Recall that whereas I use $a_1, a_2, \ldots, a_n$ to designate *act-tokens*, I use $A_1, A_2, \ldots, A_n$ to designate *act-types*, such as lying, cheating, stealing, and so on. These act-types consist in sets of all and only those act-tokens that fall under the relevant descriptions. And I use $O_1, O_2, \ldots, O_n$ to designate the sets of outcomes corresponding to all and only those act-tokens in $A_1, A_2, \ldots, A_n$, respectively.

[5] Recall that I am assuming that counterfactual determinism is true—that for each act alternative available to the agent there is some determinate fact as to what the world would be like were the agent to perform the act. See note 1 of chapter 3.

move about (i.e., perform A_3) if and only if I stay still (i.e., perform A_1) and that you will stay still (i.e., perform A_4) if and only if I move about (i.e., perform A_2), it follows that O_3 is identical to O_1 and that O_4 is identical to O_2.

Now let us suppose that the nonconsequentialist theory to be consequentialized holds that I am obligated to perform A_1 and that you are obligated to perform A_4.[6] In order for the consequentializer to hold that I am obligated to perform A_1, she must hold that O_1 outranks O_2.[7] And this implies that O_3 outranks O_4, for O_3 is identical to O_1 and O_4 is identical to O_2. Yet, for the consequentializer to hold that you are obligated to perform A_4, she must hold that O_4 outranks O_3. How, then, can the consequentializer have it both ways: that O_4 both outranks, and is outranked by, O_3? The answer is that the rankings will need to be agent-relative. On *my* ranking, O_1 outranks O_2, which implies that, on *my* ranking, O_3 outranks O_4. Nevertheless, on *your* ranking, O_4 outranks O_3, which is consistent with O_3 outranking O_4 on *my* ranking. Thus, the maximizing act-consequentialist must hold that an agent is morally permitted to perform a given act if and only if its outcome is not, *on the agent's ranking*, outranked by that of any other available alternative.[8]

§4.2 The deontic equivalence thesis

I have claimed that, for any remotely plausible nonconsequentialist theory, we can construct a version of consequentialism that is deontically equivalent to it. This, again, is the *deontic equivalence thesis* (or "DET" for short).[9] Rather than take a piecemeal approach to demonstrating the deontic equivalence thesis, I will attempt a more systematic approach, showing how consequentialism can accommodate all the various general features that can be found in various nonconsequentialist theories: moral dilemmas, supererogatory acts, agent-centered options, the self-other asymmetry, agent-centered restrictions, and special obligations. These are the features of commonsense morality.[10] If I can show that all

---

[6] I am assuming that although you *will* perform A_3 if I perform A_1, you *can* perform A_4 even if I perform A_1.

[7] O_1 and O_2 actually represent sets of outcomes. This complicates things a bit. Let us say that O_1 outranks O_2 if and only if we find that, when we compare each of the outcomes in O_1 to their most similar counterparts in O_2, some of them outrank their O_2-counterparts but none of them are outranked by their O_2-counterparts.

[8] S's evaluative ranking is not a ranking in terms of what S subjectively prefers, but rather a ranking in terms of what S ought, objectively speaking, to prefer.

[9] This thesis sometimes goes by other names, such as the "Representation Thesis" (ODDIE & MILNE 1991) and "Dreier's Conjecture" (BROWN 2004). The thesis, or some close cousin of it, has been defended and/or endorsed by Campbell Brown (2004), James Dreier (1993 and FORTHCOMING), Jennie Louise (2004), Graham Oddie and Peter Milne (1991), Douglas W. Portmore (2007 and 2009), Michael Smith (2009), and Peter Vallentyne (1988).

[10] Actually, I am not confident that commonsense morality—the morality of our commonsense moral convictions—includes moral dilemmas, but I will consider moral dilemmas regardless.

these general features can be consequentialized, then it should be easy enough to see how we could consequentialize the various deontic verdicts that are instances of these. I will proceed in the above order.

§§4.2.1 Moral dilemmas

As Peter Vallentyne notes, a "moral dilemma arises when an agent is in a choice situation in which he/she cannot satisfy the dictates of morality" (1989, p. 301). Various nonconsequentialist theories allow for moral dilemmas. Take, for instance, a *deontological theory* that includes an absolute prohibition against breaking one's promises.[11] On such a theory, a moral dilemma will arise whenever an agent makes a set of promises that cannot all be kept. Suppose, for instance, that, at t_1, I promised Cristobal that I would perform A_1 at t_5. Further suppose that, due to a lapse in memory, I promised Dolly at t_3 that I would not perform A_1 at t_5. It is now t_4, and I must decide whether or not to perform A_1 at t_5. Promise breakings are, we are supposing, absolutely prohibited, but I cannot both perform A_1 and not perform A_1 at t_5. So, no matter what, I will break one of my two promises and thereby act impermissibly.[12] I face, therefore, a moral dilemma.

Although some philosophers deny that such moral dilemmas are even conceptually possible, there are many who think that they are. Some will, therefore, consider nonconsequentialist theories that include such moral dilemmas to be at least remotely plausible. So if the deontic equivalence thesis is true, then perhaps consequentialism should be able to accommodate such moral dilemmas. I will argue that there are two types of moral dilemmas (prohibition dilemmas and obligation dilemmas), that consequentialism can accommodate only one of the two (i.e., prohibition dilemmas), but that the other (i.e., obligation dilemmas) is clearly conceptually impossible.[13]

First, let us consider obligation dilemmas. These are choice situations in which two or more of an agent's positive act alternatives are obligatory. An example

[11] As I see it, a deontological theory is a nonconsequentialist moral theory that includes at least one agent-centered constraint. See below for a definition of "agent-centered constraint."

[12] Thus, on this theory, the common assumption that there is always at least one permissible act alternative available to the agent is false. And if this common assumption is false, then it is also false to suppose that S is obligated to perform x if and only if it would be wrong for S to refrain from performing x, for, if it is false to assume that there is always at least one permissible alternative available to S, then it could be wrong for S to perform x even though it would also be wrong for S to refrain from performing x, and S cannot be obligated to do what is wrong. We should deny, then, that S is obligated to perform x if and only if it would be wrong for S to perform any available alternative and accept instead that S is obligated to perform x if and only if *both* (*i*) S is permitted to perform x and (*ii*) it would be wrong for S to perform any available alternative (VALLENTYNE 1989, p. 305).

[13] The distinction between obligation dilemmas and prohibition dilemmas as well as the forthcoming argument for obligation dilemmas being conceptually impossible come from VALLENTYNE 1989.

would be where an agent is both morally obligated to perform A_1 and morally obligated to perform A_2, can perform each of A_1 and A_2, but cannot perform both A_1 and A_2. And for this to be a genuine instance of an obligation dilemma, A_1 and A_2 must each be a *positive* act—that is, not merely the "act" of refraining from performing some act.

Consequentialism cannot accommodate such dilemmas. Consider that, on (maximizing act-) consequentialism, an act is obligatory only if its outcome outranks (on the agent's ranking) those of every alternative. So A_1 is morally obligatory only if O_1 outranks O_2. And A_2 is morally obligatory only if O_2 outranks O_1. So in order for both A_1 and A_2 to be obligatory, O_1 would have to both outrank, and be outranked by, O_2 on the same ranking.[14] And that is not possible.[15] So it is impossible for consequentialism to accommodate obligation dilemmas. But this is not at all surprising, since obligation dilemmas are conceptually impossible. To see why, note that an act is obligatory if and only if both (*i*) it is permissible and (*ii*) all its available alternatives are impermissible (VALLENTYNE 1989, p. 305).[16] From claim *ii*, it follows that, if A_1 is obligatory, then A_2, which is an available alternative, must be impermissible. But if A_2 is obligatory, then, according to claim *i*, A_2 must be permissible. So, for both A_1 and A_2 to be obligatory, A_2 would have to be both permissible and impermissible. And that is not logically possible. Let us turn, then, to those moral dilemmas that are perhaps conceptually possible: namely, prohibition dilemmas.

A prohibition dilemma is a choice situation in which all the available alternatives are impermissible. Can consequentialism accommodate such dilemmas? Yes. For instance, there will be such dilemmas whenever an agent faces a choice situation in which there are an infinite number of successively higher ranked outcomes that she can bring about. To illustrate, suppose that an agent faces a choice situation in which God will make the total aggregate utility be whatever natural number she picks and that, if she fails to pick a natural number, God will make the total aggregate utility zero. No matter what she does, then, she acts wrongly. If she picks no natural number, she acts wrongly. And if she picks some natural number, n, she acts wrongly, for had she picked $n + 1$ instead, there would have been even more aggregate utility.

Of course, this establishes only that consequentialism can accommodate some prohibition dilemmas. To establish the deontic equivalence thesis, though, I need to show not only that consequentialism can accommodate prohibition dilemmas,

---

[14] It has to be the same ranking, because there is only one agent involved, who is deciding whether to perform A_1 or A_2 at some specific time. Thus, it cannot be that we have, here, two different agent-relative or time-relative rankings.

[15] I am assuming here that the *x*-outranks-*y* relation is asymmetric. A relation, R, is asymmetric just in case: if *x*R*y*, then ~*y*R*x*.

[16] See note 12 for why the proponent of moral dilemmas cannot instead hold that S is obligated to perform *x* if and only if it would be wrong for S to refrain from performing *x*. And see VALLENTYNE 1989 (pp. 307–309) for a defense of the definition of "obligatory" given in the body of this chapter.

but also that consequentialism can accommodate the various sorts of prohibition dilemmas that any remotely plausible nonconsequentialist theory might entail. So, for instance, the consequentialist needs to be able to accommodate dilemmas of the sort that I considered at the beginning of this subsection, where, for instance, I will act wrongly if I break my promise to Cristobal by not performing A_1 at t_5 and where I will act wrongly if I break my promise to Dolly by performing A_1 at t_5.[17] To illustrate, then, let O_1 be the set of all the outcomes corresponding to the acts in A_1.[18] And let A_2 be the set of all the (positive) act-tokens, $a_2, a_3, \ldots, a_n$, that entail my not performing A_1 at t_5, and let O_2 be the set of all their corresponding outcomes. And let us assume that I am conscious and deliberating at t_4 and so must perform some positive act at t_5.[19] According to the nonconsequentialist theory to be consequentialized, it is both wrong for me to perform A_1 and wrong for me to perform A_2, and yet I must do one or the other, for A_1 and A_2 are jointly exhaustive. No matter what I do, then, I will act wrongly. How can the consequentialist accommodate such prohibition dilemmas?

To do so, the consequentialist must hold that whether O_1 outranks O_2 or vice versa depends on whether I perform A_1 or A_2.[20] More specifically, the consequentialist

---

[17] It may seem that the existence of a prohibition dilemma entails the existence of an obligation dilemma, for it may seem that a prohibition against performing x is just an obligation not to perform x. In fact, the existence of a prohibition dilemma does not entail the existence of an obligation dilemma. This is because obligation dilemmas, by definition, consist in obligations to perform two or more mutually exclusive *positive* acts, whereas the obligation not to perform x does not constitute an obligation to perform any positive act. To illustrate, suppose that I promised, at t_3, not to perform A_1 at t_5 but then died at t_4. In this case, I managed not to violate my obligation not to perform A_1 at t_5 even though I did not perform any positive act at t_5. Thus, the obligation not to perform x does not consist in an obligation to perform any positive act. And this means that the situation in which I have promised both to perform A_1 at t_5 and not to perform A_1 at t_5 constitutes a prohibition dilemma, but not an obligation dilemma.

[18] Let me just stipulate that there is only a finite set of outcomes available to me in this choice situation. Thus, it will not be possible for the consequentializer to employ the original strategy for accommodating prohibition dilemmas, which was to postulate that, for each available outcome, there is always some other available outcome that outranks it.

[19] I am assuming that intentionally remaining motionless is itself a positive act. One performs a positive act when one intentionally does something, whether it be, say, walking, running, or remaining motionless. It is possible for S to not perform a positive act, x, without performing any other positive act instead. For instance, if S is unconscious at t_5, then S is not performing x at t_5, but neither is S performing some other positive act at t_5.

[20] This might sound strange, but Campbell Brown has offered the following example to illustrate its possibility:

> Suppose... that we endorse a theory according to which agents ought always to act so as to maximise the aggregate preference satisfaction of all people, ... [and] we quite explicitly insist that only the preferences of *actual* people are to be taken into account.... Now, consider the following case. A couple would like to have a child; if they were to have a child, this would increase their preference satisfaction. However, the child would prefer that she did not exist. Moreover, the child's preference would be sufficiently strong or intense as to

must hold that O_1 outranks O_2 if and only if I perform A_2 and that O_2 outranks O_1 if and only if I perform A_1. The idea is that no matter which I perform, I should regret performing the act that I did, and, thus, I should wish that the other act's outcome obtains instead. So if I perform (or will perform) A_1, I should wish (or prefer) that O_2 obtains, but if I perform (or will perform) A_2, I should wish (or prefer) that O_1 obtains. This ensures that no matter which act I perform, its outcome will be outranked, implying that the act is impermissible. Thus, the consequentialist can, given certain assumptions, accommodate such prohibition dilemmas.[21]

§§4.2.2 Supererogatory acts, agent-centered options, and the self-other asymmetry

A supererogatory act is, as the name suggests, an act that goes above and beyond what is morally required. Clearly, satisficing consequentialism can accommodate such acts. On satisficing consequentialism, agents are morally required only to produce an outcome that is ranked sufficiently high. Producing an outcome that ranks even higher is supererogatory. But since it is doubtful that satisficing consequentialism is even tenable, the consequentializer should hope that some non-satisficing version of consequentialism, such as maximizing consequentialism, can also accommodate supererogatory acts.[22] Yet, as Michael Byron has pointed out, "It's difficult to see how a maximizing conception of morality can allow room for supererogation: If I'm required in every case to choose the best available option, how could I ever do *more* than morality required?" (BYRON 2004, p. 9) As we will see below, the answer depends on what doing *more* than is required consists in.

To illustrate, suppose that we were to define a supererogatory act as one that involves a greater self-sacrifice for the sake of others than is required.[23] In that

outweigh the preferences of the parents. . . . What ought the parents to do, according to our theory? Suppose first that they do have the child. In this case the child is an actual person, and so her preferences count in determining what the parents ought to do. And, since the child's preference outweighs the parents' preferences, our theory implies that the parents acted wrongly; they ought not to have had the child. Suppose next that the parents do not have the child. In this case, the child is a merely possible person, and so her "preferences" do not count. Thus, again, our theory implies that the parents acted wrongly. (2004, p. 33)

The idea that consequentialists can accommodate moral dilemmas in this way is Brown's.

[21] One of the assumptions is that we should reject what Erik Carlson calls the *principle of normative invariance*, which holds that an act's deontic status does not depend upon whether or not it is performed (CARLSON 1995, pp. 100–101). I make no claim concerning whether or not we should accept this principle. But, then, I also make no claim concerning whether or not we should accept prohibition dilemmas.

[22] See BRADLEY 2006 for what seems to be a decisive refutation of satisficing consequentialism.

[23] Harwood (2003, p. 182) defines supererogation in this way and, consequently, concludes that maximizing act-utilitarianism can accommodate supererogatory acts. See also VESSEL 2010 and McNAMARA 1996a, p. 433.

case, even maximizing act-utilitarianism can accommodate supererogatory acts, because sometimes an agent will have a choice between two or more maximizing acts that differ with respect to whether more of the maximal quantity of utility goes to others or to herself. Such maximizing alternatives will be morally optional on maximizing act-utilitarianism, and those that involve *more* of the maximal quantity of utility going to others as opposed to the agent will, on the above definition, be supererogatory.

But we might wonder, though, whether this definition gets it right, specifically whether it correctly specifies the relevant sense of "doing more than is required." In specifying that "doing more than is required" entails "doing more for others than is required," this definition rules out the possibility of supererogation with respect to self-regarding duties. Yet it certainly seems possible to go above and beyond what such duties require.[24] For instance, we might think that there is a duty to develop one's talents and that this is an imperfect duty, and, thus, one that does not require that we take every opportunity to develop our talents, but requires only that we develop our talents to a certain extent, taking advantage of a sufficient number of opportunities to develop our talents. But if this is right, then it is surely possible to go above and beyond the duty to develop one's talents, and yet doing so may be of no benefit to others. Here, then, is a plausible candidate for supererogation that the above definition simply rules out of court.[25]

And the definition faces another, potentially more serious, problem, for it seems that a supererogatory act must involve doing more of whatever there is *moral* reason to do more of.[26] For example, we would not think that perspiring more than is required is supererogatory, because we do not think that there is any moral reason to perspire more than is required. We do not think, for instance, that if there are two means to fulfilling some duty, then taking the means that involves more perspiration would, in virtue of that fact alone, be supererogatory. So we should think that doing more for others than is required is supererogatory only if (and because) there is some moral reason to do more for others than is required. So even if it is true that doing more for others than is required is supererogatory, this is not fundamental to the definition of "supererogatory." Instead, what is fundamental is that an act is supererogatory only if there is more moral reason to perform it than to perform some other permissible alternative.[27]

---

[24] See KAWALL 2003, PORTMORE 2007, and PORTMORE 2008a.

[25] If we think that supererogatory acts must involve self-sacrifice, then we need only imagine a case in which developing one's talents beyond the extent to which one is required to develop them involves self-sacrifice.

[26] Moral reasons are, of course, a proper subset of reasons for action. A moral reason is a reason that, morally speaking, counts in favor of, or against, performing some action. See PORTMORE 2008a and chapter 5.

[27] I leave open the question of whether there are any further necessary conditions, such as: an act is supererogatory only if it requires more self-sacrifice (or is otherwise more difficult or demanding to perform) than some other permissible alternative that one has less moral reason to do.

If this is correct, then maximizing act-utilitarianism cannot accommodate supererogatory acts, for, on maximizing act-utilitarianism, the only time that one has the option of, say, performing either a_1 or a_2 is when there is no more moral reason to perform a_1 than to perform a_2 and vice versa. On maximizing act-utilitarianism, agents can never do more than they are required to do in the relevant sense of "doing more": the sense that involves doing more of whatever it is that one has moral reason to do, for, on maximizing act-utilitarianism, the only thing that an agent has moral reason to do is to promote utility. But since maximizing act-utilitarianism requires that agents maximize utility, there is never a situation in which an agent is permitted to do anything other than what she has optimal moral reason to do. Thus, there is, on maximizing act-utilitarianism, no room for supererogatory acts—acts that there is more moral reason to perform than to perform some other permissible alternative. It remains unclear, then, how a non-satisficing consequentialist theory could accommodate supererogatory acts.

As a matter of fact, the consequentialist can accommodate supererogatory acts. To do so, she need only adopt what I call *dual-ranking act-consequentialism*:

DRAC S's performing *x* is morally permissible if and only if, and because, there is no available act alternative that would produce an outcome that S has both more moral reason and more reason, all things considered, to want to obtain than to want *x*'s outcome to obtain.[28]

As we will see in chapter 7, things are actually quite a bit more complicated than I make them out to be here. As we will see, I have been using the term "supererogatory," whereas I should probably be using the term "superperfecterogatory" instead. A superperfecterogatory act is one that goes above and beyond what perfect duty requires. The term "supererogatory," by contrast, is best reserved for acts that go above and beyond what all duty (perfect and imperfect) requires. For now, though, I will ignore this distinction and wait until chapter 7 before taking up these complicated issues.

[28] To the best of my knowledge, Ted Sider was the first to propose a version of DRAC, and he did so in order to accommodate the self-other asymmetry. His version of DRAC is called *self-other utilitarianism* (SOU): S's performing *x* is morally permissible if and only if there is no available act alternative that would produce both more utility for others and more overall utility than *x* would—see SIDER 1993, p. 128.

I am assuming that not only are there moral and non-moral reasons to perform certain actions, but also moral and non-moral reasons to prefer certain outcomes to others. It seems to me, for instance, that whereas the reason that you have to prefer an outcome in which you receive more pleasure to an otherwise identical outcome in which you receive less pleasure is a non-moral reason, the reason that you have to prefer an outcome in which children in the Third World do not starve to an otherwise identical outcome in which they do is a moral reason. Your lacking a preference for more personal pleasure would not entail a moral failing, but your lacking a preference for children not starving would. The idea that morality governs not only intentions to act, but also various other mental attitudes, such as desire, is not new. After all, we think that many moral sins involve having certain mental attitudes—e.g., lust, greed, envy, and pride.

Now, as Justin D'Arms and Daniel Jacobson (2000) have argued, moral reasons for desiring something are not of the right kind when it comes to determining whether that something is desirable. That is to say that they are not what I have called fittingness reasons. But, as I argued in chapter

I call this *dual-ranking* act-consequentialism, because, on this view, outcomes are ranked according to two auxiliary rankings, and the permissibility of actions is a function of a principal ranking that is in turn a function of these two auxiliary rankings. The two auxiliary rankings are AR_1 (a ranking of outcomes in terms of how much moral reason the agent has to want each of them to obtain) and AR_2 (a ranking of outcomes in terms of how much reason, all things considered, the agent has to want each of them to obtain).[29] And one outcome is outranked by another on the principal ranking if and only if the one is outranked by the other on both of the auxiliary rankings. Because, on DRAC, any act whose outcome is not outranked by that of some alternative on both AR_1 and AR_2 is permissible, some permissible acts have outcomes that rank higher on AR_1 than those of other permissible alternatives. And since AR_1 is a ranking of outcomes in terms of how much moral reason the agent has to act so as to bring them about, these acts are supererogatory.[30] They are acts that the agent has more moral reason to perform than to perform some other permissible alternative.[31]

To illustrate, it will be helpful to consider a substantive version of DRAC—namely, *Schefflerian utilitarianism* (SU).[32] Consider its *criterion of rightness:*

> **SU$_{cr}$** S's performing x is morally permissible if and only if there is no available act alternative that would produce both more utility for others (i.e., for those other than S) and more egoistically adjusted utility than x would, where egoistically adjusted utility includes

3, non-fittingness reasons for desiring—such as agent-relative reasons for desiring—*are* relevant in determining what one ought to do. Indeed, according to the teleological conception of practical reasons, the only sorts of reasons for desiring that are not relevant in determining what one ought to do are so-called pragmatic "reasons," which I do not even take to be genuine reasons. See §§3.1.1, including notes 9 and 11.

[29] Note that AR_1, AR_2, and the principal ranking that is function of the first two are all cardinal rankings. This is important, for, as we will see, it is these cardinal rankings that allow us to say that some supererogatory acts go to a certain extent further beyond the minimum required than other supererogatory acts do.

[30] I am assuming that if, as I argued in chapter 3, how much reason, *all things considered*, an agent has to perform an act is determined by how much reason, *all things considered*, the agent has for preferring its outcome to those of the available alternatives, then how much *moral* reason an agent has to perform an act is determined by how much *moral* reason the agent has for preferring its outcome to those of the available alternatives.

[31] Adopting DRAC's dual-ranking structure may seem unmotivated, but I address this and other objections to DRAC in chapter 5.

[32] Schefflerian utilitarianism (i.e., SU) is the view according to which all the following hold: (1) dual-ranking act-consequentialism is true; (2) S has more moral reason to want o_i to obtain than to want o_j ($j \neq i$) to obtain if and only if o_i contains more utility for others (i.e., for those other than S) than o_j does; and (3) S has more reason, all things considered, to want o_i to obtain than to want o_j to obtain if and only if o_i contains more egoistically adjusted utility than o_j does.

everyone's utility but adjusts the overall total by giving S's utility, say, ten times the weight of anyone else's.[33]

Unlike act-utilitarianism, SU accommodates both supererogatory acts and *agent-centered options*—options either to act so as to make things better overall but worse for oneself (or others) or to act so as to make things better for oneself (or others) but worse overall.[34] To illustrate, consider the following scenario in which an agent named Edouard has the following four mutually exclusive and jointly exhaustive options: a_1, a_2, a_3, and A_4. Here, A_4 is an act-type—namely, that of performing something other than a_1, a_2, or a_3. The consequences of each of these options are laid out in table 4.1.[35]

Table 4.1 $U_s(x)$ = the utility that accrues to S if S performs x.
$U_{-s}(x)$ = the utility that accrues to others if S performs x. $U(x)$ = the overall utility that is produced if S performs x. $U_{+s}(x) = U_{-s}(x) + [10 \times U_s(x)]$.

x	$U_s(x)$	$U_{-s}(x)$	$U(x)$	$U_{+s}(x)$	*deontic status*
a_1	7	**10**	17	**80**	merely permissible
a_2	2	**4**	6	**24**	impermissible
a_3	1	**15**	16	**25**	supererogatory
A_4	–1	**20**	19	**10**	supererogatory

---

[33] I call this "Schefflerian utilitarianism," because, like the theory that Scheffler (1994) argues for, it accommodates agent-centered options (or what Scheffler calls "agent-centered prerogatives"), but eschews agent-centered constraints (or what Scheffler calls "agent-centered restrictions"). Schefflerian utilitarianism (i.e., SU) does, however, differ from Scheffler's Distributive Hybrid Theory in at least two important respects: (1) it does not give priority to benefiting the worse off and (2) it incorporates not only agent-favoring options, but also agent-sacrificing options. (I explain the difference between the two below.)

Schefflerian utilitarianism is nearly identical to Jean-Paul Vessel's egoistically adjusted self-other utilitarianism—see Vessel 2010, p. 308. I published my first formulations of Schefflerian utilitarianism and defended its ability to accommodate supererogatory acts in Portmore 2007. Since then, I have adopted Vessel's apt phrase "egoistically adjusted" utility.

[34] Traditional forms of act-consequentialism allow for moral options whenever two or more acts maximize the good, but they never allow for agent-centered options, which permit agents either to act so as to make things better overall but worse for oneself (or others) or to act so as to make things better for oneself (or others) but worse overall. On traditional act-consequentialism, it is never morally permissible to make things worse overall; maximizing the overall good is, on this view, always obligatory.

[35] I have emphasized the third and fifth columns with bold-faced type since these two correspond to AR_1 and AR_2 of SU, respectively.

Schefflerian utilitarianism (i.e., SU) accommodates agent-centered options in that it permits agents to give their own utility anywhere from no weight at all up to ten times the weight of any other. Thus, Edouard can permissibly choose to do what is better for himself and perform a_1 as opposed to A_4 even though performing A_4 would be both better for others and better in terms of the impersonal good.[36] Edouard has, then, the *agent-favoring option* of performing a_1 instead of A_4, where an agent-favoring option is just an option either to promote one's own interests or to sacrifice one's own interests for the sake of doing more to promote the overall good.

Furthermore, by allowing agents to give their own utility no weight, SU accommodates *agent-sacrificing options*, where an agent-sacrificing option is just an option either to maximize the impersonal good or to sacrifice one's own interests for the sake of doing more to promote the interests of others.[37] For instance, Edouard can permissibly choose to perform a_3 as opposed to a_1, thereby providing others with a net benefit of five utiles at a cost of six utiles to himself.[38]

Thus, SU can accommodate what is known as the *self-other asymmetry*: the asymmetry found in commonsense morality between what agents are permitted to do to themselves and what agents are permitted to do to others. It seems that although an agent is not permitted to be indifferent toward the welfare of others, she is permitted to be indifferent toward her own welfare. She can, for instance, sacrifice her own hand so as to save Fay's thumb even though it would be impermissible for her to sacrifice Gustav's hand to save Fay's thumb (and even if Gustav consents to her doing so). On commonsense morality, then, agents are permitted to sacrifice their own greater good for the sake of providing others with some lesser net benefit, but they are not permitted to sacrifice someone else's greater good for the sake of providing others with some lesser net benefit—hence, the asymmetry between self and others.[39] Of course, agents are not always permitted to sacrifice their own welfare. It would, for instance, be wrong, as SU implies, for Edouard to choose to perform a_2 as opposed to a_1. Such a choice would not only be worse for Edouard, but also worse for others.[40]

Schefflerian utilitarianism (i.e., SU) can also accommodate supererogatory acts, or, at least, it can if the following is a plausible account of supererogation.

> S's performing x is supererogatory if and only if there exists some available alternative, y, such that: (*a*) S is both morally permitted to perform

---

[36] $U(a_1)$ is seventeen, whereas $U(A_4)$ is nineteen.

[37] Agent-sacrificing options permit agents to forgo their own greater good for the sake of providing others with some lesser net benefit.

[38] The benefit to others is $U_{-s}(a_3)$ minus $U_{-s}(a_1)$, which equals five. The cost to herself is $U_s(a_3)$ minus $U_s(a_1)$, which equals negative six.

[39] Another way of putting it is that whereas the fact that S's performing x would further S's self-interest does not constitute a moral reason for S to perform x, the fact that S's performing x would further someone else's self-interest does constitute a moral reason for S to perform x. For more on the self-other asymmetry, see SIDER 1993, SLOTE 1984, and SPLAWN 2001.

[40] Whereas $U_s(a_1)$ is seven, $U_s(a_2)$ is only two. And whereas $U_{-s}(a_1)$ is ten, $U_{-s}(a_2)$ is only four.

x and morally permitted to perform *y* and (*b*) S has more moral reason to perform *x* than to perform *y*.[41]

Certain acts will, on SU, meet these conditions. Schefflerian utilitarianism (i.e., SU) is, as I have stipulated, a species of DRAC. Thus, like DRAC, SU has two auxiliary rankings: (AR_1) a ranking of outcomes in terms of their utility for others, and (AR_2) a ranking of outcomes in terms of their egoistically adjusted utilities. And since SU is a species of DRAC, we can infer that AR_1 of SU is a ranking of outcomes in terms of how much moral reason the agent has to bring them about. It specifies that the more utility for others an outcome contains, the more moral reason there is to want it to obtain and to act so as to ensure that it does obtain. Thus, Edouard has more moral reason to perform a_3 than to perform a_1, a permissible alternative, for a_3 produces more utility for others. And the same holds for A_4.[42] Thus a_3 and A_4 would both be supererogatory on SU. What's more, SU allows for a range of supererogatory alternatives, where some supererogatory alternatives involve going further beyond what is required than others do.[43] For instance, A_4 involves going further beyond the minimum that morality requires than a_3 does in that there is more moral reason to perform A_4 than to perform a_3.

§§4.2.3 Agent-centered restrictions and special obligations

Remarkably, we have just seen that a certain (non-satisficing) version of consequentialism, namely, SU (which is a species of DRAC), can accommodate many of the basic features of commonsense morality, including supererogatory acts, agent-centered options, and the self-other asymmetry. But can consequentialism accommodate *agent-centered constraints* as well? An agent-centered constraint is a constraint on maximizing the good that it would be wrong to *infringe* upon even in some circumstances in which doing so would minimize comparable

---

[41] Again, as we will see in chapter 7, these conditions best describe those acts that go above and beyond what only *perfect* duty requires. In chapter 7, though, I will give an account of what it is for acts to go above and beyond what both perfect *and imperfect* duty requires. Also, I realize that some might want to add to conditions *a* and *b* a third condition: namely, (*c*) S's performing *x* is more morally praiseworthy than S's performing *y*. But I prefer to let the term "supererogatory" denote the pre-theoretic notion of going above and beyond the call of duty (i.e., that of doing more than one has to), and an act can go beyond the call of duty without being praiseworthy, as where the agent performs the act with a bad motive—see McNamara Forthcoming. In letting the term "supererogatory" refer to the pretheoretical notion of exceeding the minimum that morality demands, I follow McNamara 1996a.

[42] $U_{-s}(a_3)$ and $U_{-s}(A_4)$ are fifteen and twenty, respectively, whereas $U_{-s}(a_1)$ is only ten.

[43] On commonsense morality, there is often a range of supererogatory acts, where some supererogatory acts go further beyond the minimum required than others do (McNamara 1996a). For instance, it seems that not only is my choosing to spend my Saturdays helping the poor supererogatory, but so is my choosing to spend both my Saturdays and my Sundays helping the poor. Although both choices would seem to be supererogatory, the latter seems to go further beyond the minimum required of me than the former does.

infringements of that constraint.[44] There are two types of agent-centered constraints: *agent-centered restrictions* and *special obligations*. Agent-centered restrictions *prohibit* agents from performing certain types of acts (e.g., murder) even in
some circumstances in which doing so would minimize comparable performances
of that act-type. Special obligations, by contrast, *require* agents to do certain
things (e.g., to keep their promises) even in some circumstances in which their
failing to do so would minimize comparable failings of that type. These special
obligations often arise as the result of performing certain past acts (such as making a promise) but also come with occupying certain roles (such as certain
professional and familial roles).

To illustrate how we could fairly easily, although rather crudely, modify SU so as to
accommodate both agent-centered restrictions and special obligations in addition to
supererogatory acts, agent-centered options, and the self-other asymmetry, consider
modified Schefflerian utilitarianism (i.e., MoDSU).[45] Its *criterion of rightness* is:

MODSU$_{cr}$ S's performing x is morally permissible if and only if there is
no available act alternative that would produce both more
constraint-adjusted utility and more comprehensively
adjusted utility than x would, where the constraint-adjusted
utility of an outcome is just the sum of the utility for others,
adjusted by multiplying any disutility (or loss of utility) resulting from S's infringement of an agent-centered constraint by
five hundred, and where the comprehensively adjusted utility
of an outcome is just its constraint-adjusted utility added to
the product of S's utility times ten.

Modified Schefflerian utilitarianism (i.e., MoDSU) could easily accommodate a
non-absolute constraint against, say, committing murder.[46] Agents would, other
things being equal, be prohibited from committing murder even so as to prevent

---

[44] If there is a constraint against performing a certain act-type, then any commission of an act of
that type constitutes an *infringement* of that constraint. But not all infringements of a constraint are
wrong. All and only those infringements that are wrong constitute *violations* of that constraint. I
follow Thomson (1990, p. 122) and Zimmerman (1996, p. 181) in making this terminological
distinction.

Constraints need not be absolute. It may be permissible to infringe upon a constraint if enough
good is at stake, and it may be permissible to infringe upon a constraint if doing so would prevent a
sufficient number of comparable infringements of that constraint.

[45] Modified Schefflerian utilitarianism (i.e., MoDSU) is the view according to which all the following hold: (1) dual-ranking act-consequentialism is true; (2) S has more moral reason to want o_i to
obtain than to want o_j ($j \neq i$) to obtain if and only if o_i contains more constraint-adjusted utility than
o_j does; and (3) S has more reason, all things considered, to want o_i to obtain than to want o_j to obtain
if and only if o_i contains more comprehensively adjusted utility than o_j does.

[46] To consequentialize a nonconsequentialist theory with an absolute constraint against committing murder, we need only replace "five hundred" with "infinity" in MoDSU$_{CR}$.

up to five hundred others from each committing some comparable murder. And MODSU could easily accommodate a non-absolute constraint against failing to fulfill the special obligation that parents have to nurture their own children. Parents would, other things being equal, be prohibited from failing to nurture their own children even so as to prevent up to five hundred others from each comparably failing to nurture their children. Clearly, then, MODSU can accommodate both agent-centered restrictions and special obligations.

Of course, MODSU is terribly crude. But I offer MODSU, not as a plausible moral theory, but only as a simple illustration of how a species of DRAC could accommodate both agent-centered restrictions and special obligations. More sophisticated versions of DRAC would adopt more sophisticated principles on how to rank outcomes both in terms of how much moral reason the agent has to desire them and in terms of how much reason, all things considered, she has to desire them. Below, I will demonstrate how these more sophisticated versions of DRAC can accommodate various intuitive judgments concerning agent-centered constraints.

Let A1–A3 stand for three distinct agents. Let V1–V3 stand for three distinct potential victims. Let t_1–t_3 stand for three distinct and sequential times. And let C1 stand for some set of agent-centered constraints.[47] Assume that whenever I discuss multiple infringements of C1—whether it be multiple infringements by different agents or by the same agent at different times—each infringement of C1 is, in all morally relevant respects, comparable to the others. That is, assume that there are no morally relevant differences between each of the infringements. So, for instance, assume that what each potential victim stands to lose is the same in each case. And assume that, for each infringement, the agent's moral responsibility for that infringement is the same as it is for all the other infringements and their respective agents.

Now, consider the following schema:

4.1 It is impermissible for A1 to infringe upon C1 even if this is the only way that A1 can (short of doing something even worse) ensure that A2 and A3 do not each comparably infringe upon C1.

A number of our intuitive judgments are instances of this schema. Here are two examples:

4.1a It is impermissible for A1 to commit murder even if this is the only way that A1 can (short of doing something even worse) ensure that A2 and A3 do not each comparably commit murder.

---

[47] I talk about a set of constraints rather than a single constraint because sometimes a single act-token will violate more than one constraint. Suppose, for instance, that I promised that I would not harm Hanna. In that case, if I harm Hanna by, say, murdering her, then, in murdering her, I violate both the constraint against breaking a promise and the constraint against committing murder.

4.1b It is impermissible for A1 to break a promise even if this is the only way that A1 can (short of doing something even worse) ensure that A2 and A3 do not each comparably break a promise.

As I have already shown, versions of DRAC, such as MODSU, can account for deontic verdicts such as 4.1a and 4.1b. But although consequentialism can account for such deontic verdicts, some philosophers argue that it gives the wrong explanation for them.[48] The consequentialist's explanation for such deontic verdicts lies with, say, the fact that agents ought to have a special concern for their own agency—that is, for what they themselves do as opposed to what they merely allow to happen. Consequently, agents have more moral reason to desire that they refrain from infringing upon a constraint than to desire that each of two others refrain from comparably infringing upon the same constraint.

Contrary to this, Frances Kamm has argued that the explanation for why it is wrong, say, to murder one even so as to prevent two others from committing murder lies with the fact that the one who stands to be murdered for the sake of saving the other two has what Kamm calls a *constraining right* against being murdered—that is, a right not to be murdered even for the sake of minimizing comparable murders by oneself or by others (KAMM 1992 and KAMM 1996). Of course, the two others also possess this very same right. However, the agent only comes up against the right of *his* would-be victim, for it is only his would-be victim's right that he is considering infringing. So, on Kamm's view, the rationale for our judgment that it is wrong to murder the one so as to prevent the two others from each committing murder has nothing to do with the thought that the agent ought to have a special concern for his own agency. Rather, Kamm claims that "the agent's own act is special only in that it makes him come up against the constraining right" of his would-be victim (KAMM 1996, p. 279). This constraining right acts as a barrier against the permissibility of treating him in certain ways, such as, treating him as a means to the minimization of rights infringements overall.

There are, then, two competing explanations for deontic verdicts such as 4.1a and 4.1b:

> *The Victim-Focused Explanation:* The explanation lies with the fact that the would-be victim has a certain kind of right—specifically, a constraining right—that acts as a barrier against the permissibility of infringing upon that right even for the sake of minimizing comparable infringements of that right by oneself or by others.
>
> *The Agent-Focused Explanation:* The explanation lies with some fact other than the one stated in the victim-focused explanation, such as the

---

[48] See, for instance, BROOK 1991 and KAMM 1996, especially pp. 239–247.

fact that agents ought to have a special concern for what they do as opposed to what they merely allow to happen.[49]

Kamm thinks that the victim-focused explanation offers the better explanation, whereas a consequentialist such as myself must hold that the agent-focused explanation offers the better explanation. In support of her contention, Kamm cites the following intuitive deontic verdict:

4.2 It is impermissible for A1 to kill V3 by introducing V3 to the lethal threat that she previously initiated against V1 and V2 even if this is the only way that A1 can (short of doing something even worse) ensure that V1 and V2 are not killed by this lethal threat (KAMM 2007, p. 252).

Imagine, for instance, that A1 earlier planted a bomb that will kill V1 and V2 unless A1 now throws V3 on top of the bomb.[50] If A1 does this, V3 will die, but V1 and V2 will walk away unharmed. If, however, A1 does not do this, V1 and V2 will both die, and V3 will walk away unharmed. So A1 must choose either to be the murderer of V3 or the murderer of both V1 and V2. Intuitively, it seems wrong for A1 to throw V3 on top of the bomb, as 4.2 states. The victim-focused explanation accounts for this so long as we assume that V3 has a constraining right against being murdered. This right constrains A1 from using V3 as a means to minimizing even her (A1's) own infringements of that right.

It may seem that the agent-focused explanation, by contrast, cannot account for 4.2. After all, if agents ought to have a special concern for their own acts, then shouldn't A1 choose to minimize her own murders by throwing V3 on top of the bomb? The answer is "not necessarily," as even Kamm admits. The proponent of the agent-focused explanation can account for 4.2 by claiming that what A1 should be most concerned to minimize is not the number of people that she actually murders, but the number of people that she treats as a mere means by

---

[49] I follow Kamm in labeling these two explanations victim-focused and agent-focused—see KAMM 1996, especially pp. 239–247. Somewhat differently, Richard Brook labels the victim-focused explanation "the patient-based defense" and the agent-focused explanation "the agency-based defense"—see BROOK 1991, especially pp. 197–201. Both labeling schemes are, however, potentially misleading. For one, the proponent of the victim-focused explanation may be no more focused on the victim (or patient) than the proponent of the agent-focused explanation is. They may disagree only on what type of right that the victim (or patient) has—that is, they may disagree only as to whether or not the victim's (or patient's) right is of the sort that cannot permissibly be infringed upon even so as to minimize one's own infringements of that right. Also, note that I mean for these two explanations to exhaust the possibilities. So, strictly speaking, I should label the agent-focused explanation the "*non*-victim-focused explanation."

[50] This is what Kamm calls the "Guilty Agent Case"—see KAMM 1996, p. 242. Scanlon also relies on this case in arguing that the victim-focused explanation offers the better explanation—see SCANLON 2001, p. 47. And Brook employs a similar sort of case in arguing that the victim-focused explanation offers the better explanation—see BROOK 1991, p. 197.

attempting to murder them.[51] If this is right, then throwing V3 on top of the bomb is not what A1 should do at all. In doing this, A1 would only be increasing the number of people that she treats as a mere means, for nothing that A1 can do now can undo the fact that she has already treated each of V1 and V2 as a mere means. So treating V3 as a means to minimizing the number of people that she murders only adds to the number of people that she treats as a mere means.

To sum up, then, the consequentialist can claim that agents should be more concerned to minimize the number of people that they treat as a mere means than to minimize the number of people that they actually murder and that, therefore, A1 ought to prefer the state of affairs in which she lets V1 and V2 die from the lethal threat that she previously initiated to the state of affairs in which she saves those two by treating yet another victim, namely, V3, as a mere means.[52] The consequentialist would, thereby, be employing the agent-focused explanation to account for 4.2.

In like fashion, the consequentialist can account for the following deontic verdicts, all of which Kamm mistakenly believes will be difficult for the consequentialist to explain:

4.3 A1 is morally required to stop A2 from killing V3 even if allowing A2 to kill V3 is the only way that A1 can (short of doing something even worse) ensure that V1 and V2 are not killed by the lethal threat that A1 previously initiated (KAMM 2007, p. 252).

4.4 A1 is morally required to help V3 escape from A2, who intends to kill V3, even if allowing A2 to kill V3 is the only way that A1 can (short of doing something even worse) ensure that V1 and V2 are not killed by the lethal threat that A1 previously initiated (KAMM 2007, p. 252).

4.5 A1 is morally required to redirect the lethal threat—for example, an unstoppable trolley—that is currently threatening both V1 and V2 so that it instead threatens only V3 even if A1 is the one who initiated this lethal threat (KAMM 1996, p. 244).

In each case, the consequentialist need claim only that A1 ought to have certain preferences. Thus, to accommodate 4.3, the consequentialist will claim that agents should be more concerned with preventing others from being treated as a mere means than with minimizing the number of deaths that they are responsible for and that, therefore, A1 ought to prefer the outcome in which she stops A2 from killing V3 to the one in which she prevents V1 and V2 from being killed by the lethal threat that she previously initiated.

---

[51] See KAMM 1996, p. 244. See also BROOK 1991, pp. 207–208.

[52] I am not suggesting that it is only the number of people that one treats as a mere means that is morally relevant. Clearly, some instances of treating someone as a mere means are worse than others. For instance, attempting to murder someone is much worse than attempting to deceive someone into thinking that one is entitled to another cookie.

To account for 4.4, the consequentialist will claim that agents should be more concerned with helping people escape from would-be murderers than with minimizing the number of deaths that they are responsible for and that, therefore, A1 ought to prefer the outcome in which she helps V3 escape from A2 to the outcome in which she prevents V1 and V2 from being killed by the lethal threat that she previously initiated.

And, to account for 4.5, the consequentialist will claim that, although agents should be more concerned not to introduce any new threats than to redirect existing threats so that fewer people will die, they should, nevertheless, be concerned to do the latter. Thus, A1 ought to prefer the outcome in which V3 dies as a merely foreseen side-effect of her redirecting the unstoppable trolley onto the fewer number to the outcome in which she allows V1 and V2 to die as the intended effect of her initial act of introducing that threat. Perhaps, the thought would be that although intending to bring about a person's death as a means to achieving one's aims counts as treating that person as a mere means, doing something that has only the foreseeable consequence of bringing about that person's death does not. In any case, it should now be clear that the consequentialist can accommodate intuitions such as 4.1a, 4.1b, and 4.2–4.5.

§4.3 Beyond the deontic equivalence thesis: How consequentialist theories can do a better job of accounting for our considered moral convictions than even some nonconsequentialist theories can

Thus far, I have established that consequentialism can accommodate the same deontic verdicts that Kamm's rights-based deontology can. Kamm might nevertheless object that even if consequentialism can accommodate judgments such as 4.1a and 4.1b, it gives the wrong explanation for them. The consequentialist's explanation is the agent-focused explanation, whereas Kamm contends that the victim-focused explanation is the better explanation. Below, I will argue, contrary to Kamm, that the agent-focused explanation, not the victim-focused explanation, is the better explanation. There are two reasons why it is better. First, the agent-focused explanation can account for everything that the victim-focused explanation can account for and more. Second, unlike the agent-focused explanation, the victim-focused explanation has counterintuitive implications. I explain each in greater detail below.

Like the proponent of the victim-focused explanation, the proponent of the agent-focused explanation can account for deontic verdicts such as 4.1a, 4.1b, and 4.2–4.5. To do so, the proponent of the agent-focused explanation need only make certain claims about what agents should be most concerned to minimize. To account for 4.2, for instance, she need only claim that agents should be most concerned to minimize the number of people that they treat as a mere means. Unlike the proponent of the victim-focused explanation, however, the proponent of the agent-focused explanation is able to account for certain additional deontic verdicts: specifically, instances of 4.1 in which there is no victim associated with A1's infringement of C1.

To illustrate, consider the *Wrongful Conception Case*. A man named Larry wants very badly to have a biological son, and he can conceive only via coitus, and not through IVF or any other artificial means. But unfortunately for him, he has a rare disease, where only his X-chromosome-carrying sperm can swim. Given this, he can conceive only daughters. But suppose a new pill has just come out on the market that can help Larry get what he wants. The pill will cause a genetic mutation in Larry's sperm, converting all his X-chromosome-carrying sperm into non-swimmers and all his Y-chromosome-carrying sperm into swimmers. An unfortunate side-effect of this mutation, however, is that it causes the sons that he thereby conceives to be born with a terminal genetic disease that induces a sudden and painless death at the age of forty. Larry is so eager to have a biological son that he gladly takes the pill, consequently giving birth to a son, whom he names Matthew. Matthew lives a good life up to the age of forty, which is when he suddenly and painlessly dies of his genetic disease. Had Larry chosen instead to conceive without taking the pill, he would have conceived a daughter, whom he would have named Nicole. Nicole would have lived to the ripe old age of eighty. The quality of her life would have been, on average, no better or worse than Matthew's, but it would have been twice as long.

Let us call the act of taking the pill so as to conceive a boy who will live forty good years instead of a girl who would have lived eighty good years "A_T" (the "T" standing for "taking"). Intuitively, it seems that Larry should not, other things being equal, take the pill (thereby performing an instance of A_T) even so as to prevent two other men from each taking the pill.[53] Thus, we have, here, the following instance of 4.1:

4.1c It is impermissible for A1 to perform an instance of A_T even if this is the only way that A1 can (short of doing something even worse) ensure that A2 and A3 do not each perform a comparable instance of A_T.

Unfortunately for the proponent of the victim-focused explanation, she cannot account for 4.1c. The explanation for 4.1c cannot lie with the fact that the would-be victim has a constraining right, because, in the case of 4.1c, there is no victim, let alone an infringement upon some victim's rights. To see this, let us

---

[53] When I conducted an admittedly nonscientific poll, I found that the vast majority of participants who had intuitions such as 4.1a and 4.1b also found 4.1c to be intuitive. For the poll and some analysis, see http://peasoup.typepad.com/peasoup/2009/02/constraints-agentfocused-or-victimfo-cused-part-ii.html.

examine the Wrongful Conception Case more closely. And let us assume both that Larry is made somewhat better off as a result of taking the pill and that the only people who are possibly affected by Larry's decision are Matthew, Nicole, and himself. (It is fair to make these assumptions, for they do not seem to affect our confidence in 4.1c.) Given that Larry is somewhat better off having taken the pill, Larry is no victim. Nor is Matthew a victim, for he is not made worse off as a result of Larry's decision to take the pill. Indeed, had Larry not taken the pill, Matthew would have never been born. And, surely, we should deny that, prior to even being conceived, Matthew had the right not to be conceived just because someone else even happier than himself could have been conceived in his stead. That is a very strange right indeed, and an implausible one at that. So I do not see how Matthew could be the victim, and, more importantly, I do not see how his rights could have been infringed upon. This leaves us with Nicole. But Nicole does not exist and, thus, has no rights. So she cannot be the victim. We can conclude, then, that Larry does not infringe on anyone's rights in taking the pill and that, therefore, the explanation for the wrongness of his doing so cannot lie with the victim-focused explanation.

Of course, just because the proponent of the victim-focused explanation cannot explain something that the agent-focused explanation can does not mean that the agent-focused explanation is, *all things considered*, the better explanation. But it does mean that, *other things being equal*, the agent-focused explanation is the better explanation. As a matter of fact, though, things are not equal, but not in a way that favors the victim-focused explanation. As it turns out, the problem with the victim-focused explanation is not just that it cannot explain everything that the agent-focused explanation can explain. What's worse, the victim-focused explanation has counterintuitive implications. Consider the following schema:

4.6 It is impermissible for A1 to infringe upon C1 once at t_1, thereby harming V1, even if this is the only way that A1 can (short of doing something even worse) ensure that she does not comparably infringe upon C1 either twice at t_1 or once on each of two separate future occasions, t_2 and t_3, thereby harming V2 and V3.

If the victim-focused explanation were correct, we should expect 4.6 to be true. The constraining right that V1 possesses would make it impermissible for A1 to treat her as a means to minimizing her own infringements of C1. But, as I show below, it is intuitive to think that 4.6 is false.[54] Of course, we need to be very careful in constructing the relevant sort of test case. It is important that

---

[54] Even if I am wrong about this, all is not lost for the proponent of the agent-focused explanation. She could still account for 4.6 by claiming that agents should be more concerned to refrain from infringing upon any constraints *now* than to refrain from infringing upon more numerous constraints *later*.

A1's infringing upon C1 once be the *only* way that she can (short of doing something even worse) ensure that she does not herself *comparably* infringe upon C1 twice. If it is not, then A1 should take the more acceptable means to ensuring that she does not comparably infringe upon C1 twice. This means that we should not use as a test case one in which C1 includes an agent-centered restriction, for in order to construct a case in which A1's infringing upon some agent-centered restriction, R1, at t_1 is the *only* way that A1 can ensure that she does not *comparably* infringe upon R1 at both t_2 and t_3, we must imagine that A1 loses control of her actions such that her later infringements of R1 are involuntary.[55] And, in that case, the infringement at t_1 would not be comparable to the infringements at t_2 and t_3.

Nicolas Sturgeon nicely illustrates the problem:

> Imagine a case in which, unless I deliberately kill one innocent person now, I make it inevitable that I will deliberately kill two tomorrow. How can this be? Perhaps I am supposed to be possessed of a thirst for innocent blood, known to grow steadily in its demands if left unsated, but also to disappear forever once satisfied. Also, although apparently enough in control to make it worth my worrying conscientiously about how to cope with this unwelcome intruder into my psyche, I am somehow debarred from the option of disabling myself—by depriving myself of weapons, turning myself over to the authorities, or whatever. So the case is hard to imagine. (1996, p. 521, note 7)

And it seems even more difficult—perhaps, impossible—to imagine a case in which the only way that I can ensure that I do not *voluntarily* commit two murders in the future is to commit one murder now. If these two future murders are indeed going to be murders that I voluntarily commit, then it must be that I can refrain from committing them—that is part of what it means for them to be voluntary. And if I can refrain from committing these two murders in the future even after refraining from committing murder now, then I should refrain from murder both now and in the future.

Of course, it is easy enough to imagine a case in which I *will* voluntarily commit two future murders if I do not voluntarily commit murder now. Just imagine that I am a sane but murderous criminal who murders anyone who confronts me, and then imagine that, unless I kill Otto now, Paula and Richard will be undeterred from confronting me in the future. Thus, if I do not kill Otto now, Paula and Richard will confront me in the future, and I will, then, murder them both. But even if that is what I *will* do if I do not murder Otto, this seems like a poor

---

[55] I focus here on the diachronic case, because I do not see how it is possible that A1's infringing upon R1 once at t_1 could be the *only way* that A1 can ensure that she does not *comparably* infringe upon R1 twice at t_1.

justification for murder. I should not murder Otto so as to prevent myself from murdering Paula and Richard if I could refrain from murder altogether.[56]

To avoid having to imagine that one loses control over one's actions, we should test our intuitions regarding 4.6 using cases in which C1 is a special obligation as opposed to an agent-centered restriction, for where C1 is a special obligation it is possible to imagine a case in which A1 never loses control over her actions and yet it is true that the only way for her to ensure that she does not infringe upon C1 twice is for her to infringe upon C1 once. Moreover, when testing our intuitions, we should compare pairs of cases that differ in only one respect: specifically, with respect to whether they are an *inter-agent case* or an *intra-agent case*. *Inter*-agent cases are cases in which the agent can, by infringing upon C1, prevent more numerous others from comparably infringing upon C1. *Intra*-agent cases, by contrast, are cases in which the agent can, by infringing upon C1, prevent herself from more extensively infringing upon C1.[57]

Fortunately for us, we do not need to do the testing ourselves, for Theresa Lopez and her coauthors (2009) have already done it for us. They have constructed and performed the following experiment:[58]

Half the subjects were presented with the [following] *inter-agent* case....

Three people in Joe's community, Mark, Bill, and Frank, are planning to move over a one week period. Joe has promised Mark that he would help him move. Meanwhile David has promised Bill and Frank that he would help each of them move. When the time comes to help, it turns out that the only way for David to keep his promises to Bill and Frank is if Joe drives him, which would require Joe to break his promise to Mark.

They were then asked to indicate agreement (on a 7-point scale) with the following statement:

All things considered, Joe should break his promise to Mark, so that David can keep his promises to Bill and Frank....

[The other half of the subjects got the following *intra-agent* case.]

Three people in Joe's community, Mark, Bill, and Frank, are planning to move over a one week period. Joe has promised each of them that he would help them move. When the time comes to do so, Joe realizes that he cannot keep his promises to all three. He can either keep his promise to Mark and break his promises to Bill and Frank, or he can keep his promises to Bill and Frank and break his promise to Mark.

---

[56] Actually, things are a bit more complicated than I let on here. In chapter 7, I explore the issue with greater subtlety—see, in particular, my discussion of actualism, possibilism, and securitism in §7.1.

[57] I borrow these terms from LOPEZ ET AL. 2009. Inter-agent cases are sometimes called "multiple-agent cases," and intra-agent cases are sometimes called "single-agent cases."

[58] The case that they use, which they call the *Promise-Breaking Case*, is very similar to the one that I presented in PORTMORE 1998, pp. 12–13.

The participants who received this question were asked to rate agreement with the statement:

All things considered, Joe should break his promise to Mark, so that he can keep his promises to Bill and Frank. (LOPEZ ET AL. 2009, p. 310)

The responses to the inter-agent cases differed significantly from the responses to the intra-agent case.[59] Whereas subjects tended to agree with the claim that Joe should break his promise to Mark to ensure that he keeps his promises to Bill and Frank, subjects tended to disagree with the claim that Joe should break his promise to Mark to ensure that David keeps his (David's) promises to Bill and Frank. This experiment suggests, then, that whereas people tend to accept 4.1 and think that it is impermissible for an agent to infringe upon a constraint so as to ensure that two others do not each comparably infringe upon that constraint, people tend to reject 4.6 and think that it is permissible to infringe upon a constraint once so as to ensure that one does not comparably infringe upon that constraint twice. This gives us good reason to think that the agent-focused explanation, not the victim-focused explanation, is the better explanation for deontic verdicts such as 4.1b.[60]

I have shown, then, that not only can the consequentialist accommodate deontic verdicts such as 4.1a and 4.1b, but she can do so while providing a more plausible explanation for them than the one that rights-based deontologists such as Kamm provide. Ironically, then, it is the same intuitions (i.e., those that are instances of 4.1) that have led so many philosophers to reject traditional forms of consequentialism that now, given our new understanding of consequentialism as a theory that can accommodate agent-centered constraints, leads us to believe that commonsense morality might best be understood as a consequentialist theory.

§4.4 The implications of the deontic equivalence thesis

In the previous section, I argued that consequentialism can account for certain commonsense intuitions that rights-based deontology cannot account for, such as our intuition that Joe should break his promise to Mark to ensure that he keeps his promises to Bill and Frank in the intra-agent version of the Promise-Breaking

---

[59] As Lopez and her coauthors (2009, p. 317) report: "The mean response in the inter-agent version is 2.37 (out of 7); the mean response in the intra-agent version is 4.89. The difference between the conditions is statistically significant ($t(35) = 5.263$, $p < .001$)."

[60] See LOPEZ ET AL. 2009 for other experiments that support this contention. Particularly interesting is the fact that in one of their experiments, subjects tended to agree with the claim that it would be permissible to *lie* to ensure that one keeps two of one's own promises, while they tended to disagree with the claim that it would be permissible to lie to ensure that someone else keeps two of her promises. Thus, many think that we may infringe not only upon a special obligation but also upon an agent-centered restriction so as to minimize our overall infringements of agent-centered constraints.

Case. But if consequentialism and rights-based deontology yield different verdicts in this case, doesn't this mean that the deontic equivalence thesis (DET) is false? The answer is "no." Just because certain versions of consequentialism accommodate our *intuitive* verdict in the intra-agent version of the Promise-Breaking Case does not mean that other versions of consequentialism cannot accommodate rights-based deontology's *counterintuitive* verdict in that same case. Indeed, other versions can. To do so, the consequentialist need only claim that agents should be more concerned to ensure that they not break one promise *now* than to ensure that they not break more numerous promises *later*. So consequentialism can accommodate rights-based deontology's verdict in this case.

Given this and my arguments in the previous two sections, we should conclude that DET is true. But having done so, we still need to consider what the implications of this thesis are. Of course, one clear implication is that, for any remotely plausible set of deontic verdicts, there is some substantive version of consequentialism that generates it. But some go further and argue that another implication of DET is that every nonconsequentialist theory can be fairly regarded as a form of consequentialism, and that, therefore, we are all consequentialists.[61] In this section, I argue that this is mistaken.

If DET is true, then, for any remotely plausible substantive version of nonconsequentialism, there is some substantive version of consequentialism that is deontically equivalent to it. But even if two theories agree as to *which acts are right*, that does not mean that they agree on *what makes those acts right*. It is important to note, then, that moral theories are in the business of specifying what *makes* acts right. And so even two moral theories that are extensionally equivalent in their deontic verdicts can constitute distinct moral theories—that is, distinct theories about what *makes* acts right.

Consider Kantianism and its deontically equivalent consequentialist counterpart, which I will call *Kantsequentialism*.[62] These two theories agree as to which acts are right, but they would seem to disagree on what makes them right. On Kantianism, acts are right in virtue of their being instances of treating humanity as an end in itself. On Kantsequentialism, by contrast, acts are right in virtue of their outcomes not being outranked by that of any available alternative. Thus, they certainly appear to be two different moral theories.

We have to be careful, though, for appearances can deceive. It is clear that these two theories differ in the expressions they use to pick out the right-making features of actions, but this does not mean that the two different expressions do in fact refer to distinct right-making features.[63] Consider an analogy. One person

[61] See, for instance, BROWN 2004 and LOUISE 2004.

[62] I borrow this term from Richard Arneson. See http://philosophyfaculty.ucsd.edu/faculty/rarne son/224in97consequentialismandjustice.pdf.

[63] I have Jamie Dreier to thank for getting me to see this point. I also thank him for suggesting the following analogy concerning temperature.

might hold that what makes something the same temperature as water boiling at sea level is that its temperature is 100° Celsius, whereas another person might hold that what makes something the same temperature as water boiling at sea level is that its temperature is 212° Fahrenheit. These two people use different expressions to describe the physical property that makes something the same temperature as water boiling at sea level, but they do not disagree on what that property is, for the two expressions refer to the exact same property. Their views are, therefore, mere notational variants of the same view.[64]

Some philosophers suspect that the same is true of nonconsequentialist theories and their deontically equivalent consequentialist counterparts. To be deontically equivalent, theories must be *necessarily* coextensive in their deontic verdicts.[65] Thus, if Kantianism and Kantsequentialism are deontically equivalent, then, necessarily, an act is an instance of treating humanity as an end in itself if and only if its outcome is not outranked by that of some available alternative. But given that the two expressions on each side of the "if-and-only-if" are necessarily coextensive, we might suspect that they refer to the very same property.[66] And thus we might suspect that Kantianism and Kantsequentialism are mere notational variants of the same theory. Furthermore, if, as DET implies, every nonconsequentialist theory is necessarily coextensive with its deontically equivalent consequentialist counterpart, we might even suspect that *all* nonconsequentialist theories are mere notational variants of their deontically equivalent consequentialist counterparts. And, in that case, we really would all be consequentialists.[67]

But even if we might suspect that many nonconsequentialist theories are mere notational variants of their deontically equivalent consequentialist counterparts, it is clear that this is not true of all nonconsequentialist theories. After all, two theories are not mere notational variants of the same theory if each is true only if the other is false. And some nonconsequentialist theories are true only if their deontically equivalent consequentialist counterparts are false. This is because some nonconsequentialist theories are committed to a certain substantive view about the ranking of outcomes that is incompatible with the one that the consequentialist must adopt in order to yield the same deontic

[64] As I use the phrase "mere notational variant," two theories, T1 and T2, about what makes something F are mere notational variants if and only if T1 and T2 both hold that what makes something F is the same metaphysical property but differ only in that they use different descriptions (perhaps, synonymous descriptions—perhaps, non-synonymous descriptions) to refer to that same property.

[65] It is not enough that the two theories yield the same deontic verdicts about every act that has so far been performed in the actual world. To be deontically equivalent, the two theories must yield the same deontic verdicts in every possible world.

[66] Of course, more would need to be said to confirm this suspicion.

[67] But, as I have shown in another work, if we are all consequentialists, we are also all Kantians, all contractualists, and all virtue theorists, and all at the same time. See PORTMORE 2007, pp. 59–60. However, I no longer think that this is necessarily absurd. It would not be absurd if these are all notational variants of the same view.

verdicts that the nonconsequentialist theory yields. In such instances, the non-consequentialist theory will be true only if its deontically equivalent consequentialist counterpart is false. And, in that case, the two cannot be mere notational variants of the same view.

To illustrate, consider rule-utilitarianism, and recall that rule-utilitarianism is a nonconsequentialist theory given my convention of using "nonconsequential-ism" as shorthand for "*non*–act-consequentialism."[68] In order to consequentialize certain versions of rule-utilitarianism (viz., those that incorporate agent-centered restrictions), the consequentializer must adopt a substantive view about how out-comes rank that is incompatible with the rule-utilitarian's own substantive view about how outcomes rank. Rule-utilitarians are committed to *welfarism*, the view that one outcome is outranked by another if and only if it contains more aggregate utility. Given this commitment to welfarism, the rule-utilitarian must deny that whether one outcome outranks another depends either on who is doing the rank-ing or on whether the person doing the ranking is a murderer in one outcome but not in the other. But, in order to consequentialize rule-utilitarianism (which, in its most plausible forms, includes an agent-centered restriction against the commission of murder), this is what its deontically equivalent consequentialist counterpart theory must hold. That is, the deontically equivalent consequentialist counterpart theory must hold that, other things being equal, an agent ought to prefer an outcome in which she refrains from committing murder to an outcome in which she commits murder to prevent five others from committing murder, whereas the rule-utilitarian must hold that the latter is preferable given both that she is committed to welfarism and that welfarism commits her to the view that agents ought always to prefer the outcome with the most aggregate utility. So rule-utilitarianism and its deontically equivalent consequentialist counterpart are committed to incompatible views about how outcomes rank, and thus each can be true only if the other is false. But if each can be true only if the other is false, then they cannot be mere notational variants of the same view. So we are not all consequentialists. Some rule-utilitarians, for instance, are clearly not con-sequentialists (that is, they are clearly not act-consequentialists).[69]

§4.5 An objection

I will end this chapter by considering a common objection. Since one of the conse-quentializer's main aims is to construct a substantive version of consequentialism

---

[68] If the reader does not care for my stipulative definitions and would like an illustration involving a more stereotypically nonconsequentialist theory, then imagine welfarist Rossian pluralism. This is just Ross's deontological view combined with welfarism such that Ross's prima facie duty of benefi-cence is construed as a prima facie duty to maximize aggregate utility.

[69] For a contrary position, see DREIER FORTHCOMING.

that comports with our moral convictions, the consequentializer will need to appeal to our moral convictions in determining how outcomes rank. Otherwise, the consequentializer will be unable to ensure that outcomes rank in such a way that when this ranking is combined with consequentialism's criterion of rightness, the result is a set of deontic verdicts that comports with our moral convictions. But we might wonder whether this is legitimate. That is, we might wonder whether it is legitimate for the consequentializer to adopt one ranking over another on the basis that the former but not the latter yields intuitive deontic verdicts when combined with the following criterion of rightness:

CR An act is morally permissible if and only if its outcome is not (on the agent's ranking) outranked by that of any available alternative.[70]

The consequentialist is committed to CR. So the consequentialist must rank outcomes in a way that is compatible with both CR and the intuitive deontic judgments that she wishes to consequentialize. Now there are at least three possible procedures that she might employ to arrive at such a ranking. These are:

The Footian Procedure: Independently of any judgments that one has about how the available outcomes rank, come to some considered judgments about the permissibility of the various acts that produce them, and, to ensure that CR holds, rank their outcomes so that the only outcomes that are not outranked are those that are produced by acts that one judges to be permissible.[71]

The Anti-Footian Procedure: Independently of any judgments that one has about the permissibility of the various act alternatives available to the agent, come to some considered judgments about how their respective outcomes rank, and rank the outcomes according to these judgments alone. To ensure that CR holds, maintain that the only permissible acts are those that produce outcomes that one judges not to be outranked.[72]

---

[70] For the purposes of illustration only, I choose maximizing act-consequentialism's criterion of rightness.

[71] Of course, no one has judgments about how outcomes rank in the abstract. But, in this case, the judgment that one outcome outranks another is just the judgment that the agent ought (i.e., has most reason) to prefer the one to the other. We clearly do make such judgments. Many would, for instance, judge both that, if my child has just fallen out of the boat, I ought to prefer that she does not drown and that, if Odette can rescue only one of two groups of people drowning, then I ought to prefer that Odette rescues the group that includes my child even if the other group contains more people.

I call this the Footian Procedure, because it holds, like Foot, that the evaluative status of an outcome is determined by the deontic status of the act that produces it. More specifically, Foot (1985) held that an outcome is best only if the act that produces it is morally obligatory.

[72] The product of this procedure is what Scanlon (2001) calls "Foundational Consequentialism."

> *The Coherentist Procedure:* While keeping CR constant, revise one's
> pre-theoretical judgments both about how these outcomes rank and
> about the permissibility of the acts that produce them in light of each
> other (and in light of one's various background beliefs) until wide reflec-
> tive equilibrium is reached, and then rank the outcomes accordingly.

The Footian Procedure would yield very little, if any, normative advice beyond what our pre-theoretical deontic judgments already tell us. Thus, the consequentializer should eschew the Footian Procedure if she wants her resulting substantive theory to provide such additional normative guidance.[73] And, according to some, if a moral theory fails to provide such guidance, then this is a significant failure, as one of the things that we supposedly hope to gain from moral theorizing is the ability to better deal with moral questions about which we disagree or about which we have no confident pre-theoretical judgments.[74] But just because the consequentializer should perhaps eschew the Footian Procedure does not mean that she must eschew any appeal to our deontic judgments and adopt the Anti-Footian Procedure instead. The Coherentist Procedure is a viable alternative that, like the Anti-Footian Procedure, yields normative guidance beyond that which our pre-theoretical deontic intuitions provide.

Unlike the adherent of the Anti-Footian Procedure, the adherent of the Coherentist Procedure is willing to revise her pre-theoretical judgments about how outcomes rank in light of any potentially counterintuitive deontic verdicts it yields when combined with CR. And, unlike the adherent of the Footian Procedure, the adherent of the Coherentist Procedure is also willing to revise her pre-theoretical judgments about the deontic statuses of actions in light of any potential conflicts that may arise when she combines her pre-theoretical judgments about how

---

[73] See VAN ROOJEN 2004, pp. 164–169.

[74] See HOOKER 2000, p. 4. Although I agree that it would be *nice* if the correct moral theory were able to help us deal with moral questions about which we disagree or about which we have no confident pre-theoretical judgments, I am not convinced that the fact that some moral theory fails to provide such guidance counts against the plausibility of the theory. For instance, it seems to me that the divine command theory could be correct even if it were unable to provide us with any normative guidance. It might be, for instance, that the only way we have of determining what God's commands are is to appeal both to our moral convictions and to the fact that God commands us to act in a certain way if and only if our acting in that way is morally obligatory. In that case, the divine command theory could not help us deal with moral questions about which we disagree or about which we have no confident pre-theoretical judgments. But, for all that, it could be the correct moral theory, accurately identifying what it is that *makes* acts right and wrong. So although we may *hope* to gain from moral theorizing the ability to better deal with moral questions about which we disagree or about which we have no confident pre-theoretical judgments, it may turn out that the correct moral theory does not fulfill this hope. In any case, the point that I make here is that even if philosophers such as Hooker and van Roojen are correct in thinking that a moral theory's failure to provide normative guidance counts against the plausibility of that moral theory, this does not pose a problem for the consequentializing project, for the theory that the consequentializer comes up with will provide normative guidance.

outcomes rank with CR. Sometimes the adherent of the Coherentist Procedure will end up revising her deontic judgments in light of her more firmly held evaluative judgments (i.e., her judgments about how outcomes rank in terms of the agent's reasons for desiring them). Other times she will revise her evaluative judgments in light of her more firmly held deontic judgments. The Coherentist Procedure will, therefore, yield both new deontic judgments and new evaluative judgments.[75] Given the viability of the Coherentist Procedure, then, it seems that the consequentializer can appeal to our considered moral convictions when determining how outcomes rank without rendering her view either circular or uninformative.

There is, of course, no guarantee that the Coherentist Procedure will produce a ranking that when combined with CR yields a set of deontic verdicts that comports with all, or even most, of our considered moral convictions. But there are reasons to be optimistic. One reason is that it seems that many of our pre-theoretical judgments about how outcomes rank—that is, about how much reason the agent has to desire them—are already what is needed to render consequentialism compatible with our considered moral convictions. To illustrate, consider the following. Imagine that I visit an oracle to have my future told. The oracle's visions of the future are always accurate even if they are sometimes less than fully specific. The oracle foresees that a year from now my daughter will be drowning in a lake. The only chance I will have of rescuing her will be by using the motorboat that is always docked at the lake's pier. The oracle also foresees that a year from now

---

[75] I am assuming that sometimes we judge that an act is permissible (or impermissible) even though we judge that its outcome is (or is not) outranked. We might, for instance, judge that although I ought to prefer the outcome in which I hack into the UNOS database and move my sick child to the top of the list for receipt of a donor organ, I ought not to do this. (I thank Jussi Suikkanen for suggesting this example.) At the very least, I am assuming that sometimes our degree of confidence in our judgment that a given act is impermissible (or permissible) is greater or lesser than our degree of confidence in our judgment that its outcome is (or is not) outranked. If, contrary to these assumptions, our deontic and evaluative judgments are, from the start, in perfect accord with both CR and our background beliefs, then the Coherentist Procedure will not yield any new judgments.

I am also assuming that we have intuitions about which outcomes should be preferred to which others and that these intuitions are, to some extent, independent of our intuitions about the deontic statuses of the acts that produce them. It seems to me that we clearly do have such independent intuitions. For one, whereas our intuitions about whether an agent ought to prefer the state of affairs in which she has performed a given action to one in which she has refrained from that action varies depending on the time at which the agent is making the evaluation, our intuitions about whether or not the agent should have refrained from that action does not—see, for instance, the example concerning the woman who refused to abort her fetus with Down Syndrome, which I described in note 11 of chapter 3. For another, we have intuitions about which states of affairs are to be preferred to which others even when these states of affairs are not produced by any agent's action. For instance, we have the intuition that if I were to learn that some child at my daughter's elementary school has died in a fire, I ought to prefer that it was not my daughter who died even if, impersonally speaking, it would be better if it were her as opposed to one of her more gifted classmates who died.

Otto's two daughters will be drowning in a different lake. The only chance he will have of rescuing them is by using the motorboat that is always docked at that lake's pier. The oracle foresees that only one of us will succeed in our rescue attempt, as he foresees that one of the two motorboats will fail to start, though he cannot foresee which one it will be; this part of his vision is just too hazy.

Unfortunately, there is no way to prevent what the oracle foretells from coming true; this I have learned from the many who have tried before. All I can do, then, is to hope that I will be the one to succeed. And, intuitively, this seems exactly what I ought to hope for. That is, it seems that I ought to prefer that I will succeed even though it would be better, impersonally speaking, if Otto were the one to succeed, since if he succeeds two girls will be saved as opposed to just one.[76] This ranking of outcomes is exactly what is needed to ground, on consequentialism, a special obligation to save one's own children even when one could otherwise enable someone else to save more of their own children. If I ought to prefer that I succeed, then, on consequentialism, I should, if given the choice, save my child rather than enable Otto to save his two children.

Here's another example. Imagine that I go to the oracle a second time. This time he foretells that in a year's time I will face the choice either to commit murder so as to prevent two others from committing murder or to refrain from murder and thereby allow the two others to commit murder. The oracle foresees that I will be tempted to murder the one to prevent the two others from committing murder, but he cannot foresee whether I will ultimately give into this temptation. In this case, it seems that I ought to hope and prefer that I choose to refrain from murder. And, again, we find that this is exactly what is needed to render consequentialism compatible with our considered moral convictions—in this case, our conviction that there is an agent-centered restriction against the commission of murder.

So one reason to be optimistic about the Coherentist Procedure yielding an evaluative ranking of outcomes that renders consequentialism compatible with our considered moral convictions is the fact that many of our pre-theoretical evaluative judgments are already what they need to be in order to render consequentialism compatible with our considered moral convictions.

Another reason to be optimistic that the Coherentist Procedure will produce a ranking that when combined with CR yields a set of deontic verdicts that comports

---

[76] I very much doubt that our intuition about what I ought to prefer in this case is simply derivative of our intuition about what I ought to do in this case. After all, it is intuitive to think that I ought to prefer the state of affairs in which some stranger named Pablo saves my daughter to the state of affairs in which Pablo saves Otto's two daughters, and this is so despite its being intuitive to think that Pablo ought to save Otto's two daughters instead of my daughter. Moreover, it would be odd to think that what explains why I ought to prefer my daughter's being saved to Otto's two daughter's being saved in the original case is the fact that the relevant agent (viz., me) ought to save my daughter, but that what explains why I ought to prefer my daughter's being saved to Otto's two daughter's being saved in the Pablo case is something different altogether—after all, it cannot be the fact that the relevant agent (viz., Pablo) ought to save my daughter, for this is simply false.

with most of our considered moral convictions is the fact that our considered moral convictions will in part be shaped by this Coherentist Procedure. That is, sometimes we will on reflection reject our pre-theoretical deontic judgments precisely because they conflict with the deontic verdicts that are entailed by CR and our pre-theoretical evaluative judgments. So even if, in some instances, our pre-theoretical evaluative judgments yield deontic verdicts that conflict with our pre-theoretical deontic judgments when combined with CR, we will sometimes on reflection be willing to jettison some of these pre-theoretical deontic judgments in light of the intuitive attractiveness of moral rationalism and the teleological conception of practical reasons and their entailment of consequentialism. So, some of the pre-theoretical deontic judgments that might have otherwise made trouble for the consequentializing project will not survive our reflections. And so there is hope that the consequentializing project will succeed in advancing the cause of consequentialism by yielding a substantive version of consequentialism that comports with most, if not all, of our considered moral convictions and without our having to adopt an implausible ranking of outcomes.[77]

***

In this chapter, I have argued that any plausible nonconsequentialist theory can be consequentialized. This does not mean that we are all consequentialists, but it does mean that it is possible to construct a substantive version of consequentialism that comports with our considered moral convictions. Of course, just because it is possible to construct a substantive version of consequentialism that comports with our considered moral convictions does not mean that the resulting version of consequentialism will be plausible. A given version of consequentialism is only as plausible as its underlying ranking of outcomes. But I have argued that there are good reasons to think that the most plausible ranking of outcomes will be the one that yields a substantive version of consequentialism that comports with most, if not all, of our considered moral convictions.

This is a happy result, for, ultimately, what we are after is some version of consequentialism that comports with our considered moral convictions. After all, if the arguments from chapters 2 and 3 are correct, we must accept some version of consequentialism. Furthermore, if I have been right in thinking that utilitarianism's failure to comport with our considered moral convictions is what has gotten it in so much hot water vis-à-vis moral rationalism, then it seems that, given my arguments for moral rationalism in chapter 2, we must accept some version of consequentialism that comports with our considered moral convictions. Such a

---

[77] I am assuming that any ranking that is in wide reflective equilibrium with both our deontic judgments and our background beliefs, including our views about practical reasons and their relationship to morality—I am thinking of the teleological conception of reasons and moral rationalism, respectively—would not be an implausible ranking.

version of consequentialism would take what is best from both utilitarianism and nonconsequentialism. From utilitarianism, it would take utilitarian's compelling idea—namely, the idea that an act's deontic status is determined by the agent's reasons for preferring its outcome to those of the available alternatives such that it can never be morally wrong for her to act so as to bring about the outcome that she has most reason to want to obtain. And, from nonconsequentialism, it would take nonconsequentialism's intuitively plausible deontic verdicts and their compatibility with moral rationalism given certain plausible assumptions about what we have decisive reason to do.

Of course, consequentialism's ability to comport with our considered moral convictions (including our convictions about certain agent-centered options) is predicated not only on the plausibility of a certain ranking of outcomes, but also on the plausibility of our adopting DRAC's dual-ranking structure. And DRAC's dual-ranking structure can seem unmotivated. But things are not as they seem. There are, as I will show in the next chapter, good reasons to adopt DRAC's dual-ranking structure. Thus, in the next chapter, I will continue to defend the plausibility of consequentializing commonsense morality by defending DRAC against this and other potential objections.

5

Dual-Ranking Act-Consequentialism

Reasons, Morality, and Overridingness

Recall that, according to what I call *dual-ranking act-consequentialism,*

> **DRAC** S's performing *x* is morally permissible if and only if, and because, there is no available act alternative that would produce an outcome that S has both more moral reason and more reason, all things considered, to want to obtain than to want *x*'s outcome to obtain.

Again, I call this *dual-ranking* act-consequentialism, because, on this version of consequentialism, the permissibility of an action is a function of how its outcome ranks relative to those of its alternatives on a ranking of outcomes (i.e., the principal ranking) that is in turn a function of two auxiliary rankings: one being a ranking in terms of how much *moral* reason the agent has to want each of these outcomes to obtain, and the other being a ranking in terms of how much reason, *all things considered*, the agent has to want each of them to obtain. Clearly, these two auxiliary rankings are each evaluative: that is, they are each a ranking of outcomes in terms of the agent's reasons (or some subset of her reasons—e.g., her moral reasons) for preferring each outcome to the others. Curiously, though, DRAC's principal ranking does not seem to be a ranking of outcomes along any evaluative dimension: that is, it does not rank outcomes in terms of how much moral reason, non-moral reason, or all-things-considered reason the agent has to want each of them to obtain. What, then, motivates adopting this principal ranking and its dual-ranking structure?

It is, of course, quite common for consequentialists to adopt more sophisticated ranking principles in the hopes of reconciling consequentialism with our commonsense moral convictions. Some consequentialists, for instance, claim that the ranking of outcomes is a function of not only the amount of utility that they contain, but also the fairness of the distribution of the utility that they contain. And, by appealing to such distribution-sensitive ranking principles, consequentialism is made consistent with some of our convictions about distributive justice.

But what typically makes this more than just an ad hoc move is that the more sophisticated ranking principles are motivated by certain axiological intuitions: for instance, that we ought, other things being equal, to prefer that utility be distributed fairly. But what axiological intuitions could possibly motivate the move from traditional act-consequentialism to DRAC—specifically, the move from a single-ranking structure to a dual-ranking structure? Speaking of the principal rankings that one version of DRAC generates, Ted Sider admits that they do not "correspond to any independently important axiological facts." He says, "All I claim for their importance is their role in determining moral normative status" (1993, p. 128). In that case, though, the move to a dual-ranking structure can seem quite ad hoc.

I concede that the move from a single-ranking structure to a dual-ranking structure is not motivated by any axiological intuitions—that is, it is not motivated by our intuitions about which outcomes agents ought to prefer. Nevertheless, I will argue that the move to adopt a dual-ranking structure is motivated by more than just a concern to avoid counterintuitive implications. I will start by showing that moral reasons are not morally overriding in that non-moral reasons can, and sometimes do, prevent moral reasons, even those with considerable requiring strength, from generating moral requirements. And I will show that, given this, the consequentialist has no choice but to adopt DRAC.[1]

In §5.1, I clarify what it means to say that moral reasons are not morally overriding, drawing a distinction between *moral reasons* and *morally relevant reasons*. Then, in §5.2, I argue that those who wish to accommodate certain typical agent-centered options must deny that moral reasons are morally overriding and accept both that the reason that agents have to promote their own self-interest is a non-moral reason and that this reason can, and sometimes does, prevent the moral reason that they have to sacrifice their self-interest for the sake of doing more to promote the interests of others from generating a moral requirement. And, in §5.3, I argue that those who wish to accommodate many typical instances of supererogation must do the same. In §5.4, I show how the conclusion argued for in the previous two sections—that is, the conclusion that non-moral reasons can,

---

[1] Let me admit upfront, however, that part of my argument for moral reasons not being morally overriding is that this is something that we must hold in order to accommodate certain moral judgments. The point, though, is not to show that the case for adopting a dual-ranking structure hangs free from our moral judgments, but to show that the case for adopting a dual-ranking structure goes beyond the fact that doing so allows consequentialism to avoid counterintuitive implications. For part of the case for adopting a dual-ranking structure lies with the fact that it allows consequentialism to cohere well with a range of our moral and meta-ethical judgments, including such judgments as that there are both supererogatory acts and agent-centered options, that non-moral reasons can justify acting contrary to what there is most moral reason to do, that it is always morally permissible to do what there is most moral reason to do, and that it is always morally permissible to do what there is most reason to do, all things (and, thus, all reasons—moral and non-moral) considered.

and sometimes do, prevent moral reasons from generating moral requirements—forces us to accept a certain view about how moral and non-moral reasons function together to determine an act's deontic status, and I show that this view forces the consequentialist to adopt DRAC. Lastly, in the remaining three sections, I rebut four potential objections to DRAC.

§5.1 Some quick clarifications

To hold that moral reasons are *morally overriding* is, as you will recall from chapter 2, to hold the following thesis:

> **MO** If S has more moral reason to perform x than to perform y ($y \neq x$), then S is not morally permitted to perform y. And, thus, if S has most moral reason to perform x, then S is morally required to perform x.

If this thesis were true, then it would always be morally wrong to refrain from doing what one has most moral reason to do, even if what one has most moral reason to do is supported by only the most trivial of moral reasons and opposed by the weightiest of non-moral reasons. Suppose, for instance, that someone were to offer me a million dollars to give a lecture at a time at which I had promised to meet with a student. Assume, for the purposes of illustration, that the reason that I have to keep this promise is a moral reason, that the only reason I have to break this promise is that doing so will further my self-interest, and that the reason that I have to further my self-interest is a non-moral reason.[2] If moral reasons are morally overriding, then the non-moral reason that I have to take advantage of this unique opportunity to make a quick million is, no matter how strong, powerless to prevent the moral reason that I have to keep my promise from generating a moral requirement to do so, no matter how trivial the promise, and no matter how weak the moral reason stemming from it.

As I said in chapter 2, I think that MO is false. Those, like myself, who deny MO do so because they accept one or both of two theses that entail its falsity. After explaining what these two theses are, I am going to argue for one of them (without denying that the other might be true as well) and conclude that MO is false. But before I can explain these two theses, I need to draw a distinction and explain some terminology.

Reasons seem to play at least two normative roles in determining an act's deontic status: a requiring role and a justifying role.[3] Reasons can morally require performing acts that it would otherwise be morally permissible to refrain from performing (the requiring role), and reasons can morally justify performing acts

---

[2] As noted in chapter 2, we are to assume that I must spend the entire million on personal luxuries that will benefit only myself.

[3] They may also play an enticing role—see note 6 below.

that it would otherwise be morally impermissible to perform (the justifying role). Given these two normative roles, reasons have two potentially separable dimensions of strength: *moral requiring strength* and *moral justifying strength*. A reason has moral requiring strength to the extent that it can make it morally impermissible to refrain from performing acts that it would otherwise be morally permissible to refrain from performing, and a reason has moral justifying strength to the extent that it can make it morally permissible to perform acts that it would otherwise be morally impermissible to perform.

We can use the following criteria to determine whether one reason, R_1, has more moral requiring strength and/or more moral justifying strength than another reason, R_2:[4]

R_1 has more *moral requiring strength* than R_2 if and only if:

(i) R_1 would make it morally impermissible to do anything that R_2 would make it morally impermissible to do.

(ii) R_1 would make it morally impermissible do some things that R_2 would *not* make it morally impermissible to do.

R_1 has more *moral justifying strength* than R_2 if and only if:

(i) R_1 would make it morally permissible to do anything that R_2 would make it morally permissible to do.

(ii) R_1 would make it morally permissible do some things that R_2 would *not* make it morally permissible to do.

To illustrate the above criteria for moral requiring strength, consider that, on commonsense morality, the reason one has to refrain from killing an innocent person has more moral requiring strength than the reason one has to prevent an innocent person from dying. This is true in virtue of the following two facts: (i) If it would be immoral to do something—for instance, to push the red button rather than the green button—because it would entail failing to prevent an innocent person's death, then it would also be immoral to do that same thing if it would entail killing an innocent person. (ii) Even though it would be morally permissible to let an innocent person die in order to save one's daughter (as where both are drowning and one has only enough time to save one of the two), it would not be morally permissible to kill an innocent person in order to save one's daughter (as where one's daughter needs that person's heart to live).

To illustrate the above criterion for moral justifying strength, consider that, on commonsense morality, the reason one has to save three lives has more moral

---

[4] These are adapted from Joshua Gert's criteria for *rational* requiring strength and *rational* justifying strength. See GERT 2003, especially pp. 15–16.

justifying strength than the reason one has to save one life. This is true in virtue of the following two facts: (*i*) If it would be morally permissible to do something that would otherwise be immoral—for example, to break a promise to meet with a student—in order to save a life, then it would also be permissible to do the same in order to save three lives. (*ii*) Even though it would not be morally permissible to fail to save two lives in order to save just one (assuming that everything else is equal and, thus, that there is no reason that favors saving the one as opposed to the two), it would be morally permissible to fail to save two lives in order to save three.[5]

Having clarified what is meant by the phrases "moral requiring strength" and "moral justifying strength," I can now state one of the two theses that entail the falsity of MO:

> **NMR+MJS** *Non-moral reasons* have some (+) *moral justifying strength*. And, thus, non-moral reasons can, and sometimes do, prevent moral reasons, even those with considerable moral requiring strength, from generating moral requirements.

According to NMR+MJS, non-moral reasons can justify acting contrary to what there is most moral reason to do. Thus, if NMR+MJS is true, MO is false.

Now, NMR+MJS is not the only thesis that entails the falsity of MO, and so it is possible to deny both NMR+MJS and MO. To see how, let us assume that there are two alternatives to choose from: *x* and *y*. And let us assume that there is most moral reason to perform *x*, but most non-moral reason to perform *y*. Of course, if NMR+MJS is false, then the non-moral reasons that support performing *y* will be powerless to prevent the moral reasons that support performing *x* from generating a moral requirement to perform *x*. So, if one is going to deny both NMR+MJS and MO, then one must accept either (*a*) that there are some, admittedly weaker, moral reasons that support performing *y* and that these weaker moral reasons can prevent the stronger moral reasons that support performing *x* from generating a moral requirement to perform *x* or (*b*) that the following thesis is true:

> **MR~MRS** Some *moral reasons* have absolutely no (~) *moral requiring strength*.[6]

---

[5] Of course, John Taurek has argued that it might be permissible to save the one instead of the two if one were to flip a coin to decide which group to save—see TAUREK 1977. Nevertheless, I am claiming only that, on commonsense morality, it would be impermissible to save the one instead of the two absent some special reason for saving the one.

[6] It may be that some moral reasons are mere moral enticers: reasons that, morally speaking, count in favor of performing some act but that do not have any moral requiring strength whatsoever. These moral enticers could make doing what they entice us to do supererogatory, but they could never make doing what they entice us to do obligatory. Moral enticers would be the moral analogue of what Jonathan Dancy (2004) calls enticing reasons.

The first of these (viz., claim *a*) should be rejected. For one, the idea that the weaker moral reasons that support performing *y* could prevent the stronger moral reasons that support performing *x* from generating a moral requirement to perform *x* is implausible. For another, it seems that, in many instances, there will be no moral reason to perform *y*, and claim *a* will, therefore, be a non-starter. It seems, then, that if we want to reject both MO and NMR+MJS, we should accept claim *b*—that is, MR~MRS. By accepting MR~MRS, we can account for MO's being false. For if MR~MRS is true, then S can have most moral reason to perform *x* and yet not be morally required to perform *x* simply because the moral reasons that support performing *x* have no moral requiring strength.

I think that MR~MRS is probably true, but I will not argue for it here. Instead, I will argue for NMR+MJS. This alone is sufficient to show that MO is false. I will assume that there are various typical sorts of agent-centered options and argue that, in order to accommodate them, we must accept NMR+MJS and, thus, accept the view that non-moral reasons can, and sometimes do, affect an act's deontic status.

But let me rebut one immediate objection. Some will say that, by definition, a reason is a moral one if and only if it is relevant to determining an act's deontic status, and thus it is conceptually impossible for a non-moral reason (which, on this definition, is a reason that is not relevant to determining an act's deontic status) to be relevant to determining an act's deontic status. Of course, one could define a "moral reason" in this way, but I will adopt a different definition so as to preserve an important distinction between reasons that are relevant to determining an act's deontic status and reasons that, morally speaking, count for or against performing some action. I will call any reason that is relevant to determining an act's deontic status a *morally relevant reason*, and I will call any reason that, morally speaking, counts for or against performing some action a *moral reason*.[7]

This is an important distinction to make, because it may be that not all morally relevant reasons are moral reasons. It is possible that some reasons can justify performing acts that it would otherwise be morally impermissible to perform without themselves counting in favor of performing them, morally speaking. For instance, we might think that the fact I would personally gain from breaking a promise is not a moral reason to do so in that it does not, *morally speaking,* count in favor of my doing so.[8] Nevertheless, the reason that I have to act for personal

---

[7] Moral reasons either have some moral requiring strength or, if they do not, they are mere moral enticers. Moral enticers can make doing what they entice us to do supererogatory, but they cannot make doing what they entice us to do obligatory. Thus, a moral reason is a reason that, if sufficiently weighty, could make an act either obligatory or supererogatory. A reason that could only justify—that is, a reason that could not make an act obligatory or supererogatory but could only make an act permissible—would be a (morally relevant) non-moral reason.

[8] Nor is it the case that the fact that I would personally gain by performing the act counts against my performing it, morally speaking.

gain may be a morally relevant reason, for, perhaps, such a non-moral reason could, if sufficiently weighty, justify my breaking a promise. In any case, it would be a mistake to rule out, by definition, the very real possibility that non-moral reasons (i.e., reasons that, morally speaking, count neither for nor against any action) are relevant to determining an act's deontic status.

Having clarified the relevant terminology, I will now proceed to argue that, if we wish to accommodate many typical agent-centered options, we must accept NMR+MJS—that is, that non-moral reasons can justify acting contrary to what there is most moral reason to do. And, in the subsequent section, I will also argue that, if we wish to accommodate many typical supererogatory acts, we must accept NMR+MJS.

§5.2 Moral reasons, overridingness, and agent-centered options

An agent-centered option is a moral option either to act so as to make things better overall but worse for oneself (or others) or to act so as to make things better for oneself (or others) but worse overall. There are two types of agent-centered options: *agent-favoring options* and *agent-sacrificing options*. An agent-favoring option is a moral option either to act so as to make things better overall but worse *for oneself* or to act so as to make things better *for oneself* but worse overall. An agent-sacrificing option is a moral option either to act so as to make things better overall but worse *for others* or to act so as to make things better *for others* but worse overall. Whereas agent-favoring options permit agents to give their own interests more weight than they have from the impersonal perspective, agent-sacrificing options permit agents to give their own interests less weight than they have from the impersonal perspective.

The following is a typical instance of an agent-centered option (more specifically, an agent-favoring option): an agent has a certain sum of money that she can use to secure either a considerable benefit for herself or a far more considerable net benefit for various needy, distant strangers. Suppose, for instance, that she must choose to use the money that she has saved either to place a down payment on a new home or to help various needy, distant strangers by donating it to Oxfam.

In this and many other typical instances of agent-favoring options, the following four claims hold:

5.1 The agent has the choice to act either self-interestedly or altruistically—that is, she has the choice either to promote her own self-interest or to sacrifice her self-interest for the sake of doing more to promote the interests of others.

5.2 It is morally permissible for her to act self-interestedly.

5.3 It is also morally permissible for her to act altruistically.

5.4 The reason that she has to act altruistically is, what I will call, a *sufficient requiring reason*—a reason that has sufficient moral requiring strength to generate, absent countervailing reasons, a moral requirement to perform the act in which it counts in favor.[9]

That claims 5.1–5.3 must hold is, I take it, incontrovertible, as each follows from the definition of an "agent-favoring option." Claim 5.4, however, is in need of justification.

To see that the reason that the agent has to act altruistically is, in many typical instances, a sufficient requiring reason, consider the following two cases. In the first case, Fiona is accessing her savings account via the Internet and is about to transfer the entire balance to her escrow company so as to place the necessary down payment on her new home. She must do this if she is to purchase her new home, and she can do this simply by clicking on the TRANSFER button. However, there is an alternative. By clicking instead on the DONATE button, her savings will be transferred, not to her escrow company, but to Oxfam. Let us suppose, then, that by clicking on the DONATE button she will be providing various needy, distant strangers in the Third World with some considerable, indeed potentially life-saving, benefit (e.g., a new well with enough potable water for everyone in the village). Those who accept that there is an agent-centered option in such cases believe that, given the tremendous sacrifice involved, Fiona is not morally required to click on the DONATE button.[10] But it seems that they should also accept that the fact that her doing so would produce such a considerable benefit for these distant, needy strangers constitutes a reason of considerable moral requiring strength to click on the DONATE button. Indeed, but for the costs involved, it seems that this reason would generate a moral requirement to click on the DONATE button.

To see this, consider the second case, a variant of the first. In this case, Fiona can transfer the money to her escrow company by clicking on *either* the TRANSFER button or the DONATE button. In this case, the money that would be donated to Oxfam if Fiona clicks on the DONATE button is not hers, but that of a very rich man who has agreed to donate an equivalent sum of *his* money if, and only if,

[9] So a requiring reason is any reason that has some moral requiring strength, and a sufficient requiring reason is a requiring reason that has sufficient moral requiring strength to generate a moral requirement in the absence of countervailing reasons. It may be that all requiring reasons are sufficient requiring reasons, but I draw the distinction so as to allow for the possibility that some requiring reasons are such that individually they have insufficient moral requiring strength to generate a moral requirement but, in conjunction, they have enough combined moral requiring strength to generate a moral requirement—at least, absent countervailing considerations. Given this, we should allow that, in the above criteria for moral requiring and/or moral justifying strength, R_1 and R_2 can stand for sets of reasons and not just for individual reasons.

[10] If the reader believes that, given that lives are at stake, Fiona is morally required to click on the DONATE button, then imagine a revised version of the case in which what is at stake is just slightly less than what is needed to generate a moral requirement.

Fiona clicks on the DONATE button. Again, in either case, Fiona's money will be transferred to her escrow company, ensuring the purchase of her new home. It is just that by clicking on the DONATE button as opposed to the TRANSFER button, she also ensures that various needy strangers receive a considerable benefit. Assume that these are the only morally relevant facts.

Surely, in this case, Fiona is morally required to click on the DONATE button, for there is no good reason why she should not do so. By clicking on the DONATE button, she can purchase her new home while also providing an even more considerable net benefit for a number of others, and she can do so at no cost to herself or anyone else, for assume that if Fiona does not click on the DONATE button, the sum of money that the rich man would have otherwise donated to Oxfam will instead be burned, benefiting no one. If one thinks that beneficence is only required when the would-be beneficiaries are below a certain threshold of well-being, assume that the various needy, distant strangers that will be helped by Fiona's clicking on the DONATE button are below this threshold.

Given that we think that the reason that Fiona has to click on the DONATE button gives rise to a moral requirement in the absence of countervailing reasons, we must conclude that it is a sufficient requiring reason. Now, the only relevant difference between this case and the original one is how costly it is for Fiona to help the strangers. But surely it is implausible to suppose that Fiona's reason to help the strangers, or its moral requiring strength, diminishes as the cost of her doing so increases.[11] Suppose, for instance, that we were to increase gradually the cost of clicking on the DONATE button, from no cost at all, to ten cents, to twenty cents, to thirty cents, and so on. It is not as if there is less and less to be said in favor of Fiona's helping the strangers as the cost of her clicking on the DONATE button increases. At least, that is not what the phenomenology of the case tells us, for it feels like a case in which one reason is outweighed by another, not like a case in which one reason is undermined by another. If it were the latter,

---

[11] See KAGAN 1989, p. 49. Of course, particularists might object that a reason can have a great deal of moral requiring strength in one context (e.g., the context in which the cost of acting altruistically is quite low) but very little to no moral requiring strength in another context (e.g., the context in which the cost of acting altruistically is quite high), for particularists will deny that reasons have stable valences or strength values across possible contexts. But see GERT 2007 for an interesting and powerful response. In that article, Gert argues that the particularist "cannot merely deny that it makes sense to ascribe *stable* strength values to reasons: values that they keep from context to context. Rather, the particularist must make the blanket claim that talk of the strength of a reason makes no real sense even in a restricted context" (p. 553). This is because, when we assign a strength value to a reason, we are providing a concise representation of the way it affects the deontic statuses of acts across a range of contexts. For instance, if we assign greater moral requiring strength to one reason than to another, we are committed to a claim about how these two reasons affect the deontic statuses of acts across contexts: specifically, we must claim that the one reason would make it morally impermissible to do anything that the other reason would make it morally impermissible to do. Since this is precisely the sort of claim that particularists must deny, they must deny that talk of the strength of a reason makes any sense at all, even in particular contexts. And that is a hard bullet to bite.

then once the cost was high enough, Fiona should cease to feel any pull toward clicking on the DONATE button. But even when the cost is extremely high, the fact that clicking on the DONATE button would help these others continues to count in favor of Fiona's doing so, and with the same force as before. And there is nothing particularly special about this case. So we should conclude that, in many typical instances in which the agent has an agent-centered option, 5.4 is true.

Of course, some moral theorists who endorse agent-centered options could object that although they are committed to certain moral *principles*, they are not committed to there being any moral *reasons*, let alone to there being a sufficient requiring reason to act altruistically in such cases. They might, therefore, deny that they are committed to 5.4. But their moral principles commit them to certain moral reasons, for moral principles entail that certain facts have sufficient requiring strength. For instance, if one accepts the principle of utility (i.e., that agents are required to maximize utility), then one is thereby committed to there being a sufficient requiring reason to promote utility. The principle of utility entails that the fact that some act would promote utility is a sufficient requiring reason to perform that act. Likewise, anyone who accepts a moral principle that entails that agents are obligated to provide needy others with a significant benefit whenever their doing so would be costless both to themselves and to others is thereby committed to there being a sufficient requiring reason to act altruistically in such instances.

So, one of the assumptions that I am making is that some such moral principle is true. If this assumption were false, then Fiona would not, in the second case, be obligated to click on the DONATE button. And if that were right, then I would be wrong in saying that those who wish to accommodate many typical agent-centered options are committed to 5.4. I doubt, though, that my assumption is false. In any case, I will be assuming in what follows that some such moral principle is true and that, therefore, anyone who wishes to accommodate many typical agent-centered options must accept 5.4.

Given 5.4, we must ask: What prevents the sufficient requiring reason that the agent has to act altruistically from generating a moral requirement to act altruistically? Clearly, it must be the reason that the agent has to act self-interestedly, as this is the only countervailing reason, and we must cite some countervailing reason, since, given 5.4, we are to assume that the moral reason that the agent has to act altruistically would generate a moral requirement to act altruistically absent countervailing reasons. We must also assume that this countervailing reason to act self-interestedly must have at least as much moral justifying strength as the reason that the agent has to act altruistically has moral requiring strength—otherwise, it would not be able to prevent the reason that the agent has to act altruistically from generating a requirement to act altruistically. Lastly, we must assume that this reason to act self-interestedly must have less moral requiring strength than moral justifying strength, for, otherwise, we would end up with a moral requirement to act self-interestedly instead of a moral option to act either altruistically or self-interestedly. This is Shelly Kagan's worry. He says:

> If, in some particular case, the balance of morally relevant reasons did not favor promoting the overall good [i.e., acting altruistically] but favored instead promoting the agent's own interests [i.e., acting self-interestedly]—then it seems that these reasons would still go on to generate a moral *requirement*. Admittedly, the agent would not be morally required to promote the overall good, but she *would* be morally required to promote her interests. Yet... what we were looking for was a defense of a moral *option*, according to which the agent would still be morally permitted (although not required) to do the act with the best results overall. (1994, pp. 338–339)

The solution, as a number of philosophers have pointed out, lies with the fact that the morally relevant reasons that favor acting self-interestedly as opposed to altruistically are non-moral reasons.[12] If such non-moral reasons can prevent the moral reason that the agent has to act altruistically from generating a moral requirement, then what we end up with is a moral option rather than a moral requirement to act self-interestedly, for non-moral reasons, by definition, lack any moral requiring strength.[13] Kagan overlooks this possible solution to his worry, because he assumes that the only sorts of reasons that could prevent a moral reason from generating a moral requirement are other *moral* reasons. He says, "since we are concerned with what is required by *morality*, the relevant reasons—whether decisive or not—must be moral ones" (1989, p. 66). But Kagan's inference is unwarranted; we should not just assume that non-moral reasons are irrelevant with regard to what is required by morality.

Fortunately for the defender of agent-centered options, it is quite plausible to suppose that the fact that performing some act would further one's self-interest is not *itself* a moral reason to perform it and, thus, is not a reason of any moral requiring strength. Moral reasons are, of course, a proper subset of reasons for action. So if reasons are considerations that count for or against performing some action, then *moral* reasons are considerations that, *morally speaking*, count for or against performing some action. But there is nothing, morally speaking, that counts in favor of promoting one's self-interest per se.[14] This is not to say that one never has a moral reason to do what will further one's self-interest; one often does, as when doing one's moral duty coincides with promoting one's self-interest. The claim is only that the mere fact that performing some act would further one's self-interest does not *itself* constitute a moral reason to perform that act, for the mere fact that performing some act would be in one's self-interest is never by itself sufficient to make an act obligatory, or even supererogatory.

---

[12] See BRATMAN 1994 and SLOTE 1991.

[13] If a given reason for action did have some moral requiring strength, it would thereby count in favor of performing that act, morally speaking, and would, therefore, be a moral reason.

[14] For a more thorough defense of this claim, see PORTMORE 2003, especially section III.

Consider, for instance, that the fact that I would benefit from getting a massage does not, morally speaking, count in favor of my getting one. If I had the opportunity to get one for free and chose instead to do something less beneficial for myself, I could rightly be called foolish or imprudent, but not immoral. And the mere fact that performing some act would further one's self-interest is not only incapable of making such an act morally obligatory, it is also incapable of making such an act morally supererogatory. Consider that in those instances in which I am morally required to come to someone's aid, as where there is a child drowning in a shallow pond, ensuring that I benefit myself in the process (by, say, alerting the news media so that I might receive some reward) would not by itself constitute going above and beyond the call of duty.

Of course, some might object that there are duties to the self, and that such duties show that there is a moral reason to promote one's self-interest. But the idea that there are certain duties to the self is compatible with the thought that there is no moral reason per se to promote one's self-interest. To illustrate, take the duty to develop one's talents. It seems that this duty derives not from some duty to promote one's self-interest, but from some duty to make use of certain valuable gifts, and this explains why we are not morally obligated to develop every talent that would be of potential benefit to ourselves.

Take, for instance, the ability to walk on one's hands over great distances. This is not the sort of talent that one is morally obligated to develop. Of course, one might benefit from developing such a talent, as where one wishes to make it into *The Guinness Book of World Records*. But even so, one would not be morally required, but only prudentially required, to develop this talent. Consider also that it would have been wrong for Mozart to have wasted his unique musical gifts even if he would have been just as well off (self-interestedly speaking) being a mason instead of a musician. It seems, then, that the wrongness of wasting such great gifts lies with its wastefulness and not with its effects on the individual's self-interest. So we can admit that people are sometimes required to develop their talents (and, thus, that there are duties to the self), but we should not infer from this that the fact that some act would promote one's self-interest constitutes a moral reason for performing it. That is, we should admit that there is sometimes a moral reason to do that which will promote one's self-interest, but deny that the reason one has to promote one's self-interest is itself a moral reason.

Of course, there is no denying that, on some moral theories, such as act-utilitarianism, the reason one has to promote one's self-interest (i.e., to promote one's utility) is itself a moral reason. Nevertheless, the point of this section is to show that those moral theorists who endorse typical agent-centered options are committed to the view that the reason one has to promote one's self-interest is a non-moral reason and that such non-moral reasons can prevent moral reasons from generating moral requirements. What utilitarians think is, therefore, beside the point, since they deny the existence of agent-centered options. Unlike utilitarians, moral theorists who endorse agent-centered options typically give some credence to the sorts of intuitions that I have appealed to above. In any case, it seems that such moral theorists must hold that the reason we have to promote our self-interest is a non-moral reason if they wish to avoid, as Kagan worries, trading one moral requirement for another. We should conclude, then, that those committed to these quite typical instances of agent-centered options are further committed to:

5.5 The reason the agent has to promote her self-interest by performing the self-interested option is a non-moral reason.

But how can all of 5.1–5.5 be true? The only way is if the following is also true:

5.6 Non-moral reasons have some moral justifying strength. And, thus, non-moral reasons can, and sometimes do, prevent moral reasons, even those with considerable moral requiring strength, from generating moral require-ments. (NMR+MJS)[15]

Unless 5.6 is true, there is no way that 5.1–5.5 could all be true. To see why, con-sider the following indirect proof. If, contrary to 5.6, non-moral reasons have no moral justifying strength, then the self-interested reason the agent has to perform the self-interested option would be powerless to prevent the moral reason she has to perform the altruistic option from generating a moral requirement, for, according to 5.5, the self-interested reason she has to perform the self-interested option is a non-moral reason. Clearly, if non-moral reasons have no moral justifying

---

[15] One way this might be true is if moral rationalism is true. Moral rationalism is, you will recall, the view that an agent can be morally required to perform an act only if she has decisive reason, all things considered, to do so. If this is right, then a non-moral reason to do something other than x could prevent a moral reason to do x from generating a moral requirement to do x by tipping the balance of reasons, all things considered, in favor of doing something other than x.

Now, I have just claimed that a non-moral reason (e.g., a self-interested reason) to do something other than x can prevent a moral reason to do x from generating a moral requirement to do x by tipping the balance of reasons, all things considered, in favor of doing something other than x. David Copp, how-ever, has argued that "there is no standpoint that can claim normative priority over all other normative standpoints and render a definitive verdict on the relative significance of moral and self-interested rea-sons" (1997, p. 87). He argues that, in cases of conflict between different kinds of reasons, there is no fact as to what a person has most reason to do, all things considered. But, as I see it, moral and self-interested reasons are both reasons with *rational* requiring force. It is just that some moral reasons, and no self-in-terested reasons, have in addition to this some *moral* requiring force as well. So I do not see the problem in claiming that the rational requiring strength of the self-interested reason that one has to do something other than x could be greater than the rational requiring strength of the moral reason one has to do x such that one is rationally required to do other than x—i.e., has decisive reason, all things considered, to do other than x. See also McLEOD 2001 for a persuasive reply to Copp. And see CHANG 2004a and CHANG 2004c for how we might put both moral reasons and self-interested reasons together.

strength, then they are powerless to prevent moral reasons from generating moral requirements. And, given 5.4, we must assume that the agent has a moral reason to perform the altruistic option and that it has considerable moral requiring strength, such that it will generate a moral requirement absent countervailing reasons. But the only countervailing reason in this instance is the reason the agent has to perform the self-interested option, and, as we have just established, this non-moral reason is, assuming the falsity of 5.6, incapable of preventing the moral reason she has to perform the altruistic option from generating a moral requirement to do so. Thus, if we deny 5.6, we are forced to accept that the agent is morally required to perform the altruistic option, and that would mean that we would have to deny 5.2—that is, deny that it is morally permissible for the agent to perform the self-interested option.

So in order to accept all of 5.1–5.5, we must accept 5.6. And since we must accept all of 5.1–5.5 if we want to accommodate many typical instances of agent-centered options, it follows that, if we want to accommodate many typical instances of agent-centered options, we must accept 5.6 as well. That is, we must accept the view that non-moral reasons can, and sometimes do, prevent moral reasons, even those with considerable moral requiring strength, from generating moral requirements (i.e., NMR+MJS)—assuming, of course, that I am right to think that we should seek to accommodate such typical instances of agent-centered options.

In the next section, I will approach the same issue from a different angle, showing that, if we want to accommodate many typical instances of supererogation, we must accept NMR+MJS.

§5.3 Moral reasons, overridingness, and supererogation

Let me begin by stating two necessary conditions for an act's being supererogatory:

S's performing x is supererogatory only if there exists some available alternative, y, such that:

(a) S is morally permitted both to perform x and to perform y, and
(b) S has more moral reason to perform x than to perform y.[16]

---

[16] I leave open the question of whether there are any further necessary conditions, such as: (c) S's performing x is more morally praiseworthy than S's performing y. My preference, though, is to use the term "supererogatory" to denote the pre-theoretical notion of going above and beyond the call of duty (i.e., that of doing more than one has to), and an act can go beyond the call of duty without being praiseworthy, as where the agent performs the act with a bad motive—see MCNAMARA FORTHCOMING. Thus, conditions a and b are, I believe, jointly sufficient. In letting the term "supererogatory" refer to the pre-theoretical notion of exceeding the minimum that morality demands, I follow MCNAMARA 1996a.

Some might deny that b states a necessary condition for an act's being super-erogatory, claiming instead that an act is supererogatory if and only if it is both morally optional (condition a) and morally praiseworthy.[17] While I do not (at least, not in this chapter) want to deny (or assert) that a supererogatory act must be morally praiseworthy, I do want to argue that b states a necessary condition.

A supererogatory act is one that goes above and beyond the call of duty. Thus, an agent performs a supererogatory act only if she exceeds the minimum that morality demands—only if she does "more than she has to" (McNamara 1996a, p. 417). To illustrate, suppose that I promised to bring you some chicken-noodle soup, because you are too sick to eat anything else and are too weak to go out and buy some, let alone make some yourself. Now, the minimum that is required of me, given my promise, is that I bring you some chicken-noodle soup. And let us suppose that I could most easily do this by stopping on the way to your house to buy you some at the store. But suppose that I instead go out of my way to make you some of the best chicken-noodle soup that you have ever had, taking the time to make it from scratch. In spending half of a day making you some homemade chicken-noodle soup, I go beyond the call of duty, doing more than I have to.

Now, what I did was certainly praiseworthy, but this alone is not enough to make it supererogatory, for a supererogatory act must go beyond the call of duty and an act can be praiseworthy without going beyond the call of duty. To see this, consider the following case, which I borrow from Paul McNamara (FORTHCOMING).

> *Soldier on Point:* A soldier is on point this evening. It is her turn to guard the camp. As a general policy and by mutual agreement of everyone in the camp, the soldier on point has the choice of holding either a first or a second position, the first being slightly better with respect to protecting the camp and the second being slightly safer for the soldier on point. This evening the enemy launches a massive assault on the camp in an attempt to overrun it. Despite the grave danger involved and the temptation to run and hide, our soldier faithfully holds the second position, losing her life in the process but providing those back at the camp with sufficient time to prepare and launch a successful counter assault.

As noted in the previous chapter, I have been using the term "supererogatory" when I should prob-ably be using the term "superperfecterogatory" instead. A superperfecterogatory act is one that goes above and beyond what perfect duty requires. The term "supererogatory," by contrast, is best reserved for acts that go above and beyond what all duty (perfect and imperfect) requires. For now, though, I will ignore this distinction and wait until chapter 7 before taking up these complicated issues.

[17] Someone else might deny that b is a necessary condition, claiming instead that a supererogatory act is one that involves a greater self-sacrifice for the sake of others than is required, whether or not there is necessarily any moral reason for agents to make such self-sacrifices—see, for instance, HARWOOD 2003. For why this is problematic, see §§4.2.2.

In holding the second position, our soldier does the least that she can permissibly do—the minimum that is required of her. Doing anything less than holding the second position (such as, running and hiding) would have been impermissible. But even though our soldier did not go beyond the call of duty (as she would have had she held the first position), her actions are praiseworthy. As McNamara (FORTHCOMING) points out, "To stay on point (in either position) in the face of a high chance of death for the sake of others, knowing the advantages of running and having a much better chance of survival, is surely praiseworthy."

This suggests that for an act to be supererogatory it is not sufficient that it be only both morally optional and morally praiseworthy and that a necessary condition for an act's being supererogatory is that it goes beyond the call of duty. And given my arguments from §§4.2.2 that a supererogatory act must involve going beyond the call of duty in terms of doing more of something that there is more moral reason to do and not merely in terms of doing more of something that there is no more moral reason do (such as, perspire), we should think that b is a necessary condition for an act's being supererogatory.

A further reason to accept b as a necessary condition is that doing so nicely accounts for the normative force that supererogatory acts supposedly have. Supererogatory acts are acts that it would be good, morally speaking, to perform. Indeed, the facts that make an act supererogatory are presumably considerations that, morally speaking, count in favor of performing it as opposed to any of its non-supererogatory alternatives. But if, contrary to b, agents do not have more moral reason to perform a supererogatory act than to perform its non-supererogatory alternatives, then it is hard to see why there is supposedly something that, morally speaking, counts in favor of their doing so. So we should accept that both a and b constitute necessary conditions for an act's being supererogatory.[18]

Once we accept these two necessary conditions, however, supererogation can seem paradoxical since condition b appears to be in tension with condition a, as James Dreier has explained:

> Morality, we are inclined to think, is a matter of what reasons one has *from the moral point of view*. When there is a supererogatory act available, it would be better for you to perform it. So surely you have a reason, from the moral point of view, to perform the act. You may have some reason not to perform it, but at least typically you have no reason *from the moral point of view* [that is, no moral reason] to refrain from it (if you do have such reason, then it will ordinarily be outweighed by the reason you have to perform, because by hypothesis it is better to perform). But now it is hard to see how it could be permissible, from the moral point of view, to

---

[18] I am not alone in thinking that b is a necessary condition for an act's being supererogatory—see, for instance, DREIER 2004, HORGAN & TIMMONS 2010, RAZ 1975, and ZIMMERMAN 1993.

refrain from doing something that you have an undefeated reason (from that very point of view) to do. Everything from the moral point of view speaks in favor of your...[performing the supererogatory act], and nothing at all speaks against it.... [In] what sense is it "all right," "permissible," "not wrong" to fail...[to do so]? There seems to be no sense at all. Supererogation, according to this way of seeing things, turns out to be impossible. (2004, p. 148)

More formally, the paradox of supererogation stems from the following sort of argument:

5.7 By definition, S's performing x is supererogatory only if there exists some available alternative, y, such that: (a) S is morally permitted both to perform x and to perform y, and (b) S has more moral reason to perform x than to perform y.

5.8 If S has more moral reason to perform x than to perform y ($y \neq x$), then S is not morally permitted to perform y. (MO).

5.9 So, whenever condition b is satisfied, condition a will not be satisfied. And, yet, for an act to be supererogatory, both conditions must be satisfied. Thus, supererogation is conceptually impossible. (From 5.7 and 5.8).[19]

To dissolve the apparent paradox, the supererogationist (i.e., the person who holds that supererogation is conceptually possible) must deny 5.8, explaining why the morally undefeated reason that favors performing the supererogatory act fails to generate a moral requirement.[20] As I noted above, if one wants to deny 5.8 (i.e., MO), then one must accept either or both of the following two theses: (1) non-moral reasons have moral justifying strength and so can justify acting contrary to what there is most moral reason to do (i.e., NMR+MJS) and/or (2) some moral reasons have absolutely no moral requiring strength (i.e., MR~MRS).

There are, then, two possible (and not mutually exclusive) explanations for why the morally undefeated reason that favors performing the supererogatory act fails to generate a moral requirement to so act. If, on the one hand, NMR+MJS is false, then the only possible explanation for why the morally undefeated reason that

[19] For a similar account of the paradox of supererogation, see HORGAN & TIMMONS 2010.

[20] Of course, there can be cases in which the reason that supports some particular supererogatory act-token is not morally undefeated, as where there is another supererogatory act-token that there is even more moral reason to perform. But to simplify the presentation of things, let us assume that S's mutually exclusive and jointly exhaustive options concerning what portion of her income to donate to charity are: (x) give more than 10%, (y) give exactly 10%, and (z) give less than 10%. Assume that x is supererogatory, that y is permissible but non-supererogatory, and that z is impermissible. Thus, we must explain why the morally undefeated reasons in favor of S's performing x do not generate a moral requirement for S to perform x.

favors performing the supererogatory act fails to generate a moral requirement is that it has insufficient moral requiring strength to generate a moral requirement.[21] Call this *the insufficient-moral-requiring-strength explanation*. If, on the other hand, NMR+MJS is true, then another possible explanation for why the morally undefeated reason that favors performing the supererogatory act fails to generate a moral requirement is that the non-moral reasons there are for performing some non-supererogatory alternative prevent this morally undefeated reason from generating a moral requirement. Call this *the non-moral-reason explanation*.[22]

Philosophers such as James Dreier and Michael J. Zimmerman overlook the non-moral-reason explanation, because they assume that NMR+MJS is false.[23] According to them, non-moral reasons are irrelevant to the determination of an act's deontic status. Hence, they assume that the insufficient-moral-requiring-strength explanation is the only possible explanation.

In an effort to spell out how exactly the insufficient-moral-requiring-strength explanation might go, Dreier speculates that there might be two moral points of view, one being the point of view of justice and the other being the point of view of beneficence. Dreier further speculates that reasons stemming from justice have considerable moral requiring strength, but that reasons stemming from beneficence

---

[21] One might rightly point out that even a morally undefeated reason of considerable moral requiring strength will fail to generate a moral requirement when it is opposed by some moral reason of equal or incommensurate moral requiring strength. But this cannot explain why the morally undefeated reason that favors performing the supererogatory act fails to generate a moral requirement in those instances in which it defeats whatever moral reasons there are for performing some permissible non-supererogatory alternative. Moreover, the morally undefeated reason that favors performing the supererogatory act must defeat (not merely successfully counter) these moral reasons for performing the permissible non-supererogatory alternative if it is to meet condition *b*. Thus, assuming that non-moral reasons cannot affect an act's deontic status, the explanation for why the morally undefeated reason for performing the supererogatory alternative fails to generate a moral requirement must be that it has insufficient moral requiring strength.

[22] Both are sufficient to explain the falsity of MO, and the two are not mutually exclusive. Indeed, I think that we probably need to accept both NMR+MJS and MR~MRS if we are going to account for all intuitive cases of supererogation. On the one hand, we need, as I explain below, to appeal to NMR+MJS and the non-moral-reason explanation in order to account for cases such as the original version of the case of Fiona, as described in §5.2. And, on the other hand, we need to appeal to MR~MRS and the insufficient-moral-requiring-strength explanation in order to account for certain other cases, such as the case of Olivia as described in HORGAN & TIMMONS 2010, p. 47. For other cases in which we might need to appeal to MR~MRS and the insufficient-moral-requiring-strength explanation, see FERRY 2009 and SUIKKANEN 2009a.

[23] That Dreier rejects NMR+MJS is clear from the fact that he thinks that an act's deontic status is a function of solely moral reasons—see the first sentence in the above quote as well as what he says on p. 149 of the same article. Zimmerman, by contrast, is less explicit, but he does say that if there being more moral reason to perform the supererogatory alternative is essential to supererogation, then any theory wishing to accommodate supererogation will have to declare that there are two sets of moral reasons, deontic and non-deontic reasons (or what I am calling moral reasons with, and moral reasons without, sufficient moral requiring strength)—see ZIMMERMAN 1993, pp. 375–376.

have no moral requiring strength. According to Dreier, supererogatory acts are more beneficent, but not more just, than their non-supererogatory alternatives.[24] So although agents have better moral reason to perform a supererogatory act than to perform any of its non-supererogatory alternatives, they are not morally required to do so, for the relevant reasons (i.e., reasons of beneficence) have no moral requiring strength. What an agent is morally required to do is a function of only those reasons that have moral requiring strength (i.e., reasons of justice), and there is simply no better reason of this sort to perfom the supererogatory alternative.

The problem with Dreier's suggestion and, more generally, with the suggestion that the insufficient-moral-requiring-strength explanation is the *only* possible explanation is that both suggestions rest on the mistaken assumption that the reasons that make a supererogatory alternative morally superior to its non-super-erogatory alternatives are always moral reasons of insufficient moral requiring strength. To the contrary, it seems that in many typical instances of supereroga-tion the moral reason that favors performing the supererogatory alternative over its non-supererogatory alternatives is a sufficient requiring reason.

To illustrate, recall the case from §5.2 where Fiona must choose between acting so as to secure a considerable benefit for herself by transferring the money from her savings account to her escrow account and acting so as to secure a more con-siderable benefit for various needy, distant strangers by instead donating those funds to Oxfam. In that case, her forfeiting the chance to buy a new home and instead donating her savings to Oxfam is supererogatory. Given that Dreier and Zimmerman insist on the insufficient-moral-requiring-strength explanation, they must deny that the moral reason that favors Fiona's donating the money to Oxfam as opposed to transferring it to her escrow company is a sufficient requiring reason. If it were, then her donating the money to Oxfam would, on their view, be obligatory, not supererogatory, because, on their view, whatever non-moral reason she has to purchase a new home would be powerless to prevent a sufficient requiring reason that she has to donate the money to Oxfam from giving rise to a moral requirement to so act. But, as we have already seen in §5.2, the moral reason that favors her donating the money to Oxfam *is* a sufficient requiring reason; absent countervailing reasons, Fiona is morally *required* to donate the money to Oxfam. And there are many other similar cases in which the moral reason that the agent has to perform some beneficent and supererogatory act is a sufficient requiring reason. So if we are to account for many typical instances of supereroga-tion, we are going to have to accept the non-moral-reason explanation, thereby accepting, contrary to Dreier and others, that non-moral reasons, and not just moral reasons, are relevant to the determination of an act's deontic status. That is, we must accept NMR+MJS.

[24] Similarly, Zimmerman (1993, note 11) offers an example where he supposes that reasons of fidelity have considerable moral requiring strength but that reasons of beneficence have little to no moral requiring strength.

§5.4 A meta-criterion of rightness and how it leads us to adopt dual-ranking act-consequentialism

What we have learned from the previous two sections is that if we want to accept many typical instances of supererogatory acts and agent-centered options (and I do), then we must accept that the deontic status of an action is a function of both moral and non-moral reasons. But what might this function be? Let us call a criterion that specifies this function by providing necessary and sufficient conditions for an act's being morally permissible in terms of both moral and non-moral reasons a *meta-criterion of rightness*. Below, I will defend the following *meta*-criterion of rightness (hence, the abbreviation META), and then argue that this meta-criterion forces the consequentialist to adopt some dual-ranking version of consequentialism (e.g., DRAC):

> **META** S's performing φ is morally permissible if and only if there is no available alternative, ψ, that S has both more *requiring reason* and more reason, all things considered, to perform, where a requiring reason is just a reason that has some moral requiring strength.[25]

I will defend this meta-criterion by arguing for the following five claims, from which META can be derived:

5.10 If S has *optimal requiring reason* to perform φ, then it is morally permissible for S to perform φ.[26]

5.11 If S has *optimal reason* (all things considered) to perform φ, then it is morally permissible for S to perform φ.[27]

5.12 If it is morally permissible for S to perform ψ and S has no less requiring reason to perform an alternative, φ, than to perform ψ, then, unless there is a further alternative, χ, that S has both more requiring reason and more reason, all things considered, to perform, it is morally permissible for S to perform φ.

---

[25] It may be that not all requiring reasons are sufficient requiring reasons, for some moral reasons may have some, but not enough, moral requiring strength to generate a moral requirement absent countervailing reasons.

[26] S has optimal requiring reason to perform φ if and only if there is no alternative, ψ, such that S has more requiring reason to ψ than to φ.

[27] S has optimal reason to φ if and only if there is no alternative, ψ, such that S has more reason to ψ than to φ. By contrast, S has most (or optimific) reason to perform φ if and only if there is no alternative, ψ, such that S has at least as much reason to ψ as to φ. So whereas S can have most reason to perform only one act, S can have optimal reason to perform multiple acts, as where more than one act is tied for first place in terms how much reason there is to perform them.

5.13   If it is morally permissible for S to perform ψ and S has no less reason, all things considered, to perform an alternative, φ, than to perform ψ, then, unless there is a further alternative, χ, that S has both more requiring reason and more reason, all things considered, to perform, it is morally permissible for S to perform φ.

5.14   It is not morally permissible for S to perform φ if there is an alternative, ψ, that S has both more requiring reason and more reason, all things considered, to perform.[28]

Claim 5.10 is hardly controversial, as it follows rather straightforwardly from the definition of a "requiring reason." By definition, only requiring reasons are capable of generating moral requirements. So even if an agent had more non-requiring reasons (where such reasons include non-moral reasons as well as moral reasons with no moral requiring strength) to do other than that which she has optimal requiring reason to do, these reasons could not generate a moral requirement to do otherwise. And if the agent is not morally required to do other than that which she has optimal requiring reason to do, then it follows that it is permissible for her to do what she has optimal requiring reason to do.

Claim 5.11 is, by contrast, considerably more controversial, but only if we are unwilling to concede that non-moral reasons can justify acting contrary to what one has most moral reason to do. Once we concede this (and I have argued that we must concede this—that is, I have argued for NMR+MJS), there is no more plausible claim about when non-moral reasons justify performing an act that would otherwise be impermissible. For if the non-moral reasons in favor of performing a given act do not make that act morally permissible when they successfully counter all other reasons (moral and non-moral), then when? Therefore, we should accept 5.11, acknowledging that it is always morally permissible to do what one has optimal reason to do, all things considered. In any case, 5.11 is entailed by moral rationalism, which I defended in chapter 2.

If only 5.10 and 5.11 were true, then agents would have rather limited options. At most, agents would have, in any given situation, only two options: (1) the option to do what they have optimal requiring reason to do and (2) the option to

---

[28] More formally and accurately, the argument has the following form: $\forall x \forall y \{(Py \,\&\, {\sim}Ryx) \rightarrow [{\sim}\exists z(Rzx \,\&\, Azx) \rightarrow Px]\}$, $\forall x \forall y \{(Py \,\&\, {\sim}Ayx) \rightarrow [{\sim}\exists z(Rzx \,\&\, Azx) \rightarrow Px]\}$, $\forall x[\exists z(Rzx \,\&\, Azx) \rightarrow {\sim}Px]$, $\exists x Px \therefore \forall x[Px \leftrightarrow {\sim}\exists z(Rzx \,\&\, Azx)]$, where "Px" stands for "it is morally permissible for S to perform x," "Ryx" stands for "S has more requiring reason to perform y than to perform x," and "Ayx" stands for "S has more reason, all things considered, to perform y than to perform x." Strictly speaking, then, 5.10 and 5.11 are superfluous, although they will help with the explication below. Also, although not explicitly stated above, I am assuming that there is some morally permissible alternative available to S (i.e., $\exists x Px$). I thank G. Shyam Nair, Errol Lord, and especially Peter Marchetto for helping me with this argument.

do what they have optimal reason to do, all things considered.[29] (In those situations in which agents have optimal requiring reason to perform precisely one act, an act which they also happen to have optimal reason to do, all things considered, they would have no options at all.) To illustrate, suppose that there is a burning building with twelve children trapped inside. Assume that a man named Alex knows this and has, consequently, called the fire department. Nevertheless, it is clear to Alex that they probably will not arrive soon enough and that all the children will very likely perish unless he acts now and rescues them himself. Unfortunately, Alex lacks the proper fire-fighting equipment, and so there is no way for him to rescue the children without suffering severe injuries in the process. Moreover, we will assume that the more trips that he makes into the burning building the more severe and life-threatening his injuries will be. He can rescue, at most, two children per trip, one under each arm. Given the great costs associated with each trip, we should assume that what he has most reason to do, all things considered, is to refrain from making any trips into the burning building. But we should also assume that what he has most requiring reason to do is to save all twelve children, making the necessary six trips into the burning building. So, if only 5.10 and 5.11 were true, Alex would be required to make either zero or six trips into the building, thereby rescuing either none or all of the children.[30]

But, surely, if it is permissible for him to refrain from entering the building at all (rescuing no children), then it is permissible for him to enter the burning building once and rescue two of the children. To account for this, we should accept 5.12 in addition to 5.10 and 5.11, for 5.12 says that if it is morally permissible for S to perform ψ and S has no less requiring reason to perform φ than to perform ψ, then we should presume that S is also permitted to perform φ. For instance, if it is permissible for Alex to save no children and he has no less (and, indeed, more) requiring reason to save two, then presumably it is also permissible for him to save the two. The only instances in which this presumption of permissibility will prove false are those in which S has both more requiring reason and more reason, all things considered, to do something else—say, χ—instead. In that case, S should choose to perform χ over φ.

To illustrate, let us suppose: (1) that α_1 is the act-set that consists in standing around outside while waiting for the fire fighters to arrive, rescuing none of the children, (2) that α_2 is the act-set that consists in entering the burning building once and rescuing two of the children, and (3) that α_3 is the act-set that consists

---

[29] Strictly speaking, there could be more than two options if there were more than one act that was tied for first place either in terms of what there is optimal requiring reason to do or in terms of what there is optimal reason to do, all things considered.

In PORTMORE 2003, I defended a view according to which an act is permissible if and only if it is either what the agent has optimal requiring reason to do or what the agent has optimal reason to do, all things considered. I now reject that view and accept META instead.

[30] This is what Ted Sider's self-other utilitarianism implies. See SIDER 1993.

in entering the burning building once and rescuing a completely unimportant trash bin.[31] Given 5.11, it is permissible for Alex to perform α_1; it is, after all, what he has optimal (i.e., most) reason to do, all things considered—or, at least, so we are assuming. Given 5.12, it is also permissible for Alex to perform α_2, as he has no less (and, indeed, more) requiring reason to perform α_2 than to perform the permissible α_1, and there is no alternative that he has both more requiring reason and more reason, all things considered, to perform. He has more reason, all things considered, to perform α_2 than to perform any act that involves his taking more trips into the burning building, and he has more requiring reason to perform α_2 than to perform any act that involves his taking fewer trips into the burning building. Thus, according to 5.12, it also permissible for Alex to perform α_2. But it is not permissible for Alex to perform α_3, for α_2 is an alternative that Alex has both more requiring reason and more reason, all things considered, to perform. It is clear that there is more requiring reason to perform α_2 than to perform α_3, for it is clear that there is more requiring reason to save two children than there is to save a trash bin. And it is clear that Alex has more reason, all things considered, to perform α_2 than to perform α_3, because, even if α_2 and α_3 are on a par in terms of non-moral reasons, it is clear that there is more moral reason and thus more reason, all things considered, to perform α_2. So although there is a presumption in favor of its being permissible to do φ if there is no less requiring reason to do φ than to do some other permissible alternative, ψ, this presumption does not hold when there is yet another alternative, χ, that the agent has both more requiring reason and more reason, all things considered, to perform than to perform φ. And this is just what 5.12 says.

We should also, I believe, accept 5.13. If it is morally permissible for S to perform ψ and S has no less reason, all things considered, to perform φ, then presumably it is also permissible for S to perform φ. To illustrate, consider again the above case, and this time let us add to the above suppositions the following three: (4) that α_4 is the act-set that consists in making six trips into the burning building, rescuing all twelve children, (5) that α_5 is the act-set that consists in making five trips into the burning building, rescuing ten of the children, and (6) that α_6 is the act-set that consists in making five trips into the burning building, rescuing ten of the children while taking some extra time on the fifth trip to rummage through the garbage, during which time the children are inhaling more smoke, increasing their risk of developing respiratory problems. Given 5.10, it is permissible for Alex to perform α_4; it is, after all, what he has optimal (indeed, optimific) requiring reason to do. Given 5.13, it is also permissible for Alex to perform α_5, as he has no less (and, indeed, more) reason, all things considered, to perform α_5 than to perform α_4 (a permissible alternative), and there is no alternative that he has both more requiring reason and more reason, all things considered, to perform. He has

---

[31] This example is inspired by one of Kagan's—see KAGAN 1989, pp. 16 and 240.

more reason, all things considered, to perform α_5 than to perform any alternative act-set that involves his taking more trips into the burning building and he has more requiring reason to perform α_4 than to perform any alternative act-set that involves his taking fewer trips into the burning building. Thus, according to 5.13, it is also permissible for Alex to perform α_5. But it is not permissible for Alex to perform α_6, for α_5 is an alternative that Alex has both more requiring reason and more reason, all things considered, to perform. There is more requiring reason to perform α_5 than to perform α_6, because there is a requiring reason for Alex to minimize the children's chances of developing respiratory problems.[32] And it is clear that Alex has more reason, all things considered, to perform α_5 than to perform α_6, because not only is there more moral reason to perform α_5, but also more nonmoral reason to perform α_5—after all, Alex has a non-moral reason to avoid the unpleasantness of rummaging through the garbage as well as a non-moral reason to avoid inhaling more smoke. So although there is a presumption in favor of its being permissible to do φ if there is no less reason, all things considered, to do φ than to do some other permissible alternative, ψ, this presumption does not hold when there is yet another alternative, χ, that the agent has both more requiring reason and more reason, all things considered, to perform than to perform φ. And this is just what 5.13 says.

Lastly, we should accept 5.14, which says that it is not morally permissible for S to perform φ if there is an available alternative, ψ, that S has both more requiring reason and more reason, all things considered, to perform. First, if there is more requiring reason for S to perform ψ, then some reason would have to justify S's performing φ instead. But, by hypothesis, there is more reason, all things considered, for S to perform ψ than for S to perform φ. So unless we think that the mere fact that S has *some* reason to perform φ is enough to justify doing so even though there is both more requiring reason and more reason, all things considered, to perform ψ, we should accept 5.14.

Given 5.10–5.14, we should accept META as our meta-criterion of rightness, for this is what is entailed by 5.10–5.14.[33] Of course, coming up with a meta-criterion of rightness is only the first step along the path toward developing a substantive moral theory. The next step would be to come up with both a substantive account of when there is more requiring reason to perform one act than to perform another and a substantive account of when there is more reason, all things considered, to perform one act than to perform another. Only then would the meta-criterion yield substantive deontic verdicts. One way of doing this, the consequentialist's way, is to hold that an agent's reasons for performing various alternative actions are a function of her reasons for desiring their associated out-

[32] What if there were just as much requiring reason to perform α_6 as there is to perform α_5? In that case, α_6 would be stupid and irrational, but not immoral.

[33] More accurately, I should say that META is what is entailed by 5.12–5.14 plus the assumption that there is some morally permissible alternative available to S—see note 28.

comes. When we combine such a teleological conception of practical reasons with the above meta-criterion, we get DRAC's *criterion of rightness*:

> **DRAC$_{cr}$** S's performing x is morally permissible if and only if there is no available act alternative that would produce an outcome that S has both more moral reason and more reason, all things considered, to want to obtain than to want x's outcome to obtain.[34]

So DRAC's dual-ranking structure is not unmotivated. Indeed, the act-consequentialist has no choice but to adopt DRAC if she is to accommodate NMR+MJS. It might be objected, though, that my arguments for NMR+MJS presuppose that there are agent-centered options of the sort that commonsense morality takes there to be, the sort of which 5.1–5.5 are true. But I do not see why the consequentialist cannot help herself to this given that her main nonconsequentialist rivals all presuppose that there are such agent-centered options and so are committed to the truth of 5.1–5.5. So these non-consequentialist rivals cannot object that 5.1–5.5 are not true. And if they are true, then the consequentialist has a principled reason for making the move to a dual-ranking structure.

Of course, even DRAC is not all that substantive. There is still very little flesh on its bones. To add a bit more flesh, we would have to give both a substantive account of when there is more moral reason to desire one outcome than to desire another and a substantive account of when there is more reason, all things considered, to desire one outcome than to desire another. One way to do this is to adopt what I have called *Schefflerian utilitarianism* (SU) and its *criterion of rightness*:

> **SU$_{cr}$** S's performing x is morally permissible if and only if there is no available act alternative that would produce both more utility for others (i.e., for those other than S) and more egoistically adjusted utility than x would, where egoistically adjusted utility includes everyone's utility but adjusts the overall total by giving S's utility, say, ten times the weight of anyone else's.[35]

---

[34] If there are both requiring and non-requiring moral reasons for desiring an outcome, and if what an agent has requiring reason to do is a function of what she has requiring reason to want as opposed to what she has moral reason (in general) to want, then I will need to replace "moral reason" with "requiring reason" in my formulation of DRAC here and elsewhere. In §§7.1.5, I suggest that we should indeed make this replacement.

[35] Again, Schefflerian utilitarianism (SU) is the view according to which all the following hold: (1) dual-ranking act-consequentialism is true; (2) S has more moral reason to want o_i to obtain than to want o_j ($j \neq i$) to obtain if and only if o_i contains more utility for others (i.e., for those other than S) than o_j does; and (3) S has more reason, all things considered, to want o_i to obtain than to want o_j to obtain if and only if o_i contains more egoistically adjusted utility than o_j does, where egoistically adjusted utility includes everyone's utility but adjusts the overall total by giving S's utility, say, ten times the weight of anyone else's.

On SU, agents are never required to promote their own well-being, not even when they can do so at no cost to others. But, on SU, agents are sometimes required to promote the well-being of others, as when they can do so at no cost to themselves. So whereas the reason that agents have to promote the well-being of others has considerable moral requiring strength, the reason that agents have to promote their own well-being has absolutely no moral requiring strength. Nevertheless, the moral justifying strength of the reason that agents have to promote their own well-being is ten times that of the reason they have to promote, to the same extent, the well-being of others.[36] It is the strong justificatory force of this reason that accounts for SU's ability to accommodate a wide range of agent-favoring options. And it is the complete lack of requiring force associated with the reason that agents have to promote their own well-being that accounts for SU's ability to accommodate a wide range of agent-sacrificing options.

Despite SU's ability to accommodate such a wide range of options, a number of philosophers have objected to SU (or, at least, to a theory that is relevantly similar to it). In the next three sections, I will address these objections and show why they all fail. I do this, not because I ultimately endorse SU, but because these objections to SU apply equally to the theory that I do endorse—namely, commonsense consequentialism. So unless I can show that these objections against SU fail, my theory will be in trouble as well. Nevertheless, I will keep the focus on SU for now, because it is considerably less complicated than my own theory, and, thus, doing so will greatly simplify my discussion of the objections.

§5.5 Norcross's objection

On SU, there is a *pro tanto* duty of beneficence, for there is always more requiring reason to promote the utility of others than to refrain from doing so. Nevertheless, agents are not always required to promote the utility of others, as sometimes the self-sacrifice involved is too great. To illustrate, suppose that S must choose whether or not to perform x, where x is some altruistic act. And let us suppose that the difference in overall utility for others if S performs x as opposed to $\sim x$ is n. On SU, S is permitted to refrain from performing x so long as the amount of utility that S would sacrifice in performing x is greater than or equal to one-tenth of n. If, however, the amount of utility that S would sacrifice in performing x is less than one-tenth of n, S would be required to perform x. Interestingly, then, although there can, on SU, be more or less moral reason to perform an act, an act cannot be more or less wrong. On SU, right and wrong is an all-or-nothing affair.

Alastair Norcross (2006a, 2006b) has argued that consequentialists should reject such a theory. He cites the following two reasons. First, a theory that held

---

[36] Remember that I picked the number ten only for the purposes of illustration. The actual multiplier might be different.

both that there was a duty of beneficence (e.g., a duty to give some percentage of one's income to charity) and that rightness and wrongness was an all-or-nothing affair "would have to say that there was a *threshold*, e.g., at 10 percent, such that if one chose to give 9 percent one would be wrong, whereas if one chose to give 10 percent one would be right. If this distinction is to be interesting, it must say that there is a *big* difference between right and wrong, between giving 9 percent and giving 10 percent, and a small difference between pairs of right actions [e.g., between giving 10 versus 11 percent], or pairs of wrong actions [e.g., between giving 8 versus 9 percent]" (NORCROSS 2006b, 41). And Norcross argues that the consequentialist should deny that the difference between giving 8 percent and giving 9 percent is any less significant than the difference between giving 9 percent and giving 10 percent. After all, in each case, the difference in terms of how much good would be done is exactly the same—that is, assuming a fixed income. Thus, if the consequentialist had to choose between convincing only one of two people to give an extra 1 percent, where one is currently giving 9 percent and the other is currently giving 8 percent, she should be indifferent, for, either way, the result will be that the same amount of additional money goes to charity.[37]

Second, Norcross claims that another "related reason to reject an all-or-nothing line between right and wrong is that the choice of any point on the scale of possible options as a threshold for rightness will be *arbitrary*" (NORCROSS 2006b, p. 41). Thus, Norcross would claim not only that SU's current multiplier of ten is arbitrary (which, of course, it is), but also that any alternative multiplier that we might replace it with would be equally arbitrary (which I deny). And since we should reject arbitrary moral distinctions, we should, Norcross would argue, reject SU no matter what multiplier it employs.

Neither of these are good reasons for rejecting SU.[38] To see why, consider that "right" and "wrong" (i.e., "permissible" and "impermissible") might be like "worth it" and "not worth it." For instance, it might be worth it to trade one's services— let us say an hour of babysitting—for $10, but not worth it to trade those services for $9. It is not that there is a bigger difference between $9 and $10 than there is between $8 and $9. But a $1 increase in the offered payment from $9 to $10 can make all the difference as to whether or not it is worth it to trade one's services for the offered payment. This is true even if a $1 increase in the offered payment from $8 to $9 makes no difference as to whether or not it is worth it to trade one's services for the offered payment. Norcross seems to assume that if the distinction between, say, what is worth it and what is not worth it is to be an interesting one,

---

[37] As Rob Lawlor (2009b, p. 104) points out, Norcross is conflating two separate issues here: (1) the issue of whether convincing someone to give an extra 1 percent would make a difference as to whether that someone acts permissibly and (2) the issue of whether we ought to care about the permissibility of someone's actions over and above what good those actions would do.

[38] For a more detailed and thorough discussion of the flaws in Norcross's arguments, see LAWLOR 2009a and LAWLOR 2009b.

the difference between $9 and $10 would have to be greater than the difference between $8 and $9. But although there is no greater difference between these two pairs of possible payments, the difference between the first pair, but not the second, can make all the difference concerning whether or not it is worth it to trade one's services for the offered payment.

Furthermore, there is nothing arbitrary about the $10 threshold; the threshold is set at the point at which it becomes worth it to trade one's services for the offered payment. Likewise, there need not be anything arbitrary about the 10 percent threshold (or whatever we should replace it with); the threshold is set at the point at which it would become contrary to reason to give any more to charity. In both cases, then, the threshold lies where an increase in one of the two competing factors tips the balance from not worth it to worth it or from permissible to impermissible. Whether it is worth it to trade an hour of babysitting for a certain amount of money depends on whether one has at least as much reason to want to receive that amount of money as to want to spend that hour doing something else. Likewise, whether it is permissible to refrain from performing some self-sacrificing and beneficent act depends, according to SU, on whether one has at least as much reason, all things considered, to want to avoid such a self-sacrifice as to want to provide those others with that degree of benefit.[39] In both cases, there comes a point when the reasons for acting one way justify acting that way as opposed to the other way. There is nothing at all arbitrary about such a point.[40] So Norcross is mistaken in thinking that the consequentialist cannot accept some interesting and non-arbitrary threshold for rightness—that threshold lies at the point at which any further self-sacrifice for the sake of others would be supererogatory as opposed to obligatory.

§5.6 Splawn's objection

Consider the case depicted in table 5.1, where an agent named Bonnie has the following three mutually exclusive and jointly exhaustive options: a_1, a_2, and A_3, where A_3 is an act-type—namely, that of performing some act other than either a_1 or a_2.

---

[39] I am assuming both that moral reasons (such as the moral reason one has to benefit others) and non-moral reasons (such as the non-moral reason one has to avoid self-sacrifice) are commensurable and that non-moral reasons sometimes outweigh moral reasons such that what one has most reason to do, all things considered, is contrary to what one has most moral reason to do. Furthermore, I am assuming that when there is more reason, all things considered, to act contrary to what one has most moral reason to do, it is permissible to do so. That is, I am assuming both NMR+MJS and META, both of which I have argued for above. For more on the commensurability of moral and non-moral reasons, see McLEOD 2001 and CHANG 2004a.

[40] Rob Lawlor makes the same point—see LAWLOR 2009b, p. 106. I originally made this point and the one above in my lectures on scalar consequentialism, which were posted on 4/4/2008 at http://www.public.asu.edu/~dportmor/Satisficing%20Consequentialism.pdf.

Table 5.1 $U_s(x)$ = the utility that accrues to S if S performs x. $U_{-s}(x)$ = the utility that accrues to others if S performs x. $U(x)$ = the overall utility that is produced if S performs x. $U_{+s}(x)$ = $U_{-s}(x)$ + $[10 \times U_s(x)]$.

x	$U_s(x)$	$U_{-s}(x)$	$U(x)$	$U_{+s}(x)$	deontic status
a_1	10	**−50**	−40	**50**	merely permissible
a_2	−10	**100**	90	**0**	supererogatory
A_3	−5	**49**	44	**−1**	impermissible

On SU, A_3 is impermissible, because a_2 is an alternative that would produce both (1) more utility for others than A_3 would and (2) more egoistically adjusted utility than A_3 would—that is, both (1) $U_{-s}(a_2) > U_{-s}(A_3)$ and (2) $U_{+s}(a_2) > U_{+s}(A_3)$. Yet A_3 is considerably better for others than a_1 is ($U_{-s}(A_3) > U_{-s}(a_1)$), and a_1 is a permissible alternative. So why, Clay Splawn (2001) wonders, is it permissible for S (i.e., Bonnie) to perform a_1 but not A_3? Sure, it is more costly for S to perform A_3 than it is for S to perform a_1, but Splawn claims that we should accept the following plausible-sounding principle: "it is always permissible for an agent to make a self-sacrifice so long as that sacrifice does not bring about worse consequences for others" (2001, p. 330). Splawn claims that any theory that fails to accommodate this plausible-sounding principle fails to accommodate the self-other asymmetry.[41] He says, "Isn't it *exactly* the suggestion of the self-other asymmetry that sacrificing one's own good for the benefit of others is permissible? And isn't that *exactly* what [A_3] is: a considerable self-sacrifice on the part of S in order to bring about some good for others?" (2001, p. 330). And, yet, I claimed in chapter 4 that SU does accommodate the self-other asymmetry. In response, I will argue that Splawn's plausible-sounding principle is, in fact, *implausible* and that, contrary to what Splawn claims, a theory does not need to accommodate this implausible principle in order to accommodate the self-other asymmetry.

To see why the principle is implausible, we will need to get clear on what precisely it says, specifically, what we are supposed to be comparing when we judge that a self-sacrificing act does or does not "bring about worse consequences for others." One suggestion might be that we are comparing what the total well-being for others would be were the agent to interfere with ongoing causal processes by performing the self-sacrificing act with what it would be were the agent to refrain from interfering with ongoing causal processes and omit the self-sacrificing act. But I do not think that this is what Splawn has in mind, and, in any case, the principle is clearly implausible on such an interpretation. Consider again the burning

---

[41] The objection was originally raised against Ted Sider's self-other utilitarianism, but it applies equally to SU. See SIDER 1993.

building case from above and suppose that Alex takes only one trip into the burning building, rescuing the trash bin instead of the two children. Did he act wrongly? Well, had he not performed this self-sacrificing act, the consequences would not have been worse for others (on this interpretation), for had he done nothing and just waited for the fire fighters to arrive, the two children would have still died. So, on this interpretation of the principle, taking one trip into the burning building and rescuing the trash bin instead of the two children is permissible, which is just absurd.

A more plausible suggestion, therefore, might be that we are, for each available alternative, to compare what the total well-being for others would be were the agent to perform that alternative with what it would be were the agent to perform the self-sacrificing act in question, and so long as there is at least one alternative where others would be no worse off, then the self-sacrificing act is deemed permissible. On this interpretation of the principle, it is permissible for Bonnie to perform A_3 (as Splawn thinks it should be), for there is at least one alternative where others would be no worse off: namely, a_1. Indeed, not only would others be no worse off, they would in fact be better off: $U_{-s}(A_3) > U_{-s}(a_1)$. The problem, though, with this interpretation is that it ignores the fact that a_2 is a more attractive alternative. So although it would be permissible for Bonnie to perform A_3 were a_1 the only available alternative, it is arguably impermissible for Bonnie to perform A_3 given that a_2 is an available alternative. It is true that Bonnie does better by others by performing A_3 instead of a_1, but she can do even better by others by performing a_2. And what justification does she have for not doing even better by others by performing a_2? Given that Bonnie has more reason, all things considered, to perform a_2 than to perform A_3, there would seem to be no good reason why Bonnie should not perform a_2 instead of A_3. Thus, Bonnie has no excuse for not doing more for the sake of others by performing a_2 instead of A_3. Sure, a_2 is more costly, but, by hypothesis, we are supposing that the reason that Bonnie has to avoid this extra cost is insufficient to defeat the reason Bonnie has to do a_2—namely, that a_2 will do more good for others. So although it is often permissible to make a self-sacrifice so as to benefit others, it is not permissible to do so when one can do something else that will benefit others even more and without having to make any greater of a self-sacrifice than one has decisive reason to make.

So when Splawn asks, "What possible justification could be given for saying that [A_3] is morally wrong?" (2001, p. 330), the answer is that there is both more requiring reason and more reason, all things considered, to perform a_2 instead. In choosing A_3 over a_2, Bonnie would be unreasonably selfish. Bonnie would be benefiting herself by five utiles at a cost of fifty-one utiles for others. So even if we grant, as SU does, that Bonnie has ten times more reason to benefit herself than to benefit others, we must still concede that Bonnie has more reason to benefit others by fifty-one utiles than she has to benefit herself by five utiles. And, thus, we should concede that A_3 is wrong.

What's more, we find that, on this interpretation, Splawn's plausible-sounding principle falls victim to the same counterexample that it did on the first interpretation. On this second interpretation, it is also permissible to enter the burning building and save the trash bin instead of the two children, for waiting for the fire department is an available option that is no worse for others than entering the burning building and rescuing the trash bin is. Indeed, the only way to interpret Splawn's principle so that it does not get this implausible result is to hold that we are, for each available alternative, to compare what the total well-being for others would be were the agent to perform that alternative with what it would be were the agent to perform the self-sacrificing act, and then to hold that if there is even one alternative where others would be worse off, then the self-sacrificing act is *impermissible*. But, on this interpretation, A_3 would, contrary to what Splawn says, be impermissible, for others are worse off on A_3 than on a_2. Since Splawn insists that the principle implies that A_3 is permissible, this cannot be how Splawn wants us to interpret the principle. So we must accept one of the first two interpretations. But, in that case, the principle has counterintuitive implications, implying that it is permissible to enter the burning building once and save the trash bin instead of the two children. We should not, then, think that SU is objectionable in that it violates Splawn's principle. Nor should we conclude that SU fails to incorporate the self-other asymmetry in failing to accommodate Splawn's principle.

§5.7 Violations of the transitivity and independence axioms

SU holds that an act is morally permissible if and only if its outcome is not outranked by that of any available act alternative. And it holds that one outcome outranks another if and only if it contains both more utility for others and more egoistically adjusted utility than the other does. Interestingly, then, SU's is-not-outranked-by relation (let us call it "the $\succeq$ relation") violates the transitivity axiom, according to which, if $A \succeq B$ and $B \succeq C$, then $A \succeq C$.[42] To illustrate, consider, again, the scenario depicted in table 5.1. None of the outcomes in O_3 (i.e., the set of outcomes corresponding to the set of acts in A_3) are outranked by o_1 (i.e., a_1's outcome) and o_1 is not outranked by o_2 (i.e., a_2's outcome), but each of the outcomes in O_3 is outranked by o_2. So SU's is-not-outranked-by relation (i.e., the $\succeq$ relation) is intransitive. But this is not problematic. We should not expect the $\succeq$ relation to be a transitive relation. If the $\succeq$ relation were equivalent to the at-least-as-good-as relation, then we would expect the $\succeq$ relation to be transitive. But to say that one outcome is not outranked by another on SU's ranking principle is not

---

[42] And the same holds, more generally, for DRAC's is-not-outranked-by relation, but I will focus on SU for the purposes of illustration.

to say that the one is at least as good as the other, for SU's ranking principle is not a ranking of outcomes in terms of their goodness. So I do not see why we should expect the $\succeq$ relation to be transitive.

The transitivity axiom is not the only axiom of expected utility theory that is violated by SU. On SU, the does-not-have-a-higher-deontic-status-than relation (let us call it "the $\subseteq$ relation") violates the independence axiom: if, for any set of available alternatives in which A and B are the only alternatives, A $\subseteq$ B, then, for any set of available alternatives in which A and B both appear, A $\subseteq$ B. To illustrate, suppose that a_1 and A_3 were the only available alternatives. In that case, a_1 would not have a higher deontic status than any of the acts in A_3, for, where a_1 and A_3 are the only available alternatives, both are, on SU, permissible. But where a_2 is also an available alternative, a_1 does have a higher deontic status than the acts in A_3. Where a_2 is an available alternative, SU entails both that a_1 is permissible and that A_3 is impermissible. And let me just stipulate that, as I will use the phrase "higher deontic status," a permissible act always has a higher deontic status than an impermissible one. Thus the $\subseteq$ relation violates the independence axiom.

The thought behind the independence axiom is that adding more alternatives should not affect how two alternatives rank relative to each other in terms of their deontic status; the relative ranking between two alternatives is *independent* of what other available alternatives there are. But whereas we should perhaps expect preferences and utility to obey the independence axiom, we should not expect SU (or any other version of DRAC) to do so. To see why, we need only turn again to my response to Splawn's objection. In that response, I gave good reasons to think that how two alternatives rank relative to one another should depend on what other alternatives are available. Performing any of the acts in A_3 would not be unreasonably selfish if a_1 were the only available alternative. But performing one of the acts in A_3 would be unreasonably selfish if a_2 were an available alternative. So we should not think that the relative ranking between two alternatives is independent of what other available alternatives there are.[43]

***

We continue to look for some version of consequentialism that comports with our considered moral convictions. Given the arguments from chapters 2 and 3, we are led to accept some version of consequentialism—that is, some version of the view that an act's deontic status is determined by the agent's reasons for and against preferring its outcome to those of the available alternatives, such that, if S is morally required to perform x, then, of all the outcomes that S could bring about, S has

---

[43] I thank Ted Sider for pointing out the need to address violations of the transitivity and independence axioms.

most (indeed, decisive) reason to desire that x's outcome obtains. And we are looking for some non-traditional version of consequentialism, for, as we saw in chapter 1, traditional versions of consequentialism fail to comport with our considered moral convictions and, consequently, run afoul of moral rationalism, which is something I argued for in chapter 2. Now, as we saw in the previous chapter, the key to accommodating certain considered moral convictions (such as the conviction that there are agent-centered options and supererogatory acts) on a consequentialist theory is to adopt a consequentialist theory with a dual-ranking structure, a theory such as DRAC. But there are several objections to doing so. In this chapter, I have tried to address most of them.

The main objection has been that DRAC's dual-ranking structure seems unmotivated. In response to this objection, I have argued that an act is morally permissible if and only if there is no available alternative that the agent has both more requiring reason and more reason, all things considered, to perform. And I have argued that, given this, the consequentialist must adopt DRAC's dual-ranking structure. I have also defended DRAC against four other objections: Norcross's objection, Splawn's objection, and two objections concerning violations of the axioms of expected utility theory. There remains, however, at least one other important objection. Shelly Kagan has argued that if one accounts for agent-centered options, as the proponent of DRAC does, by asserting that the reason that agents are not always morally obligated to promote the overall good is that they sometimes have more reason, all things considered, to promote their own good, then what you get is a rational requirement for them to promote their own good, when what we wanted was both a moral, and a rational, option for them to pursue either their own interests or the greater good. In the next chapter, I will rebut this objection.

6

Imperfect Reasons and Rational Options

In the previous chapter, I argued that in order to account for many typical agent-centered options we must hold that the fact that an act would promote the agent's self-interest is a non-moral reason and that, when this non-moral reason successfully counters the moral (requiring) reason that she has to act altruistically, it morally justifies her acting self-interestedly as opposed to altruistically. But it does so without generating a moral requirement to act self-interestedly, for such non-moral reasons are, by definition, without any moral requiring strength. The result, then, is a moral option to act either altruistically or self-interestedly.

In this chapter, I explain and rebut an important objection to this account of agent-centered options.[1] In the process, I develop a new theory of objective rationality, one that accounts for how agents rationally ought to act when their future actions are not under their present deliberative control.[2] This new theory will serve not only to enable me to rebut this important objection, but also to introduce the general structural features of commonsense consequentialism, the moral theory that I will be arguing for in the next and final chapter.

§6.1 Kagan's objection: Are we sacrificing rational options to get moral options?

In response to those who have given the sort of account of agent-centered options that I argued for in the last chapter (e.g., Michael Slote), Shelly Kagan has raised the following important objection:

---

[1] Some of the material in this chapter is drawn from PORTMORE FORTHCOMINGb. However, it is important to note that the view that I endorsed in PORTMORE FORTHCOMINGb—namely, the Future-Course-of-Action Theory (or "FCAT")—is not the one that I presently endorse. In its place, I have come to accept *securitism*, a view that I describe below.

[2] S's φ-ing at some later time is under S's present deliberative control if and only if whether S φs at that later time depends on the immediate outcome of S's present deliberations—that is, depends on which attitudes (e.g., intentions) she forms directly in response to her present deliberations.

Slote is arguing, in effect, that whenever the agent has a moral option, then from the rational point of view the reasons the agent has for favoring her own interests outweigh the reasons that support promoting the greater good [that is, support acting altruistically]. . . . But if this is so, then what if anything prevents these reasons from grounding a rational *requirement* to favor her interests in each such case? (1991, p. 927)[3]

If the answer is that nothing would, then this would seem to be an unacceptable result, for it would mean that in such cases "it would be rationally forbidden— irrational—to choose to do the morally preferable act" (KAGAN 1991, pp. 927– 928). This would seem unacceptable for at least two reasons. First, it seems unacceptable to suppose that, whenever there is a moral option, performing the morally preferable option is necessarily rationally forbidden.[4] Second, it seems unacceptable to suppose that, whenever there is a moral option, there is a rational requirement to perform the self-interested option, for what we want to account for is the intuition that there is *both* a moral, *and a rational*, option to act either altruistically or self-interestedly.

Nevertheless, Kagan's objection to Slote is, as stated, a bit too quick, for, contrary to what Kagan says, Slote need not claim that, from the rational point of view, the non-moral reason the agent has to act self-interestedly *outweighs* the moral reason the agent has to act altruistically. Slote could instead claim that these two opposing reasons exactly balance out. If so, Slote could plausibly claim that the fact that there is just as much overall reason to act self-interestedly as to act altruistically accounts for the lack of a moral requirement to act altruistically. Moreover, since there is just as much reason, all things considered, to perform the one as the other, there will be a rational option to do either.

As convenient as this might be, it is implausible to suppose that we could account for a rational option whenever there is a moral option by claiming that the relevant reasons always exactly balance out. As Kagan rightly points out, such ties would be too rare to account for the wide range of options we take there to be. To illustrate, suppose that I could save some stranger from having to endure great physical pain by sacrificing $500.[5] If Slote were to suppose that the reasons for and against sacrificing the $500 exactly balance out and that this is what accounts for both the moral and rational option to do either, then, if the tie were broken, there would cease to be an option anymore. Suppose, for instance, that the

---

[3] Kagan is responding to Slote 1991.

[4] Kagan does not deny that performing the morally preferable (and supererogatory) option is sometimes rationally forbidden—see KAGAN 1991, p. 928. What he finds implausible is the idea that all, or even most, supererogatory acts are rationally forbidden.

The account of supererogation that I gave in PORTMORE 2003 did have the implication that all supererogatory acts are rationally forbidden, and both Michael Byron and Betsy Postow rightly objected to it for this reason. See BYRON 2005 and POSTOW 2005, pp. 245–253.

[5] I borrow this example from KAGAN 1989, pp. 374–375.

situation were to change such that there was now slightly more reason for or against making the sacrifice, as where either the amount of pain that the stranger faces or the amount of money that I would need to pay to prevent it has increased slightly. In that case, it seems that we must admit that there is now most reason, all things considered, to perform one of the two alternatives. Yet we think that making such an altruistic self-sacrifice remains rationally optional even after the strength and/or number of the reasons for or against making the self-sacrifice increases slightly. And if there is an option both before and after the strength and/or number of the reasons that support just one of the two alternatives increases, we cannot account for such options by supposing that the relevant reasons exactly balance out.

So Kagan's objection amounts to the following. If the reasons in favor of each alternative are not exactly balanced out, then it seems that one or the other alternative will be the one that there is most reason, all things considered, to perform, and, if so, that alternative will be rationally required even if it is not morally required. And the reasons in favor of each alternative only rarely exactly balance out. Therefore, this strategy for defending agent-centered options involves trading, in most instances, a moral requirement for a rational requirement, when what we were looking for was both a moral, and a rational, option to act either altruistically or self-interestedly.

It is important to realize, though, that the problem of accounting for rational options given the implausibility of supposing that the relevant reasons always exactly balance out is a difficult philosophical problem that befalls anyone interested in accounting for what Joseph Raz calls:

> *The Basic Belief:* This is the belief that, in most typical choice situations, the relevant reasons do not require performing one particular alternative, but instead permit performing any of numerous alternatives.[6]

It seems, for instance, that I could now, in accordance with reason, do any of the following: watch TV, read a novel, practice the piano, volunteer for Oxfam, work on this book, play with my daughter, or prepare for my next lecture. But how are we to account for this? It seems that there could be such rational options only if there were exactly equal reason to perform each of the optional alternatives, and yet it is difficult to believe that such is the case.[7] For instance, it is difficult to believe that I

---

[6] See RAZ , p. 100.

Raz calls it the *basic* belief, because it seems to be sufficiently entrenched in our commonsense thinking that we should give it "credence unless it can be shown to be incoherent or inconsistent with some of our rightly entrenched views" (1999, p. 100). As he sees it, then, the basic belief is one of our starting points, and so our task is to explain why it is true rather than to defend its truth.

[7] Here and throughout the book, my focus is on objective rationality, not subjective rationality. An act is objectively rational if and only if the agent has sufficient reason to perform it—that is, if and only if the agent is objectively rationally permitted to perform it (see §1.4). The reader should assume

have just as much reason to watch TV as to either volunteer for Oxfam or work on this book. After all, volunteering for Oxfam seems vastly superior to watching TV in terms of the amount of impersonal good that it would do, and working on this book seems vastly superior to watching TV in terms of the amount of good it would do me—assume that I am not at this moment too tired to work productively on the book.[8] Moreover, the fact that, in many of these choice situations, the relevant alternatives remain rationally optional even after there has been an increase in the number and/or strength of the reasons that favor just one of the alternatives shows that their optional status could not have been due, in the first place, to a perfect balance of reasons (GERT 2008, p. 14). For instance, it seems that it would still be rationally permissible for me to continue to work on this book even if there were a slight increase in the strength and/or number of reasons that favor just one of the other options, as where, say, Oxfam institutes a new policy of giving each volunteer a delicious cookie. So the puzzle is to explain how, in most choice situations, there could be so many rationally optional alternatives if, as seems to be the case, there is not exactly equal reason to perform each one of them.

It seems, then, that the problem of accounting for rational options is not any more serious for the defender of agent-centered options than it is for anyone else who accepts the basic belief. And if the problem is not specific to the above account of agent-centered options, then it is no objection to this account that it encounters the same problem that anyone wishing to account for rational options faces. Moreover, since this problem is quite general, those who endorse this account of agent-centered options, such as myself, can appeal to the same potential solutions that others appeal to in accounting for the basic belief, and there are, as we will see presently, quite a few of them.

There are at least four possible solutions to the problem of accounting for the basic belief. First, we could adopt a satisficing conception of rationality, where it is rationally permissible to perform any act that is supported by sufficiently weighty reasons. Given this conception of rationality, we could account for the basic belief by claiming that, in most choice situations, there are sufficiently weighty reasons to perform all of the seemingly rationally optional alternatives. Moreover, the defender of agent-centered options could hold that although the non-moral reason that the agent has to act self-interestedly outweighs the moral reason that she has to act altruistically (thereby preventing it from generating a moral requirement), there is still a rational option to do both, for both are supported by sufficiently weighty reasons.

---

that, unless otherwise qualified, I am talking about objective rationality whenever I use the word "rational" or any of its variants.

[8] Indeed, it seems that we *know* that my watching TV is not the alternative that I have most reason to perform. Thus, our belief that the relevant reasons permit my watching TV cannot be explained in terms of any kind of epistemic uncertainty as to whether or not it is the alternative that I have most reason to perform.

Second, we could claim that reasons for action have not only two separable dimensions of moral strength but also two separable dimensions of rational strength: *rational requiring strength* and *rational justifying strength*. Roughly speaking, a reason has rational justifying strength to the extent that it can make it rationally permissible to perform acts that it would otherwise be irrational to perform, and a reason has rational requiring strength to the extent that it can make it irrational to refrain from performing acts that it would otherwise be rationally permissible to refrain from performing.[9] If we were, then, to claim that, in most choice situations, some of the relevant reasons have a great deal of rational justifying strength but very little to no rational requiring strength, we could thereby account for the basic belief.

Interestingly, Joshua Gert (2004) argues that, in comparison to self-interested reasons for avoiding nontrivial harms, altruistic reasons have little to no rational requiring strength, but just as much rational justifying strength when the amount of harm at stake for others is comparable to the amount of harm at stake for oneself. Thus, on Gert's view, one is rationally permitted to sacrifice one's own life to save the lives of two others even though one would not be rationally required to sacrifice much, if anything, to save those two lives.

If this is right, then the defender of agent-centered options can claim that, given its considerable *moral* justifying strength, the non-moral reason that the agent has to safeguard her own self-interest prevents the moral reason that she has to act altruistically from generating a moral requirement to act altruistically, but that it does so without thereby generating a rational requirement to act self-interestedly, for its *rational* requiring strength is exceeded by the rational justifying strength of her moral reason to act altruistically. And although the moral reason she has to act altruistically has sufficient rational justifying strength to make acting altruistically rationally permissible, it has insufficient rational requiring strength to make acting altruistically rationally required, for, as Gert claims, altruistic reasons have very little to no rational requiring strength. So, on Gert's view, we end up with a rational option to act either altruistically or self-interestedly.

Third, we could claim that, in most choice situations, the relevant reasons are either not at all, or only very imprecisely, comparable (or commensurable). When two competing reasons are incomparable, they neither defeat one another nor exactly balance out (and, furthermore, they would not be on a par). And since whenever the competing reasons for various act alternatives fail to defeat each other, it accords with reason to perform any one of them, claiming that, in most choice situations, the relevant reasons are incomparable and thus fail to defeat each other allows us to account for the basic belief. If this is right, then the defender of agent-centered options could account for rational options by making

---

[9] See GERT 2003 and GERT 2004.

the following claims: (1) the sorts of reasons that support supererogatory acts are typically altruistic (or impartial) reasons, (2) the sorts of reasons that support their permissible non-supererogatory alternatives are typically self-interested (or partial) reasons, and (3) these two types of reasons are not at all, or only very imprecisely, comparable. Indeed, Henry Sidgwick (1966) made these three claims. He held that impartial reasons and self-interested reasons are wholly incomparable, and this led him to accept a kind of *dualism of practical reason*, where it is always objectively rational to do either what would be impartially best or what would be self-interestedly best. And, recently, Derek Parfit (2011, pp. 131–137) has argued that some form of dualism about practical reason is correct, but that Sidgwick was wrong to think that impartial and self-interested reasons are wholly incomparable. Parfit argues that they are instead only very imprecisely comparable. In either case, though, there would, in most instances, be a rational option to act either altruistically or self-interestedly.

Fourth, we could account for the basic belief by supposing that the relevant reasons are *imperfect reasons*—reasons that do not support performing any specific alternative, but instead support performing any of the alternatives that would each constitute an equally effective means of achieving the same worthy end. Of course, it may seem that acting self-interestedly and acting altruistically cannot plausibly be interpreted as two ways of pursuing the same worthy end, nor as two ways of acting on the same reason. But things are not as they seem. If we recognize that our agency is extended over time and that, at a more general level of description, we can choose between two temporally extended courses of action, one that includes acting self-interestedly now and acting altruistically later and another that includes acting altruistically now and acting self-interestedly later, then it does seem plausible to construe these two courses of action as two ways of trying to achieve the same thing: specifically, a reasonable balance between altruistic pursuits and self-interested pursuits over time. If we think that any reasonably choice-worthy course of action will contain both altruistic acts and self-interested acts, then it does not matter whether I perform an altruistic act now and a self-interested act later or vice versa so long as, in the end, I perform a sufficient number of each.[10]

To sum up, then, Kagan's objection poses no more serious a problem for the defender of agent-centered options than it does for anyone else concerned to account for the basic belief. Moreover, there are, as I have shown, a number of potential solutions to the problem of accounting for the basic belief, and the defender of agent-centered options could potentially avail herself of any one of them. Now, I have not assessed whether any of these proposed solutions is satis-

---

[10] "Reasonably choice-worthy" can be given either a maximizing or a satisficing interpretation. On the maximizing interpretation, a course of action is reasonably choice-worthy if and only if it is maximally choice-worthy. On the satisficing interpretation, a course of action is reasonably choice-worthy if and only if it is sufficiently choice-worthy.

factory. But whether or not a satisfactory solution can be found, the defender of
agent-centered options need not fear Kagan's objection. If, on the one hand, a satisfactory solution can be found, then it seems likely that the defender of agent-
centered options will be able to avail herself of that solution and thereby meet
Kagan's objection. If, on the other hand, a satisfactory solution is nowhere to be
found, then the defender of agent-centered options will have to admit, as Kagan
worries, that there will be a rational option to act either altruistically or self-interestedly only in those rare instances in which the reasons supporting each alternative
exactly balance out. But, in that case, Kagan's objection cuts no ice, for, if the basic
belief is something that we must ultimately abandon, then everyone (whether they
endorse agent-centered options or not) will have to admit that there are rational
options only when the relevant reasons exactly balance out.

Since, as I have just argued, the defender of agent-centered options need not be
concerned with whether or not a satisfactory solution to the problem of accounting
for the basic belief can be found, it may seem that I should just stop here and
remain neutral regarding whether there is such a solution and, if so, what it is. But
such a tactic, although legitimate, is one that many readers would find unsatisfy-
ing. After all, some potential solutions to the problem of accounting for the basic
belief might cohere better with the claims and arguments in this book than others
do. So it would be good to know which solution I advocate and to what extent it
coheres with the other theses of this book. Thus, I will, below, try to develop and
defend what I take to be the best solution to the problem of accounting for the
basic belief. In the process, I will be defending a particular theory of (objective)
rationality: namely, *rational securitism* (hereafter, simply "securitism"). Securitism
will not only serve to account for the basic belief and for the fact that our moral
options are typically rationally optional as well, but it will also serve as a model for
my favored theory of morality—namely, commonsense consequentialism—which
is a version of moral securitism (the moral analogue of securitism). As we will see
in the next chapter, securitism and commonsense consequentialism share many of
the same structural features. So explaining and defending securitism in this chapter
will make it easier for me to explain and defend commonsense consequentialism in
the next. Besides, part of the case for commonsense consequentialism is that
coheres well with other theses argued for in this book, including securitism.

§6.2 Imperfect reasons and rational options

Often times, what an agent has most reason to do is determined by facts about
what she has most reason to achieve. But such facts often fail to support any
specific alternative, for there is often more than one way to achieve the same
result. To illustrate, consider the following three examples. First, the fact that
I need to get to the airport provides me with a reason to take any of the following
equally attractive means to getting there: a bus, a taxi, or a train—assume that

these are all equally attractive given their comparative cost, comfort, and convenience.[11] Second, the fact both that I have a paper that needs to be finished in a month's time and that I will most likely finish it by then if and only if I implement a policy of spending two hours a day working on it provides me with a reason to spend two hours (any two hours) each day over the next month working on it. And, third, the fact that I need to spend one of the next two days grading exams and the other painting the backyard fence in order to meet certain important deadlines provides me with a reason either (1) to spend tomorrow grading exams and the next day painting the backyard fence or (2) to spend tomorrow painting the backyard fence and the next day grading exams.

These three sorts of reasons are what I call *imperfect reasons*, for they are analogous to imperfect duties in that they allow for significant leeway in how one chooses to comply with them.[12] Just as the imperfect duty of beneficence requires only that one be beneficent to a certain extent but leaves it up to one's discretion to whom and on which occasions to be beneficent, imperfect reasons speak in favor of achieving some worthy end but leave it up to one's discretion which of the equally attractive means to achieving this end to take.

Imperfect reasons arise in what Joshua Gert calls *multiple-option cases*, cases in which there is more than one equally attractive means to achieving the same worthy end (2003, p. 10). In multiple-option cases, it is rationally permissible to take any of the equally attractive means to achieving this end, for the relevant reasons are imperfect reasons, which do not support performing any particular act, but instead support performing any of the acts that constitute an equally attractive means to achieving the same worthy end. That there are multiple-option cases where the relevant reasons are imperfect reasons is, I take it, uncontroversial. But if the existence of multiple-option cases is as uncontroversial as I claim, we might wonder why philosophers such as Raz (1999) and Gert (2003) have held that we cannot account for the basic belief simply by appealing to them. The answer is that they each believe that multiple-option cases are insufficiently numerous to account for the basic belief.

To demonstrate this, Raz cites a case in which a woman named Mary has the opportunity to see a powerful performance of a good play at her local theater tonight but decides to stay home instead (1999, p. 99). Raz's view is that both alternatives—going to the theater and staying home—are rationally permissible. And although he admits that many reasons are imperfect reasons (or what he calls reasons that "are not time-specific"), he denies that such reasons allow us to account for the basic belief. He says:

---

[11] I borrow this example from GERT 2003, p. 10.

[12] Jonathan Dancy calls such reasons "unfocused" reasons, and Raz calls a subclass of such reasons "reasons that are not time-specific"—see DANCY 2004 (p. 100) and RAZ 1999 (p. 100), respectively. I first introduced the notion of an imperfect reason as well as the idea that it could be employed to account for rational options in PORTMORE 2000.

In many cases the reasons for doing one thing or another are not time-specific: the same reasons and the same opportunity to conform to them will apply on a number, sometimes an indefinite number, of occasions. This does not, however, explain the basic belief. Quite apart from the fact that delay is not costless, the basic belief applies to time-specific reasons as well. Mary, in our example, does not have to go to the play even on the last evening of its run. She may still just not feel like it and do something else instead. (1999, p. 100)

Likewise, Gert believes that the set of cases in which there are rational options is significantly broader than the set of multiple-option cases. Gert believes, for instance, that it is rationally permissible both to sacrifice $200 to prevent forty children from suffering from serious malnutrition for forty days and to refuse to do so, choosing instead to spend that money on oneself (2003, pp. 8–9). As he sees it, this is a case in which there is a rational option, but he denies that it is a multiple-option case. He says:

Multiple-option cases depend crucially on the fact that the class of rationally justified options in any given case can plausibly be seen as ways of doing the *same thing*. In the examples that were used to motivate the justifying/requiring distinction, on the other hand, the pairs of justified options were always of the following form.

(a) Make a sacrifice for an altruistic reason.
(b) Do not make the sacrifice.

Such pairs cannot plausibly be construed as alternate ways of pursuing the same end or acting on the same reasons. (2003, p. 13)[13]

This, I will argue, is mistaken. I will show that options *a* and *b* can be construed as two alternative ways of pursuing the same end and of acting on the same reason.

As Gert admits, it is crucial to get the level of description right when assessing the rational status of an act, for whether it is true that I am doing what I am rationally required to be doing depends on how we describe what it is that I am doing (2003, pp. 13–14). To illustrate, consider again the case where I must get to the airport, and let us assume that I happen to be taking a taxi to get there. If we ask whether I am rationally required to be doing *what I am doing*, the answer will depend on the level of description. If, on the one hand, we describe *what I am doing* as taking a taxi to the airport, the answer will be "no," because taking the bus is an equally attractive means of getting to the airport and I am rationally permitted to do that instead. If, on the other hand, we describe *what I am doing*, more

---

[13] The letters *a* and *b* are not italicized in the original.

generally, as going to the airport, the answer will be "yes," because I am rationally required to go to the airport (or so we are supposing). So, at one level of description, I am rationally required to be doing *what I am doing*, and, at another, I am not.

The same can be said of Gert's example (and, as we will later see, of Raz's example as well). At a more general level of description, there are two courses of action that I might take over time, one that involves my acting self-interestedly now and altruistically later and another that involves my acting altruistically now and self-interestedly later, and it is plausible to construe these two courses of action as two ways of trying to achieve the same thing: a reasonable balance between altruistic acts and self-interested acts over time. If we think that the order in which I perform such acts is unimportant and that what is important is only that I end up striking a reasonable balance between the two types of acts, then it does not matter whether I act self-interestedly now and altruistically later or vice versa so long as, in the end, I perform a sufficient number of each over time.

In Raz's case, we can say something similar. If we acknowledge that Mary conceives of her agency as being extended over time, then we should think that, at the relevant level of description, the pertinent choice is not between seeing this play on its last night and staying home, but between two courses of action, containing both a certain amount of relaxation and a certain amount of cultural enrichment. So even though this is a good play and it is Mary's last opportunity to see it, this will not be Mary's last opportunity to do something as entertaining and culturally enriching as seeing this play. And surely she is not rationally required to take advantage of every such opportunity. So if we take a broader view of things, we should think that what each of us, including Mary, should be trying to do is to strike a reasonable balance between various worthy pursuits, such as relaxation and cultural enrichment, over time. It is important to note, then, that if Mary stays home tonight and relaxes, there will be other opportunities for her to similarly enrich herself, and that, if she goes to the play, there will be other opportunities for her to get some relaxation. What is important, then, is not that she takes advantage of any specific opportunity for relaxation or cultural enrichment, but that she takes advantage of both sorts of opportunities sufficiently often over time.

To illustrate, suppose that Mary decides to stay home tonight while intending to take advantage of some future opportunity to do something culturally enriching. If we then ask whether she is rationally required to be doing *what she is doing*, the answer will depend, as it did above, on the level of description. If, on the one hand, we describe *what she is doing* as staying home tonight while intending to do something culturally enriching on some future night, the answer will be "no," because she is permitted instead to go to the theater tonight while intending to relax at home on some future night, which is an equally attractive means of striking a reasonable balance between relaxation and cultural enrichment over time. If, on the other hand, we describe *what she is doing*, more generally, as implementing a plan to strike some reasonable balance between relaxation and cultural enrichment over time, then the answer will be "yes," because she is rationally required to strike such a balance over time. So, at one level of description, she is rationally required to be doing *what she is doing*, and, at another, she is not. So it seems that if we view Mary's options from a suitably general level of description, we find that this is a multiple-option case after all.

So while admitting that there are multiple-option cases, Raz and Gert claim that such cases are insufficiently numerous to account for the basic belief, and so they resort to more controversial claims in trying to account for the basic belief: in Raz's case, to the claim that there are widespread incommensurabilities among reasons, and, in Gert's case, to the claim that reasons have two separable dimensions of rational strength (i.e., rational requiring strength and rational justifying strength). I will, however, argue that multiple-option cases are sufficiently numerous to account for the basic belief and, thus, that we need not appeal to such controversial claims in accounting for the basic belief. My argument will be that Raz and Gert fail to appreciate the fact that most typical choice situations are multiple-option cases, because they fail to view our choices from the appropriate level of description: that of choosing between various courses of action over time. To be clear, I am not going to argue that the controversial claims that Raz and Gert appeal to in accounting for the basic belief are false or even that they are not needed to account for something else. I will argue only that they are not needed to account for the basic belief and, thus, that we can account for the basic belief with only the theoretical apparatus that all sides agree on: imperfect reasons and multiple-option cases. Also, I should warn the reader that I will not be defending the basic belief. As Raz points out, our task is to explain why it is true, and that is what I aim to do and with as few assumptions as possible.

In the next section, I present my own theory of objective rationality—namely, securitism. I then show, in the subsequent section, how this theory enables us to account for the basic belief. In the last section, I explore securitism's suppositions and implications, defending it against various potential objections.

§6.3 Securitism

§§6.3.1 Objective rationality

Before I state my theory, let me be clear on what it is a theory about. It is a theory about what it is *objectively* rational to do. Objective rationality is about what agents ought to do in the most fundamental and unqualified sense. So it is not about what they morally ought to do, nor is it about what they prudentially ought to do. Instead, it is about what they objectively ought to do, all things considered—see §1.4. Thus, to say that an act is objectively irrational is to say that the "action absolutely should not be performed" (GERT 2004, p. 137).

Some suggest that we should understand objective rationality in terms of advisability: objectively irrational actions are those that no fully informed and well-meaning advisor would recommend performing on the assumption that the agent would take the advice.[14] More precisely, though, we should understand the notion of objective rationality in terms of reasons: an act is objectively rational if and only if the agent has sufficient reason to perform it—that is, if and only if the agent is objectively rationally permitted to perform it (again, see §1.4).[15] The objective rational status of an act is, then, purely a function of the reasons there are for and against performing it, irrespective of whether or not the agent is aware of them.

The subjective rational status of an act, by contrast, depends not on what reasons there are, but on what reasons the agent takes there to be or, alternatively, on the practical mental functioning of the agent. On the former view, an act is subjectively rational if and only if the agent has beliefs whose truth would give her sufficient reason to perform it. And when the agent has inconsistent beliefs, the act will be subjectively rational relative to some beliefs, but subjectively irrational relative to others (PARFIT 2011, pp. 112–113). On the latter view, an act is subjectively rational if and only if it does not indicate some failure in the practical mental functioning of the agent (GERT 2004, p. 160). I will not take a stand on which, if either, account of subjective rationality is correct. For my purposes, it is important only that we have a clear understanding of objective rationality, of which I now offer a theory.

Let me warn the reader, though, that the theory that I am about to offer is unusual in a number of ways. So there will be a fair bit of explanation involved, and it will not be until the next section that I will explore the theory's implications concerning the basic belief.

§§6.3.2 Doing the best we can

According to many normative theories, we are to assess the normative status of an action by comparing it with the available alternatives—the available alterna-

---

[14] See GERT 2004 (p. 140) for more on this idea. I add the qualification "on the assumption that the agent will take the advice" to eliminate the worry that in some cases the agent might be predisposed to rebel against such advice. I should also add that the advice needs to be complete. That is, it will not do to advise an agent merely to do x if doing x without simultaneously intending or doing y would be disastrous. What's more, we must realize that an agent's reasons for doing x could potentially diverge from an advisor's reasons for advising her to do x, and the objective rationality of an agent's doing x is a function of her reasons for doing x, not the advisor's reasons for advising her to do x. At best, then, the advice model is just an often-useful (but also sometimes misleading) heuristic for getting a grip on our intuitions about what is objectively rational. It must, however, be used cautiously. For more on this issue, see §1.4.

[15] Another helpful way of understanding this notion, which was suggested to me by Peter de Marneffe, is as follows: an act is objectively rational if and only if the set of true propositions provide sufficient reason for the agent to perform it. I am assuming, here, that a reason for S to φ is just some fact that counts in favor of S's φ-ing. Thus, there can be reasons for S to φ of which S is completely unaware, for S can be completely unaware that the relevant reason-constituting facts obtain.

tives being those that are, in the relevant sense, open to the agent. On such a theory, the objective rational status of an action is determined by comparing how much reason there is to perform it to how much reason there is to perform each of the available alternatives. More specifically, the theory might hold that an act is rationally permissible if and only if there is no available alternative that there is even more reason to perform. Such a theory is, I think, quite promising. In any case, it is the sort of theory that I will explore here.

Once we accept such a theory, the first question to ask is: Which are the available alternatives, such that one ought to perform the best of them—that is, the one that there is most reason to perform? One common answer is that the available alternatives are those that the agent *can* perform. Thus, a number of philosophers have claimed that we ought to do the best we can.[16] The relevant sense of "can" here is the one that concerns the debate over whether or not "ought" implies "can." Following Michael J. Zimmerman, I will call the alternatives that a subject, S, can, in this sense, perform "personally possible" for S (ZIMMERMAN 1996, pp. 46–47). The idea that S ought to do the best that is personally possible for her is plausible only if "ought" implies "personally possible" and nothing more restrictive than "personally possible." For suppose that "ought" implies not only "personally possible," but also "F," where "F" stands for a predicate denoting some other more restrictive sense of "available" such that the set of acts that are F is a proper subset of those that are personally possible. If such is the case, then there would be some acts that are personally possible for S but which S cannot be obligated to perform: specifically, those that are personally possible for S but are not F. If there is such an F, then we must reject the idea that agents ought to do the best that they can (i.e., the best that is personally possible for them).[17] Below, I will argue that there is such an F and that "F" stands for "scrupulously securable." But, first, let me explain some terminology.

To illustrate the difference between what is scrupulously securable by an agent and what is personally possible for that agent, consider the following. Suppose that I am on a low-fat, low-carbohydrate diet. It is now 2 P.M., and I am thinking that I should grill up some low-calorie vegetables and a lean boneless, skinless chicken breast for tonight's dinner. If this is what I am going to have for dinner, I will need to get into my car, drive to the grocery store, buy the necessary ingredients, drive back home, marinate the chicken, cut up the vegetables, fire up the grill, wait for it to heat up, grill the chicken and vegetables, serve them, and eat them. But suppose that, as a matter of fact, no matter what, at 2 P.M., I plan or intend to do later, I will not end up eating grilled chicken and vegetables for dinner

---

[16] See, for instance, FELDMAN 1986 and ZIMMERMAN 1996.

[17] I am assuming that "F" does not stand for something like "the best of those that the agent can perform," for it would be odd to suppose that the available alternatives from which the agent must choose include only the best of those that she can perform. After all, why would only the best be available?

tonight. For, as a matter fact, I am going to end up eating pizza instead. What is going to happen is this: while in the midst of preparing the chicken and vegetables at 5 P.M., I am going to get very hungry. And, in this state, I am going to be overcome by the temptation to go off my diet and will throw the chicken and vegetables back in the fridge, turn off the grill, and order pizza. It is not that I could not grill and eat the chicken and vegetables. Indeed, I could in that, if I were to intend at 5 P.M. to continue with my plan to grill and eat chicken and vegetables, then that is exactly what I would do. It is just that, as a matter of fact, I will at 5 P.M. abandon my plan and order pizza instead, and there is no action/intention that I might perform/have at 2 P.M. that is going to change this fact.

In this case, my eating grilled chicken and vegetables at 6 P.M. is, as of 2 P.M., personally possible for me. It is personally possible for me, for there is a series of steps that I could take that culminate in my eating grilled chicken and vegetables at 6 P.M. tonight, and the following is true of each one of these steps: having taken the previous step or steps, I could take the next step in that, were I to intend to take the next step, I would succeed in doing so. That is, having gotten into my car, I would then drive to the grocery store if I were to intend to do so. And having arrived at the grocery store, I would then buy the necessary ingredients if I were to intend to do that. And so on and so forth.

Nevertheless, my eating grilled chicken and vegetables at 6 P.M. is not, as of 2 P.M., scrupulously securable by me, for, as we are supposing, no matter what I intend at 2 P.M. to do later, I will not end up eating grilled chicken and vegetables at 6 P.M. Even if I were at 2 P.M. to form the most resolute intention to stick with my plan, it is a fact about my psychology that I would abandon it in the face of the ensuing desire to eat pizza. Thus, there is absolutely nothing that I can intend at 2 P.M. to do later that will result in my eating chicken and vegetables at 6 P.M.—or so we are assuming. Of course, there are things that I could intend at 2 P.M. to do later that would prevent me from eating pizza at 6 P.M. I could, for instance, intend at 2 P.M. to commit some crime later in front of a police officer so that I will end up in jail by 6 P.M. Nevertheless, there is nothing that I could intend at 2 P.M. to do later that would ensure that I end up eating grilled chicken and vegetables at 6 P.M.—this is not something they serve in jail. Thus, my sitting in jail at 6 P.M. is, as of 2 P.M., scrupulously securable by me, but my eating grilled chicken and vegetables at 6 P.M. is not.

In the above example, I have been assuming that there is no set of background attitudes that I could permissibly form or maintain that would enable me to bring about, through my present intentions, that I eat grilled chicken and vegetables at 6 P.M. This is important because what I am able to bring about through my present intentions depends on what my background attitudes are. For instance, whereas I am unable bring about, through my present intentions, that I eat grilled chicken and vegetables at 6 P.M. given my rational belief that my going off my diet on this particular occasion would be no big deal, I would, nevertheless, be able to bring this about were I to have the irrational belief that my life depends on my eating grilled chicken and vegetables at 6 P.M. If I were to have this irrational belief, then my present intention would be sufficient to ensure that I eat grilled chicken and vegetables at 6 P.M. For although I am going to be beset by a very strong desire to eat pizza at around 5 P.M., the strength of this desire will pale in comparison with the strength of my desire to continue living, and, thus, I will have no problem continuing with my plan to eat grilled chicken and vegetables. So it is only because I rationally believe that my going off my diet on this particular occasion would be no big deal that I am unable to secure, through my present intentions, that I eat grilled chicken and vegetables at 6 P.M. Given this rational belief, the desire that I have to stick to my diet will be overpowered by the ensuing desire to eat pizza, causing me to abandon my plan to eat grilled chicken and vegetables.

It is important to realize, then, that which future actions an agent can secure through her present intentions depends on what her background attitudes are. Given this, there is a distinction to be made between what is securable by an agent and what is scrupulously securable by that agent.[18] Roughly speaking, something is securable by an agent if and only if there is both some set of intentions and some set of background attitudes such that if she were to have those intentions and those background attitudes, that something would be brought about. By contrast, something is *scrupulously* securable by an agent if and only if there is both some set of intentions and some set of *permissible* background attitudes such that if she were to have both those intentions and those permissible background attitudes, that something would be brought about. Since, in the above example, we are assuming that there is no set of background attitudes that I am permitted to have that would enable me to bring about, through my present intentions, that I eat grilled chicken and vegetables at 6 P.M., my eating grilled chicken and vegetables at 6 P.M. is not, as of the present, scrupulously securable by me. I am assuming, though, that there could be some set of impermissible background attitudes (e.g., one that includes the belief that my life depends on my eating grilled chicken and vegetables at 6 P.M.) that I either have or have the capacity to form that would enable me to bring about, through my present intentions, that I eat grilled chicken and vegetables at 6 P.M. If so, my eating grilled chicken and vegetables at 6 P.M. would be, as of the present, securable by me.

With this example in mind, I can now define the relevant notions more precisely. Let "α_i" and "α_j" be variables that range over sets of actions. The acts in these sets may be simple or compound, synchronous or asynchronous, consecutive or inconsecutive. Furthermore, let us define a *schedule of intentions* extending

---

[18] I thank Jacob Ross for getting me to see that which future actions an agent can secure through her present intentions depends on what her background attitudes are and, thus, that there is an important distinction to be made between what is securable and what is scrupulously securable. Through his insightful comments on an earlier draft of this chapter and the ensuing discussion that we had over email, Ross has helped shape much of my latest thinking on this issue.

over a time-interval, T, as a function from times in T to sets of intentions. And let us say that S's intentions *follow* a certain schedule of intentions, I, extending over T just in case, for every time t_i belonging to T, S has at t_i all and only the intentions that I specifies for t_i. Let us also say that S *carries out* an intention to perform α_i if and only if S performs α_i. Lastly, let us say that S's φ-ing *involves* S's ψ-ing just in case it follows from S's φ-ing that S ψs, in the sense that, necessarily, if S φs then S ψs. Thus, my raising my arm quickly involves my raising my arm. And my carrying out the intention to both open the door and step outside involves my stepping outside.[19] The definitions of "securable," "personally possible," and "scrupulously securable" are, then, as follows:

6.1 A set of actions, α_j, is, as of t_i, *securable* by S if and only if there is a time, t_j, that either immediately follows t_i or is identical to t_i, a set of actions, α_i (where α_i may, or may not, be identical to α_j), and a set of background attitudes, B, such that the following are all true: (1) S would perform α_j if S were to have at t_j both B and the intention to perform α_j; and (2) S has at t_i the capacity to continue, or to come, to have at t_j both B and the intention to perform α_j.

6.2 A set of actions, α_j, is, as of t_i, *personally possible* for S if and only if there is some schedule of intentions, I, extending over a time-interval, T, beginning at t_i such that the following are all true: (*a*) if S's intentions followed schedule, I, then S would carry out all the intentions in I; (*b*) S's carrying out all the intentions in I would involve S's performing α_j; (*c*) S has just before t_i the capacity to continue, or to come, to have the intentions that I specifies for t_i; and (*d*) for any time t_j in T after t_i ($t_i < t_j$), if S's intentions followed I up until t_j, then S would have just before t_j the capacity to continue, or to come, to have the intentions that I specifies for t_j.[20]

6.3 A set of actions, α_j, is, as of t_i, *scrupulously securable* by S if and only if there is a time, t_j, that either immediately follows t_i or is identical to t_i, a set of actions, α_i (where α_i may, or may not, be identical to α_j), and a set of background attitudes, B, such that the following are all true: (1) S would perform α_j if S were to have at t_j both B and the intention to perform α_j; (2) S has at t_i the capacity to continue, or to come, to have at t_j both B and the intention to perform α_j; and (3) S would continue, or come, to have at t_j B (and, where α_i is not identical to α_j, the intention to perform α_i as well) if S both were at t_i aware of all the relevant reason-constituting facts and were at t_i to respond to these facts/reasons in all and only the ways that they prescribe, thereby coming to have at t_j all those

---

[19] I borrow the definitions of "follows," "involves," "carries out," and "schedule of intentions" from J. ROSS FORTHCOMING.

[20] I borrow this definition, with minor modifications, from J. ROSS FORTHCOMING, but the general idea of personal possibility comes from Goldman (1978, p. 193) and Zimmerman (1996, p. 46).

attitudes that, given those facts, she has decisive reason to have and only those attitudes that she has, given those facts, sufficient reason to have.[21]

Each of these definitions needs clarifying. I will start by making five clarificatory points about 6.1.

Clarifying 6.1: First, by "attitudes," I mean to be referring to only a subclass of attitudes—namely, *judgment-sensitive attitudes*, which are those attitudes that are sensitive to one's judgments about reasons (SCANLON 1998, p. 20). These are the attitudes that an ideally rational agent would come to have whenever she judges that there are decisive reasons to have them and that an ideally rational agent would cease to have whenever she judges that there are insufficient reasons to have them. Judgment-sensitive attitudes include attitudes such as fear, desire, belief, and admiration. Hunger, however, is not a judgment-sensitive attitude, for it does not respond to our judgments about reasons (SCANLON 1998, p. 20). The judgment that one has already had plenty to eat and, thus, that one has no reason to be hungry is not the sort of thing that would cause even an ideally rational agent to cease to be hungry.

Since it is only our judgment-sensitive attitudes that are under our control in the sense of their being responsive to our judgments about reasons (the sense that is relevant both to their being under our control and to our being responsible for them), these are the only sorts of mental states that can positively affect what we are able to secure.[22] Consider that if I cannot, through my present intentions, ensure that I will stick to my diet given my incredible hunger, then my keeping to my diet is not something that is, as of the present, securable by me. For how hungry I am is not something that I can *directly* control. By contrast, if the reason that I cannot, through my present intentions, ensure that I will stick to my diet is that I have the irrational belief that the pizza in front of me is low in fat and carbohydrates, then my keeping to my diet is, as of the present, securable by me. For this belief is, we will suppose, under my control in that I am capable of both recognizing and responding appropriately to the reasons there are for thinking that the pizza is high in fat and carbohydrates and can, thereby, come to have the rational belief that this is so.[23] And let us suppose that, were I to come to have this rational belief,

---

[21] Here, I am assuming counterfactual determinism. That is, I am assuming that for any event, *e* (including actions, sets of actions, and the formations of intentions), there is some determinate fact as to what the world would be like if *e* were to occur. Of course, this is controversial. So, depending on what sorts of events may be indeterminate and whether so-called "counterfactuals of freedom" can be true even if we have libertarian free will, I may need to substitute "would likely" for "would" in the relevant subjunctive conditionals.

[22] For a defense of the view that judgment-sensitive attitudes, such as beliefs and desires, are under our control (although not under our volitional control), see HIERONYMI 2006, PETTIT & SMITH 1996, A. M. SMITH 2010, and STEUP 2008.

[23] I, of course, acknowledge that this belief is not under my volitional control. That is, I cannot come to have this belief merely by deciding or intending to have this belief.

I would then be able to ensure, through my present intentions, that I stick to my diet. Thus, what is positively securable by an agent depends on her judgment-sensitive attitudes, but not on those attitudes or mental states that are not sensitive to her judgments about reasons.

Second, let me clarify that to say that S *performs* a set of actions α_j is just to say that S performs each act in that set. Suppose, for instance, that I plan to spend this morning working on this chapter and tomorrow morning grading exams. I perform this set of actions if and only if I spend this morning working on this chapter and tomorrow morning grading exams.

Third, note that condition 2 in 6.1 (and 6.3 as well) is needed given the following sort of case. Suppose that S is at t_i in a persistent vegetative state. Presumably, given S's immutable, unconscious state at t_i, no set of actions is, as of t_i, securable by S. Yet the following counterfactual may be true: S would perform α_j if S were to have at t_j both B and the intention to perform α_j. For, in the closest possible world in which S has at t_j both B and the intention to perform α_j (a world in which S is not in a persistent vegetative state at t_j), S performs α_j. Thus, condition 1 would be met and so we must add to it: (2) S has at t_i the capacity to continue, or to come, to have at t_j both B and the intention to perform α_j. Adding this condition allows us to account for the fact that a set of actions will not be, as of t_i, securable by S unless S has at t_i the capacity to form (or to continue to have) the relevant attitudes and intention—a capacity that those in a persistent vegetative state lack.

Of course, there are other ways of lacking the capacity to form the relevant attitudes and intention besides being in a persistent vegetative state. For instance, S could be conscious and capable of deliberating but lack the concepts needed to form the relevant attitudes and intention. Or S could be conscious but lack the capacity to recognize and/or respond appropriately to the reasons there are for having the relevant attitudes and intention. In that case, whether S forms the relevant attitudes and intention would not be under her *rational control*, where S has rational control over whether or not she φs only if both (*a*) she has the capacity to recognize and assess the relevant reasons and (*b*) her φ-ing is at least moderately responsive to her assessments concerning these reasons (A. M. SMITH 2010).[24] As I see it, then, S's having the relevant concepts as well as S's having rational control over whether or not she forms the relevant attitudes and intention are both prerequisites for her having the capacity to come to have B and the intention to perform α_j.

Fourth, note that I am assuming that "intentions" should be construed broadly so as to include plans, policies, resolutions, and the like. We should construe intentions in this way, for we are planning agents. We conceive of our agency as being extended over time, and because of this, we often plan, undertake, and then, finally, complete temporally extended activities and projects (BRATMAN

---

[24] For what being at least moderately reasons-responsive consists in, see FISCHER & RAVIZZA 1998, pp. 62–91 and especially 243–244.

2007, p. 21). We do not simply act from moment to moment. Instead, we form future-directed intentions and adopt both plans and policies, which help us to organize and coordinate our activities over time (BRATMAN 2007, p. 26).

As Michael Bratman explains, "plans typically concern relatively specific courses of action extended over time" (2007, p. 27). For instance, one might plan to spend the morning grading exams and the afternoon playing golf. Policies, by contrast, involve a general commitment "to a certain kind of action on certain kinds of potentially recurrent occasions—for example, to buckling up one's seat belt when one drives, or to having at most one beer at dinner" (BRATMAN 2007, p. 27). Besides plans and policies, there are also resolutions. A resolution is an intention that one has resolved not to reconsider even in the face of anticipated temptation to do so (HOLTON 2009, pp. 9–12).[25] For instance, someone might resolve to exercise or to refrain from eating sweets.

Fifth, it is important to note that the relevant intention here is not the intention to perform α_j, but the intention to perform α_i, which may or may not be identical to α_j. Thus, 6.1 (and 6.3 as well) allows that a set of actions, α_j, can be, as of t_i, securable (or scrupulously securable) by S even though S lacks at t_i the capacity to form the intention to perform α_j. To illustrate, consider Sean, a boy who, on his twelfth birthday (that is, at t_i), decides that he wants to earn a PhD in mathematics. And let us assume that α_j is the fully specified set of acts that Sean would need to perform in order to achieve his goal. Now, at t_i, Sean is only twelve and so certainly does not know, with much specificity, what all he needs to do to earn a PhD in mathematics. For instance, he does not know that he is going to need to prove Gödel's incompleteness theorems on his comprehensive exams. Indeed, as of t_i, he has not even heard of Gödel's incompleteness theorems. Given this, Sean lacks at t_i the capacity to form the intention to perform each specific act in α_j. For one, α_j includes acts that Sean cannot at t_i intend to perform, simply because Sean does not at t_i have the requisite concepts. Sean cannot, for instance, intend to prove Gödel's incompleteness theorems when he does not even have the concept of a theorem, let alone the concept of a formal system's being incomplete. For another, α_j is simply too large and too complex for Sean to hold consciously before his mind in the way that is necessary for intending to perform each specific act in α_j. Thus, Sean lacks at t_i the capacity to come to have at t_j the intention to perform α_j.

Nevertheless, 6.1 allows that α_j can be, as of t_i, securable (or scrupulously securable) by Sean. It will be securable so long as there is a time, t_j, that either immediately follows t_i or is identical to t_i, a set of actions, α_i (where α_i may, or may not, be identical to α_j), and a set of background attitudes, B, such that the following are all true: (1) S would perform α_j if S were to have at t_j both B and the

---

[25] On one plausible view, a resolution involves both a first-order intention to perform a certain action and a second-order intention not to let that first-order intention be deflected by anticipated contrary inclinations—see HOLTON 2009, pp. 11–12.

intention to perform α_j; and (2) S has at t_i the capacity to continue, or to come, to have at t_j both B and the intention to perform α_i. Suppose, then, that the intention to perform α_i simply consists in the intention to earn a PhD in mathematics and that Sean has at t_i the capacity to come to have at t_j this intention. And let us assume that if Sean were at t_j to intend to earn a PhD in mathematics, he would, given his background attitudes and other facts about him, perform the very large and complex set of actions that is required to do so, including, let us assume, proving Gödel's incompleteness theorems on his comprehensive exams. In that case, 6.1 implies that Sean's performing α_j is, as of t_i, securable by him even though he lacks at t_i the capacity to form the intention to perform α_j.

Clarifying 6.2: The main difference between those sets of actions that are securable and those that are merely personally possible is that the latter class is often considerably larger than the former class. For although every set of actions that is, as of t_i, securable by S will also be, as of t_i, personally possible for S, the converse does not hold. Some sets of actions that are not, as of t_i, securable by S will, as of t_i, be personally possible for S. To illustrate, consider Erika, a six-year-old girl who knows next to nothing about chess. Erika's beating the Russian grandmaster Anatoly Karpov at chess is personally possible but not securable.[26] It is personally possible for her in that there is a series of moves that she could make (e.g., moving her king's knight to f3) that culminates in her beating Karpov, and the following is true of each these moves: having made the previous move (or moves), she would succeed in making some particular move next were she to intend to make that move. That is, there is a schedule of intentions, I (e.g., one that involves her intending at t_1 to make a certain move, her intending at t_3 to make another particular move, her intending at t_7 to make yet another particular move, and so on), that meet all the conditions in 6.2 and that, if carried out, involves her beating Karpov. Nevertheless, Erika's beating Karpov is not securable by her. For, as we will suppose, she lacks at the age of six the intellectual capacity to form the complicated intention to perform the series of moves that would culminate in her beating Karpov, and although she certainly has the capacity to form some less complicated intention, such as the intention to beat Karpov, her forming such an intention would not result in her beating Karpov—that is, even if she were to form the intention to beat Karpov, she would fail to do so, or so we shall assume. Thus, her beating Karpov is personally possible for her but not securable by her.

Clarifying 6.3: 6.3 differs from 6.1 only in that it includes the following additional condition: (3) S would continue, or come, to have at t_j B (and, where α_i is not identical to α_j, the intention to perform α_i as well) if S both were at t_i aware of all the relevant reason-constituting facts and were at t_j to respond to these facts/reasons in all and only the ways that they prescribe, thereby coming to have at t_j all those attitudes that, given those facts, she has decisive reason to have and only

---

[26] This example is inspired by one from HOWARD-SNYDER 1997.

those attitudes that she has, given those facts, sufficient reason to have.[27] Thus, it is the addition of this third condition that differentiates what is scrupulously securable from what is securable. To illustrate the need for this third condition, consider the following case.[28]

> *The Mind-Reading Psycho:* Sam is a mind-reading psycho who has Teresa locked up inside his house. Victor is outside with his gun. Victor cannot get in unless Sam lets him in. And Sam will let Victor in at t_2 if and only if Sam reads Victor's mind and finds that Victor wants at t_1 to kill Teresa. Now, the only way that Teresa will escape with her life is if Sam lets Victor inside at t_2. For Victor, unlike Sam, is slow and weak, and, once inside, Teresa will be able to overpower Victor, take his gun, and use his gun to escape from both Sam and Victor. Absent Victor's gun, though, Teresa will be unable to escape and will be killed by Sam. So, Teresa will escape with her life if and only if Victor gets inside at t_2. And Victor will get inside at t_2 if and only if he wants at t_1 to kill Teresa. At t_0, Victor does happen to want to kill Teresa. But whether he will continue to have at t_1 the desire to kill Teresa depends entirely on whether or not he recognizes and responds appropriately to the reasons that he has for not wanting to kill Teresa. As a matter of fact, he fails to recognize and/or respond appropriately to these reasons, although he has, we will suppose, the capacity to do so.[29] Consequently, Victor is able to get inside, and Teresa escapes.

In this case, Victor's going inside the house at t_2 is, as of t_0, securable by Victor. However, it is not, as of t_0, scrupulously securable by Victor. For, in order to get inside the house, Victor must continue to have at t_1 the desire to kill Teresa, and this is impermissible. In fact, he has decisive reason to desire that he not kill Teresa, and if he were at t_0 aware of the relevant reason-constituting facts and responded appropriately to them he would by t_1 cease to desire to kill Teresa. The fact that Victor's going inside the house at t_2 is not, as of t_0, scrupulously securable by Victor has, I believe, important implications with respect to Victor's obligations. After all, it seems implausible to suppose that Victor is, as of t_0, obligated to enter the house given both that Victor will be unable to enter the house unless he

---

[27] Note that some, but not all, people with merely sufficient (i.e., sufficient but not decisive) reason to φ (where, say, φ is some attitude in *B*) would φ if they were made aware of all the relevant reason-constituting facts and were to respond appropriately to them. This is because S's having merely sufficient reason to φ entails that it is both objectively permissible for S to φ and objectively permissible for S not to φ. What is important, then, according to condition 3 is whether S is one of those people who would φ if she were made aware of all the relevant reason-constituting facts and were to respond appropriately to them.

[28] This case is based on one that Jacob Ross suggested to me.

[29] See FISCHER & RAVIZZA 1998 for what is required to have such a capacity.

continues to have at t_1 the desire to kill Teresa and that Victor ought *not*, as of t_0, to continue to have at t_1 the desire to kill Teresa. And it cannot be that Victor ought to perform an option that continues to be available to him only in virtue of his continuing to have an attitude that he ought not to continue to have.[30] Since I think that Victor is not, as of t_0, obligated to enter the house despite the fact that this is the best course of action that is, as of t_0, securable by him, I must hold that "obligatory" implies not merely "securable," but also "scrupulously securable." I will now defend this view.

§§ 6.3.3 "Obligatory" implies "scrupulously securable"

As I said above, I think "ought" implies not only "personally possible," but also "scrupulously securable." More precisely, I think that S's being objectively obligated, as of t_i, to φ at t_j implies not only that S's φ-ing at t_j is, as of t_i, personally possible for S, but also that S's φ-ing at t_j is, as of t_i, scrupulously securable by S. Why do I think this? There are at least three arguments that I find persuasive.

The first of these is what I call the *argument from blameworthiness*. Suppose, contrary to what I think, that the range of alternatives that an agent can be obligated, as of t_i, to perform is wider than those that are, as of t_i, scrupulously securable by her. In that case, an agent could have, say, an obligation at t_i to φ at t_j ($t_i <$ t_j) even though her φ-ing at t_j is not, as of t_i, scrupulously securable by her. This would be an obligation that she could fail to fulfill even if she had at t_i, and at every time prior to t_i, all those attitudes that she had decisive reason to have and only those attitudes that she had sufficient reason to have. And so if she fails to φ at t_j while meeting the relevant criteria for being responsible for such inaction, she will be blameworthy for having failed to fulfill this obligation that she supposedly had at t_i even though she had at t_i, and at every time prior to t_i, all those attitudes that she had decisive reason to have and only those attitudes that she had sufficient reason to have. I find this quite implausible.

It seems to me that if an agent is going to be blameworthy for having failed to fulfill an obligation that she supposedly had at t_i, then she must have been guilty of having made some mistake prior to or at t_i, a mistake in virtue of which she failed to fulfill the obligation. But if she had all the attitudes (desires, beliefs, intentions, etc.) that she had decisive reason to have and only the attitudes that she had sufficient reason, then I do not see how she has made any mistake at all. Of course, someone might suggest that we could rightly blame her for failing to fulfill the obligation that she had at t_i to φ at t_j given that she made some mistake *after* t_i that resulted in her failing to φ at t_j. But unless there was some other mistake that she made prior to or at t_i that resulted in her making that mistake *after* t_i, then I do not see how we can rightly blame her for failing to fulfill some obligation that she supposedly had *at* t_i. If her failure to fulfill the obligation is attribut-

---

[30] I thank Jacob Ross for convincing me of this.

able only to some mistake that she makes *after t_i*, then we should think that this obligation must be one that she had *after t_i*. And it is this later obligation, and not some obligation that she supposedly had at or before t_i, that she is blameworthy for failing to fulfill in virtue of the mistake that she made after t_i.

I am focusing, here, on the agent's attitudes, because it seems to me that it is only our attitudes that are most directly under our (rational) control. And, thus, it is our attitudes that we are ultimately responsible for (see A. M. SMITH 2005 and A. M. SMITH 2008). Consider that whereas an agent can come to intend to φ by responding appropriately to her reasons to φ, whether she actually φs (as opposed to merely intending to φ) depends not only on how she responds to the relevant reasons but also on various contingencies that are entirely outside of her (rational) control, such as whether she suffers from some unexpected paralysis or is a disembodied brain in a vat. So I think that ultimately what an agent should be held responsible for are her judgment-sensitive attitudes (i.e., the attitudes that are under her rational control), and if these attitudes are what her reasons dictate that they ought to be, then she is completely without fault and, therefore, blameless. So, as I see it, an agent can be blamed for failing to fulfill an obligation to perform a certain act only if her failure to perform that act can be traced back either to her failing to have some attitude that she had decisive reason to have or to her having some attitude that she had insufficient reason to have.

More formally, the argument is this:

6.4 If the range of alternatives that an agent can be obligated, as of t_i, to perform were wider than those that are, as of t_i, scrupulously securable by her, then an agent who had, at all times leading up to and including time t_i, all those attitudes that she had decisive reason to have and only those attitudes that she had sufficient reason to have could be blameworthy for failing to fulfill an obligation that she had at t_i.

6.5 An agent who had, at all times leading up to and including time t_i, all those attitudes that she had decisive reason to have and only those attitudes that she had sufficient reason to have could not be blameworthy for failing to fulfill an obligation that she had at t_i.

6.6 Therefore, the range of alternatives that an agent can be obligated, as of t_i, to perform can be no wider than those that are, as of t_i, scrupulously securable by her.

As I said, I take there to be at least three cogent arguments for the claim that S's being objectively obligated, as of t_i, to φ at t_j implies that S's φ-ing at t_j is, as of t_i, scrupulously securable by S. The second of these arguments concerns the practical nature of both morality and rationality. Thus, I call it the *argument from practicality*. It draws inspiration from similar arguments by David Copp and Holly S. Goldman (now Holly M. Smith)—see COPP 2003 (pp. 271–275) and GOLDMAN 1978 (pp. 194–195). Because normative principles are supposed to be practical, the range of actions that a normative principle can assess, from the standpoint of a given time t_i, can be no wider than the range of actions that are accessible for guidance at t_i itself. And I believe that it is plausible to suppose that an action is accessible for guidance at t_i if and only if it is, as of t_i, scrupulously securable by the agent. For a requirement to perform an action that was not, as of t_i, scrupulously securable by the agent would be of no practical use to the agent, because the agent could not bring herself to perform the required action even by coming to have at t_i (or immediately subsequent to t_i) all those attitudes that she has decisive reason to have and only those attitudes that she has sufficient reason to have. Consider, for instance, that if an agent's φ-ing at t_j is not, as of t_i, scrupulously securable by her, then she cannot, at t_i, either effectively intend to φ at t_j or effectively intend to do anything else that would result in her φ-ing at t_j—at least, not while maintaining a permissible set of background attitudes.[31] It seems, then, that such a prescription would be utterly useless, for not even an agent who was at t_i aware of all the relevant reason-constituting facts and appropriately responsive to these facts could bring herself to fulfill the obligation. And if there is no intention that she can form at t_i (in conjunction with some set of permissible background attitudes) that will ensure that she fulfills her putative obligation at t_i to φ at t_j, then what practical use can she make of such an obligation? None, it would seem.

The third argument is one that I owe, in broad strokes, to Richard Yetter Chappell (2009). I call it the *argument from irrationality*, because it begins with the plausible assumption that it is irrational for an agent to intend at t_i to φ if she knows that she will not φ even if she intends at t_i to φ.[32] In other words, it is irrational to form what one knows would be an ineffective intention. This means that no agent who is at t_i both perfectly rational and fully informed about her present alternatives would ever form at t_i the intention to perform an act that is not, as of t_i, scrupulously securable by her. For being fully informed about her present alternatives she would know that such an intention would, given her rational background attitudes, be ineffective, and her knowing this precludes her from rationally forming such an intention.[33] So unless we want to hold that an agent

---

[31] A subject, S, can at t_i effectively intend to do x at t_j if and only if S would do x at t_j if S were to intend at t_i to do x at t_j.

[32] Many philosophers have endorsed either this thesis or some stronger thesis that entails it. J. H. Sobel claims that "a person cannot intend an action she is sure that she will not do" (1994, p. 239). R. Jay Wallace claims that "the intention to do x requires at least the belief that it is *possible* that one do x" (2001, p. 20). Michael Bratman claims that "there will normally be irrationality in intending to A and believing that one will not A" (1987, p. 38). Gilbert Harman (1976, p. 432) and J. David Velleman (1989) have each claimed that intending to φ entails the belief that one will φ.

[33] I mean for her present alternatives to include not only various alternative actions, but also various alternative intentions. Note, though, that to say that S is at t_i both perfectly rational and fully informed about her present alternatives does not imply that S has been perfectly rational in the past or will be perfectly rational in the future. Indeed, part of what is entailed in S's being, at t_i, fully informed about her present alternatives is knowing what she would do at future times given her predictable lack of perfect rationality at those future times.

can, as of t_i, be objectively rationally required to perform an act that she cannot rationally intend to perform while being both perfectly rational and fully informed about her present alternatives, we must deny that an agent can, as of t_i, be objectively rationally required to perform an act that is not, as of t_i, scrupulously securable by her.[34] And, of course, we should deny that an agent can, as of t_i, be objectively rationally required to perform an act that she cannot rationally intend to perform while being both perfectly rational and fully informed about her present alternatives, for, surely, an agent who is both perfectly rational and fully informed about her present alternatives will form, at t_i, the intention to perform any act that she is, as of t_i, objectively rationally required to perform—provided, of course, that she has the capacity to form that intention. Therefore, we must deny that an agent can, as of t_i, be objectively rationally required to perform an act that is not, as of t_i, scrupulously securable by her.

In thinking about these three arguments, it might be helpful to consider how each would apply to the diet case from above. I will take them in reverse order, starting with the argument from irrationality. Let us assume (1) that I have at 2 P.M. the capacity to intend both to eat grilled chicken and vegetables at 6 P.M. as well as to perform all the acts that are a necessary means to my doing so and (2) that I am at 2 P.M. both perfectly rational and fully informed about my present alternatives. Being fully informed about my present alternatives, I know that, no matter what I now (at 2 P.M.) intend to do, I will not end up eating grilled chicken and vegetables at 6 P.M. And knowing this and being perfectly rational, I cannot rationally intend at 2 P.M. to eat chicken and vegetables at 6 P.M., for it is irrational to form what one knows would be an ineffective intention. And, if I cannot rationally form, at 2 P.M., the intention to eat grilled chicken and vegetables at 6 P.M., then I do not see how I could be, as of 2 P.M., objectively rationally required to eat grilled chicken and vegetables at 6 P.M. How can I be objectively rationally required to do what I cannot form the intention to do when both perfectly rational and fully informed about my present alternatives? It is true that my eating grilled chicken and vegetables at 6 P.M. is, as of 2 P.M., personally possible for me, but it is not, as of 2 P.M., scrupulously securable by me. There is nothing that I can at 2 P.M. do or intend to do while maintaining a rational set of background attitudes that will ensure that I eat grilled chicken and vegetables at

[34] As will become obvious shortly, I do think that an agent can, as of t_i, be objectively rationally required to perform a set of actions that she cannot intend to perform, for it may be that the required set of actions is either too large or too complex for her to intend to perform given her limited cognitive capacities. Nevertheless, I think that such obligations are possible only when the agent has the capacity to form some significantly simpler intention that is sufficient to ensure that she will perform the larger and more complex set of actions. More importantly, I am assuming that it would be possible for her—at least, if her capacities were improved—to *rationally* intend to perform even this larger and more complex set of actions while being both perfectly rational and fully informed about her present alternatives.

6 P.M. Indeed, the situation is worse: no matter what, at 2 P.M., I do or intend to do, I will not eat grilled chicken and vegetables at 6 P.M. so long as I maintain a rational set of background attitudes. But, then, how can I be, as of 2 P.M., under an objective obligation to eat grilled chicken and vegetables at 6 P.M. when, knowing this, rationality prohibits me from intending at 2 P.M. to eat grilled chicken and vegetables at 6 P.M.—an intention that I am otherwise capable of forming?

Next, consider the argument from practicality, and let us assume, for the purposes of seeing how this argument applies to the diet case, that I am at 2 P.M. both aware of all the relevant reason-constituting facts and am appropriately responsive to these facts, thereby coming to have all the attitudes that I have decisive reason to have and only the attitudes that I have sufficient reason to have. But assume that my having such a rational set of attitudes is insufficient to ensure that I will eat grilled chicken and vegetables at 6 P.M. For as we are supposing my eating grilled chicken and vegetables at 6 P.M. is not, as of 2 P.M., scrupulously securable by me. So now suppose that you tell me at 2 P.M. that I am, as of the present, objectively rationally required to eat grilled chicken and vegetables at 6 P.M. What am I supposed to do with this "information"? Given that my eating grilled chicken and vegetables at 6 P.M. is not, as of the present, scrupulously securable by me, there is nothing that I can do with it, for there is no presently available action or intention that would lead to my fulfilling this putative obligation—at least, not while also fulfilling whatever other obligations that I have vis-à-vis my background attitudes. Such an obligation would seem, then, to be utterly useless. And even if *objective* obligations need not be of any practical use to actual agents, they should at least be of practical use to ideal agents (i.e., those who aware of all the relevant reason-constituting facts and appropriately responsive to them), and, as I have said, we are to assume that I am such an agent.

Lastly, for the purposes of seeing how the argument from blameworthiness applies to the diet case, let us further assume that not only do I have at 2 P.M. all the attitudes that I have decisive reason to have and only the attitudes that I have sufficient reason to have, but also that I have had, at all times prior to 2 P.M., all those attitudes that I have had decisive reason to have and only those attitudes that I have had sufficient reason to have. Assume, then, that my weakness of will is not attributable to any mistake on my part, such as my not previously intending to develop a strong will, but is instead attributable to some phenomena completely outside of my rational control—such as, a genetically induced chemical imbalance in my brain. How, then, can we rightly blame me for failing to fulfill the putative obligation that I have at 2 P.M. to eat grilled chicken and vegetables at 6 P.M. For in virtue of what mistake am I to be blamed for not eating grilled chicken and vegetables at 6 P.M.? It seems that there is none.

§§6.3.4 Securitism

Given the above arguments, we should hold that S's being objectively obligated, as of t_i, to φ at t_j implies that S's φ-ing at t_j is, as of t_i, scrupulously securable by S. And, thus, we need a theory of objective rationality that accounts for this fact. I hope to offer such a theory, which I will call (rational) *securitism*. But before I can state the theory, I need to add one more definition to those given above: a set of actions, $α_i$, that is, as of t_i, available to S (i.e., available either in the sense of being personally possible for S or in the sense of being scrupulously securable by S) is a *maximal set of actions* if and only if there is no other set of actions, $α_i$, that is, as of t_i, available to S such that performing $α_i$ involves performing $α_j$ but not vice versa.[35]

I can now state *securitism* as follows:

> **Sec** It is, as of t_i, objectively rationally permissible for S to perform a non-maximal set of actions, $α_j$, beginning at t_j ($t_i < t_j$) if and only if, and because, at least one of the objectively rationally permissible maximal sets of actions that are, as of t_i, scrupulously securable by S involves S's performing $α_j$.[36]

This theory has two rather unusual features. First, it tells us to apply normative principles directly only to maximal sets of actions. We, then, assess a non-maximal set of actions indirectly in terms of whether or not there is some permissible maximal set of actions that involves the agent's performing it. Second, securitism relativizes permissions—and, consequently, obligations—to times.[37] I will explain each of these features below. But, before I do, it is important to note that securitism is not itself a substantive view, for it does not tell us how to assess maximal sets of actions (hereafter: "MSAs"). Securitism is, for instance, neutral with regard to whether the correct normative principles are teleological or non-teleological.

---

[35] What I call a "maximal set of actions" is what Jacob Ross (FORTHCOMING) calls a "maximally specific option." As he points out, "options can be more or less specific. Right now I have the option of *raising my arm*. I also have the more specific options of *raising my arm quickly* and of *raising my arm and raising my leg*. And I have the more general options of *moving my arm* and of *raising my arm or raising my leg*." I am indebted to Ross for helping me arrive at this more precise definition.

[36] Since $t_i < t_j$, Sec tells us only whether S is permitted to perform some prospective act, not whether S was, *ex post facto*, permitted to have performed the act that she did perform. To find out whether S has violated some obligation in having performed some act, we need to ask whether there was, as of some time prior to its performance, an obligation for her to refrain from performing that act. If there was and if that obligation was never canceled (as where one is released from a promise), we can judge, *ex post facto*, that she was wrong to have performed that act.

I defend securitism in greater detail in PORTMORE 2011. See J. ROSS FORTHCOMING, though, for some potential problems concerning securitism (or what he calls "scrupulous securitism").

[37] An act is obligatory if and only if it is the only permissible available alternative—see note 12 in chapter 4.

Of course, given my arguments in chapter 3, I would favor a teleological version of securitism, according to which a given maximal set of actions, MSA_j, is, as of t_i, objectively rationally permissible if and only if, and because, its outcome is not, on S's evaluative ranking, outranked by that of any other MSA that is, as of t_i, scrupulously securable by S.[38] But, for the purposes of this chapter, I will pretend to be neutral as to how MSAs are to be assessed.

Focusing, then, on securitism in general and not on any particular substantive version of securitism, I still need to explain its two unusual features, starting with the fact that it holds that normative principles are to be applied directly only to MSAs. To understand why securitism has this unusual feature, we must first understand why it would be inadequate for a normative theory to assess only *minimal acts*.

Minimal acts are the most basic acts. They are the indivisible atoms of action. Most actions are not minimal acts, as most acts are composed of a number of other more basic acts. For instance, the act of firing a semiautomatic handgun is a compound act that is comprised of a sequence of more basic actions: inserting the magazine, releasing the slide, taking off the safety, taking aim, and squeezing the trigger. Minimal actions, by contrast, do not consist of other more basic acts. As Jordan Howard Sobel explains:

> A *minimal* action is one which, once begun, cannot be stopped by its agent short of completion: once initiated a minimal action is to this extent out of its agent's control. All instantaneous actions are necessarily minimal: for example,...placing a bet. And some non-instantaneous actions are contingently minimal: for example,...beheading by guillotine. (1976, p. 198)

It is fairly obvious that a normative theory must do more than just assess minimal acts. Most of our practical deliberations concern non-minimal acts. For instance, an agent might deliberate about whether to fire a semi-automatic handgun. Or she might deliberate about whether to accelerate while turning right. Or she might deliberate about whether to grade this morning and mow the lawn

---

[38] More specifically, I endorse *teleological maximizing securitism* (TMS): the view according to which all the following are true: (*a*) it is, as of t_i, objectively rationally permissible for S to perform a non-maximal set of actions, α_j, beginning at t_j ($t_i < t_j$) if and only if, and because, it is, as of t_i, objectively rationally permissible for S to perform a maximal set of actions, MSA_j, that involves S's performing α_j; (*b*) it is, as of t_i, objectively rationally permissible for S to perform a maximal set of actions, MSA_j, if and only if, and because, MSA_j is one of the optimal MSAs that is, as of t_i, scrupulously securable by S; (*c*) MSA_j is one of the optimal MSAs that is, as of t_i, scrupulously securable by S if and only if, and because, MSA_j's prospect is not, on S's t_i-relative evaluative ranking, outranked by that of any alternative MSA that is, as of t_i, scrupulously securable by S; and (*d*) MSA_j's prospect is not, on S's t_i-relative evaluative ranking, outranked by that of any alternative MSA that is, as of t_i, scrupulously securable by S if and only if, and because, there is no alternative MSA that is, as of t_i, scrupulously securable by S whose prospect S has at t_i more reason, all things considered, to desire.

tomorrow morning or vice versa. And most of our intentions are intentions to perform non-minimal acts. For instance, I intend to turn the alarm on when I leave the house this morning and then lock the door behind me. And many of our intentions take the form of plans that involve performing sets of actions that extend over substantial periods of time. For instance, this Thursday, I plan on dropping off my daughter at school in the morning, returning home to pack, driving down to Tucson in the early afternoon, picking up my friend at the airport there, and then afterward heading for the Westward Look Resort, which is where we will both be attending a workshop. Since our deliberations and intentions often concern such sets of actions, an adequate normative theory must be able to assess them and not just minimal acts.

There are three possible approaches to using normative principles to assess both minimal actions as well as sets of actions. These are:

The Bottom-Up Approach: Use normative principles to directly assess the permissibility of only minimal acts and then agglomerate to determine the permissibility of non-minimal acts.

The Across-the-Board Approach: Use normative principles to directly assess the permissibility of minimal acts, maximal sets of acts, and everything in between.

The Top-Down Approach: Use normative principles to directly assess the permissibility of only maximal sets of acts and then distribute to determine the permissibility of non-maximal sets of actions, including those that contain only one minimal act.

Securitism employs the top-down approach. To defend securitism, then, I must explain why this approach is superior to the other two alternatives. I will start by considering the bottom-up approach. The problem with this approach is that it must rely on the following implausible principle, which holds that *permissibility agglomerates* over *conjunction* (hence, "PAC"):

PAC $[P(S, t_i, x_1), P(S, t_i, x_2), \ldots, \& \ P(S, t_i, x_n)] \rightarrow P[S, t_i, (x_1, x_2, \ldots, \& \ x_n)]$.

Here, "$P(S, t_i, x_i)$" stands for "S is, as of t_i, permitted to perform x_i."

To see why PAC is implausible, we need to consider only one simple example, which I will call *The Two Medicines*. Assume that Zeke is suffering from a potentially fatal disease. Fortunately, Zeke can cure himself either by taking medicine M1 at t_3 (call this a_1) or medicine M2 at t_5 (call this a_2). He must, however, be careful not to do both, for this would be a lethal combination. Here, then, is a case where, contrary to PAC, an agent is, as of t_1, permitted to perform a_1 and is also, as of t_1, permitted to perform a_2, but is not, as of t_1, permitted to perform both a_1 and a_2. We should, therefore, reject PAC and the approach that presupposes it: namely, the bottom-up approach.

The across-the-board approach does not fare any better. The problem with this approach is that it commits us to denying the following plausible principle, which holds that *permissibility distributes* over *conjunction* (hence: PDC):

PDC $P[S, t_i, (x_1, x_2, \ldots, \& x_n)] \rightarrow [P(S, t_i, x_1), P(S, t_i, x_2), \ldots, \& P(S, t_i, x_n)]$.

To illustrate the problem, consider the following egoistic normative principle:

EGO It is, as of t_i, objectively rationally permissible for S to perform φ if and only if, and because, there is no alternative act that is, as of t_i, personally possible for S that would produce more utility for S than φ would.

If we adopt EGO and take the across-the-board approach, letting "φ" range over minimal acts, maximal sets of actions, and everything in between, then we must reject PDC. To see why, consider the following case, which I base loosely on a case from JACKSON & PARGETTER 1986 (p. 235):

Professor Procrastinate: Professor Procrastinate receives at t_1 an invitation to review a book. He is the best person to do the review and has the time to do it. The best thing for him and for others would be if he accepts the invitation at t_2 and then writes the review when the book arrives at t_4. The second best thing for him and for others would be if he declines the invitation at t_2. The worst thing for him and for others would be if he accepts the invitation at t_2 and then never writes the review, and this is what would in fact happen were he to accept the invitation at t_2. Assume, then, that although Professor Procrastinate's accepting the invitation at t_2 and then writing the review at t_4 is, as of t_1, personally possible for him, it is not, as of t_1, scrupulously securable by him. That is, there is, as of t_1, nothing that he can do or intend to do while maintaining a permissible set of background attitudes that would ensure that he accepts the invitation at t_2 and then writes the review at t_4. No matter how resolute he is at t_1 in his intention to write the review at t_4, he will end up forever procrastinating, thereby failing to ever write the review.

If we take the across-the-board approach and let "φ" range over, among other things, compound acts, EGO implies that it is, as of t_1, permissible for Professor Procrastinate both to accept the invitation at t_2 and to write the review at t_4, for performing this compound act would produce more utility for Professor Procrastinate than any other relevant alternative would. (Here, the relevant alternatives are: (1) both to accept the invitation at t_2 and to refrain from writing the review at t_4; (2) both to decline the invitation at t_2 and to refrain from writing the review at t_4; and (3) both to ignore the invitation at t_2 and to refrain from writing the review at t_4—writing the review at t_4 without accepting the invitation at t_2 is not, I am supposing, an option.) Yet, if we take this across-the-board approach and, thus, let "φ" range over individual acts as well, EGO also implies that it is, as of t_1, impermissible for Professor Procrastinate to accept the invitation at t_2, for doing so would produce less utility for Professor Procrastinate than the only relevant alternative (i.e., declining the invitation) would.

These two implications are jointly incompatible with PDC. Thus, adopting EGO while taking the across-the-board approach forces us to deny PDC. Of course, I have considered only one possible normative principle, namely EGO, but it should be fairly obvious how the result generalizes, for the only way that the top-down approach differs from the across-the-board approach is that the former, but not the latter, ensures that PDC will hold.

I find that denying PDC is high price to pay for adopting the across-the-board approach and so I think that we should reject this approach. But not everyone agrees with me. Some think that it is perfectly plausible to deny PDC. For instance, Jackson and Pargetter claim that there are obvious counterexamples to this sort of principle. The particular principle that they are concerned with is the one that says that "ought" distributes over conjunction, but everything they say with respect to this principle applies to PDC, mutatis mutandis. They say:

> Perhaps an overweight Smith ought to stop smoking and eat less, but it may not be true that he ought to stop smoking. For it may be that were he to stop smoking he would compensate by eating more. It is clear to many overweight smokers, and to their doctors, that they ought to stop smoking and eat less, while it is far from clear to them that they ought to stop smoking. (JACKSON & PARGETTER 1986, p. 247)

Assuming that, typically, S ought to intend to φ if S both ought to φ and has the capacity to intend to φ and that this case is a typical one, then Jackson and Pargetter's remarks suggest both (*i*) that Smith ought, as of t_0, to intend both to stop smoking and to eat less and (*ii*) that Smith ought, as of t_0, to intend not to stop smoking.[39] But this cannot be right, because there is a consistency requirement on intentions. "There is, in particular, a rational demand that one's inten-

---

[39] There may be atypical cases where, although S both ought to φ and has the capacity to intend to φ, S ought not to intend to φ. For instance, someone might hold that Sergio ought to act spontaneously and has the capacity to intend to act spontaneously but ought not to intend to act spontaneously, for such an intention would only be self-defeating. Nevertheless, it is implausible to suppose that smoking and eating less are like acting spontaneously in that they can be done only by not directly intending to do them. Moreover, I am not convinced that such atypical cases are genuine possibilities. In the case of Sergio, for instance, I am inclined to deny that Sergio ought to act spontaneously and hold instead only that he ought to act in whatever way that might cause him to act spontaneously. Perhaps, what he ought to do is to have a couple stiff drinks.

tions, taken together with one's beliefs, fit together into a consistent model of one's future" (BRATMAN 2009, p. 29). We can state this demand more precisely if we stipulate that when someone intends to φ the propositional content of her intention is the proposition that she φs. The requirement, then, is that S ought rationally to be such that the set consisting of all the propositional contents of S's beliefs and all the propositional contents of S's intentions is logically consistent (J. ROSS 2009, p. 244). Now, clearly implications i and ii violate this requirement. Thus, an agent cannot rationally intend not to stop smoking while also intending both to stop smoking and eat less. It seems, then, that Jackson and Pargetter should accept PDC, because otherwise they are committed to the mistaken view that agents are sometimes rationally permitted to have intentions with logically inconsistent propositional contents when, in fact, it is manifestly irrational to have such intentions.

Jackson and Pargetter go wrong, I believe, in thinking that Smith ought, as of t_0, to stop smoking and eat less. If we assume, as they seem to, that if Smith were to stop smoking he would necessarily compensate by eating more, then we should deny that Smith's stopping smoking and eating less is, as of t_0, scrupulously securable by Smith. And since, as I argued above, "ought" implies "scrupulously securable," we should deny their claim that Smith ought, as of t_0, to stop smoking and eat less. And if we do that, we find that this is no counterexample to PDC after all.

The only way to ensure that PDC holds short of accepting the implausible bottom-up approach is to accept the top-down approach. This is the approach that securitism takes. In the case of Professor Procrastinate, securitism implies, given certain plausible assumptions about how to assess maximal sets of actions, that Professor Procrastinate should, as of t_1, decline the invitation. But it denies that Professor Procrastinate should, as of t_1, both accept the invitation and write the review. It denies this, because this is not, as of t_1, scrupulously securable by Professor Procrastinate.

As I mentioned above, securitism has a second unusual feature: it relativizes permissions—and, consequently, obligations—to times. This is necessary because obligations can change over time. For instance, the following is possible: S was, as of t_1, obligated to perform x but is not, as of t_2, obligated to perform x. Obligations can change over time, because both what is personally possible and what is scrupulously securable can change over time and "obligatory" implies both "personally possible" and "scrupulously securable." To illustrate, consider the following:

> Suppose that Smith ought to give her students a list of paper topics on Wednesday. If Smith's obligations do not change over time, then it is always the case that Smith ought to provide the list on Wednesday. Wednesday comes, however, and Smith arrives in class without the list. If "ought" implies "can," it then follows that Smith is able on

Wednesday to give the class the list. Yet although this is something that Smith was once able to do, she is no longer able to do it. (CURRAN 1995, p. 72)

So we either have to reject the plausible view that "ought/obligation" implies "can/personally possible" as well as "scrupulously securable" or accept that obligations and permissions need to be time-indexed. I prefer the latter.[40]

Although securitism has some unusual features not found in other more traditional theories, I think that this is a merit of the view. Traditional theories often fail to account for the fact that our options and hence our obligations change over time. And they often fail to provide criteria for assessing sets of actions, despite the fact that we often deliberate about, and form intentions to perform, sets of actions. For these reasons, I think that securitism is a promising alternative to such traditional normative theories. It is also promising in that it can, as I will show below, account for the basic belief.

§6.4 Securitism and the basic belief

Securitism allows us to account for the basic belief, for, on securitism, it turns out that most choice situations are multiple-option cases, cases in which there is more than one way for the agent to ensure that she performs some rationally permissible maximal set of actions (MSA). Consider, for instance, that S will, on securitism, have the rational option to act either altruistically or self-interestedly at t_1 provided that there is both a rationally permissible MSA that is, as of t_0, scrupulously securable by S in which S acts altruistically at t_1 and a rationally permissible MSA that is, as of t_0, scrupulously securable by S in which S acts self-interestedly at t_1. Furthermore, S will, on securitism, have the rational option of performing any of numerous self-interested acts at t_1 (e.g., watching TV, working on a book, going to the theater, etc.) provided that there is, in each case, a rationally permissible MSA that is, as of t_0, scrupulously securable by S in which S performs that self-interested act at t_1. And the same goes for S's performing any of numerous altruistic acts at t_1.

But will these provisos hold? The answer, I believe, is "yes." We should think that, in most choice situations, there are rationally permissible MSAs in which S performs various different types of self-interested acts as well as rationally permissible MSAs in which S performs various different types of altruistic acts, for no matter what specific criteria we think should be used to assess the permissibility of MSAs, it is clear that in assessing MSAs it often does not matter whether

[40] See GOLDMAN 1976 for more on this issue.

the first act in that set is of one type or another so long as, in the end, the same balance among the various types is achieved.[41]

Thus, the basic belief only seemed puzzling, because we were taking too narrow a view of our choices. If we consider my choice of what to do from a perspective that ignores the fact that my agency is extended over time, it does seem difficult to believe that I have just as much reason to watch TV as to volunteer for Oxfam or to work on this book. But when we take the broader view and compare MSAs that all involve the same (or roughly the same) proportion of relaxing acts, altruistic acts, and career-furthering acts, just in different temporal sequences, we see that they are all equally well supported by reason, for they each constitute an equally effectual means to my performing a rationally permissible MSA.[42] Thus, I have, on securitism, the rational option of performing any one of them now—assuming, of course, that each is, as of now, scrupulously securable by me.[43]

To take a more concrete example, suppose that I am, as of t_0, rationally permitted to perform either a_1 or a_4 at t_1 but that I am, as of t_0, rationally required to perform one of these two at t_1. This means that if we were to look at all of the MSAs that are, as of t_0, scrupulously securable by me, we would find (1) that there is, at least, one rationally permissible MSA in which I perform a_1 at t_1, (2) that there is, at least, one rationally permissible MSA in which I perform a_4 at t_1, and (3) that there is no rationally permissible MSA in which I perform neither a_1 nor a_4 at t_1. So my options are:

(A) Undertake some rationally permissible MSA that involves my performing a_1 at t_1 and, thus, perform a_1 at t_1.

(B) Undertake some rationally permissible MSA that involves my performing a_4 at t_1 and, thus, perform a_4 at t_1.

(C) Undertake some rationally impermissible MSA that involves neither my performing a_1 at t_1 nor my performing a_4 at t_1 and, thus, perform neither a_1 nor a_4 at t_1.

This is clearly a multiple-option case, for there is more than one way for me to achieve the same end: that of undertaking some rationally permissible MSA. One

---

[41] I admit that sometimes that which I perform now will affect whether a reasonable balance will be achieved in the end, for sometimes the only way to ensure that I will do two things is to get the less attractive option over with first. In such instances, procrastination with respect to the less attractive option is irrational. I will have more to say about this in §§6.5.5.

[42] I believe that a number of MSAs, containing *different* proportions of relaxing acts, altruistic acts, and career-furthering acts, can all be rationally permissible. I will have more to say about this in §§6.5.2.

[43] I am assuming that much of the time our present intentions are effective. Thus, I am assuming, for instance, that if I were to intend this morning to relax this afternoon and work this evening, then that is what I would do and that, if I were instead to intend this morning to work this afternoon and relax this evening, then I would do that instead.

way is by opting for A, and another is by opting for B. And the reason that I have to perform a_1 (or a_4) at t_1 (viz., that doing so is a means to my performing a rationally permissible MSA) is an imperfect reason, for it is equally a reason for me to perform a_4 (or a_1) at t_1.

Return now to Gert's case, where the permissible options are:

(*a*) Make a sacrifice for an altruistic reason.

(*b*) Do not make the sacrifice [italics mine]. (2003, p. 13)

Gert denies that this is a multiple-option case, for he claims that "such pairs cannot plausibly be construed as alternate ways of pursuing the same end or acting on the same reasons" (2003, p. 13). However, he gives no argument for this claim; he must just think that it is obvious. But it is not at all obvious. Indeed, as I have shown, options *a* and *b* could be two alternative ways of pursuing the end of performing some rationally permissible MSA. Furthermore, options *a* and *b* can be construed as two alternative ways of acting on the same reason: specifically, the imperfect reason that I have to perform any set of actions that constitutes a means to my performing a rationally permissible MSA. Indeed, Gert's options *a* and *b* could just be my options A and B above.

Of course, if securitism is to account for the basic belief, it must do more than just account for options *a* and *b* being rationally optional, it must also account for the fact that they remain rationally optional even after the strength and/or number of reasons in favor of just one of them has increased slightly. Suppose, for instance, that I am choosing between (*a**) volunteering for Oxfam today and relaxing tomorrow and (*b**) relaxing today and volunteering for Oxfam tomorrow. Call option *a** "VOLUNTEER-RELAX" and call option *b** "RELAX-VOLUNTEER." Assume that both options are rationally permissible, for it does not matter which I do today and which I do tomorrow, as the same ends will be achieved either way. But now suppose that things have just changed. Suppose that although Oxfam has always provided each volunteer with a pre-packaged cookie, Oxfam has just announced a new special incentive for volunteering today: today and *today only* each volunteer will receive a freshly baked cookie. It seems, then, that I now have an additional reason to perform VOLUNTEER-RELAX as opposed to RELAX-VOLUNTEER: namely, I will receive a more delicious cookie if I do.[44] So the question arises: If, previously, there was a rational option for me to perform either RELAX-VOLUNTEER or VOLUNTEER-RELAX when Oxfam was not offering a freshly baked cookie to those who volunteer today, why isn't VOLUNTEER-RELAX now rationally required given that there is this new and additional reason for performing this option? Can securitism account for these two options (RELAX-VOLUNTEER and

---

[44] Whereas there is no reason to prefer receiving a cookie today to receiving one on some later day, there is a reason to prefer receiving a freshly baked cookie today to receiving a pre-packaged one on some later day—or so I will assume.

VOLUNTEER-RELAX) being rationally permissible both before and after the addition of this new reason for performing VOLUNTEER-RELAX?

Interestingly, securitism can and without appealing to satisficing, incommensurability, or anything else similarly controversial—provided, that is, that we accept the following two plausible assumptions, which I label "A1" and "A2":

A1 If it is rationally permissible for an agent with options (a) φ-ψ and (b) ψ-φ to perform whichever one she prefers (that is, to perform φ and ψ in whichever order—either (a) φ-ψ or (b) ψ-φ—she feels like performing them), and if it is rationally permissible for her preference to shift from one option to the other, then she has, in the ordinary sense, the rational option of performing either (a) φ-ψ or (b) ψ-φ even though she is, in some stricter sense, rationally required to perform the preferred option.

A2 Some slight increase in the number and/or strength of the reasons that favor the non-preferred option is typically insufficient to outweigh the strength of the reasons that the agent has to perform the preferred option.[45]

Given A1 and A2, securitism can account for the fact that RELAX-VOLUNTEER remains rationally optional even after there is some slight increase in the strength and/or number of the reasons that favor VOLUNTEER-RELAX, as where Oxfam is providing, today and *today only*, each volunteer with a freshly baked cookie. To illustrate, assume that all the rationally permissible MSAs that are, of this moment, scrupulously securable by me include my performing whichever option I prefer. So if, on the one hand, I prefer RELAX-VOLUNTEER to VOLUNTEER-RELAX, then all the rationally permissible MSAs that are presently scrupulously securable by me will include my performing RELAX-VOLUNTEER. But if, on the other hand, I prefer VOLUNTEER-RELAX to RELAX-VOLUNTEER, then all the rationally permissible MSAs that are presently scrupulously securable by me will include my performing VOLUNTEER-RELAX.

Now let us suppose that, in fact, I prefer RELAX-VOLUNTEER to VOLUNTEER-RELAX. In that case, all the rationally permissible MSAs that are presently scrupulously securable by me will include my performing RELAX-VOLUNTEER. And even if

---

[45] Let me stipulate that the "preferred option" is the one that would best satisfy the agent's preferences over time. But if no kind of desire/preference could ever provide an agent with a reason for action, then we should take "the preferred option" to stand for "the option that would provide the agent with the most enjoyment over time given her rationally optional likes and dislikes." For an argument that the kind of desire that is at play here can provide an agent with a reason for action, see CHANG 2004b. I do not want to endorse her argument, though. Instead, I prefer to remain neutral on the issue.

Oxfam offers the new enticement of a freshly baked cookie, it will still be that all the rationally permissible MSAs that are presently scrupulously securable by me include my performing RELAX-VOLUNTEER, for, as A2 states, this slight increase in the strength of the reasons that favor my performing VOLUNTEER-RELAX is insufficient to outweigh the strength of the reasons that I have to go with my preferred option—namely, RELAX-VOLUNTEER.

Of course, the reader may wonder: In what sense is there a rational option to perform VOLUNTEER-RELAX if all the rationally permissible MSAs that are presently scrupulously securable by me include my performing RELAX-VOLUNTEER instead? The answer is: "in the ordinary sense." As A1 states, if I am rationally permitted to perform whichever option I prefer, and if I am rationally permitted to prefer either one, then I have, in the ordinary sense, the rational option to perform either. This is just what it means to have a rational option. When we say, for instance, that Grace has the rational option to choose either soup or salad with her entrée, we do not mean that it would be rational for her to choose soup even if she prefers salad. Rather, what we mean is that she has the rational option of choosing whichever one she prefers and that she is not rationally required to have, or to stick with, one preference as opposed to the other. If this is right, then an agent has a rational option so long as the antecedents in A1 are met. And, as I have just argued, they are, on securitism, met in the case in which I am choosing between RELAX-VOLUNTEER and VOLUNTEER-RELAX.[46] What's more, it seems that, given A2, securitism implies that these two options remain rationally optional (in the ordinary sense given by A1) even after there is a slight increase in the number and/or strength of the reasons that favor just one of them.[47]

Things get a bit more interesting, however, when we increase the stakes. Suppose, for instance, that Oprah Winfrey is offering, today and today only, to give to each volunteer a brand-new car. If so, it would seem foolish of me to pass up this unique opportunity to receive a free car, even if I would, other things being

---

[46] But what if my performing VOLUNTEER-RELAX as opposed to RELAX-VOLUNTEER would have disastrous consequences down the road? Suppose that I am going to meet a potential new friend named Harvey if and only if I volunteer today. And let us suppose that I am going to be driving through a certain intersection at a certain time (on my way to Harvey's house) if and only if I meet him. Lastly, assume that a drunk driver is going run through this intersection against the red light at precisely this time, such that, if I am there too, I am going die in a horrible automobile accident. In that case, the antecedents in A1 would not, on securitism, be met. On securitism, I would, in such a case, be objectively rationally required to perform RELAX-VOLUNTEER regardless of which option I happen to prefer, although I may be subjectively rationally permitted to perform VOLUNTEER-RELAX given my ignorance of these disastrous future consequences. The idea that I am objectively rationally required to perform RELAX-VOLUNTEER in this case seems, upon reflection, to be the correct result. Note, then, that although I am concerned to defend the basic belief, I am not concerned to defend the view that we have as many rational options as we initially take ourselves to have. Indeed, I hold, on the basis of reflection, that we likely have fewer rational options than we initially take ourselves to have.

[47] This account of rational options is one that I borrow from BRATMAN 1994, pp. 330–331. See also PORTMORE 2003, pp. 328–331.

equal, prefer RELAX-VOLUNTEER to VOLUNTEER-RELAX. Here, then, there seems to be more than just a slight increase in the strength and/or number of the reasons that favor my performing VOLUNTEER-RELAX. Thus, whatever reason I have to perform my preferred option (viz., RELAX-VOLUNTEER) is not going to be strong enough to outweigh the reason that I now have to perform my non-preferred option (viz., VOLUNTEER-RELAX). So securitism would seem to imply that I am now, given Winfrey's offer, rationally required to perform VOLUNTEER-RELAX. And this seems to be the correct result.

But, now, consider a variation on this case in which Bill Gates is offering, today and today only, to donate an extra $200 to Oxfam for each person who volunteers *today*. And let us assume that this extra $200 would be enough to provide measles immunizations for an additional ten children. It may seem that, here too, the new and additional reason that I now have for performing VOLUNTEER-RELAX constitutes more than just a slight increase in the strength and/or number of the reasons for doing so. And, thus, securitism may seem to imply that I am rationally required to perform VOLUNTEER-RELAX even if I would, other things being equal, prefer to perform RELAX-VOLUNTEER. This, I suspect, will seem counterintuitive, but let me suggest that securitism need not have this putative implication, as I now explain.

Securitism will have this counterintuitive implication only if the additional reason that Gates's offer provides constitutes more than just a slight increase in the strength of the reasons for my performing VOLUNTEER-RELAX. But it seems to me that the strength of my reasons for taking advantage of this special opportunity to help others varies greatly depending on whether or not my doing so is essential to my taking the welfare of others as one of my ultimate ends. If, on the one hand, my taking advantage of this particular opportunity is essential to my counting as someone who takes the welfare of others as an ultimate end, then I will likely have most reason to complete an MSA in which I take advantage of the opportunity that Gates's offer provides—that is, one that involves my performing VOLUNTEER-RELAX. But if, on the other hand, my taking advantage of this particular opportunity is not essential to my counting as someone who takes the welfare of others as an ultimate end, then I will likely have most reason to complete whichever MSA would best further my interests, which could be one that involves my performing RELAX-VOLUNTEER instead. Or so I will argue.

It seems to me, as well as to others who have been similarly inspired by Kant's remarks on imperfect duties, that we are both morally and rationally required to adopt the welfare (or happiness) of others as an ultimate end.[48] That is, we are required "to make the happiness of others a serious, major, continually relevant,

---

[48] I borrow the term "an ultimate end" from Robert Noggle, who uses it to refer to "an intrinsic end that is a fundamental and indispensible part of the agent's life" (2009, p. 8). An agent's ultimate ends may include such things as the happiness of others, the well-being of her loved ones, and the perfection of herself.

life-shaping end" (HILL 2002, p. 206).[49] And this requirement in turn entails a further one: to act throughout our lives so as to exhibit a sufficient propensity to promote the happiness of others. Having such a propensity is, after all, constitutive of having adopted the happiness of others as an ultimate end. If, for instance, someone with the usual abilities and opportunities does nothing to promote the happiness of others, this would show that she has not truly adopted the happiness of others as an ultimate end (HILL 2002, p. 204).

It is important to note, though, that having a propensity to A does not imply that one takes advantage of every favorable opportunity to A, as Robert Noggle explains:

> To say that Fred has a propensity to drink alcohol does not mean that Fred drinks whenever possible or even at every favorable opportunity. Fred may retain a propensity to drink even if he sometimes turns down drinks at parties that are good opportunities for drinking. Thus, one or a few failures to A even at good opportunities for Aing need not raise any doubts about a person having a propensity to A. However a pattern of continual failures to A despite many favorable opportunities *would* cast doubt on the claim that a person has a propensity to A. (2009, p. 7)

Likewise, it seems that unless I have exhibited a pattern of failing to take advantage of good opportunities to help others, I can turn down this particular opportunity to help others, performing RELAX-VOLUNTEER, and still count as having adopted the welfare of others as an ultimate end. And this is so even if my performing VOLUNTEER-RELAX represents a particularly good opportunity for me to benefit others in that Gates is going to donate an extra $200 if I do. So, in this case, it seems that I would count as someone who takes the welfare of others as an ultimate end whether I perform RELAX-VOLUNTEER or VOLUNTEER-RELAX. Thus, my performing VOLUNTEER-RELAX simply is not essential to my counting as someone who takes the welfare of others as an ultimate end.

Furthermore, it seems to me that, in those instances in which I will count as having taken the welfare of others as an ultimate end either way, the primary determiner of whether I should perform an MSA that involves my performing VOLUNTEER-RELAX or one that involves my performing RELAX-VOLUNTEER is which option would best promote my self-interest, which in turn is likely determined by which I prefer.[50] Here, we come close to what James Griffin calls a

---

[49] I think that we are also required to adopt other things as ultimate ends—things such as our own perfection and the happiness and perfection of our children.

[50] This does not mean that that it will be objectively rational for me to continue to put off helping others until my doing so is no longer consistent with my having adopted the welfare of others as an ultimate end. In some instances, it will be in my self-interest to help others sooner rather than later, as where, for instance, I prefer VOLUNTEER-RELAX to RELAX-VOLUNTEER.

discontinuity in value. Take two values A and B. These values are *discontinuous* if "so long as we have enough of B any amount of A outranks any further amount of B" (1986, p. 85). Of course, we do not quite have a discontinuity in value here, for I do not think that the priority is absolute. It seems to me that even if one has enough beneficence in one's life to count as leading a life that is full and meaningful, a life that is exceedingly better in terms of beneficence could outrank even a life that is somewhat better in terms of one's self-interest.[51] Likewise, a life that is moderately better in terms of beneficence could outrank a life that is only the slightest bit better in terms of one's self-interest. Nevertheless, so long as we restrict ourselves to MSAs in which one counts as having taken the welfare of others as an ultimate end, then the rationally permissible MSAs will *tend* to be the ones that are best in terms of one's self-interest.

So, despite initial appearances, it seems that the additional reason that Gates's offer provides for my performing VOLUNTEER-RELAX as opposed to RELAX-VOL-UNTEER amounts to no more than a slight increase in the strength of the reasons to do so—at least, this is so assuming that I have not regularly failed to take advantage of good opportunities to promote the welfare of others and that I plan to perform a set of actions that will ensure that I perform an MSA in which I take advantage of such opportunities sufficiently often.[52] And thus it is both this fact and A2 that explains why my performing RELAX-VOLUNTEER remains rationally permissible even after Gates provides me with an additional reason to perform VOLUNTEER-RELAX instead.

Of course, it may be that were Gates to offer to donate enough extra money for my volunteering today, it would, then, cease to make sense for me to perform RELAX-VOLUNTEER, for it may be that certain opportunities are so exceptionally good that one could not count as having adopted the welfare of others as an ultimate end and yet pass them up.[53] But the chance to ensure that Oxfam receives an

---

[51] The talk of "enough beneficence" can be misleading. The idea is not that there is some cap on how much beneficence can be required of us such that once we have exceeded this cap we can no longer be required to do anything more for the sake of others. This is implausible, for it seems that no matter how much we have already done for the sake of others, we could still be required to do more, as where, for instance, we happen upon a child drowning in a shallow pond, whom we can save at very little cost to ourselves. So although we do need to be sufficiently beneficent to count as having adopted the welfare of others as an ultimate end, the fact that the duty of beneficence consists in the duty to make the welfare of others "a serious, major, continually relevant, life-shaping end" (HILL 2002, p. 206) means that this duty is never over and done with—see NOGGLE 2009, especially p. 12.

[52] If I have exhibited a pattern of failing to take advantage of good opportunities to help others, then there will come a point at which I can no longer continue to do so and still count as having adopted the welfare of others as an ultimate end. At this point, taking advantage of this opportunity is, given my past neglect, rationally required.

[53] Also, if the example were changed so that I could ensure that Oxfam receives an extra $200 by sacrificing merely the fulfillment of some very trivial preference (such as, the slight preference I have to write out addresses in print as opposed to cursive), I might, then, be required to make this small sacrifice (thereby sacrificing some very small portion of my self-interest) even if my doing so is not

additional \$200 does not seem to be this sort of "golden opportunity," as there are typically plenty of other such opportunities to ensure that Oxfam receives an additional \$200.[54]

These are, at any rate, my views on the matter. If readers have other views about how to assess the rational permissibility of MSAs, they should apply them, not my views, when evaluating securitism. The point has been to show only that securitism need not imply that, in the case in which Gates offers to contribute an extra \$200 for each of those who volunteer today, I am rationally required to perform VOLUNTEER-RELAX. Of course, some readers may not agree with some of my assumptions, but, regardless, they should think that securitism has counterintuitive implications only if they think either (1) that there are instances in which an agent is rationally permitted to perform a certain course of action even though she is rationally prohibited from performing any MSA in which she performs that course of action or (2) that there are instances in which an agent is rationally prohibited from performing a certain course of action even though she is rationally permitted to perform some MSA in which she performs that course of action. So, for instance, one should think that securitism has counterintuitive implications in the Gates Case only if one thinks either (1) that I am rationally permitted to perform RELAX-VOLUNTEER even though there is no rationally permissible MSA in which I perform RELAX-VOLUNTEER or (2) that I am rationally prohibited from performing RELAX-VOLUNTEER even though there is some rationally permissible MSA in which I perform RELAX-VOLUNTEER.

§6.5 Securitism's suppositions and implications

In this the last section of the chapter, I wish to explore securitism further. Doing so will help us to better understand the theory as well as to stave off some potential misconceptions about the view. I will start by considering whether securitism must make any implausible suppositions to account for the basic belief. To account for the basic belief, securitists must suppose that what matters most is that agents perform maximal sets of actions (MSAs) that achieve a reasonable balance between various worthy ends and that it often matters very little, if at all, in which order these ends are pursued. Some might worry, though, that securitists must implausibly further suppose that the best way to balance the various competing ends will be the same for each of us and that, for each of us, there will be only one

---

essential to my leading a full and meaningful life. As I say above, it seems to me that even if one has enough beneficence in one's life to count as leading a full and meaningful life, a life that is moderately better in terms of beneficence may outrank a life that is only the slightest bit better in terms of one's self-interest.

[54] Again there is no cap on the amount of beneficence that can be required of us. Thus, no matter how beneficent one has been in the past, there may be certain "golden opportunities" that everyone is required to take advantage of—see NOGGLE 2009, p. 12.

way to optimally balance these ends. I show that this is not the case. I also show that although securitism presupposes that some very complex and highly speci-fied MSAs are obligatory, it does not presuppose that agents can form the inten-tion to perform each and every act that is included in such MSAs. Lastly, I turn to securitism's implications with regard to end-of-life decisions, procrastination, and Warren Quinn's self-torturer puzzle. I argue that securitism has plausible implications in each instance.

§§6.5.1 Does securitism implausibly suppose that the best way to balance the various competing factors in our lives is the same for each of us?

We all have to balance various competing factors in our lives: such as career, family, entertainment, personal projects, and the welfare of others. But it would be a mis-take to suppose that the best way to balance these competing factors is going to be the same for each of us. It is not as if the best MSA for each of us is going to contain the same proportions of various worthy pursuits, as where, say, 40% of the acts in such an MSA would be focused on furthering one's career, another 40% would be focused on our family and friends, and the remaining 20% would be focused on helping others. As I see it, there are no universally ideal proportions.

What is important is that each of us leads a life that is full and meaningful, but there are many different paths to such a life. Living a full and meaningful life requires that each of us adopt certain ultimate ends—the welfare of others being one of them. But the fact that we should each have this as our end does not entail that we should each dedicate the same percentage of our resources to helping others. Indeed, someone with abundant resources and limited familial obligations would be required to perform an MSA in which a much higher percentage of her actions are focused on helping strangers than, say, someone else with limited resources and a disabled child to care for.

So we are not each required to dedicate the same percentage of our resources to a given end. Nor are we required to adopt the same specific set of ends. Even if there are certain broadly construed ends that we should each adopt in order to live full and meaningful lives, these ends will, in practice, yield different derivative ends for different people. Take the end of developing one's talents. For one person, it will mean adopting the development of one's musical gifts as an end. For another, it will mean adopting the development of one's philosophical talents as an end. So, different people will need to take different paths to a full and mean-ingful life. Moreover, of those MSAs that one could perform so as to put one on the path to leading a full and meaningful life, some will be more choice-worthy than others given one's individual psychological traits. Consider, for instance, that although we all need enjoyment in our lives, we enjoy different things. Whereas some find skydiving exhilarating, others find it terrifying.

In sum, the best way to balance various competing factors in our lives is going to vary from person to person, for a lot is going to depend on each person's individual circumstances and psychological traits. In virtue of this, which MSAs, with which sorts of proportions of various sorts of activities, will be rationally permissible will vary from one individual to another.

§§6.5.2 Does securitism implausibly suppose that, for each of us, there is only one way to optimally balance the various competing factors in our lives?

As noted above, how any individual should optimally balance the various competing factors in her life is going to depend a great deal on her own individual circumstances and psychological traits. But even given a particular set of circumstances and psychological traits, there can be more than one way to optimally balance two or more competing factors. For instance, trading $30,000 for a Honda Accord might, for a given individual, be just as good as trading $70,000 for a Jaguar XJ. Each of these two trades may strike, what is for her, an optimal tradeoff between savings and luxury. Likewise, there may be more than one way for a person to strike an optimal balance between, say, altruism and self-interest. Imagine, for instance, a young doctor who must choose to work either for the Mount Sinai Medical Center in New York or for Doctors without Borders in Africa. The former offers the chance to live in greater material comfort and to employ more sophisticated medical techniques, whereas the latter trades less of these goods for the opportunity to do more good. Both, then, involve a certain trade-off between altruism and self-interest, but both trade-offs may be just as good. So, on securitism, it may be that, for each person, there is a range of different trade-offs among various competing goods that all count as optimal.

§§6.5.3 Does securitism implausibly suppose that agents can form the intention to perform each and every act that is included in some very large and complex MSA?

Securitism presupposes that MSAs can be permissible, impermissible, and even obligatory. Yet, in most instances, it would be impossible for a human agent to intend to perform each and every act in which these MSAs consist. This is because many of these MSAs include literally millions of acts performed over multiple decades. Given the limits of human comprehension, no human could ever form the intention to perform each and every act contained within such large and complex MSAs.

A human agent could, however, form the intention to achieve an end (or set of ends) that requires her to perform such a very large and complex set of actions. To illustrate, consider that, when I was younger, I formed the intention to earn a PhD in philosophy and that this was an end that I could achieve only by performing a very large and complex set of actions. At the time, I had only the foggiest notion of all that I would need to do to succeed. So even though I did not form the intention to perform some highly specified set of actions culminating in my receiving a PhD in philosophy, I did form the general intention to do pretty much whatever it takes (within reason) to earn a PhD in philosophy. And this intention, we will suppose, is what led me down the path that culminated in my having performed the very large and complex set of actions needed to earn a PhD in philosophy. These sorts of general intentions are not at all beyond human limits, and this is all that the proponent of securitism needs. On securitism, I am obligated to perform some MSA, because there is some fairly general intention (say, the intention to pursue a PhD in philosophy) that will—or, at least, will likely—lead me to perform each and every act included within the obligatory MSA.

§§6.5.4 Is it problematic that securitism implies that as we approach the end of our lives our rational options narrow considerably?

Suppose that I am deciding whether to spend this Sunday at the beach with my family or at home alone watching football on TV. On securitism, both would typically be rationally optional, for there would typically be both a rationally permissible MSA that is presently scrupulously securable by me in which I spend today watching TV and spend some later day doing something with my family and a rationally permissible MSA that is presently scrupulously securable by me in which I spend today doing something with my family and spend some later day watching TV (or doing something else similarly relaxing). What is important is that I take advantage of both opportunities to relax and opportunities to spend time with my family and that I do each sufficiently often, but it does not generally matter which I do on any particular occasion.

But now suppose that this is my last day of life. In that case, I have no future opportunities beyond today. And so the choice is no longer between doing one of these activities today and the other on some later day, but is instead between doing one of them today and the other never again. And I am inclined to think that if my choice is between spending my last day with my family and spending it alone watching TV, I ought spend it with my family even if, not knowing that my death is imminent, I happen to prefer, other things being equal, to spend the day alone watching TV.[55]

Far from being objectionable, this implication seems to be a merit of the view. After all, I cannot see how any fully informed and well-meaning advisor would recommend that I spend my last day alone watching TV. Surely, there is something better I could be doing on my last day! So I think that securitism is right to imply that as we approach the end of our lives our rational options narrow considerably.[56]

---

[55] Of course, given that I am going to die today, other things are not equal.

[56] And note that if the explanation for the basic belief lay with the incommensurability of values (Raz) or the fact that reasons have two potentially separable dimensions of rational strength (Gert), then we should not expect a narrowing of one's options as one approaches the end of one's life.

But now consider a different sort of case. Suppose that I am on my deathbed dictating my last will and testament. And let us assume that I have already provided for my family's continued financial security, as I have taken out a rather substantial life-insurance policy with them as the beneficiaries. Some might claim that, having provided for my family's financial security, I am rationally permitted to do almost anything with my estate that would not be harmful, leaving it to any individual or organization or even using it to purchase some extravagant funeral for myself—one in which, say, my body is blasted out into space (see COCHRANE 2009).

I am not so sure. First, let us take the case in which I have so far exhibited throughout my life a sufficient concern for others, having clearly adopted the welfare of others as one of my ultimate ends. Since having such a concern for others does not necessitate taking advantage of every good opportunity to help others, I could pass up this (my last) opportunity to help others and still count as having led a full and meaningful life. Given this, it seems that it might be rationally permissible for me to use the money for my own benefit by, say, creating an open-access, digital archive of my work. Of course, it might also be permissible for me to donate my entire estate to charity. Which of these two options would in the end be best would depend, I think, on which would best serve my interests, which in turn would depend on whether I happen to care more about helping others to an even greater extent than I already have or more about ensuring that my work is made widely available. I do not, however, think that it would be rationally permissible for me to leave my estate to some random well-to-do stranger or to spend it on some extravagant funeral in which my body is blasted out into space. Given my particular cares and concerns, either action would seem positively foolish.

Now, consider the case in which I have not lived a life in which I have exhibited having adopted the welfare of others as one of my ultimate ends. Unfortunately, nothing I can do now will change this. I was required to have adopted the happiness of others as "a serious, major, continually relevant, life-shaping end" (HILL 2002, p. 206), and I did not. The best I can do now is to atone for this moral failure. So the question becomes: Which course of action is more choice-worthy—the one in which I atone for my previous selfishness by leaving most, if not all, of my estate to some charitable organization or the one in which I continue to act for my own benefit, using the money to set up a digital archive of my work? I think that the former is more choice-worthy. And if this is right, then (maximizing) securitism implies that it would be rationally impermissible for me to use the money for my own benefit.[57]

Of course, all this is based on the assumption that there is no rationally permissible MSA that is presently scrupulously securable by me in which I use the money for my own benefit instead of donating it to charity. But if the reader thinks otherwise, then she should think that securitism has different implica-

---

[57] Maximizing securitism holds that a given MSA is objectively rationally permissible if and only if there is not more reason to perform some alternative MSA. We do not have to adopt maximizing securitism, but it is interesting to see how even maximizing securitism can account for the basic belief.

tions. For instance, if it turns out that I am wrong and that, even in this case, the MSA in which I use the money to set up the digital archive of my work is in fact rationally permissible, then securitism will imply that using my estate to do this is rationally permissible. Again, the reader should think that securitism is unacceptable only if her views on what it is, as of the present, rationally permissible to do is incompatible with her views about which of the presently scrupulously securable MSAs are rationally permissible.

§§6.5.5 What does securitism imply about procrastination?

Securitism has plausible implications concerning the rational permissibility of procrastination. To illustrate, suppose that there are two things that I need to get done today: exercise and finish grading some exams. Let us suppose that I usually exercise in the morning, because I find that if I put it off until the afternoon, I often lack the willpower to exercise. But let us suppose that I really prefer to finish my grading this morning and put off exercising until this afternoon, which is when the weather is supposed to be ideal for a run. Whether it is permissible for me to put off exercising until this afternoon depends, according to securitism, on whether there is some plan, resolution, or other intention that I could form now that would ensure that I finish grading this morning and exercise this afternoon. If there is, then that is what I should plan on doing. If there is not, if the only way to ensure that I both exercise and finish grading today (short of forming some irrational background attitudes) is to plan on exercising this morning and finish grading this afternoon, then this is what I ought to do.

Securitism, thus, plausibly supposes that whether it is objectively rationally permissible for an agent to put something off for later depends on whether she can effectively intend to do so. If her present intention will be effective in ensuring that she succeeds in doing it later, then it is permissible, other things being equal, for her to put it off. But if there is no present intention that would ensure that she succeeds in doing it later, then she should not, other things being equal, put it off and should instead do it now.[58]

§§6.5.6 What does securitism imply about cases such as Warren Quinn's case of the self-torturer?

Consider Warren Quinn's famous puzzle of the self-torturer:

> Suppose there is a medical device that enables doctors to apply electric current to the body in increments so tiny that the patient cannot feel

---

[58] I include these other-things-being-equal clauses because the objective rational status of putting something off does not just depend on whether one can effectively intend to do so. It also depends on whether some disastrous unforeseen consequence would result from your putting it off.

them. The device has 1001 settings: 0 (off) and 1...1000. Suppose someone (call him the self-torturer) agrees to have the device, in some conveniently portable form, attached to him in return for the following conditions: The device is initially set at 0. At the start of each week he is allowed a period of free experimentation in which he may try out and compare different settings, after which the dial is returned to its previous position. At any other time, he has only two options—to stay put or to advance the dial one setting. But he may advance only one step each week, and he may *never* retreat. *At each advance he gets $10,000.*

Since the self-torturer cannot feel any difference in comfort between adjacent settings, he appears to have a clear and repeatable reason to increase the voltage each week. The trouble is that there *are* noticeable differences in comfort between settings that are sufficiently far apart. Indeed, if he keeps advancing, he can see that he will eventually reach settings that will be so painful that he would then gladly relinquish his fortune and return to 0.

The self-torturer is not alone in his predicament. Most of us are like him in one way or another. We like to eat but also care about our appearance. Just one more bite will give us pleasure and will not make us look fatter; but very many bites will. And there may be similar connections between puffs of pleasant smoking and lung cancer, or between pleasurable moments of idleness and wasted lives. (1990, p. 79)

As Quinn notes, although the self-torturer's situation is highly unusual, most of us face similar predicaments on a regular basis. It is important, then, for a theory of objective rationality to offer plausible suggestions as to what one should do when facing such predicaments. Securitism does. To see this, let us assume that the self-torturer will, after the 1,000 weeks are over, rightly regret having advanced the dial as many times as he did if and only if he advances the dial more than n times. Given Quinn's stipulations, it is clear that $n < 1,000$. Now suppose that the self-torturer faces the decision of whether to advance the dial a step during some particular week short of n weeks into it. According to securitism, the self-torturer should advance a step this particular week only if there is some intention to φ such that, if the self-torturer were to intend now to φ, he would end up advancing no more than n times altogether. Suppose, then, that it is the first week and the setting is at zero. Suppose that the self-torturer has played around with various settings and determined that the best trade-off between pain and money lies with advancing the dial exactly n steps. Suppose, then, that he resolves to advance the dial the next n weeks and to stop after the nth week. There are two possibilities. Perhaps, his resolution will hold. Perhaps, he will advance n weeks, and come the following week he will not reconsider his intention to advance only n steps and will stand firm at n steps. If this is what would happen, then the self-torturer is permitted, other things being equal, to advance a step each of the next n weeks.

However, there is another possibility. After advancing the first n weeks, the self-torturer might be tempted to reconsider his earlier intention to stop after the nth week. He might, then, try advancing the dial a step the following week and find that there is no discernable difference. Finding that there is no discernable difference and wanting an additional $10,000, perhaps he will reconsider his earlier intention and decide to advance another step beyond n steps. Perhaps, he continues to do this. In the end, he ends up in so much pain that he would gladly return all the money to return to the zero setting. If this is what would happen, then securitism implies that the self-torturer should not advance a step this week—assuming, of course, that he can prevent this from happening by not advancing a step this week. Thus, securitism plausibly implies that whether the self-torturer should advance a step this week depends on whether his resolution to advance no more than n steps will hold firm even if he advances this week. If it will, he should, other things being equal, advance. If it will not, he should not. And this all seems quite plausible.

***

In this chapter, I have argued that we can account for the basic belief without appealing to any controversial assumptions such as the assumption that, in most choice situations, the relevant reasons are incommensurable or have two separable dimensions of strength (rational justifying strength and rational requiring strength). I have argued that we can account for the basic belief by appealing to only that which all sides agree on: that there are multiple-option cases and that in such cases the relevant imperfect reasons provide equal reason for pursuing each of the equally attractive means to achieving the relevant end. I have argued that, ultimately, what agents have most reason to do is to perform rationally permissible maximal sets of acts (MSAs). And the reason an agent has to perform some rationally permissible MSA is an imperfect reason, for it equally supports all the various other particular acts that each constitutes a means to performing some rationally permissible MSA. Since, in most choice situations, many of the available act alternatives constitute a way of acting on this imperfect reason, we find that the relevant reasons permit performing any of these various act alternatives. And this, I have argued, is how we can best account for the basic belief.

In the process of making these arguments, I have developed and defended a new theory of objective rationality, which I call (rational) securitism. I have argued that this theory is promising not only because it enables us to account for the basic belief, but also because it provides plausible verdicts as to both the permissibility of procrastination and the permissibility of advancing a step in Quinn's self-torturer case. Moreover, securitism allows us to meet Kagan's objection while holding onto the account of agent-centered options that I defended in the previous chapter.

In the next chapter, I apply the lessons learned in this chapter—in particular, (*i*) that "obligatory" implies "scrupulously securable," (*ii*) that permissions and obligations must be time-indexed, and (*iii*) that we need to be able to assess not only the deontic statuses of minimal acts but also that of MSAs and of everything in between—to moral theory, arguing that they have important implications for how we should best formulate utilitarianism as well as consequentialism, more generally.

7

Commonsense Consequentialism

In this chapter, I return to the theory with which I began the book: maximizing act-utilitarianism. Applying the lessons learned over the last six chapters, I suggest a series of incremental improvements on the theory, eventually arriving at what I take to be the most plausible version of utilitarianism: namely, *commonsense utilitarianism*. I then show how, by abstracting from this theory, we can arrive at what I take to be the most plausible version of consequentialism: namely, *commonsense consequentialism*. This theory is, I believe, quite promising. I show just how promising it is via a comparison with traditional act-consequentialism. Lastly, I end the chapter and the book by summarizing what has been shown and explaining what remains to be shown.

§7.1 The best version of act-utilitarianism: Commonsense utilitarianism

§§7.1.1 Maximizing act-utilitarianism

One of the simplest and most traditional consequentialist theories is *maximizing act-utilitarianism* (MAU), the view both (1) that traditional act-consequentialism is true and (2) that an act maximizes the good if and only if it maximizes aggregate utility. Its *criterion of rightness* is as follows:

> **MAU$_{cr}$** It is objectively morally permissible for S to perform an act, x, if and only if there is no alternative act that is personally possible for S that would produce more aggregate utility than x would.

Maximizing act-utilitarianism (i.e., MAU) is unsatisfactory for a number of reasons, not the least of which is that it conflicts with moral rationalism given certain plausible assumptions about what agents have decisive reason to do—see chapter 2. But it also fails for a couple of technical reasons.

First, it fails to index permissions to times despite the fact that it makes permissibility a function of what is personally possible for the agent, which is something that can change over time. To illustrate the problem, suppose that x is, as of t_1, the best alternative that is personally possible for me. Maximizing act-utilitarianism (i.e., MAU) implies, then, that I am obligated to perform x and that my performing y, an inferior alternative, is impermissible. But suppose that, by the time that t_3 rolls around, things will have changed such that x is no longer personally possible for me and y is now (as of t_3) the best alternative that is personally possible for me. Surely, it cannot be that I am still obligated to perform x. After all, "obligatory" implies "personally possible," and x is no longer (as of t_3) personally possible for me. So is y obligatory or impermissible? The answer seems to be that y was, as of t_1, impermissible but is, as of t_3, obligatory. It seems impossible, then, to answer such questions without indexing permissions (and hence also obligations) to times, which is something MAU fails to do.

Second, MAU fails to provide criteria for assessing the deontic statuses of various sets of actions despite the fact that we deliberate about whether to perform sets of actions and form intentions to perform sets of actions. Unfortunately, MAU is mostly silent with regard to the deontic statuses of sets of actions, for the variable "x" ranges over only individual actions (types and tokens). Of course, MAU does render a verdict with regard to certain sets of actions: specifically, those that constitute some larger, individual act. Take, for instance, the act of firing a semiautomatic handgun. This compound act is comprised of a sequence of more basic actions: inserting the magazine, releasing the slide, taking aim, and squeezing the trigger. Insofar as this sequence of actions constitutes the larger, compound act of firing a semiautomatic handgun, MAU renders a verdict as to its deontic status. But, as noted in the previous chapter, not all sets of actions make up some larger, individual act. For instance, the set of actions that I intend to perform today— drop off my daughter at school in the morning, return home to pack, leave the house by 11 A.M., stop to get gas, head down to Tucson, grab some lunch along the way, pick up my friend Dave at Tucson International Airport, and then head over to the Westward Look Resort for the workshop that we will both be attending— does not constitute any *individual* action. Thus, MAU is silent as to its deontic status. Yet this is a set of actions about which I have deliberated. Moreover, it is a set of actions that I intend to perform. Surely, then, an adequate moral theory should tell me whether it is a set of actions that I am permitted to perform.

§§7.1.2 Revised maximizing act-utilitarianism

These two technical problems can be easily solved. We need only to adopt what I call *revised maximizing act-utilitarianism* and its *criterion of rightness*:

RMAU$_{cr}$ It is, as of t_i, objectively morally permissible for S to perform a set of actions, α_j, beginning at t_j ($t_i < t_j$) if and only if there is no alternative set of actions that is, as of t_i, personally possible for S that would produce more aggregate utility than α_j would.

This revised version of maximizing act-utilitarianism (i.e., RMAU) does index permissions to times, and it does allow us to assess the deontic statuses of all possible sets of actions. Nevertheless, it is not without its own problems.

One problem is that it violates the following plausible principle of deontic logic, which holds that *permissibility distributes* over *conjunction* (hence, "PDC"):

PDC $P[S, t_i, (x_1, x_2, \ldots, \& x_n)] \rightarrow [P(S, t_i, x_1), P(S, t_i, x_2), \ldots, \& P(S, t_i, x_n)]$,

where, if you will recall from chapter 6, "$P(S, t_i, x_i)$" stands for "S is, as of t_i, permitted to perform x_i." To see that it violates PDC, consider the following revised version of the procrastination example from chapter 6:

> *Professor Procrastinate II:* Professor Procrastinate receives, at t_1, an invitation to review a book. He is the best person to do the review and has the time to do so. If he both accepts the invitation at t_2 and then teaches a seminar on the book at t_3, he will write the review at t_4, which is what would be best both for him and for others. However, he is, as a matter of fact, going to teach at t_3 a course on logic as opposed to a seminar on the book—the result being that he is going to become so engrossed at t_4 in redesigning his logic course that he will put off writing the review indefinitely. Assume, then, that although Professor Procrastinate's accepting the invitation at t_2, teaching a seminar on the book at t_3, and writing the review at t_4 is, as of t_1, personally possible for him, it is not, as of t_1, scrupulously securable by him. For there is, as of t_1, nothing that he can do or intend to do that will, given any set of permissible background attitudes, secure his performance of this course of action. Indeed, no matter how resolute he is, at t_1, in his intention to teach a seminar on the book at t_3 and write the review at t_4, he will instead end up being overcome both by the temptation to teach logic at t_3 and by the temptation to redesign his logic course at t_4. And, thus, he will end up perpetually procrastinating, failing to ever write the review. It would be better, then, if he were to decline the invitation at t_2. For it would be better to do this than to accept the invitation at t_2 and end up never writing the review, which is precisely what would happen if he were to accept the invitation.

The situation is depicted graphically in figure 7.1. The points on the graph labeled "P_1," "P_2," and "P_3" represent choice points. The branches stemming from each choice point represent the set of mutually exclusive and jointly exhaustive act alternatives that are, as of that point, securable by Professor Procrastinate—assume, if necessary, that God will cause Professor Procrastinate to cease to exist should he intend to do anything other than the acts depicted in the graph and that, therefore, the branches on the graph represent his *only* options. Thus, at P_1, he must choose to perform either a_1 or a_2, but not both.

a_1 = accept the invitation a_4 = teach logic

a_2 = decline the invitation a_5 = write the book review

a_3 = teach a seminar on the book a_6 = redesign the logic course

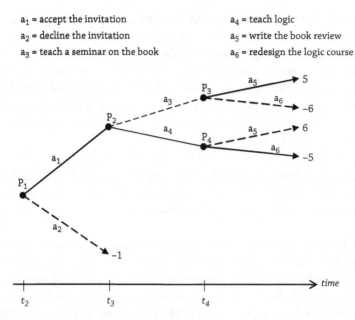

Figure 7.1

Solid lines represent acts that Professor Procrastinate would choose to perform were he to reach the relevant choice point. Dashed lines represent acts that Professor Procrastinate could, but would not, choose to perform were he to reach the relevant choice point. Thus, if Professor Procrastinate were to reach P_3, he would, as the solid line represents, choose to perform a_5, not a_6. But he could perform a_6 in that, if he were to intend at t_4 to perform a_6, that is what he would do.

Time is represented by the line at the bottom. So, as one can see from the graph, a_1's time-interval extends from t_2 to t_3, and a_3's time-interval extends from t_3 to t_4.

Lastly, the numerals to the right of each arrow represent the utility of the corresponding compound acts. Thus, Professor Procrastinate's performing a_1 would produce minus five utiles, for Professor Procrastinate would end up performing the compound act, a_1-and-a_4-and-a_6, if he were to perform a_1. Likewise, we can see from the graph that his performing a_1-and-a_3 would produce five utiles, for he would end up performing the compound act, a_1-and-a_3-and-a_5, if he were to perform a_1-and-a_3.

According to RMAU, Professor Procrastinate is not, as of t_1, objectively morally permitted to perform a_1, as there is an alternative—namely, a_2—that would produce more utility than a_1 would. Professor Procrastinate's performing a_1 would produce minus five utiles, whereas his performing a_2 would produce only minus one utiles. Although RMAU implies that Professor Procrastinate is not, as of t_1, objectively morally permitted to perform a_1, RMAU implies that he is, as of

t_1, objectively morally permitted (indeed, required) to perform a_1-and-a_3, as the only alternative to this compound act is a_1-and-a_4, which is suboptimal. Professor Procrastinate's performing a_1-and-a_4 would produce minus five utiles, whereas his performing a_1-and-a_3 would produce five utiles.[1] Since RMAU implies that Professor Procrastinate is, as of t_1, objectively morally permitted to perform a_1-and-a_3 but is not, as of t_1, objectively morally permitted to perform a_1, it is clear that RMAU violates PDC. And violating PDC is, as I explained in chapter 6, a high price to pay for accepting any theory.

What's worse, though, is that RMAU implies that agents can avoid an obligation to perform a better course of action simply by failing to come to have the intention that they ought to come to have. To see this, consider yet another version of the procrastination example from chapter 6:

> *Professor Procrastinate III:* Professor Procrastinate receives, at t_0, an invitation to review a book. He is the best person to do the review and has the time to do it. If he both accepts the invitation at t_2 and then teaches a seminar on the book at t_3, he will write the review at t_4, which is what would be best both for him and for others. However, as a matter of fact, he is going to teach logic at t_3, and this will result in his becoming so engrossed in redesigning his logic course at t_4 that he will put off writing the review indefinitely. Now, the only reason that he is going to end up teaching logic at t_3 is that this is what he is going intend at t_1 to do. If he were instead to come to intend at t_1 to teach a seminar on the book, as he could and should, then he would do that instead. Nevertheless, given that he will actually intend at t_1 to teach logic, what he would do were he to accept the invitation is to teach logic at t_3, redesign his logic course at t_4, and never get around to writing the review.

The situation is depicted graphically in figure 7.2. The dash-dotted line between P_1 and P_5 represents the fact that $a_1(\&i_2)$ is not actually an option that Professor Procrastinate can choose, at will, to perform, for i_2 is an intention, not an action. Intentions, unlike actions, are not under the agent's volitional control. An agent cannot choose, at will, what to intend any more than she can choose, at will, what to believe.[2] Professor Procrastinate's choice, then, is between performing a_1 and performing a_2, and not between performing a_1 with this or that intention.

---

[1] Professor Procrastinate's performing a_1-and-a_4 is the only alternative to his performing a_1-and-a_3, for alternatives must be both agent-identical and time-identical. Two sets of actions are *agent-identical* if and only if they have the same agent. And two sets of actions are *time-identical* if and only if they persist over the exact same interval (or intervals) of time. Technically, there are other alternatives involving a_2 (e.g., a_2-and-a_4), but I am assuming these are all suboptimal.

[2] Of course, agents can choose to perform acts that will cause them to have certain beliefs. Suppose, for instance, that I could pay someone to hypnotize me into believing that p. This, then,

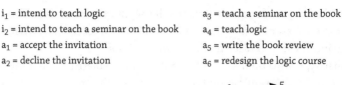

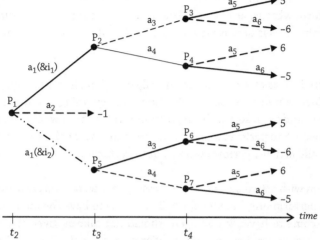

Figure 7.2

Although intentions are not under an agent's volitional control, they are, like beliefs, attitudes for which there can be reasons. Moreover, intentions are judgment-sensitive attitudes, meaning that they are responsive to an agent's judgments about reasons. Given this, we will suppose that S has rational control over whether or not she intends at t_1 to teach a seminar on the book at t_3 and would, therefore, be responsible for failing to do so.[3] Thus, it is fair to say that Professor Procrastinate ought, as of t_0, to intend at t_1 to teach a seminar on the book at t_3, for he has decisive reason to do so. Now, surely, Professor Procrastinate's failure to come to have this intention does not excuse him from being obligated to perform what is, as of t_0, the best course of action that is scrupulously securable by him: namely, accepting the invitation at t_2, teaching a seminar on the book at t_3, and writing the review at t_4.[4] To secure his performance of this (the best) course of action, Professor Procrastinate need only to intend at t_1 to perform this course

would be a case in which I chose to perform an act that caused me to believe that *p*. But, in this case, it is the physical act of my paying this person, not the mental "act" of my believing that *p*, that I chose, at will, to perform. For more on this topic, see HIERONYMI 2006.

[3] Again, for more on this notion of control, see HIERONYMI 2006, PETTIT & SMITH 1996, A. M. SMITH 2010, and STEUP 2008.

[4] I am assuming that his writing the review would be sufficiently good both for him and for others that there is decisive reason for him to write the review.

of action, which is, as of t_0, an attitude that he ought to come to have. The problem, then, is that Professor Procrastinate will intend at t_1 to teach logic, when he ought instead to intend at t_1 to teach a seminar on the book.[5]

Implausibly, RMAU implies that Professor Procrastinate's impending failure to intend at t_1 to teach a seminar on the book excuses him from being, as of t_0, obligated to perform what is, as of t_0, the best course of action that is scrupulously securable by him. This is because RMAU is a version of the following implausible view:

> *Actualism:* It is, as of t_i, objectively (morally or rationally) permissible for S to perform a non-maximal set of actions, α_j, beginning at t_j ($t_i < t_j$) if and only if, and because, the maximal set of actions that S would actually perform were S to perform α_j is no worse than the maximal set of actions that S would actually perform were S not to perform α_j.

The problem with actualism is that it takes as given certain future actions that an agent will perform only because she will not come to have the intentions that she ought to come to have. But an agent should not take as given those future actions that are under her present deliberative control. That is, Professor Procrastinate should not take as given that he will be teaching logic at t_3 when whether or not he is going to teach logic at t_3 depends on whether, in response to his reasons, he forms at t_1 the intention to teach a seminar on the book instead. Thus, when Professor Procrastinate deliberates about whether to accept the invitation, he should not reason to the conclusion that he ought to decline the invitation on the assumption that he would never get around to writing the review if he were to accept the invitation. For whether or not this assumption is true depends on what he will, at t_1, intend to teach at t_3, and, in deliberating at t_0 about what to do in the future, he should not hold fixed future intentions that are currently under his present deliberative control (CARLSON 1999, p. 265). That is, he should not, in his present deliberations, treat as fixed that which depends on his present deliberations. And whether he will intend at t_1 to teach logic at t_3 and, thus, whether he will teach logic at t_3 depends on his present deliberations.

So rather than think that he should decline the invitation because he is going to teach logic at t_3 and thereby become so engrossed in revising his logic course at t_4 that he will never get around to writing the review, he should think that he ought, as of t_0, both to accept the invitation at t_2 and to teach a seminar on the book at t_3. And these thoughts should lead him to form the intention at t_1 both to accept the invitation at t_2 and to teach a seminar on the book at t_3, thereby ensuring that he will write the review at t_4. The thought, then, is that an agent should hold

---

[5] I am a compatibilist. So my holding that he ought, as of t_0, to form the intention at t_1 to teach a seminar on the book at t_3 is compatible with my stipulation that he is determined to form the intention at t_1 to teach logic at t_3.

fixed her performance of x at t_j while rationally deliberating at t_i if and only if her performance of x at t_j does not depend on the outcome of her rational deliberations at t_i.

The general problem with actualist views such as RMAU, then, is that they imply that agents can avoid incurring certain obligations simply by failing to come to have the attitudes that they ought to come to have. The attitude in question need not be an intention, as in the case of *Professor Procrastinate III*. It could instead be some other judgment-sensitive attitude, such as a desire or a belief.[6] Consider, for instance, yet another twist on the above example. Suppose that the only reason that Professor Procrastinate would not write the review even if he were to accept the invitation is that he believes, due to wishful thinking, that if he procrastinates for long enough, the book's publisher will eventually offer him a $100,000 incentive to finish the review. Given this irrational belief, it may be that even if he were to intend at t_1 both to accept the invitation at t_2 and to write the review at t_3, he would change his mind about writing the review by the time that t_3 rolls around, deciding to hold out for the money. So, on RMAU, he would not, as of t_0, be under an obligation to accept the invitation at t_2. For what would actually happen were he to accept the invitation at t_2 (i.e., his procrastinating indefinitely) is worse than what would happen were he not to accept the invitation at t_2 (i.e., their finding the next best person to write the review). But it is implausible to suppose that he can avoid an obligation to write the review simply by failing to believe what he ought to believe—specifically, that he will never be offered any money to finish the review. And were he to come to have this belief, which is the belief that he ought to come to have, he would, then, have no problem mustering the will to sit down and write the review—or so I am assuming. The problem, then, is that actualist views such as RMAU allow agents to avoid obligations by failing to come to have the attitudes that they ought to come to have—attitudes that are essential to their securing a better course of action.

§§7.1.3 Maximizing securitist utilitarianism

So although RMAU avoids some of the technical problems that plagued MAU, it is clearly not the best version of utilitarianism. It has counterintuitive implications in cases such as *Professor Procrastinate II* and *Professor Procrastinate III*.

A view that avoids these counterintuitive implications as well as the technical problems that plagued MAU is *maximizing securitist utilitarianism*:

> **MSU** The view according to which all the following are true: (*a*) it is, as of t_i, objectively morally permissible for S to perform a non-maximal set of actions, α_j, beginning at t_j ($t_i < t_j$) if and only if, and because, it is, as of t_i, objectively morally permissible for S to

---

[6] I thank Jacob Ross for pointing this out to me.

perform a maximal set of actions, MSA_j, that involves S's performing α_j; (b) it is, as of t_i, objectively morally permissible for S to perform a maximal set of actions, MSA_i, if and only if, and because, MSA_i is one of the optimal MSAs that is, as of t_i, scrupulously securable by S; (c) MSA_i is one of the optimal MSAs that is, as of t_i, scrupulously securable by S if and only if, and because, MSA_i's outcome is not, on S's evaluative ranking, outranked by that of any alternative MSA that is, as of t_i, scrupulously securable by S; and (d) MSA_i's outcome is not, on S's evaluative ranking, outranked by that of any alternative MSA that is, as of t_i, scrupulously securable by S if and only if, and because, there is no alternative MSA that is, as of t_i, scrupulously securable by S whose outcome contains more aggregate utility than MSA_i's outcome does.

Like RMAU, MSU rightly implies that, in *Professor Procrastinate II*, Professor Procrastinate is not, as of t_1, objectively morally permitted to perform a_1 (that is, to accept the invitation). But, unlike RMAU, MSU does not counterintuitively imply that PDC is false, for, unlike RMAU, MSU does not further imply that Professor Procrastinate is, as of t_1, objectively morally permitted to perform a_1-and-a_3 (that is, to accept the invitation and teach a seminar on the book). In *Professor Procrastinate II*, none of the objectively morally permissible maximal sets of actions that are, as of t_1, scrupulously securable by Professor Procrastinate involves his performing a_1-and-a_3 for the simple reason that his performing a_1-and-a_3 is not, as of t_1, scrupulously securable by him. So MSU is superior to RMAU in that it does not violate PDC.

Maximizing securitist utilitarianism (i.e., MSU) is also superior to RMAU in that it does not imply that agents can avoid obligations simply by failing to come to have the attitudes that they ought to come to have. Thus, in *Professor Procrastinate III*, MSU, unlike RMAU, implies that Professor Procrastinate is, as of t_1, objectively morally obligated to perform a_1 (that is, to accept the invitation).[7] The MSAs that

---

[7] Although Professor Procrastinate has an *unconditional* moral obligation, as of t_1, to *accept* the invitation, he has a *conditional* obligation, as of t_1, to *decline* the invitation if he is not going to write the review. What's more, there is even a sense in which Professor Procrastinate ought, as of t_1, to decline the invitation: the relevant sense of "ought" being what Caspar Hare (2011) calls the "ought of omniscient desire" or "ought[OD]." Professor Procrastinate ought[OD], as of t_1, to decline the invitation, for this is what an omniscient being with the appropriate interests would want him to do—after all, an omniscient being would know that Professor Procrastinate would not write the review even if he were to accept the invitation. By contrast, the sense in which Professor Procrastinate ought, as of t_1, to accept the invitation is what Hare calls the "ought of most reason" or "ought[MR]." This is the sense of "ought" that I have been concerned with throughout this book. As I see it, S ought[MR] to perform x if and only if performing x is what a normatively conscientious person would do if she faced S's choice of alternatives and was aware of all the relevant reason-constituting facts. See HARE 2011 for other interesting ways in which the ought[OD] and the ought[MR] can come apart.

are, as of t_1, scrupulously securable by Professor Procrastinate are: (1) a_1-and-a_4- and-a_6 with minus five utiles, (2) a_2-and-a_4-and-a_6 with minus one utiles, and (3) a_1-and-a_3-and-a_5 with five utiles.[8] According to MSU, then, the only objectively morally permissible MSA is a_1-and-a_3-and-a_5, which produces the most utility of the three. Thus, Professor Procrastinate is, as of t_1, objectively morally obligated to perform a_1 given that every objectively morally permissible MSA that is, as of t_1, scrupulously securable by Professor Procrastinate involves his performing a_1.

So MSU is clearly superior to its actualist counterpart—namely, RMAU. But besides actualism and securitism, there is also the following view:

> *Possibilism:* It is, as to t_i, objectively (morally or rationally) permissible for S to perform a non-maximal set of actions, α_j, beginning at t_j ($t_i < t_j$) if and only if, and because, at least one of the optimal maximal sets of actions that is, as of t_i, personally possible for S involves S's performing α_j.

Thus, to determine whether MSU is the best version of utilitarianism, we need to know not only whether it is superior to its actualist counterpart (viz., RMAU), but also whether it is superior to its possibilist counterpart—namely, *maximizing possibilist utilitarianism:*

MPU The view according to which all the following are true: (*a*) it is, as of t_i, objectively morally permissible for S to perform a non-maximal set of actions, α_j, beginning at t_j ($t_i < t_j$) if and only if, and because, it is, as of t_i, objectively morally permissible for S to perform a maximal set of actions, MSA_j, that involves S's performing α_j; (*b*) it is, as of t_i, objectively morally permissible for S to perform a maximal set of actions, MSA_i, if and only if, and because, MSA_i is one of the optimal MSAs that is, as of t_i, personally possible for S; (*c*) MSA_i is one of the optimal MSAs that is, as of t_i, personally possible for S if and only if, and because, MSA_i's outcome is not, on S's evaluative ranking, outranked by that of any alternative MSA that is, as of t_i, personally possible for S; and (*d*) MSA_i's outcome is not, on S's evaluative ranking, outranked by that of any alternative MSA that is, as of t_i, personally possible for S if and only if, and because, there is no alternative MSA that is, as of t_i, personally possible for S whose outcome contains more aggregate utility than MSA_i's outcome does.

Maximizing possibilist utilitarianism (i.e., MPU) is inferior to MSU. The problem with MPU, and with possibilism in general, is that it is unrealistic. As Holly Goldman

---

[8] To ensure that these are MSAs, we should just assume that Professor Procrastinate will die at t_5 no matter what he does. Also, I am assuming that Professor Procrastinate would perform a_4-and-a_6 if he were to perform a_2.

notes, "there seems little point in prescribing an act which puts the agent in a position to do great things if the same act also puts him in a position to do something disastrous, and he would choose the latter rather than the former [no matter what other permissible attitudes he forms]" (1976, p. 468). Consider again *Professor Procrastinate II*. MPU implies that Professor Procrastinate is, as of t_1, objectively morally required to accept the invitation (that is, to perform a_1), because this would put him in the position to perform the best subsequent course of action—namely, a_4-and-a_5. But why should Professor Procrastinate put himself in the position to perform the best subsequent course of action (viz., a_4-and-a_5) if this also puts him in the position to perform the worst subsequent course of action (viz., a_4-and-a_6) and, as a matter of fact, he is going to choose to perform the worst course of action regardless of his background attitudes? I could see the point in MPU's prescribing that Professor Procrastinate performs a_1 now if there was some presently available set of intentions and permissible background attitudes that would result in his following up with the best subsequent course of action. But, in *Professor Procrastinate II*, there is no presently available set of intentions and permissible background attitudes that would result in his following up with the best subsequent course of action. And, in that case, it seems pointless for MPU to prescribe that he performs a_1.[9]

Another problem with MPU, and with possibilism in general, is that it implausibly implies that there is the following sort of asymmetry: how some future agent would behave in response to S's φ-ing is relevant to whether S should φ if that future agent is someone other than S, but not if that future agent is S. But why should it matter whether that future agent is S or someone else if regardless there is no presently available set of intentions and permissible background attitudes that will change how this future agent is going to behave in response to S's φ-ing? If, in neither case, does S have any control over what that future agent will do, why should the two cases be treated differently?[10]

Of course, only in those instances in which that future agent is S is it possible for S to have present deliberative control over what that future agent is going to do, as where, say, S will ψ at some future time, t_3, if and only if, and because, S forms, as a result of her present deliberations, the intention to φ at t_1. But even if S does sometimes have present deliberative control over whether or not she will ψ at t_3, it is important to realize that this is not always the case. For, sometimes, no matter what presently available set of intentions or permissible background

---

[9] MPU also implies that Erika from §§6.3.2 (the six-year-old who knows next to nothing about chess) would be obligated to beat Karpov at chess if something important—say, someone's life—were to depend on her doing so. Yet the idea that she could be obligated, as of t_1, to do something that is not, as of t_1, securable (let alone scrupulously securable) by her is quite implausible. Again, such a prescription seems utterly useless given that she lacks, as of t_1, the capacity to form the sort of intention that would result in her beating Karpov.

[10] A number of philosophers have made this point. See, for instance, GOLDMAN 1976 (p. 469) and WOODARD 2009 (pp. 219–220).

attitudes S forms at t_1, S is (or is not) going to ψ at t_3. What is relevant, then, is not whether the future agent is S or someone else but whether that future agent's behavior is under S's present deliberative control. If it is not, then, contrary to possibilism, whether S should φ depends on what that future agent would do if S were to φ. The thought, then, is that if S is no more able at t_0 to prevent her future self from ψ-ing at t_3 in response to her φ-ing at t_1 than she is able at t_0 to prevent some future other from ψ-ing at t_3 in response to her φ-ing at t_1, then her obligation at t_0 to φ (or not to φ) at t_1 depends just as much on what her future self would (as opposed to could) do at t_3 in response to her φ-ing at t_1 as it does on what that future other would (as opposed to could) do at t_3 in response to her φ-ing at t_1.

Thus, possibilism, unlike securitism, fails to distinguish between those cases in which S has present deliberative control over what she does in the future and those cases in which she does not. It focuses instead on the irrelevant distinction between whether the future agent is S or someone else. Thus, there is, according to possibilism, no relevant distinction to be made between Professor Procrastinate's situation in *Professor Procrastinate II* and his situation in *Professor Procrastinate III*. In both cases, Professor Procrastinate's accepting the invitation to review the book at t_2 and writing the review at t_4 is, as of t_1, personally possible for him. And, on possibilism, that is all that matters. The fact that, in *Professor Procrastinate II*, Professor Procrastinate would not write the review at t_4 if he were to accept the invitation at t_2 is, according to possibilism, completely irrelevant even though there is, as of t_1, no presently available set of intentions and background attitudes that could alter this fact. But surely this unalterable fact is relevant. Professor Procrastinate should, as of t_1, treat his future procrastination as unalterable if there is, as of t_1, no presently available set of intentions and background attitudes that could ensure that he does not procrastinate at t_4. It is only in *Professor Procrastinate III* that Professor Procrastinate should treat his future procrastination as alterable. For it is only in that case that there is, as of t_1, some way for Professor Procrastinate to ensure that he does not procrastinate—specifically, by forming the intention at t_1 both to accept the invitation at t_2 and to teach a seminar on the book at t_3.

Possibilism also ignores the way we in fact reason about practical matters. We often reason that we ought not to φ because φ-ing would put us in a position in which we are going, no matter how resolute we are now, to give into temptation and do something even worse than not φ-ing (GOLDMAN 1976, pp. 469–470). Thus, in *Professor Procrastinate II*, Professor Procrastinate should, knowing his tendency to procrastinate, reason that he ought to decline the invitation. And we often reason that we ought to plan now on ψ-ing in the future since our ψ-ing in the future will prevent us from being tempted to do the wrong thing. Thus, in *Professor Procrastinate III*, Professor Procrastinate should reason that he ought to teach a seminar on the book at t_3 so that he will not be tempted at t_4 to redesign his logic course as opposed to write the review. And this should lead him to form the intention at t_1 to teach a seminar on the book at t_3. It seems, then, that possibilist theories such as MPU fail to capture the way that we in fact reason about practical matters. Thus, MSU seems superior to MPU not only in that it rightly distinguishes between those cases in which one's future behavior is under one's present deliberative control and those cases in which it is not, but also in that it better captures the way we in fact reason about practical matters.

So we have seen that MSU is superior to both its actualist and possibilist counterparts: that is, to RMAU and MPU, respectively. Nevertheless, I do not think that MSU is, in its present formulation, the best version of utilitarianism. For, as it currently stands, it cannot account for the basic features of commonsense morality: agent-favoring options, agent-sacrificing options, special obligations, agent-centered restrictions, supererogatory acts, and the self-other asymmetry. We should, then, apply the lessons that we learned in chapter 4 and reformulate MSU so as to accommodate these basic features of commonsense morality. We can do so by combining MSU with the structural features of MoDSU (from §§4.2.3) that enabled it to accommodate the basic features of commonsense morality. When we do, we get what I call *commonsense utilitarianism*.

§§7.1.4 Commonsense utilitarianism

Commonsense utilitarianism (or "CSU" for short) is that version of utilitarianism that accommodates more of our commonsense moral intuitions than any other version of utilitarianism does. The following is an initial stab at formulating the view:

> **CSU** The view according to which all the following are true: (*a*) it is, as of t_i, objectively morally permissible for S to perform a non-maximal set of actions, α_j, beginning at t_j ($t_i < t_j$) if and only if, and because, it is, as of t_i, objectively morally permissible for S to perform a maximal set of actions, MSA_i, that involves S's performing α_j; (*b*) it is, as of t_i, objectively morally permissible for S to perform a maximal set of actions, MSA_i, if and only if, and because, MSA_i is one of the optimal MSAs that is, as of t_i, scrupulously securable by S; (*c*) MSA_i is one of the optimal MSAs that is, as of t_i, scrupulously securable by S if and only if, and because, MSA_i's outcome is not, on S's evaluative ranking, outranked by that of any alternative MSA that is, as of t_i, scrupulously securable by S; and (*d*) MSA_i's outcome is not, on S's evaluative ranking, outranked by that of any alternative MSA that is, as of t_i, scrupulously securable by S if and only if, and because, there is no alternative MSA that is, as of t_i, scrupulously securable by S whose outcome contains both more constraint-adjusted utility and more comprehensively adjusted utility than MSA_i's outcome does, where the constraint-adjusted utility of an outcome is just the sum of the utility for others, adjusted by multiplying any disutility (or loss of utility) resulting from S's infringements of an agent-centered constraint by five hundred, and where the comprehen-

sively adjusted utility of an outcome is just its constraint-adjusted utility added to the product of S's utility times ten.[11]

This is only an initial stab at formulating commonsense utilitarianism. Commonsense utilitarianism will undoubtedly need to be much more nuanced than this. But even if the above formulation is rather simplistic, it is good enough for our present purposes. Commonsense utilitarianism illustrates how a utilitarian theory can accommodate the basic features of commonsense morality: agent-favoring options, agent-sacrificing options, special obligations, agent-centered restrictions, supererogatory acts, and the self-other asymmetry. In this respect it is like MoDSU from chapter 4. But it is superior to MoDSU in that it is securitist, indexes permissions to times, and provides criteria for assessing everything from a minimal act to a maximal set of actions.

To illustrate how commonsense utilitarianism can accommodate the basic features of commonsense morality, consider the scenario depicted in table 7.1, which is very similar to the one depicted in table 4.1 of chapter 4.[12] In the scenario depicted in table 7.1, there are four mutually exclusive and jointly exhaustive maximal sets of actions that are, as of t_0, scrupulously securable by an agent named Ernesto: MSA_1, MSA_2, MSA_3, and MSA_4.

Commonsense utilitarianism accommodates agent-centered options in that it permits agents to give their own utility anywhere from no weight at all up to ten

Table 7.1 $U_o(\varphi)$ = the utility that will accrue to others, excluding $U_i(\varphi)$, as a result of S's performing φ. $U_i(\varphi)$ = the disutility (or loss of utility) that will accrue to others as a result of S's infringing on any agent-centered constraint by performing φ. $U_{con}(\varphi)$ = $U_o(\varphi)$ + $[500 \times U_i(\varphi)]$. $U_s(\varphi)$ = the utility that will accrue to S as a result of S's performing φ. $U_{com}(\varphi)$ = $U_{con}(\varphi)$ + $[10 \times U_s(\varphi)]$.

MSA_i	$U_o(\varphi)$	$U_i(\varphi)$	$U_{con}(\varphi)$	$U_s(\varphi)$	$U_{com}(\varphi)$	deontic status
MSA_1	10	0	**10**	7	**80**	merely permissible
MSA_2	24	–1	**–476**	50	**24**	impermissible
MSA_3	15	0	**15**	1	**25**	supererogatory
MSA_4	20	0	**20**	–1	**10**	supererogatory

[11] I am assuming, here, that the proponent of CSU holds both that the more constraint-adjusted utility an outcome contains the more moral reason there is for the agent to desire that it obtains and that the more comprehensively adjusted utility an outcome contains the more reason there is, all things considered, for the agent to desire that it obtains.

[12] I have emphasized the fourth and sixth columns with bold-faced type since these two represent the two auxiliary rankings of which permissibility is, according to commonsense utilitarianism, a function.

times the weight of any other. Thus, Ernesto can permissibly choose to do what is better for himself and perform MSA_1 even though his performing MSA_4 would be both better for others and better overall.[13] Ernesto has, then, the agent-favoring option of performing MSA_1 instead of MSA_4. Furthermore, by allowing agents to give their own utility no weight, commonsense utilitarianism accommodates agent-sacrificing options, which permit agents to forgo their own greater good for the sake of providing others with some lesser net benefit. For instance, Ernesto can permissibly choose to perform MSA_3 as opposed to MSA_1, thereby providing others with a net benefit of five utiles at a cost of six utiles to himself.[14] Thus, commonsense utilitarianism, like MODSU, accommodates what is known as the self-other asymmetry.

Commonsense utilitarianism can also accommodate agent-centered constraints, which include both special obligations and agent-centered restrictions. According to commonsense utilitarianism, there will, for instance, be a non-absolute restriction against committing murder. Agents would, other things being equal, be prohibited from committing murder even so as to prevent up to five hundred others from each committing some comparable murder. And, according to commonsense utilitarianism, there will be a non-absolute constraint against failing to fulfill the special obligation that parents have to nurture their own children. Parents would, other things being equal, be prohibited from failing to nurture their own children even so as to prevent up to five hundred others from each comparably failing to nurture their children. Clearly, then, commonsense utilitarianism can accommodate both agent-centered restrictions and special obligations.

Commonsense utilitarianism can even accommodate the notion of going above and beyond the call of duty—or, at least, it can if the following is a plausible account of *super*erogation with respect to *maximal* sets of actions:

> **SUPER-MAX** It is, as of t_i, supererogatory for S to perform a maximal set of actions, MSA_j, beginning at t_j $(t_i < t_j)$ if and only if, and because, there is some alternative maximal set of actions, MSA_i, also beginning at t_j $(t_i < t_j)$ such that: (a) it is, as of t_i, both objectively morally permissible for S to perform MSA_j and objectively morally permissible for S to perform MSA_i and (b) S has more moral reason to perform MSA_j than to perform MSA_i.

Certain maximal sets of actions will, on commonsense utilitarianism, meet conditions a and b. To see this, note that commonsense utilitarianism has two

---

[13] Whereas $U_o(MSA_1)$ is ten, $U_o(MSA_4)$ is twenty. And the total utility produced by Ernesto's performing MSA_1 is seventeen, whereas the total utility produced by Ernesto's performing MSA_4 is nineteen.

[14] The benefit to others is $U_o(MSA_3)$ minus $U_o(MSA_1)$, which equals five. The cost to himself is $U_s(MSA_3)$ minus $U_s(MSA_1)$, which equals negative six.

auxiliary rankings: (AR_1) a ranking of outcomes in terms of their constraint-adjusted utility, and (AR_2) a ranking of outcomes in terms of their comprehensively adjusted utility. The first ranking, AR_1, is a ranking of outcomes in terms of how much moral reason the agent has to bring them about. It specifies that the more constraint-adjusted utility an outcome contains the more moral reason there is to want it to obtain and, thus, to act so as to bring it about. And the second ranking, AR_2, is a ranking of outcomes in terms of how much reason, all things considered, the agent has to bring them about. It specifies that the more comprehensively adjusted utility an outcome contains the more reason there is, all things considered, to want it to obtain and, thus, to act so as to bring it about.

Given this, Ernesto has more moral reason to perform MSA_3 than to perform MSA_1, a permissible alternative, for MSA_3 produces more constraint-adjusted utility than MSA_1 does. And the same holds for MSA_4.[15] Thus, MSA_3 and MSA_4 are both supererogatory on commonsense utilitarianism. What's more, commonsense utilitarianism allows for a range of supererogatory alternatives, where some supererogatory alternatives go further beyond the minimum required than others do. For instance, MSA_4 involves going further beyond the minimum that morality requires than MSA_3 does. In this scenario, Ernesto is required to produce at least ten units of constraint-adjusted utility, and MSA_4 produces ten additional units beyond this minimum, whereas MSA_3 produces only five additional units beyond this minimum.

§§7.1.5 Supererogatory versus superperfecterogatory

Unfortunately, SUPER-MAX does not provide criteria for determining whether some non-maximal set of actions is supererogatory. So we cannot yet assess whether commonsense utilitarianism accommodates the intuitive idea that various non-maximal sets of acts are supererogatory. Perhaps, though, the problem could be easily solved by adopting the following principle, which holds that *supererogatoriness* distributes over *conjunction*:

SupDC $SUP[S, t_i, (\alpha_1, \alpha_2, \ldots, \& \alpha_n)] \rightarrow [SUP(S, t_i, \alpha_1), SUP(S, t_i, \alpha_2), \ldots, \& SUP(S, t_i, \alpha_n)]$,

where "$SUP(S, t_i, \alpha_i)$" stands for "S's performing α_i is, as of t_i, supererogatory."

In fact, this will not do, for SupDC is false.[16] SupDC is false in virtue of the fact that there are imperfect duties, which can be fulfilled only by performing certain sets of actions over time. Thus, it is possible for a set of actions to go beyond the call of some imperfect duty even though none of the acts within that set go beyond the call of duty themselves. Take, for instance, the (imperfect) duty of beneficence.

---

[15] Whereas $U_{con}(MSA_3)$ and $U_{con}(MSA_4)$ are fifteen and twenty, respectively, $U_{con}(MSA_1)$ is only ten.

[16] Paul McNamara has noted the fact that SupDC is false—see 1996a, p. 432.

In general, it does not require that you take advantage of any particular opportunity to help others, but it does require that you take advantage of such opportunities with sufficient regularity—at least, it does assuming that you have certain typical abilities and opportunities. So, for instance, even if it would clearly go beyond the call of duty for Kimo to donate $200 to charity each and every month given that $200 amounts to nearly half of the disposable income that he has each month, his donating $200 on any particular occasion would not in and of itself go beyond the call of duty. If, in the past fifty years, the only thing that Kimo has ever done to help others is to donate $200 on January 1, 2000, then this act of charity would not itself count as going above and beyond the call of duty. Indeed, given that this is all that he has ever done, he has surely fallen well short of what is minimally required by the (imperfect) duty of beneficence. The fact that he has done so little despite both the means and opportunity to do considerably more demonstrates that he has not made "the happiness of others a serious, major, continually relevant, life-shaping end" (HILL 2002, p. 206), which is what the duty of beneficence requires.

So, given the nature of the duty of beneficence, that it is an imperfect duty, a duty to adopt the happiness of others as "a serious, major, continually relevant, life-shaping end," it follows that an agent can go beyond the call of the duty of beneficence only by performing a temporally extended set of actions that goes beyond what is minimally required to count as having adopted the welfare of others as "a serious, major, continually relevant, life-shaping end." But although such a set of actions would be supererogatory, it does not follow that any of the individual acts within that set go beyond the call of duty themselves. Thus, SUPDC is false. And this means that what I had, in earlier chapters, been calling a *supererogatory act* is more accurately called a *superperfecterogatory act*—that is, an act that goes beyond the call of only what perfect duty requires.[17] More precisely, a *superperfec*terogatory act is defined as follows:

> **SUPERF** It is, as of t_i, superperfecterogatory for S to perform a set of actions, α_j, beginning at t_j $(t_i < t_j)$ if and only if, and because, there is some alternative set of actions, α_i, also beginning at t_j $(t_i < t_j)$ such that: (a) it is, as of t_i, both objectively morally permissible for S to perform α_j and objectively morally permissible for S to perform α_i and (b) S has more moral reason to perform α_j than to perform α_i.

Kimo's donating $200 to charity on January 1, 2000, was superperfecterogatory, for he was not morally required to do so. He was, we will suppose, morally permitted to have spent that $200 on himself.[18] But although this act was

---

[17] I borrow this term and the distinction from SINNOTT-ARMSTRONG 2005, p. 204.

[18] Not all permissible acts are superperfecterogatory. To illustrate, suppose that Lorenzo and Melissa are both drowning and that I can save only one of the two, as they are so far apart that there

superperfecterogatory, it was not supererogatory. Kimo did not thereby go beyond the call of duty, for he did not thereby exceed what the duty of beneficence requires. So, in contrast to superperfecterogatory acts, we can define a *super*erogatory set of actions—a set that goes above and beyond the call of both perfect and imperfect duty—as follows:

> **SUPER** It is, as of t_i, supererogatory for S to perform a set of actions, α_j, beginning at t_j $(t_i < t_j)$ if and only if, and because, both of the following hold: (1) in performing α_j, S does not thereby only minimally or partially fulfill some positive duty, and (2) there is some alternative set of actions, α_i, also beginning at t_j $(t_i < t_j)$ such that: (*a*) it is, as of t_i, both objectively morally permissible for S to perform α_j and objectively morally permissible for S to perform α_i and (*b*) S has more moral reason to perform α_j than to perform α_i.[19]

There are a number of aspects to this definition that are in need of clarification. First, α_i and α_j are alternatives only if they have the same agent and extend for the same intervals of time—that is, only if they are both agent-identical and time-identical. Second, in φ-ing, S does thereby only *minimally fulfill* some positive duty, D, if and only if S's φ-ing fulfills D and there is no more moral reason for S to φ than to do anything else that would fulfill D. Third, in φ-ing, S does thereby only *partially fulfill* some positive duty, D, if and only if S's φ-ing is a proper subset of some set of actions by which S minimally fulfills D. Fourth, a *positive duty* is one that can be fulfilled only by performing some set of actions. This contrasts with a *negative duty*, which can be fulfilled only by refraining from performing some set actions.

To see both how SUPER yields intuitively plausible verdicts in a range of cases and how commonsense utilitarianism can accommodate these plausible verdicts and thereby accommodate various supererogatory non-maximal sets of actions, it will be helpful to work through a few examples, which I present below. Assume that none of the morally relevant details have been left out of their descriptions. Assume that certain alternatives have been left out only when they are vastly inferior to the others and are, therefore, morally irrelevant. And assume, as noted above, that, on commonsense utilitarianism, the more constraint-adjusted utility an outcome contains the more moral reason there is for the agent to want it to obtain and, thus, to act so as to bring it about. Lastly, assume that the imperfect duty of beneficence is a kind of agent-centered constraint: specifically, a kind of

---

is no way to reach both of them in time. Let us further suppose that I am morally obligated to save one of the two. And let us assume that there is no more moral reason to save the one than the other. Finally, assume that, after tossing a coin to decide whom to save, I save Melissa. Saving Melissa was permissible, but it was not superperfecterogatory, for, although there was another alternative that I was permitted to do instead (viz., to save Lorenzo), I had no more moral reason to save Melissa than to save Lorenzo.

[19] This definition is inspired in part by the one found in MELLEMA 1991.

special obligation that one may not permissibly infringe upon even so as to pre-vent more numerous others from comparably infringing upon it. Assume, then, that it is impermissible to fail to adopt the happiness of others as "a serious, major, continually relevant, life-shaping end" even if doing so will prevent more numerous others from doing the same. Here, then, are the cases.

Case 1 (The Generous Donation): Suppose that over the remainder of my life I donate \$120 per month to Oxfam even though my circumstances are such that I could minimally fulfill my duty of beneficence by donating only \$100 per month, on average, over my entire adult life.[20] Further assume that I do not minimally or partially fulfill any positive duty by donating an additional \$20 a month over the remainder of my life. Assume, then, that I have not, for instance, promised anyone that I would donate an additional \$20 a month. And assume that, throughout my adult life, I have always given at least \$100 a month to charity. Thus, I am not obli-gated to give more in future months so as to make up for giving less than \$100 in past months. Lastly, assume that the relevant alternatives and their associated utilities are as depicted in table 7.2.

In this case, SUPER rightly implies that my donating an additional \$20 a month over the remainder of my life is supererogatory. And commonsense utilitarianism accommodates this verdict. My performing α_3 is supererogatory, for common-sense utilitarianism implies that α_2 and α_3 are both permissible and that there is more moral reason for me to perform α_3 than to perform α_2, as α_3 produces more constraint-adjusted utility.

Table 7.2 α_1 = **my donating \$90 per month over the remainder of my life.** α_2 = **my donating \$100 per month over the remainder of my life.** α_3 = **my donating \$120 per month over the remainder of my life.** $U_o(\varphi)$ = **the utility that will accrue to others, excluding $U_i(\varphi)$, as a result of S's performing φ.** $U_i(\varphi)$ = **the disutility (or loss of utility) that will accrue to others as a result of S's infringing on any agent-centered constraint by performing φ.** $U_{con}(\varphi)$ = $U_o(\varphi)$ + **[500 × $U_i(\varphi)$].** $U_s(\varphi)$ = **the utility that will accrue to S as a result of S's performing φ.** $U_{com}(\varphi)$ = $U_{con}(\varphi)$ + **[10 × $U_s(\varphi)$].**

α_i	$U_o(\varphi)$	$U_i(\varphi)$	$U_{con}(\varphi)$	$U_s(\varphi)$	$U_{com}(\varphi)$	deontic status
α_1	90	−10	**−4,910**	30	**−4,610**	impermissible
α_2	100	0	**100**	20	**300**	merely permissible
α_3	120	0	**120**	0	**120**	supererogatory

[20] Strictly speaking, the duty of beneficence requires only that agents adopt the welfare of others as an ultimate end, but, from this duty, it follows that those with certain abilities and opportunities have a duty to act in whatever way is constitutive of their having adopted the welfare of others as an ultimate end.

Case 2 (The Minimal Donation): Assume that everything is as it is in *The Generous Donation* except that in this case I donate an average of only $100 a month over the remainder of my life. Again, the relevant alternatives and their associated utilities are as depicted in table 7.2.

In this case, SUPER rightly implies that my donating an average of only $100 a month over the remainder of my life (that is, my performing α_2) is merely permissible, and not supererogatory. And commonsense utilitarianism accommodates this verdict, for, on commonsense utilitarianism, there is no more moral reason for me to perform α_2 than to perform any other permissible alternative. After all, α_2 produces no more than the minimum amount of constraint-adjusted utility that I am required to produce.

Case 3 (The Loan): Suppose that I owe my friend $1,000, which is the amount that he loaned me exactly one year ago. Since that time, our fortunes have reversed. He has hit upon some difficult financial times, and I have unexpectedly inherited a fortune from my recently deceased uncle. Given our changes in fortune, I promised my wife that I would repay his loan immediately and with $200 in interest, and this despite the fact that our original agreement did not call for the payment of any interest and did not call for repayment until two years' time had elapsed. Regardless, I keep my promise to my wife and immediately pay my friend $1,200. Assume that the relevant alternatives and their associated utilities are as depicted in table 7.3.

In this case, SUPER rightly implies that my immediately paying my friend $1,200 is obligatory, and not supererogatory. In immediately paying back my friend's loan with interest, I more than minimally fulfill my duty to repay his loan, but I only minimally fulfill my duty to keep my promise to my wife. And, thus, I did nothing supererogatory in immediately paying my friend $1,200.[21] Commonsense utilitarianism accommodates this verdict, for commonsense

Table 7.3 α_1 = my paying my friend $1,000 a year from now. α_2 = my immediately paying my friend $1,200. $U_o(\varphi)$ = the utility that will accrue to others, excluding $U_i(\varphi)$, as a result of S's performing φ. $U_i(\varphi)$ = the disutility (or loss of utility) that will accrue to others as a result of S's infringing on any agent-centered constraint by performing φ. $U_{con}(\varphi)$ = $U_o(\varphi)$ + [500 × $U_i(\varphi)$]. $U_s(\varphi)$ = the utility that will accrue to S as a result of S's performing φ. $U_{com}(\varphi)$ = $U_{con}(\varphi)$ + [10 × $U_s(\varphi)$].

α_i	$U_o(\varphi)$	$U_i(\varphi)$	$U_{con}(\varphi)$	$U_s(\varphi)$	$U_{com}(\varphi)$	*deontic status*
α_1	1,000	−200	**−99,000**	200	**−97,000**	impermissible
α_2	1,200	0	**1,200**	0	**1,200**	obligatory

[21] This is, of course, consistent with the fact that my promising my wife to repay him immediately and with interest was supererogatory.

utilitarianism implies that the only relevant alternative, namely, α_1, is impermissible, making α_2 obligatory.

Case 4 (The Daughters): Suppose that I promised my friend Omar that I would help one of his two daughters—that is, either Paloma or Rene—with their homework. And assume that there is actually more moral reason for me to help Paloma, for she would benefit more from my help. Yet let us suppose that there is also more non-moral reason for me to help Paloma, as it is no more difficult for me to help Paloma than it is for me to help Rene and I would, in fact, prefer to help Paloma in that I enjoy her company more. Assume that the relevant alternatives and their associated utilities are as depicted in table 7.4.

SUPER implies that my helping Paloma is obligatory, not supererogatory. Although I have more moral reason to help Paloma than to help Rene, helping Paloma does not constitute a supererogatory act, for, as commonsense utilitarianism implies, my helping Rene is impermissible and, thus, my helping Paloma is obligatory. Helping Rene is impermissible on commonsense utilitarianism, because there is an alternative (viz., α_3) that I have both more moral reason and more reason, all things considered, to perform. I have more moral reason to help Paloma because she would benefit more from my help than Rene would. And I have more reason, all things considered, to help Paloma, because this would be better not only for Paloma but also for me given that I prefer her company.

It may seem, though, that my helping Paloma should be optional, not obligatory.[22] Now, although I admit that it can seem this way, I am not so sure. It is, after all, plausible to suppose that, other things being equal, it is generally wrong to sacrifice one's own greater good if this will only make things worse for others

Table 7.4 α_1 = **my helping neither Paloma nor Rene.** α_2 = **my helping Rene.** α_3 = **my helping Paloma.** $U_o(\varphi)$ = **the utility that will accrue to others, excluding** $U_i(\varphi)$, **as a result of S's performing** φ. $U_i(\varphi)$ = **the disutility (or loss of utility) that will accrue to others as a result of S's infringing on any agent-centered constraint by performing** φ. $U_{con}(\varphi) = U_o(\varphi) + [500 \times U_i(\varphi)]$. $U_s(\varphi)$ = **the utility that will accrue to S as a result of S's performing** φ. $U_{com}(\varphi) = U_{con}(\varphi) + [10 \times U_s(\varphi)]$.

α_i	$U_o(\varphi)$	$U_i(\varphi)$	$U_{con}(\varphi)$	$U_s(\varphi)$	$U_{com}(\varphi)$	deontic status
α_1	0	-5	**-2,500**	3	**-2,470**	impermissible
α_2	5	0	**5**	1	**15**	impermissible
α_3	10	0	**10**	2	**30**	obligatory

[22] Both Michael Ferry (2009) and Jussi Suikkanen (2009a) have raised this objection against the view that I offered PORTMORE 2003.

overall. And this is precisely what I would be doing if I helped Rene instead of Paloma. My helping Rene is less good for others overall, since Paloma would benefit more from my help. And it would be less good for me as well, since I would enjoy helping Paloma more than I would enjoy helping Rene. So, in helping Rene, I would be sacrificing my own greater good only to bring about less good for others. And, in general, such behavior seems wrong. We might think, though, that in this specific case what is at stake in my helping Paloma rather than Rene is insufficient to generate a moral requirement to help her. In essence, the claim would be that the moral reason that I have to help Paloma instead of Rene has no moral requiring strength. I am not sure whether this is the right thing to say about this particular case, but I certainly want to allow that some moral reasons have no moral requiring strength.

Here's my thinking. There are both requiring and non-requiring moral reasons for desiring an outcome, and what an agent has requiring reason to *do* is a function of only what she has requiring reason to *want*.[23] We might think, for instance, that although you have a moral reason to prefer, other things being equal, the outcome in which an acquaintance, named Lee, is slightly cheered by your complimenting him on his stylish shoes, this reason is not such that you would be guilty of any moral infraction if you did not prefer this outcome to an otherwise equal outcome in which he does not receive your compliment and is not thereby cheered. Although minimally decent people will, in general, prefer that others are better off, they need not be concerned (at least, not always) with such trivial benefits to others.

This contrasts with cases in which there clearly is a requiring reason to prefer one outcome to another. Take, for instance, the preference for children not starving. To lack this preference would be a significant failing. Lacking this preference indicates a serious flaw in one's moral character, and, insofar as one is responsible for failing to develop a good moral character and/or is responsible for failing to recognize and respond appropriately to the moral reasons that there are for preferring that children not starve, one would be blameworthy for lacking a preference for children not starving.[24] Here, then, there seems to be a requiring reason for preferring that children not starve.

If we accept that there is such a distinction between requiring and non-requiring moral reasons for desiring, then we will need to abandon commonsense utilitarianism. The problem with commonsense utilitarianism is that it does not permit us to draw a distinction between those moral reasons with and those moral reasons without moral requiring strength. And that is not commonsense utilitarianism's only problem. Another problem with commonsense utilitarianism is that it implausibly assumes that an agent's reasons for and against desiring an outcome is solely

---

[23] Recall that a requiring reason is just a reason with some moral requiring strength.

[24] I do not think that volitional control over one's preferences is a necessary condition for being blameworthy for lacking a preference. For more on this issue, see, for instance, SCANLON 1998, A. M. SMITH 2005, and A. M. SMITH 2008.

a function of people's utilities. To the contrary, it seems that sometimes agents have a reason to desire that an outcome not obtain, not because it is an outcome in which anyone's utility has been diminished, but because it is an outcome in which a constraint has been infringed upon. For instance, it seems that an agent has a reason to desire that she not infringe upon the constraint against breaking a promise even if breaking the given promise would not adversely affect anyone's utility. Commonsense utilitarianism cannot accommodate such intuitions.

Both problems can be fixed if we abstract away from commonsense utilitarianism, arriving at what I call *securitist consequentialism*. In the next section, I will explain securitist consequentialism and the argument for it. Since securitist consequentialism is but only a skeleton of a moral theory, I will spend the following section putting some more meat on its bones, arriving at commonsense consequentialism. Commonsense consequentialism has all the advantages of commonsense utilitarianism but none of its disadvantages. It is, I believe, the most plausible version of consequentialism.

§7.2 Securitist consequentialism and the argument for it

One of the lessons learned from the above is that we should accept *moral securitism:*

> **MS** It is, as of t_i, objectively morally permissible for S to perform a non-maximal set of actions, α_j, beginning at t_j $(t_i < t_j)$ if and only if, and because, at least one of the objectively morally permissible maximal sets of actions that are, as of t_i, scrupulously securable by S involves S's performing α_j.

Moral securitism is the moral analogue of (rational) securitism (see chapter 6), but, as with (rational) securitism, moral securitism is not very substantive. We need, then, to decide what substantive version of moral securitism to accept. Given the arguments from the first two chapters, I think that we should accept the following teleological version of moral securitism, namely, *securitist consequentialism:*

> **SC** The deontic status of a non-maximal set of actions, α_j, beginning at t_j $(t_i < t_j)$ is determined by the reasons there are for and against the agent's preferring certain outcomes to others, such that, if S is, as of t_i, morally required to perform α_j, then, of all the outcomes that S could bring about by performing some MSA that is, as of t_i, scrupulously securable by S, S has most reason to desire some subset of those that would result from S's performing an MSA that involves S's performing α_j.

The argument for SC runs as follows:

7.1 The deontic status of a non-maximal set of actions, α_j, beginning at t_j $(t_i < t_j)$ is determined by the agent's reasons for and against performing α_j, such that, if S is, as of t_i, morally required to perform α_j, then S has most reason, all things considered, to perform α_j. (MR^1).

7.2 An agent's reasons for and against performing α_j are determined by her reasons for and against preferring certain outcomes to others, such that if S has most reason to perform α_j, then, of all the outcomes that S could bring about by performing some MSA that is, as of t_i, scrupulously securable by S, S has most reason to desire some subset of those that would result from S's performing an MSA that involves S's performing α_j. (TCR^4).

7.3 Therefore, the deontic status of a non-maximal set of actions, α_j, beginning at t_j $(t_i < t_j)$ is determined by the reasons there are for and against the agent's preferring certain outcomes to others, such that, if S is, as of t_i, morally required to perform α_j, then, of all the outcomes that S could bring about by performing some MSA that is, as of t_i, scrupulously securable by S, S has most reason to desire some subset of those that would result from S's performing an MSA that involves S's performing α_j. (SC).

This argument is similar to the one given for act-consequentialism in §1.2 and reiterated in §2.3. The original premises have, however, been revised, which accounts for the conclusion's being securitist consequentialism as opposed to act-consequentialism. Let me now explain why we should accept these revised premises, starting with 7.1 (MR^1), which is a revised version of moral rationalism (MR)—the view that an act's deontic status is determined by the reasons there are for and against performing it, such that, if S is morally required to perform x, then S has most reason (indeed, decisive reason) to perform x. The problem with MR is that it is unnecessarily narrow in that it focuses exclusively on individual actions. We should broaden it to cover sets of actions. We can do so by replacing it with MR^1. And we do not lose anything in the process, for the same considerations that support the contention that an agent can be morally required to perform an individual act, x, only if she has decisive reason to perform x also support the broader contention that an agent can be morally required to perform a set of actions, α_j, only if she has decisive reason to perform α_j.

To illustrate, suppose that we are wondering whether S is morally required to perform α_j. Given the arguments in chapter 2, we should hold that S is morally required to perform α_j only if S has decisive reason to perform α_j. To think otherwise would be to allow that S could be morally required to perform α_j even though S has sufficient reason to perform some alternative—say, α_i. And we should reject this possibility, for it would entail that S could be morally blameworthy for having freely and knowledgeably performed α_i even though she was led to do so by flawlessly exercising her capacity to respond appropriately to the relevant reasons—the very capacity in virtue of which she is morally account-able for having performed α_i. But to hold someone accountable for having per-formed α_i in virtue of her possessing a certain capacity that, when exercised flawlessly, leads her to perform α_i is inappropriate. We should, then, endorse the broader 7.1 and not just the narrower MR, for the same arguments that were given in support of MR in Chapter 2 can, mutatis mutandis, be given in support of 7.1 (MR^1) as well.

Let us turn now to 7.2 (TCR^4). Premise 7.2 is a revised version of our original formulation of the teleological conception of practical reasons (viz., TCR)—the view according to which S has more reason to perform a_i than to perform a_j just when, and because, S has more reason to desire that o_i obtains than to desire that o_j obtains. There are two problems with TCR. First, it is too narrow in that it focuses exclusively on individual acts. We should broaden it to encompass act-sets. Second, it is formulated on the assumption that actualism is true.[25] But, as I have argued above, securitism is superior to both actualism and possibilism. We should, therefore, reformulate TCR so that it is compatible with securitism, as is the case with 7.2. For these two reasons, we should accept 7.2 (TCR^4) as opposed to TCR. Again, we do not lose anything in the process, for the arguments that were given in support TCR in chapter 3 could just as well be given in support of 7.2 (TCR^4), mutatis mutandis.

Given that we should both accept 7.1 (MR^1) as opposed to MR and accept 7.2 (TCR^4) as opposed to TCR, it follows that we should accept securitist consequen-tialism (SC) as opposed to act-consequentialism (AC), for 7.3 (SC) is entailed by the conjunction of 7.1 and 7.2.

§7.3 Commonsense consequentialism and how it compares with traditional act-consequentialism

Although securitist consequentialism is a substantive version of moral securitism, it still is not all that substantive as versions of consequentialism go, for it does not tell us how to rank outcomes. Drawing on the insights garnered from chapter 5 and the above, we should, I believe, rank outcomes as dual-ranking act-consequential-ism does. By adopting its dual-ranking structure, we can ensure that the resulting theory will, as does dual-ranking act-consequentialism, accommodate the basic features of commonsense morality, such as supererogatory acts, agent-centered options, and the self-other asymmetry. But, unlike dual-ranking act-consequen-tialism, we should distinguish between requiring and non-requiring reasons for desiring an outcome. For, as we learned in §§7.1.5, not all moral reasons for desiring an outcome have moral requiring strength—that is, not all moral reasons for

---

[25] This is because o_i is just the outcome that *would* obtain were S to perform a_i, and likewise for o_j and a_j.

desiring an outcome are such as to make one blameworthy for lacking that desire even in the absence of countervailing reasons for not having that desire.

The result of conjoining securitist consequentialism with a dual-ranking structure, while allowing that there are both requiring and non-requiring reasons for desiring an outcome, is what I call *commonsense consequentialism*:

> **CSC** The view according to which all the following are true: (*a*) it is, as of t_i, objectively morally permissible for S to perform a non-maximal set of actions, α_j, beginning at t_j ($t_i < t_j$) if and only if, and because, it is, as of t_i, objectively morally permissible for S to perform a maximal set of actions, MSA_i, that involves S's performing α_j; (*b*) it is, as of t_i, objectively morally permissible for S to perform a maximal set of actions, MSA_i, if and only if, and because, MSA_i is one of the optimal MSAs that is, as of t_i, scrupulously securable by S; (*c*) MSA_i is one of the optimal MSAs that is, as of t_i, scrupulously securable by S if and only if, and because, MSA_i's outcome is not, on S's evaluative ranking, outranked by that of any alternative MSA that is, as of t_i, scrupulously securable by S; and (*d*) MSA_i's outcome is not, on S's evaluative ranking, outranked by that of any alternative MSA that is, as of t_i, scrupulously securable by S if and only if, and because, there is no alternative MSA that is, as of t_i, scrupulously securable by S whose outcome S has both more requiring reason and more reason, all things considered, to want to obtain.[26]

Clause *a* ensures that commonsense consequentialism takes the top-down approach to assessing permissibility. Clause *b* ensures that commonsense consequentialism is a maximizing version of moral securitism. Clause *c* ensures that it is a teleological/consequentialist version of maximizing moral securitism that employs an agent-relative ranking of outcomes. And clause *d* ensures that this ranking of outcomes is a function of two auxiliary evaluative rankings, one a ranking of outcomes in terms of how much requiring reason the agent has to desire that each obtains and the other a ranking of outcomes in terms of how much reason, all things considered, the agent has to desire that each obtains.

Since commonsense consequentialism is a bit unwieldy, it might be useful to think of commonsense consequentialism as a three-step procedure (although it is, of course, a criterion of rightness, not a decision procedure):

---

[26] Again, for the sake of simplifying the discussion, I am assuming that counterfactual determinism is true and that, therefore, there is some unique determinate outcome associated with any given MSA. Of course, I should allow for the possibility that counterfactual determinism is false. Thus, strictly speaking, commonsense consequentialism should be formulated in terms of *prospects* as opposed to *outcomes*. In the final and most precise formulation of commonsense consequentialism (viz., CSC*) that is given later on in this chapter, I do formulate the view in terms of prospects.

Step 1: Survey all the various MSAs that are, as of t_i, scrupulously securable by S.

Step 2: For each of these MSAs, determine whether or not the MSA is objectively morally permissible. A given MSA is objectively morally permissible if and only if there is no other MSA whose outcome S has both more requiring reason and more reason, all things considered, to want to obtain.[27]

Step 3: Judge that S is, as of t_i, objectively morally permitted to perform a non-maximal set of actions, α_j, beginning at t_j $(t_i < t_j)$ if and only if at least one of the objectively morally permissible MSAs that are, as of t_i, scrupulously securable by S involves S's performing α_j.

To acquire a better understanding of commonsense consequentialism, it will be helpful to compare it to *traditional act-consequentialism* and its *criterion of rightness*:

TAC$_{cr}$ S's performing x is morally permissible if and only if S's performing x would maximize the good (impersonally construed).[28]

As I explain below, commonsense consequentialism departs from traditional act-consequentialism in five important respects. The first two concern how the two theories differ in their criteria for determining moral permissibility, the next two concern how they differ in their methods for ranking outcomes, and the last concerns how they differ in their abilities to accommodate certain basic features of commonsense morality.

§§7.3.1 Whereas traditional act-consequentialism offers a criterion for evaluating only individual actions, commonsense consequentialism offers a criterion for evaluating sets of actions

Traditional act-consequentialism's criterion of rightness (i.e., TAC$_{cr}$) is a criterion for evaluating only individual actions (types and tokens). Unfortunately, though, not all sets of actions constitute larger individual actions. And, thus, TAC$_{cr}$ is unable to evaluate certain sets of actions. Yet, as we have learned, this is something that any adequate moral theory must be able to do if it is going to account for

---

[27] Recall that S has optimal reason to φ if and only if there is no available alternative, ψ, such that S has more reason to ψ than to φ.

[28] Traditional act-consequentialism's criterion of rightness (i.e., TAC$_{cr}$) is not equivalent to traditional act-consequentialism, for one can both accept TAC$_{cr}$ and reject act-consequentialism, as where one holds that agents should maximize the good but denies that agents always have most reason to desire that the good be maximized. Of course, one cannot both accept traditional act-consequentialism and reject act-consequentialism, because traditional act-consequentialism is, by definition, a species of act-consequentialism; traditional act-consequentialism holds both that act-consequentialism is true and that an act produces an outcome that the agent has optimal reason to want to obtain if and only if it maximizes the good.

many of our typical moral judgments, as we often do make moral judgments concerning various sets of actions. It is fortunate, then, that commonsense consequentialism avoids this problem, for, unlike TAC$_{cr}$, commonsense consequentialism's criterion of rightness is formulated using the variable, α_j, which ranges over sets of actions.

It is because commonsense consequentialism can assess the deontic statuses of sets of actions that it is compatible with the idea that there are imperfect duties, duties that can be fulfilled only by performing certain sets of actions over time. For instance, you cannot fulfill the duty of beneficence by performing any single beneficent act. To fulfill this duty, you must act in such a way as to demonstrate that you have adopted the happiness of others as a major, *ongoing*, and life-shaping end, and the only way to do that is to complete some fairly extended set of actions that demonstrates an ongoing commitment to promoting the welfare of others.

§§7.3.2 Whereas traditional act-consequentialism is a form of direct consequentialism, commonsense consequentialism is a form of indirect consequentialism

Commonsense consequentialism is a version of securitist consequentialism, which is a form of *indirect consequentialism*. Whereas, on *direct consequentialism* (i.e., act-consequentialism), the deontic status of an individual action is determined by how its outcome ranks relative to those of the available alternatives on some evaluative ranking of outcomes, on *indirect consequentialism*, the deontic status of an individual action is determined by whether or not it accords with some ideal set of rules (rule-consequentialism) or stems from some ideal set of motives (motive consequentialism) or is contained within some ideal set of MSAs (securitist consequentialism). The ideal set of rules, motives, or MSAs is in turn selected on the basis of how their associated outcomes rank relative to those of the available alternatives on some evaluative ranking of outcomes. Hence, the consequences are only indirectly relevant in assessing the deontic statuses of individual actions.

To illustrate, consider rule-consequentialism. It holds that an individual act is morally permissible if and only if it accords with the ideal set of rules. And, on at least one version of rule-consequentialism, the ideal set of rules is the one "whose internalization by the overwhelming majority of everyone everywhere in each new generation has maximum expected value in terms of well-being (with some priority for the worst off)" (HOOKER 2000, p. 32). Similarly, securitist consequentialism holds that an individual act is morally permissible if and only if it is contained within the ideal set of MSAs. And, on securitist consequentialism, the ideal set of MSAs (i.e., the permissible MSAs) consists in all and only those MSAs whose outcomes are not, on the agent's evaluative ranking, outranked by that of any alternative MSA that is scrupulously securable by the agent.

Being a version of securitist consequentialism as opposed to act-consequentialism is what enables commonsense consequentialism to endorse moral securitism: the view that it is, as of t_i, objectively morally permissible for S to perform a non-maximal set of actions, α_j, beginning at t_j ($t_i < t_j$) if and only if, and because, at least one of the objectively morally permissible maximal sets of actions that are, as of t_i, scrupulously securable by S involves S's performing α_j. As I argued above, we should endorse moral securitism given the problems associated with its two main rivals: actualism and possibilism.

§§7.3.3 Whereas traditional act-consequentialism ranks outcomes along a single evaluative dimension, commonsense consequentialism ranks outcomes according to a function of two auxiliary rankings, each along a different evaluative dimension

If moral rationalism (MR) is true, then it is always morally permissible to do what there is most reason to do, all things considered. This and the fact that moral reasons are not rationally overriding implies that they are not morally overriding either—that is, that non-moral reasons can, and sometimes do, prevent moral reasons, even those with substantial moral requiring strength, from generating moral requirements. Thus, non-moral reasons serve to limit what we can be morally required to do. If, for instance, the non-moral reasons that you have to perform some self-interested act, x, outweigh the moral reasons that you have to perform some altruistic alternative act, y, then you cannot be morally required to sacrifice your self-interest and perform y as opposed to x. (Of course, you would not be morally required to perform x either, for you would also be permitted to do what you have more moral reason to do rather than what you have less moral reason to do.)

The upshot of all this is that the deontic status of an action is a function of both moral reasons and non-moral reasons. That function, I have argued in chapter 5, is given by the following *meta*-criterion of rightness:

> **META** S's performing φ is morally permissible if and only if there is no available alternative, ψ, that S has both more requiring reason and more reason, all things considered, to perform.

And, in that same chapter, I argued that the only way to accommodate META within a consequentialist framework is to hold that one outcome outranks another, on the agent's evaluative ranking, if and only if she has both more requiring reason and more reason, all things considered, to want the one to obtain than to want the other to obtain. Thus, on commonsense consequentialism, the ranking of outcomes is a function of two auxiliary rankings: one a ranking in terms of how much requiring reason the agent has to desire that they obtain and the other in terms of how much reason, all things considered, the agent has to desire that they obtain.

As I showed in chapter 4, this dual-ranking structure allows the consequential-ist to accommodate agent-centered options (of both the agent-favoring and the agent-sacrificing varieties), for it provides agents with the option to give their interests more (as in the case of agent-favoring options) or less (as in the case of agent-sacrificing options) weight than the equivalent interests of others. Traditional act-consequentialism's criterion of rightness (i.e., TAC_{cr}), by contrast, ranks outcomes along a single evaluative dimension: their impersonal value. Thus, unlike commonsense consequentialism, there is no way for TAC_{cr} to accommodate options to give one's own interests anything but the weight that they have from the impersonal perspective.

§§7.3.4 Whereas traditional act-consequentialism ranks outcomes according to their value, commonsense consequentialism ranks outcomes according to how much reason the agent has to desire that they obtain

Suppose that I can effect only one of two possible worlds: either the one in which I save my own daughter (call this w_1) or the one in which I ensure that some stranger saves his slightly more gifted daughter (call this w_2). And let me just stipulate that w_2 is slightly better than w_1, as the stranger's daughter would con-tribute slightly more impersonal good to the world than my daughter would. We will assume, though, that everything else is equal. Now, despite the fact that w_2 is slightly better than w_1, it seems that I have more reason to desire that w_1 be actualized than to desire that w_2 be actualized, for it seems that the reason that I have to desire the world in which my daughter is saved outweighs the reason that I have to desire the world in which there is slightly more impersonal good. And it is not just that I have more reason, *all things considered*, to desire that w_1 be actualized. Given the moral importance of the special relationship that I have with my daughter, I also have more *requiring* reason to desire that w_1 be actualized. Indeed, if I did not care more about the preservation of my daugh-ter's life than I did about such small increases in the impersonal good, I would be open to moral criticism. Parents ought, morally speaking, to care more about the preservation of their children's lives than they do about such small increases in the impersonal good.

If all this is right, then commonsense consequentialism and traditional act-consequentialism will sometimes rank these two worlds differently. On tradi-tional act-consequentialism, there is only one possible ranking of these two worlds, and, on that ranking, w_2 outranks w_1. On commonsense consequential-ism, by contrast, there is potentially a different ranking for each agent, as each agent is to rank outcomes according to how much reason she has to desire that each of them obtains. Since one agent can have more reason than another to desire that a certain outcome obtains, different agents can end up with different rankings. This is true in the above example. On my evaluative ranking, w_1 out-ranks w_2, but, on the stranger's evaluative ranking, w_2 outranks w_1. Thus, whereas traditional act-consequentialism holds that we all have the same goal of bringing about the best possible outcome, commonsense consequentialism holds that each individual agent has the potentially distinct goal of bringing about the outcome that *she* has most reason to desire. It is because commonsense consequentialism, unlike traditional act-consequentialism, holds that each agent has her own ranking of outcomes that commonsense consequentialism, unlike TAC_{cr}, can accommodate agent-centered constraints, such as the special obligation that parents have to ensure that they save their own children even at the cost of fewer children being saved by their parents.

The problem with ranking outcomes according to their value, then, is that it excludes from consideration all agent-relative reasons. This is because the value of a possible world correlates with only a subset of an agent's reasons for desiring its actualization—specifically, a subset of her agent-neutral reasons for desiring its actualization.[29] But agents can have agent-relative reasons for desiring its actualization, as is the case with my reasons for desiring w_1—the possible world in which my daughter is saved. Moreover, these agent-relative reasons can tip the balance such that agents sometimes have better overall reason to prefer a worse world to a better world, as is the case where I have better overall reason to prefer w_1 to w_2. And, as I argued in chapter 3, if I have better overall reason to prefer w_1 to w_2, then I have better overall reason to *do* what will actualize w_1 as opposed to what will actualize w_2. Given this and the arguments for moral rationalism from chapter 2, we should conclude, contrary to what TAC_{cr} implies, that I cannot be obligated to act so as to actualize w_2 as opposed to w_1 even though w_2 has more impersonal value. The lesson, then, is that if we want to take into account all of our reasons for desiring a given outcome and, thereby, all of our reasons for acting so as to produce that outcome, we must rank outcomes according to how much reason the agent has to desire that they obtain as opposed to how valuable they are.

§§7.3.5 Whereas traditional act-consequentialism cannot accommodate the basic features of commonsense morality, commonsense consequentialism can

Commonsense consequentialism can accommodate all the basic features of commonsense morality: agent-centered restrictions, special obligations, agent-favoring options, agent-sacrificing options, and supererogatory acts. Let me briefly illustrate each in turn. To account for an agent-centered restriction against, say, the commission of murder, the proponent of commonsense consequentialism need only claim that, other things being equal, S has both more requiring reason and more reason, all things considered, to prefer the outcome of an MSA in which

---

[29] It is only a subset of her reasons, because we must not only meet the partiality challenge, but also solve the wrong-kind-of-reasons problem. See chapter 3.

she refrains from murdering some individual to the outcome of an otherwise identical MSA in which she instead murders that individual so as to prevent less than n others from each committing a comparable murder—where n marks the threshold for this non-absolute restriction.[30] To account for the special obligation that, say, parents have to nurture their own children, the proponent of commonsense consequentialism need only claim that, other things being equal, S has both more requiring reason and more reason, all things considered, to prefer the outcome of an MSA in which she nurtures her own children to the outcome of an otherwise identical MSA in which she instead abandons her own children so as to ensure that less than n others nurture their children—where n marks the threshold for this non-absolute special obligation.

To account for the agent-favoring option that S currently has, say, to perform either an altruistic act or a self-interested act, the proponent of commonsense consequentialism need only claim that there is both a morally permissible MSA scrupulously securable by S in which she presently performs an altruistic act and a morally permissible MSA scrupulously securable by her in which she presently performs a self-interested act, for, in either case, a reasonable balance between altruism and egoism will be achieved.

To account for the agent-sacrificing option that S currently has, say, to use her last dose of painkillers so as to alleviate either some stranger's mild headache or her own more severe headache, the proponent of commonsense consequentialism need only claim that, other things being equal, she has more requiring reason to prefer the outcome of an MSA in which she alleviates the stranger's headache, but more reason, all things considered, to prefer the outcome of an otherwise identical MSA in which she instead alleviates her own more severe headache. And, to account for the fact that it would be supererogatory for her to alleviate the stranger's headache, the proponent of commonsense consequentialism need only both accept that S has more requiring reason to prefer the outcome of an MSA in which she uses her last dose of painkillers to alleviate the stranger's mild headache and accept the account of supererogation that I gave above. We see, then, that commonsense consequentialism shares with dual-ranking act-consequentialism the ability to accommodate the basic features of commonsense morality.

---

[30] Note the ease with which commonsense consequentialism can account for the fact that agent-centered restrictions have thresholds: at some point, the agent-neutral reason that one has to want there to be fewer infringements of the restriction overall outweighs the agent-relative reason that one has to want there to be no personal infringements of that restriction. Deontological views have a much more difficult time accounting for thresholds—see, for instance, ELLIS 1992. Commonsense consequentialism can with similar ease account for why some agent-centered restrictions are more stringent than others, such that one can permissibly infringe upon one but not the other in instances where the two conflict. The proponent of commonsense consequentialism can claim, for instance, that the agent-relative reason that one has to refrain from committing murder outweighs, other things being equal, the agent-relative reason one has to refrain from breaking a promise.

§7.4 What has been shown and what remains to be shown

I have argued for a rationalist conception of the authority of morality, for a tel-eological conception of practical reasons, for a teleological conception of morality, and for a teleological conception of (objective) rationality. Below, I give the final and most precise formulations of these views, taking into account both (*i*) the fact that these views should be formulated in terms of *prospects* as opposed to *outcomes* given the possibility that counterfactual determinism is false and, thus, the possibility that there is more than one outcome associated with a given action or set of actions and (*ii*) the fact that these prospects should be ranked in terms of the agent's time-relative ranking given that there are not only agent-relative, but also time-relative, reasons for preferring one prospect to another.[31]

MR* *Moral Rationalism:* The deontic status of α_j is determined by the agent's rea-sons for and against performing α_j, such that, if S is, as of t_i, morally required to perform α_j, then S has at t_i most (indeed, decisive) reason, all things con-sidered, to perform α_j.

TCR* *The Teleological Conception of (Practical) Reasons:* An agent's reasons for and against performing α_j are determined by her reasons for and against prefer-ring certain outcomes to others, such that S has at t_i more reason to per-form a_i than to perform a_j just when, and because, S has at t_i more reason to desire p_i than to desire p_j, where p_i and p_j are the prospects of a_i and a_j, respectively.

CSC* *Commonsense Consequentialism:* The view according to which all the follow-ing are true: (*a*) it is, as of t_i, objectively morally permissible for S to per-form a non-maximal set of actions, α_j, beginning at t_j ($t_i < t_j$) if and only if, and because, it is, as of t_i, objectively morally permissible for S to perform a maximal set of actions, MSA_i, that involves S's performing α_j; (*b*) it is, as of t_i, objectively morally permissible for S to perform a maximal set of actions, MSA_i, if and only if, and because, MSA_i is one of the optimal MSAs that is, as of t_i, scrupulously securable by S; (*c*) MSA_i is one of the optimal MSAs that is, as of t_i, scrupulously securable by S if and only if, and because, MSA_i's prospect is not, on S's t_i-relative evaluative ranking, outranked by that of any alternative MSA that is, as of t_i, scrupulously securable by S; and (*d*) MSA_i's prospect is not, on S's t_i-relative evaluative ranking, outranked by that of any alternative MSA that is, as of t_i, scrupulously securable by S if and only if, and because, there is no alternative MSA that is, as of t_i,

---

[31] For why we need to take facts *i* and *ii* into account, see notes 5 and 11 of chapter 3, respectively.

scrupulously securable by S whose prospect S has at t_i both more requiring reason and more reason, all things considered, to desire.[32]

TMS *Teleological Maximizing Securitism:* The view according to which all the following are true: (*a*) it is, as of t_j, objectively rationally permissible for S to perform a non-maximal set of actions, α_j, beginning at t_j $(t_i < t_j)$ if and only if, and because, it is, as of t_i, objectively rationally permissible for S to perform a maximal set of actions, MSA_i, that involves S's performing α_j; (*b*) it is, as of t_i, objectively rationally permissible for S to perform a maximal set of actions, MSA_i, if and only if, and because, MSA_i is one of the optimal MSAs that is, as of t_i, scrupulously securable by S; (*c*) MSA_i is one of the optimal MSAs that is, as of t_i, scrupulously securable by S if and only if, and because, MSA_i's prospect is not, on S's t_i-relative evaluative ranking, outranked by that of any alternative MSA that is, as of t_i, scrupulously securable by S; and (*d*) MSA_i's prospect is not, on S's t_i-relative evaluative ranking, outranked by that of any alternative MSA that is, as of t_i, scrupulously securable by S if and only if, and because, there is no alternative MSA that is, as of t_i, scrupulously securable by S whose prospect S has at t_i more reason, all things considered, to desire.

I have shown that these four theses form a coherent whole that together provide a systematic account of our commonsense intuitions about morality, rationality, and the relationship between the two. Moral rationalism (i.e., MR*), for instance, accounts for our intuition that morality, unlike the law, is rationally authoritative. The teleological conception of reasons (i.e., TCR*) systemically accounts for our commonsense intuitions about what we have reason to do. Commonsense consequentialism (i.e., CSC*) systematically accounts for our commonsense intuitions about what we (objectively) morally ought to do, providing, in the process, a systematic account of all the basic features of commonsense morality: imperfect duties, special obligations, supererogatory acts, agent-favoring options, agent-sacrificing options, agent-centered restrictions, and the self-other asymmetry. Lastly, teleological maximizing securitism (i.e., TMS) systematically accounts for our commonsense intuitions about what we (objectively) rationally ought to do, providing, in the process, what is perhaps the most plausible explanation for the basic belief—the belief that, in most typical choice situations, the relevant reasons do not require performing one particular alternative, but instead permit performing any of numerous alternatives.

---

[32] S has at t_i more (requiring) reason to desire MSA_1's prospect, p_1, than to desire MSA_2's prospect, p_2, if and only if $\Sigma_i [Pr(o_i/MSA_1) \times D_{s\text{-}t}(o_i)]$ is greater than $\Sigma_i [Pr(o_i/MSA_2) \times D_{s\text{-}t}(o_i)]$, where MSA_i is some maximal set of actions, $Pr(o_i/MSA_i)$ is the objective probability of o_i's obtaining given S's performance of MSA_i, and $D_{s\text{-}t}(o_i)$ is the S-relative t_i-relative desirability value of o_i, which is just a measure of how much (requiring) reason S has at t_i to desire that o_i obtains.

I have shown that maximizing, teleological theories—whether they be about reasons, morality, or rationality—are extremely ecumenical and accommodating. These theories can accommodate our commonsense intuitions about reasons, morality, and rationality while remaining compatible with a wide range of theses about the nature of value, morality, and persons—even those that have seemed to some (e.g., Anderson and Scanlon) antithetical to the teleological approach. I have shown, for instance, that these theses are compatible with the view that the primary bearers of value are not states of affairs but instead persons, animals, and things, and that our basic evaluative attitudes—attitudes such as love, respect, and admiration—are non-propositional attitudes that we take up toward persons, animals, and things. Surprisingly, then, we find that these teleological theories are compatible with even the idea that persons, not states of affairs, have intrinsic value and that we respond appropriately to their value by loving, respecting, and admiring them. Moreover, these theories are compatible with the view that we are morally prohibited from acting in ways that fail to express our respect for persons even when our doing so would prevent more numerous others from acting in ways that are comparably disrespectful to persons. What's more, these theories have the ability to surpass some of their non-teleological rivals in accommodating our commonsense intuitions, doing a better job, for instance, of accommodating our commonsense intuitions about intra-agent cases.[33]

Admittedly, though, these teleological views (i.e., TCR*, CSC*, and TMS) will be compatible with our commonsense intuitions only if certain assumptions about what agents have reason to desire are correct. The real question, then, is whether what agents have reason to desire is such that, when inputted into these teleological theories, the output is plausible deontic verdicts. I have suggested that this is so. I have suggested, for instance, that it is intuitive to think that, other things being equal, an agent ought to prefer the state of affairs in which she saves her loved one to the state of affairs in which she enables some stranger to save her (the stranger's) loved one, even if the latter would be slightly better, impersonally speaking. We would, I think, fault an agent for lacking such a preference, thinking either that she is not responding appropriately to the reasons that their loving relationship provides or that she must not truly love her putative "loved" one. And, as I argued in chapter 4, this view about what agents have reason to desire is precisely the one that the consequentialist needs to ground the special obligation that agents have to save their own loved ones.

I also argued, again in chapter 4, that even in those cases in which our pre-theoretical judgments about what we have reason to desire are not quite what is needed to generate plausible deontic verdicts when inputted into a teleological theory such as commonsense consequentialism, we might, on reflection, come to a different judgment about what there is reason to desire in light of the intuitive

---

[33] See §4.3.

attractiveness of moral rationalism and the teleological conception of practical reasons and their entailment of consequentialism. Of course, all this is highly speculative. Ideally, what we want is a fully developed theory about what agents have reason to desire and to be shown that such a theory, when conjoined with theories such as commonsense consequentialism and teleological maximizing securitism, yields plausible deontic verdicts. Unfortunately, I have no such theory to offer.[34] There will, then, be some skepticism as to whether these teleological theories will in fact do all that I say that they can. This is understandable.

I should remind my readers, though, that my aim has not been to convince them that commonsense consequentialism is the most plausible moral theory or that teleological maximizing securitism is the most plausible theory of objective rationality. To have any hope of succeeding in such ambitious aims, I would have to provide and then defend a fully developed theory about what agents have reason to desire. What's more, I would need to survey all their rivals and do a thorough assessment of how commonsense consequentialism and teleological maximizing securitism compare to them. I have done neither. But, then, my aim has been considerably less ambitious. I hope only to have developed the most plausible versions of these theories and to have shown that these theories are attractive and promising and so deserving of further consideration. The advantages and disadvantages of theories that take the deontic statuses of actions to be a function of the value of their outcomes have been well explored, but the same cannot be said of the advantages and disadvantages of theories that take the deontic statuses of actions to be a function of how much reason agents have to want their outcomes to obtain—theories such as dual-ranking act-consequentialism, commonsense consequentialism, and teleological maximizing securitism. My hope is to have gotten this exploration underway and to have uncovered enough to demonstrate that such theories merit further exploration.

---

[34] I do, however, have some ideas about where we might begin to look for such a theory—see PORTMORE 2005, section 3.

GLOSSARY

Across-the-board approach: The approach to assessing permissibility whereby normative principles are applied directly to minimal acts, maximal sets of acts, and everything in between. (Contrast *top-down approach* and *bottom-up approach*.)

Act: Something that an agent does because she intends to do it.

Act alternative: See *alternative act*.

Act-consequentialism (AC): The view that an act's deontic status is determined by the agent's reasons for and against preferring its outcome to those of the available alternatives, such that, if S is morally required to perform *x*, then, of all the outcomes that S could bring about, S has most (indeed, decisive) reason to desire that *x*'s outcome obtains. (Contrast *personal value teleology* and *impersonal value teleology*.)

Act-set: A set of one or more acts that are all jointly performable by a single agent.

Act-token: A particular act performed by a particular agent at a particular time. (Contrast *act-type*.)

Act-type: A universal that can, in general, be instantiated by a number of distinct act-tokens. (Contrast *act-token*.)

Actualism: The view that it is, as of t_i, objectively (morally or rationally) permissible for S to perform a non-maximal set of actions, α_j, beginning at t_j $(t_i < t_j)$ if and only if, and because, the maximal set of actions that S would actually perform were S to perform α_j is no worse than the maximal set of actions that S would actually perform were S not to perform α_j. (Contrast *securitism* and *possibilism*.)

Agent-centered constraint: A constraint on maximizing the good that it would be wrong to infringe upon even in some circumstances in which doing so would minimize comparable infringements of that constraint. Examples include *special obligations* and *agent-centered restrictions*.

Agent-centered option: A moral option either to act so as to make things better overall but worse for oneself (or others) or to act so as to make things better for oneself (or others) but worse overall. Examples include *agent-favoring options* and *agent-sacrificing options*.

Agent-centered restriction: A type of agent-centered constraint that prohibits agents from performing certain act-types (such as murder) even in some circumstances in which performing the given act-type is the only way to minimize comparable performances of that act-type. (See also *special obligation*.)

Agent-favoring option: A type of agent-centered option that provides one with a moral option either to act so as to make things better overall but worse for oneself or to act so as to make things better for oneself but worse overall. (Contrast *agent-sacrificing option*.)

Agent-identical: Having the same agent.

Agent-sacrificing option: A type of agent-centered option that provides one with a moral option either to act so as to make things better overall but worse for others or to act so as to make things better for others but worse overall. (Contrast *agent-favoring option*.)

Agglomeration Principle (PAC): The principle according to which permissibility agglomerates over conjunction, such that: $[P(S, t_i, x_1), P(S, t_i, x_2), \ldots, \& \ P(S, t_i, x_n)] \rightarrow P[S, t_i, (x_1, x_2, \ldots, \& \ x_n)]$, where "$P(S, t_i, x_i)$" stands for "S is, as of t_i, permitted to perform x_i." (Contrast *distribution principle*.)

Aggregate utility of an act: The sum of all the utility it produces minus the sum of all the disutility it produces.

Alternative acts: Acts that are agent-identical, time-identical, mutually exclusive, and jointly exhaustive.

Asymmetric relation: A relation, R, is asymmetric just in case: if xRy, then $\sim y$Rx.

Available: That which is a relevant option. Possibilities for what constitutes a relevant option include: that which is *securable* by the agent, that which is *scrupulously securable* by the agent, and that which is *personally possible* for the agent.

Basic belief: The belief that, in most typical choice situations, the relevant reasons do not require performing one particular alternative, but instead permit performing any of numerous alternatives.

Best alternative: See *optimific alternative*.

Better for: For all subjects S and all states of affairs p and q, it is better for S that p is the case than that q is the case if and only if the set of all the right kind of reasons to prefer, for S's sake, its being the case that p to its being the case that q is weightier than the set of all the right kind of reasons to prefer, for S's sake, its being the case that q to its being the case that p (SCHROEDER 2008b).

Better that: For all states of affairs p and q, it is better that p is the case than that q is the case if and only if the set of all the right kind of reasons to prefer its being the case that p to its being the case that q is weightier than the set of all the right kind of reasons to prefer its being the case that q to its being the case that p (SCHROEDER 2008b).

Blameworthy: Being worthy of moral blame. S is blameworthy for performing x if and only if it is appropriate (i.e., fitting) for S to feel guilt about having performed x and appropriate for others to feel indignation in response to S's having performed x and, if they were thereby wronged, also to resent S for having performed x.

Bottom-up approach: The approach to assessing permissibility whereby normative principles are applied only to minimal acts and the agglomeration principle is used to assess the permissibility of non-minimal acts. (Contrast *top-down approach* and *across-the-board approach*; see also *agglomeration principle*.)

Carries out: S carries out an intention to perform α_i if and only if S performs α_i.

Commonsense consequentialism (CSC*): The view according to which all the following are true: (*a*) it is, as of t_i, objectively morally permissible for S to perform a non-maximal set of actions, α_j, beginning at t_j ($t_i < t_j$) if and only if, and because, it is, as of t_i, objectively morally permissible for S to perform a maximal set of actions, MSA$_j$, that involves S's performing α_j; (*b*) it is, as of t_i, objectively morally permissible for S to perform a maximal set of actions, MSA$_j$, if and only if, and because, MSA$_j$ is one of the optimal MSAs that is, as of t_i, scrupulously securable by S; (*c*) MSA$_j$ is one of the optimal MSAs that is, as of t_i, scrupulously securable by S if and only if, and because, MSA$_j$'s prospect is not, on S's t_i-relative evaluative ranking, outranked by that of any alternative MSA that is, as of t_i, scrupulously securable by S; and (*d*) MSA$_j$'s prospect is not, on S's t_i-relative evaluative ranking, outranked by that of any alternative MSA that is, as of t_i, scrupulously securable by S if and only if, and because, there is no alternative MSA that is, as of t_i, scrupulously securable by S whose prospect S has at t_i both more requiring reason and more reason, all things considered, to desire. (See also *prospect* and *more reason to desire*.)

Commonsense utilitarianism (CSU): The view according to which all the following are true: (a) it is, as of t_i, objectively morally permissible for S to perform a non-maximal set of actions, α_j, beginning at t_j $(t_i < t_j)$ if and only if, and because, it is, as of t_i, objectively morally permissible for S to perform a maximal set of actions, MSA_i, that involves S's performing α_j; (b) it is, as of t_i, objectively morally permissible for S to perform a maximal set of actions, MSA_i, if and only if, and because, MSA_i is one of the optimal MSAs that is, as of t_i, scrupulously securable by S; (c) MSA_i is one of the optimal MSAs that is, as of t_i, scrupulously securable by S if and only if, and because, MSA_i's outcome is not, on S's evaluative ranking, outranked by that of any alternative MSA that is, as of t_i, scrupulously securable by S; and (d) MSA_i's outcome is not, on S's evaluative ranking, outranked by that of any alternative MSA that is, as of t_i, scrupulously securable by S if and only if, and because, there is no alternative MSA that is, as of t_i, scrupulously securable by S whose outcome contains both more constraint-adjusted utility and more comprehensively adjusted utility than MSA_i's outcome does. (See also *constraint-adjusted utility* and *comprehensively adjusted utility*.)

Compound act: An act that has two or more simpler acts as parts. Examples include (1) assembling a model airplane and (2) chewing gum while walking. (Contrast *minimal act*.)

Comprehensively adjusted utility: The sum of the constraint-adjusted utility added to the product of S's utility times ten. (See also *constraint-adjusted utility*.)

Consequentialism: See *act-consequentialism*.

Consequentialist prudence: The view that S's performing x is prudent if and only if S's performing x would maximize S's utility.

Consequentialize: To construct a substantive version of consequentialism that is deontically equivalent to some nonconsequentialist theory. (See also *deontically equivalent*.)

Constraining right: A potential victim, V, has a constraining right against being φ-ed (e.g., murdered) if and only if V has a right not to be φ-ed even in some circumstances in which the agent's φ-ing V would minimize comparable commissions of φ by herself or others.

Constraint: See *agent-centered constraint*.

Constraint-adjusted utility: The sum of the utility for others, adjusted by multiplying any disutility (or loss of utility) resulting from S's infringements of any agent-centered constraints by five hundred.

Counterfactual determinism: The view that, for any event e (including actions, sets of actions, and the formations of intentions), there is some determinate fact as to what the world would be like if e were to occur.

Decisive moral reason: S has decisive moral reason to φ if and only if S's reasons are such as to make S objectively morally required to φ. (Contrast *sufficient moral reason*.)

Decisive reason: S has decisive reason to φ if and only if S's reasons are such as to make S objectively rationally required to φ. (Contrast *sufficient reason*.)

Defeat: To say that the reasons that favor φ-ing defeat the reasons that favor ~φ-ing is to say that the reasons that favor φ-ing prevail over the reasons that favor ~φ-ing, such that the agent has decisive reason to φ. (Contrast *successfully counter*.)

Deontic equivalence thesis (DET): The thesis that, for any remotely plausible nonconsequentialist theory, there is a substantive version of consequentialism that is deontically equivalent to it.

Deontic moral value: A measure of how much (objective) moral reason there is to perform an act.

Deontic status: All acts have one of the following two deontic statuses: (1) permissible or (2) impermissible. Additionally, all permissible acts have one of the following two deontic statuses: (a) optional or (b) obligatory. And all optional acts have one of the following two deontic statuses: (i) merely permissible or (ii) supererogatory.

Deontic value: A measure of how much (objective) reason there is to perform an act.

Deontically equivalent: Two theories are deontically equivalent if and only if they agree about the deontic status of every (actual or possible) act. That is, for any deontic predicate (such as, permissible, impermissible, optional, obligatory, or supererogatory), both theories are in perfect agreement as to the set of actions that are in the extension of that predicate.

Deontological theory: A nonconsequentialist moral theory that includes at least one agent-centered constraint.

Direct consequentialism: The view that the deontic status of an individual action is determined by how its outcome ranks relative to those of the available alternatives on some evaluative ranking of outcomes. An example is act-consequentialism. (Contrast *indirect consequentialism*.)

Distribution principle (PDC): The principle according to which permissibility distributes over conjunction, such that: $P[S, t_i, (x_1, x_2, \ldots, \& x_n)] \rightarrow [P(S, t_i, x_1), P(S, t_i, x_2), \ldots, \& P(S, t_i, x_n)]$, where "$P(S, t_i, x_i)$" stands for "S is, as of t_i, permitted to perform x_i." (Contrast *agglomeration principle*.)

Disutility: A measure of whatever it is that diminishes a subject's welfare. (Contrast *utility*.)

Dual-ranking act-consequentialism (DRAC): The view that S's performing x is morally permissible if and only if, and because, there is no available alternative that would produce an outcome that S has both more moral reason and more reason, all things considered, to want to obtain than to want x's outcome to obtain.

Effectively intend: S can at t_i effectively intend to do x at t_j $(t_i < t_j)$ if and only if S would do x at t_j if S were to intend at t_i to do x at t_j.

Egoism: See *ethical egoism*.

Egoistically adjusted utility: That which includes everyone's utility but adjusts the overall total by giving S's utility, say, ten times the weight of anyone else's.

Ethical egoism: The view both (1) that act-consequentialism is true and (2) that an act produces an outcome that S has optimal reason to want to obtain if and only if it maximizes S's utility. (Contrast *rational egoism*.)

Evaluative ranking: A ranking of outcomes (or prospects) in terms of the agent's reasons (or some subset of her reasons—e.g., her moral reasons) for preferring each to the others.

Expectably best: That which has the highest expected deontic value.

Expectably morally best: That which has the highest expected deontic moral value.

Expected deontic moral value: That which is determined by multiplying the subjective probability that some practical moral comparative is true by the deontic moral value of that action if it is true, doing the same for all of the other practical moral comparatives, and adding up the results (SEPIELLI 2009, pp. 7 and 11). (See also *practical moral comparatives*.)

Expected deontic value: That which is determined "by multiplying the subjective probability that some practical comparative is true by the objective [i.e., deontic] value of that action if it is true, doing the same for all of the other practical comparatives, and adding up the results" (SEPIELLI 2009, pp. 7 and 11). (See also *practical comparatives*.)

Explanatory reasons for action: The facts that explain why an agent performed an act. Examples include *motivating reasons for action*. (Contrast *normative reasons for action*.)

Fittingness reasons: Those reasons that are relevant to determining whether, and to what extent, an outcome is valuable/desirable (i.e., fitting to value/desire).

Follows: S's intentions follow a certain schedule of intentions, I, extending over a time-interval, T, just in case, for every time t_i belonging to T, S has at t_i all and only the intentions that I specifies for t_i (J. ROSS FORTHCOMING).

Freely performs: S freely performs x if and only if S performs x having the relevant sort of control over whether or not she performs x—that is, the sort of control that is necessary for her being an appropriate candidate for praise or blame with respect to her having performed x.

Good: A state of affairs, p, is good if and only if it is better than most of the states of affairs in some contextually supplied comparison class (SCHROEDER 2008b).

Good for: A state of affairs, p, is good for a subject, S, if and only if it is better for S than most of the states of affairs in some contextually supplied comparison class (SCHROEDER 2008b).

Imperfect reasons: Reasons that do not support performing any specific alternative, but instead support performing any of the alternatives that would each constitute an equally effective means of achieving the same worthy end.

Impermissible: That which is not permissible.

Impersonal-value teleology: The view an act's deontic status is determined by the impersonal value of its outcome, such that, if S is morally required to perform x, then S's performing x would produce the most good, impersonally construed. (Contrast *act-consequentialism* and *personal-value teleology*.)

Indirect consequentialism: The view that the deontic status of an individual action is determined by whether or not it, say, accords with the ideal set of rules (rule-consequentialism), stems from the ideal set of motives (motive consequentialism), or is included in one of the MSAs in the ideal set of scrupulously securable MSAs (securitist consequentialism), where the ideal set of rules, motives, or scrupulously securable MSAs is in turn selected on the basis how their associated outcomes rank relative to those of the alternatives on some evaluative ranking. (Contrast *direct consequentialism*.)

Infringement: If there is a constraint against performing a certain act-type, then any commission of an act of that type constitutes an infringement of that constraint. (Contrast *violation*.)

Inter-agent cases: Cases in which the agent can, by infringing upon a set of constraints, C1, prevent more numerous others from comparably infringing upon C1.

Intra-agent cases: Cases in which the agent can, by infringing upon a set of constraints, C1, prevent herself from more extensively infringing upon C1.

Involves: S's φ-ing involves S's ψ-ing just in case it follows from S's φ-ing that S ψs, in the sense that, necessarily, if S φs then S ψs (J. ROSS FORTHCOMING).

Judgment-sensitive attitude: An attitude that is sensitive to one's judgments about reasons for and against it.

Knowledgeably performs: S knowledgeably performs x if and only if S performs x knowing all the relevant facts—the relevant facts being the facts the ignorance of which would otherwise either inculpate or exculpate S for performing x.

Maximal set of actions (MSA): A set of actions, α_j, that is, as of t_i, available to S (i.e., available either in the sense of being personally possible for S or in the sense of being scrupulously securable by S) is a maximal set of actions if and only if there is no other set of actions, α_i, that is, as of t_i, available to S such that performing α_i involves performing α_j but not vice versa.

Maximizes: S's φ-ing maximizes X if and only if there is no available alternative that would produce more X than φ would.

Maximizing act-utilitarianism (MAU): The view both (1) that traditional act-consequentialism is true and (2) that an act maximizes the good if and only if it maximizes aggregate utility.

Maximizing possibilist utilitarianism (MPU): The view according to which all the following are true: (*a*) it is, as of t_i, objectively morally permissible for S to perform a non-maximal set of actions, α_j, beginning at t_j ($t_i < t_j$) if and only if, and because, it is, as of t_i, objectively morally permissible for S to perform a maximal set of actions, MSA$_i$, that involves S's performing α_j; (*b*) it is, as of t_i, objectively morally permissible for S to perform a maximal set of actions, MSA$_i$, if and only if, and because, MSA$_i$ is one of the optimal MSAs that is, as of t_i, personally possible for S; (*c*) MSA$_i$ is one of the optimal MSAs that is, as of t_i, personally possible for S if and only if, and because, MSA$_i$'s outcome is not, on S's evaluative ranking, outranked by that of any alternative MSA that is, as of t_i, personally possible for S; and (*d*) MSA$_i$'s outcome is not, on S's evaluative ranking, outranked by that of any alternative MSA that is, as of t_i, personally possible for S if and only if, and because, there is no alternative MSA that is, as of t_i, personally possible for S whose outcome contains more aggregate utility than MSA$_i$'s outcome does.

Maximizing securitist utilitarianism (MSU): The view according to which all the following are true: (*a*) it is, as of t_i, objectively morally permissible for S to perform a non-maximal set of actions, α_j, beginning at t_j ($t_i < t_j$) if and only if, and because, it is, as of t_i, objectively morally permissible for S to perform a maximal set of actions, MSA$_i$, that involves S's performing α_j; (*b*) it is, as of t_i, objectively morally permissible for S to perform a maximal set of actions, MSA$_i$, if and only if, and because, MSA$_i$ is one of the optimal MSAs that is, as of t_i, scrupulously securable by S; (*c*) MSA$_i$ is one of the optimal MSAs that is, as of t_i, scrupulously securable by S if and only if, and because, MSA$_i$'s outcome is not, on S's evaluative ranking, outranked by that of any alternative MSA that is, as of t_i, scrupulously securable by S; and (*d*) MSA$_i$'s outcome is not, on S's evaluative ranking, outranked by that of any alternative MSA that is, as of t_i, scrupulously securable by S if and only if, and because, there is no alternative MSA that is, as of t_i, scrupulously securable by S whose outcome contains more aggregate utility than MSA$_i$'s outcome does.

Merely permissible: That which is optional but not supererogatory.

Merely sufficient reason: S has merely sufficient reason to φ if and only if S has sufficient, but not decisive, reason to φ—that is, if and only if S's reasons are such as to make it both objectively rationally permissible for S to φ and objectively rationally permissible for S not to φ. (Contrast *decisive reason* and *sufficient reason*.)

Meta-criterion of rightness: A criterion that provides both necessary and sufficient conditions for an act's being morally permissible in terms of both moral and non-moral reasons.

Minimal act: An act that, once begun, cannot be stopped by its agent short of completion. Examples include all instantaneous actions, such as placing a bet, as well as some non-instantaneous actions, such as beheading by guillotine (J. H. SOBEL 1976, p. 198). (Contrast *compound act*.)

Minimally fulfills: In φ-ing, S does thereby only minimally fulfill some positive duty, D, if and only if S's φ-ing fulfills D and there is no more moral reason for S to φ than to do anything else that would fulfill D. (See also *positive duty*.)

Modified Schefflerian utilitarianism (MODSU): The view according to which all the following hold: (1) dual-ranking act-consequentialism is true; (2) S has more moral reason to want o_i to obtain than to want o_j ($j \neq i$) to obtain if and only if o_i contains more constraint-adjusted utility than o_j does; and (3) S has more reason, all things considered, to want o_i to obtain than to want o_j to obtain if and only if o_i contains more comprehensively adjusted utility than o_j does.

Moral dilemma: A situation in which there is no way for an agent to satisfy the dictates of morality (VALLENTYNE 1989, p. 301). Examples include *obligation dilemmas* and *prohibition dilemmas*.

Moral enticer: See *morally enticing reason*.

Moral justifying strength: One reason, R_1, has more moral justifying strength than another, R_2, if and only if both (*i*) R_1 would make it morally permissible to do anything that R_2 would make it morally permissible to do and (*ii*) R_1 would make it morally permissible do some things that R_2 would not make it morally permissible to do. (Contrast *moral requiring strength*.)

Moral option: An instance in which an agent is morally permitted to perform more than one alternative.

Moral rationalism (MR*): The deontic status of α_j is determined by the agent's reasons for and against performing α_j, such that, if S is, as of t_i, morally required to perform α_j, then S has at t_i most (indeed, decisive) reason, all things considered, to perform α_j.

Moral reason: A reason that, morally speaking, counts in favor of an agent's φ-ing. Such a reason would, if unopposed and sufficiently weighty, be capable of making φ either morally obligatory or morally supererogatory. (Contrast *morally relevant reason*.)

Moral requiring strength: One reason, R_1, has more moral requiring strength than another, R_2, if and only if both (*i*) R_1 would make it morally impermissible to do anything that R_2 would make it morally impermissible to do and (*ii*) R_1 would make it morally impermissible do some things that R_2 would not make it morally impermissible to do. (Contrast *moral justifying strength*.)

Moral securitism (MS): The view that it is, as of t_i, objectively morally permissible for S to perform a non-maximal set of actions, α_j, beginning at t_j ($t_i < t_j$) if and only if, and because, at least one of the objectively morally permissible maximal sets of actions that are, as of t_i, scrupulously securable by S involves S's performing α_j. (Contrast *securitism*.)

Morally best alternative: The alternative that the agent has most moral reason to perform. (Contrast *optimific alternative*.)

Morally blameworthy: See *blameworthy*.

Morally enticing reason: A reason that, morally speaking, counts in favor of φ-ing but that does not have any moral requiring strength. (Contrast *requiring reason*.)

Morally overriding: Moral reasons are morally overriding if and only if, for all y, S would not be morally permitted to perform y if there were some x ($x \neq y$) that S had more moral reason to perform. (Contrast *rationally overriding*.)

Morally relevant reason: Any reason that is relevant to determining an act's deontic status. Examples include moral reasons as well as any non-moral reasons that have some moral justifying strength. (Contrast *moral reason*.)

More reason to desire: S has at t_i more (requiring) reason to desire the prospect of her performing α_1 (viz., p_1) than to desire the prospect of her performing α_2 (viz., p_2) if and only if $\Sigma_i[Pr(o_i/\alpha_1) \times D_{\text{s-t}}(o_i)]$ is greater than $\Sigma_i[Pr(o_i/\alpha_2) \times D_{\text{s-t}}(o_i)]$, where α_i is some set of actions, $Pr(o_i/\alpha_i)$ is the objective probability of o_i's obtaining given S's performance of α_i, and $D_{\text{s-t}}(o_i)$ is the S-relative t_i-relative desirability value of o_i, which is just a measure of how much (requiring) reason S has at t_i to desire that o_i obtains.

More requiring reason: "S has more requiring reason to φ than to ψ ($\psi \neq \varphi$)" is short for "the set of all the reasons that S has to φ has greater moral requiring strength than the set of all the reasons that S has to ψ ($\psi \neq \varphi$)."

Most reason: See *optimific reason*.

Motivating reasons for action: The facts that motivated an agent to perform an act—that is, the facts that the agent took to be her reasons for performing the act. These are a subclass of *explanatory reasons for action*. (Contrast *normative reasons for action*.)

Motive consequentialism: The view that the deontic status of an action is determined by whether or not it stems from the ideal set of motives, where the ideal set of motives is in turn selected on the basis how their associated outcomes rank relative to those of the alternatives on some evaluative ranking.

Multiple-option case: A case in which there is optimal reason to achieve some end and more than one equally attractive means to achieving that end.

Murder: The act of intentionally killing an innocent person.

Negative act: The intentional omission of some physical act. (Contrast *positive act*.)

Negative duty: A duty that can be fulfilled only by refraining from performing some set of actions. (Contrast *positive duty*.)

Nonconsequentialism: A moral theory that is not act-consequentialist. An example is *rule-consequentialism*.

Non-moral reason: A reason that is not a moral reason. (Contrast *moral reason*.)

Non-requiring reason: A reason that has absolutely no moral requiring strength. (Contrast *requiring reason*.)

Normative reasons for action: A fact that counts in favor of an agent's performing an action. (Contrast *explanatory reasons for action* and *motivating reasons for action*.)

Objective ought: S objectively ought to perform *x* if and only if performing *x* is what a normatively conscientious person would do if she faced S's choice of alternatives and was aware of all the relevant reason-constituting facts. In other words, S objectively ought to perform some alternative if and only if it is the best alternative—the alternative that she has most reason to perform. (Contrast *subjective ought*.)

Objective rationality: The objective rational status of an act is purely a function of the (objective) reasons there are for and against performing it, irrespective of whether or not the agent is aware of them. (Contrast *subjective rationality*.)

Objective reason: See *reason*.

Objectively morally impermissible: That which there is decisive moral reason to refrain from.

Objectively morally permissible: That which is not objectively morally impermissible.

Objectively rationally impermissible: That which there is decisive reason to refrain from.

Objectively rationally permissible: That which is not objectively rationally impermissible. (See also *objective rationality*.)

Obligation dilemma: A moral dilemma in which two or more of the agent's positive act alternatives are obligatory. (Contrast *prohibition dilemma*.)

Obligatory: That which is the only permissible available alternative.

Optimal alternative: The alternative, φ, is optimal if and only if there is optimal reason to perform φ. (Contrast *optimific alternative*.)

Optimal reason: S has optimal reason to φ if and only if there is no alternative, ψ, such that S has more reason to ψ than to φ. (Contrast *optimific reason*.)

Optimific alternative: The alternative, φ, is optimific (or best) if and only if there is optimific reason to perform φ. (Contrast *optimal alternative*.)

Optimific reason: S has optimific (or most) reason to φ if and only if S has more reason to perform φ than to perform any other available alternative. (Contrast *optimal reason*.)

Optional: That which one is permitted both to perform and to refrain from performing.

Outcome: The outcome associated with S's φ-ing is the outcome that would obtain were S to φ—that is, the possible world that would be actual were S to φ.

Overridingness: To say that one type of reason, say, *m*-reasons, overrides another, say, *n*-reasons, with respect to a certain kind of normative status, *N*, is to say that, in any situation in which both types of reasons are present and an act, x, has a certain N-status, no modification of the situation that involves affecting only what n-reasons there are will change x's N-status. That is, if m-reasons override n-reasons with respect to an act's N-status, then even the weakest m-reason overrides the strongest n-reason in the determination of that act's N-status.

Partially fulfills: In φ-ing, S does thereby only partially fulfill some positive duty, D, if and only if S's φ-ing is a proper subset of some set of actions by which S minimally fulfills D. (See also *minimally fulfills* and *positive duty*.)

Performs a set of actions: S performs a set of actions, α_j, if and only if S performs every act in that set.

Permissible: That which is not impermissible, or, in other words, that which one is not obligated to refrain from.

Personal-value teleology: The view that an act's deontic status is determined by the personal value of its outcome, such that, if S is morally required to perform x, then S's performing x would produce the most good for S. (Contrast *impersonal-value teleology* and *act-consequentialism*.)

Personally possible: A set of actions, α_j, is, as of t_i, personally possible for S if and only if there is some schedule of intentions, I, extending over a time-interval, T, beginning at t_i such that the following are all true: (*a*) if S's intentions followed schedule, I, then S would carry out all the intentions in I; (*b*) S's carrying out all the intentions in I would involve S's performing α_j; (*c*) S has just before t_i the capacity to continue, or to come, to have the intentions that I specifies for t_i; and (*d*) for any time t_j in T after t_i ($t_i < t_j$), if S's intentions followed I up until t_j, then S would have just before t_j the capacity to continue, or to come, to have the intentions that I specifies for t_j (J. ROSS FORTHCOMING). (Contrast *securable* and *scrupulously securable*; see also *follows*, *involves*, *carries out*, and *schedule of intentions*.)

Plan: An intention to perform some act or set of actions in the future. For instance, one might plan to spend tomorrow morning playing golf.

Policy: An intention to perform a certain kind of action in certain potentially recurring situations—for example, to buckling up one's seat belt when one drives (BRATMAN 2007, p. 27).

Positive act: The intentional performance of some physical act. (Contrast *negative act*.)

Positive duty: A duty that can be fulfilled only by performing some set of actions. (Contrast *negative duty*.)

Possibilism: The view that it is, as of t_i, objectively (morally or rationally) permissible for S to perform a non-maximal set of actions, α_j, beginning at t_j ($t_i < t_j$) if and only if, and because, at least one of the optimal maximal sets of actions that is, as of t_i, personally possible for S involves S's performing α_j. (Contrast *actualism* and *securitism*.)

Practical comparative: Anything of the form: the balance of reasons favors S's doing x as opposed to y.

Practical moral comparative: Anything of the form: the balance of moral reasons favors S's doing x as opposed to y.

Pragmatic reasons for S to φ: Reasons that are provided by facts about the consequences of S's φ-ing.

Present deliberative control: S's φ-ing at some later time is under S's present deliberative control if and only if whether S φs at that later time depends on the immediate outcome of S's present deliberations—that is, depends on which attitudes she forms directly in response to her present deliberations.

Principle of normative invariance: The view that an act's deontic status does not depend on whether or not it is performed.

Prohibition dilemma: A moral dilemma in which all of the agent's positive act alternatives are impermissible. (Contrast *obligation dilemma*.)

Proper subset: One set of actions, α_j, is a proper subset of another, α_i, if and only if every element in α_j is also an element in α_i but not every element in α_i is an element in α_j—that is, if and only if $\alpha_j \subset \alpha_i$.

Prospect: The prospect of S's performing some set of actions, α_i, is a probability distribution over the set of possible outcomes associated with S's performing α_i. (See also *more reason to desire*.)

Rational control: S has rational control over whether or not she φs only if both (1) she has the capacity to recognize and assess the relevant reasons and (2) her φ-ing is at least moderately responsive to her assessments concerning these reasons. (Contrast *volitional control*.)

Rational-desire teleology: See *act-consequentialism*.

Rational egoism: The view that S has sufficient reason to perform x if and only if, and because, S's performing x would maximize S's utility. (Contrast *ethical egoism*.)

Rational justifying strength: A reason, R_1, has more rational justifying strength than another, R_2, if and only if both (*i*) R_1 would make it rationally permissible to do anything that R_2 would make it rationally permissible to do and (*ii*) R_1 would make it rationally permissible do some things that R_2 would not make it rationally permissible to do. (Contrast *rational requiring strength*.)

Rational requiring strength: One reason, R_1, has more rational requiring strength than another, R_2, if and only if both (*i*) R_1 would make it rationally impermissible to do anything that R_2 would make it rationally impermissible to do and (*ii*) R_1 would make it rationally impermissible do some things that R_2 would not make it rationally impermissible to do. (Contrast *rational justifying strength*.)

Rational securitism: See *securitism*.

Rationally overriding: Moral reasons are rationally overriding if and only if, for all y, S would not be rationally permitted to perform y if there were some x ($x \neq y$) that S had more moral reason to perform. (Contrast *morally overriding*.)

Reason: There is a reason for S to φ if and only if there is some fact that counts in favor of S's φ-ing, where φ is some judgment-sensitive attitude.

Reasons for action: See *normative reasons for action*.

Requiring reason: A reason that has some moral requiring strength. (Contrast *non-requiring reason*.)

Resolution: An intention that one has resolved not to reconsider even in the face of anticipated temptation to do so. On one plausible view, a resolution involves both a first-order intention to perform a certain action and a second-order intention not to let that first-order intention be deflected by anticipated contrary inclinations—see HOLTON 2009, pp. 11–12.

Restrictions: See *agent-centered restrictions*.

Rule-consequentialism: The view that the deontic status of an action is determined by whether or not it accords with the ideal set of rules, where the ideal set of rules is in turn selected on the basis how their associated outcomes rank relative to those of the alternatives on some evaluative ranking.

Schedule of intentions extending over a time-interval, *T*: A function from times in T to sets of intentions (J. ROSS FORTHCOMING).

Schefflerian utilitarianism (SU): The view according to which all the following hold: (1) dual-ranking act-consequentialism is true; (2) S has more moral reason to want o_i to obtain than to want o_j ($j \neq i$) to obtain if and only if o_i contains more utility for others (i.e., for those other than S) than

o_j does; and (3) S has more reason, all things considered, to want o_i to obtain than to want o_j to obtain if and only if o_i contains more egoistically adjusted utility than o_j does. (See also *egoistically adjusted utility*.)

Scrupulously securable: A set of actions, α_j, is, as of t_i, scrupulously securable by S if and only if there is a time, t_j, that either immediately follows t_i or is identical to t_i, a set of actions, α_i (where α_i may, or may not, be identical to α_j), and a set of background attitudes, B, such that the following are all true: (1) S would perform α_j if S were to have at t_j both B and the intention to perform α_i; (2) S has at t_i the capacity to continue, or to come, to have at t_j both B and the intention to perform α_i; and (3) S would continue, or come, to have at t_j B (and, where α_i is not identical to α_j, the intention to perform α_i as well) if S both were at t_i aware of all the relevant reason-constituting facts and were at t_j to respond to these facts/reasons in all and only the ways that they prescribe, thereby coming to have at t_j all those attitudes that, given those facts, she has decisive reason to have and only those attitudes that she has, given those facts, sufficient reason to have. (Contrast *securable* and *personally possible*.)

Securable: A set of actions, α_j, is, as of t_i, securable by S if and only if there is a time, t_j, that either immediately follows t_i or is identical to t_i, a set of actions, α_i (where α_i may, or may not, be identical to α_j), and a set of background attitudes, B, such that the following are all true: (1) S would perform α_j if S were to have at t_j both B and the intention to perform α_i; and (2) S has at t_i the capacity to continue, or to come, to have at t_j both B and the intention to perform α_i. (Contrast *personally possible* and *scrupulously securable*.)

Securitism (SEC): The view that it is, as of t_i, objectively rationally permissible for S to perform a non-maximal set of actions, α_j, beginning at t_j ($t_i < t_j$) if and only if, and because, at least one of the objectively rationally permissible maximal sets of actions that are, as of t_i, scrupulously securable by S involves S's performing α_j. (Contrast *actualism*, *possibilism*, and *moral securitism*.)

Securitist consequentialism (SC): The view that the deontic status of a non-maximal set of actions, α_j, beginning at t_j ($t_i < t_j$) is determined by the reasons there are for and against the agent's preferring certain outcomes to others, such that, if S is, as of t_i, morally required to perform α_j, then, of all the outcomes that S could bring about by performing some MSA that is, as of t_i, scrupulously securable by S, S has most reason to desire some subset of those that would result from S's performing an MSA that involves S's performing α_j. (Contrast *act-consequentialism*.)

Self-other asymmetry: Whereas the fact that S's performing x would further S's self-interest does not constitute a moral reason for S to perform x, the fact that S's performing x would further someone else's self-interest does constitute a moral reason for S to perform x.

Self-other utilitarianism: The view that S's performing x is morally permissible if and only if there is no available act alternative that would produce both more utility for others and more overall utility than x would.

Set of actions: See *act-set*.

Simple act: See *minimal act*.

Special obligations: Obligations that are specific to individuals given their particular relationships and history. Examples include obligations arising out of past acts (e.g., the obligation to keep one's promises) as well as the obligations that come with occupying certain roles (e.g., professional and familial obligations). A special obligation is a type of agent-centered constraint. Thus, there is a special obligation to perform a certain act-type (e.g., a special obligation to save one's own child) if and only if agents are required to perform that act-type even in some circumstances in which their failing to perform that act-type is the only way to minimize comparable failures to perform that act-type.

Subjective ought: S subjectively ought to perform x if and only if performing x is what a normatively conscientious person would do if she were in the exact same situation that S is in, facing S's choice of alternatives and all the normative and non-normative uncertainty that goes along with being in S's epistemic position. (Contrast *objective ought*.)

Subjective rationality: On Parfit's view, an act is subjectively irrational if and only if the agent has beliefs whose truth would give her decisive reasons not to perform the act. And when the agent has inconsistent beliefs, the act will be subjectively rational relative to some beliefs but subjectively irrational relative to others (PARFIT 2011, pp. 112–113). On Gert's view, an act is subjectively irrational if and only if it indicates some failure in the practical mental functioning of the agent (GERT 2004, p. 160). (Contrast *objective rationality*.)

Successfully counter: To say that the reasons to φ successfully counter the reasons to ψ ($\psi \neq \varphi$) is to say that the reasons to φ prevent the reasons to ψ from being decisive by, say, equaling, outweighing, undermining, or silencing them. Another possibility is that the reasons to φ are incommensurable with the reasons to ψ such that there is sufficient reason both to φ and to ψ. (Contrast *defeat*.)

Sufficient moral reason: S has sufficient moral reason to φ if and only if S's reasons are such as to make S objectively morally permitted to φ. (Contrast *decisive moral reason*.)

Sufficient reason: S has sufficient reason to φ if and only if S's reasons are such as to make S objectively rationally permitted to φ. In other words, S has sufficient reason to φ if and only if S does not have decisive reason to refrain from φ-ing. (Contrast *decisive reason* and *merely sufficient reason*.)

Sufficient requiring reason: A reason that has sufficient moral requiring strength to generate, absent countervailing reasons, a moral requirement to perform the act of which it counts in favor.

Supererogatory: S's φ-ing is supererogatory if and only if, in φ-ing, S goes above and beyond the call of both perfect and imperfect duty—that is, if and only if, in φ-ing, S does more than duty requires. (Contrast *superperfecterogatory*.)

Superperfecterogatory: S's φ-ing is superperfecterogatory if and only if, in φ-ing, S goes above and beyond the call of perfect duty—that is, if and only if, in φ-ing, S does more than perfect duty requires. (Contrast *supererogatory*.)

Teleological conception of (practical) reasons (TCR*): An agent's reasons for and against performing α_j are determined by her reasons for and against preferring certain outcomes to others, such that S has at t_i more reason to perform a_i than to perform a_j just when, and because, S has at t_i more reason to desire p_i than to desire p_j, where p_i and p_j are the prospects of a_i and a_j, respectively.

Teleological maximizing securitism (TMS): The view according to which all the following are true: (*a*) it is, as of t_i, objectively rationally permissible for S to perform a non-maximal set of actions, α_j, beginning at t_j ($t_i < t_j$) if and only if, and because, it is, as of t_i, objectively rationally permissible for S to perform a maximal set of actions, MSA_i, that involves S's performing α_j; (*b*) it is, as of t_i, objectively rationally permissible for S to perform a maximal set of actions, MSA_i, if and only if, and because, MSA_i is one of the optimal MSAs that is, as of t_i, scrupulously securable by S; (*c*) MSA_i is one of the optimal MSAs that is, as of t_i, scrupulously securable by S if and only if, and because, MSA_i's prospect is not, on S's t_i-relative evaluative ranking, outranked by that of any alternative MSA that is, as of t_i, scrupulously securable by S; and (*d*) MSA_i's prospect is not, on S's t_i-relative evaluative ranking, outranked by that of any alternative MSA that is, as of t_i, scrupulously securable by S if and only if, and because, there is no alternative MSA that is, as of t_i, scrupulously securable by S whose prospect S has at t_i more reason, all things considered, to desire. (See also *prospect* and *more reason to desire*.)

Time-identical: Persisting over the exact same interval (or intervals) of time.

Top-down approach: The approach to assessing permissibility whereby normative principles are applied only to maximal sets of actions and the distribution principle is used to determine the permissibility of non-maximal sets of actions. (Contrast *bottom-up approach* and *across-the-board approach*; see also *distribution principle*.)

Traditional act-consequentialism (TAC): The view both (1) that act-consequentialism is true and (2) that an act produces an outcome that the agent has optimal reason to want to obtain if and only if it maximizes the good (impersonally construed).

Transitive: A relation, R, is transitive just in case: if xRy and yRz, then xRz.

Ultimate end: "An intrinsic end that is a fundamental and indispensible part of the agent's life" (NOGGLE 2009, p. 8).

Undefeated reason: S has an undefeated reason to φ if and only if S has sufficient reason to φ.

Utile: The smallest possible measure of utility, equivalent to someone's experiencing the mildest of pleasures for the briefest of moments.

Utilitarianism: See *maximizing act-utilitarianism*.

Utility: A measure of whatever it is that enhances a subject's welfare. (Contrast *disutility*.)

Value abstractism: The view that the sole or primary bearers of intrinsic value are certain abstracta—facts, outcomes, states of affairs, or possible worlds. (Contrast *value concretism*.)

Value concretism: The view that the fundamental bearers of intrinsic value are concrete entities (e.g., persons, animals, and things). (Contrast *value abstractism*.)

Violation: Any infringement of a constraint that is morally wrong. (Contrast *infringement*.)

Volitional control: S has volitional control over whether or not she φs only if both (1) she has the capacity to intend to φ and (2) whether or not she φs depends on whether or not she intends to φ. (Contrast *rational control*.)

REFERENCES

Alexander, L. (2008). "Scalar Properties, Binary Judgments." *Journal of Applied Philosophy* 25: 85–104.

Anderson, E. (1996). "Reasons, Attitudes, and Values: Replies to Sturgeon and Piper." *Ethics* 106: 538–554.

———. (1993). *Value in Ethics and Economics*. Cambridge, Mass.: Harvard University Press.

Arneson, R. (2002). "The End of Welfare as We Know It? Scanlon versus Welfarist Consequentialism." *Social Theory and Practice* 28: 315–336.

Bennett, J. (1980). "Accountability." In Z. V. Straaten (ed.), *Philosophical Subjects: Essays Presented to P. F. Strawson*, pp. 14–47. Oxford: Clarendon Press.

Bradley, B. (2006). "Against Satisficing Consequentialism." *Utilitas* 18: 97–108.

Bratman, M. E. (2009). "Intention, Belief, Practical, Theoretical." In S. Robertson (ed.), *Spheres of Reason*, pp. 29–62. Oxford: Oxford University Press.

———. (2007). *Structures of Agency*. New York: Oxford University Press.

———. (1994). "Kagan on 'The Appeal to Cost'." *Ethics* 104: 325–332.

———. (1987). *Intention, Plans, and Practical Reason*. Cambridge, Mass.: Harvard University Press.

Brink, D. O. (1997). "Kantian Rationalism: Inescapability, Authority, and Supremacy." In G. Cullity and B. Gaut (eds.), *Ethics and Practical Reason*, pp. 255–291. New York: Oxford University Press.

Brook, R. (1991). "Agency and Morality." *Journal of Philosophy* 88: 190–212.

Broome, J. (1991). *Weighing Goods*. Oxford: Basil Blackwell.

Brown, C. (2004). "Consequentialise This." Unpublished manuscript dated September 10, 2004.

Bykvist, K. (2009). "Objective versus Subjective Moral Oughts." Unpublished manuscript. Retrieved May 9, 2009, from http://ethics-etc.com/wp-content/uploads/2009/05/bykvist.doc.

———. (2003). "Normative Supervenience and Consequentialism." *Utilitas* 15: 27–49.

Byron, M. (2005, April). "Alternative Consequentialisms, Part 2: Position-Relative Consequentialism." Unpublished paper presented at Lingnan University, Hong Kong.

———. (2004). "Introduction." In M. Byron (ed.), *Satisficing and Maximizing*, pp. 1–13. Cambridge: Cambridge University Press.

Carlson, E. (1999). "Consequentialism, Alternatives, and Actualism." *Philosophical Studies* 96: 253–268.

———. (1995). *Consequentialism Reconsidered*. Dordrecht: Kluwer Publishers.

Chang, R. (2004a). "Putting Together Morality and Well-Being." In P. Baumann and M. Betzler (eds.), *Practical Conflicts: New Philosophical Essays*, pp. 118–158. Cambridge: Cambridge University Press.

———. (2004b). "Can Desires Provide Reasons for Action?" In R. J. Wallace, P. Pettit, S. Scheffler, and M. Smith (eds.), *Reason and Value: Themes from the Moral Philosophy of Joseph Raz*, pp. 56–90. Oxford: Oxford University Press.

———. (2004c). "All Things Considered." *Philosophical Perspectives* 18: 1–22.

Chappell, R. Y. (2009). "'Why is it that'...." (7:32 PM, November 30, 2009). Comment to a blog-post: Richard Yetter Chappell's "Actualism and Complex Actions," *Philosophy, et cetera*. Retrieved December 28, 2009, from "http://www.philosophyetc.net/2009/11/actualism-and-complex-actions.html?showComment=1259627528000#c1022235661064585180".

Cochrane, A. (2009). "Explaining the Basic Belief." Unpublished manuscript dated March 26, 2009.

Copp, D. (2003). "'Ought' Implies 'Can', Blameworthiness, and the Principle of Alternate Possibilities." In D. Widerker and M. McKenna (eds.), *Moral Responsibility and Alternative Possibilities: Essays on the Importance of Alternative Possibilities*, pp. 265–299. Burlington, VT: Ashgate.

———. (1997). "The Ring of Gyges: Overridingness and the Unity of Reason." *Social Philosophy and Policy* 14: 86–106.

Curran, A. (1995). "Utilitarianism and Future Mistakes: Another Look." *Philosophical Studies* 78: 71–85.

Dancy, J. (2004). "Enticing Reasons." In R. J. Wallace, P. Pettit, S. Scheffler, and M. Smith (eds.), *Reason and Value: Themes from the Moral Philosophy of Joseph Raz*, pp. 91–118. Oxford: Oxford University Press.

D'Arms, J., and D. Jacobson. (2000). "Sentiment and Value." *Ethics* 110: 722–748.

Darwall, S. (2006a). *The Second-Person Standpoint: Morality, Respect, and Accountability*. Cambridge, Mass.: Harvard University Press.

———. (2006b). "Morality and Practical Reason: A Kantian Approach." In D. Copp (ed.), *The Oxford Handbook of Ethical Theory*, pp. 282–320. Oxford: Oxford University Press.

Dorsey, D. (FORTHCOMING). "Weak Anti-Rationalism and the Demands of Morality." *Noûs*.

Dreier, J. (FORTHCOMING). "In Defense of Consequentializing." *Oxford Studies in Normative Ethics*.

———. (2004). "Why Ethical Satisficing Makes Sense and Rational Satisficing Doesn'." In M. Byron (ed.), *Satisficing and Maximizing*, pp. 131–154. Cambridge: Cambridge University Press.

———. (1993). "Structures of Normative Theories." *The Monist* 76: 22–40.

Ellis, A. (1992). "Deontology, Incommensurability, and the Arbitrary." *Philosophy and Phenomenological Research* 52: 855–875.

Eyal, N. (2008). "Non-Consequentialist Utilitarianism." *Kadish Center for Morality, Law & Public Affairs. ISUS-X, Tenth Conference of the International Society for Utilitarian Studies*. Retrieved August 21, 2008, from http://repositories.cdlib.org/kadish/isus_x/by_N_Eyal.

Feldman, F. (1986). *Doing the Best We Can: An Essay in Informal Deontic Logic*. Dordrecht: D. Reidel Publishing Company.

Ferry, M. (2009). "Does Morality Demand Our Very Best? On Moral Prescriptions and the Line of Duty." Retrieved August 9, 2009, from http://www.colorado.edu/philosophy/center/RoME_2009_full_papers.shtml.

Fischer, J. M., and M. Ravizza. (1998). *Responsibility and Control: A Theory of Moral Responsibility*. Cambridge: Cambridge University Press.

Foot, P. (2001). *Natural Goodness*. Oxford: Clarendon Press.

———. (1985). "Utilitarianism and the Virtues." *Mind* 94: 196–209.

Gert, J. (2008). "Michael Smith and the Rationality of Immoral Action." *Journal of Ethics* 12: 1–23.

———. (2007). "Normative Strength and the Balance of Reasons." *Philosophical Review* 116: 533–562.

———. (2004). *Brute Rationality: Normativity and Human Action*. Cambridge: Cambridge University Press.

———. (2003). "Requiring and Justifying: Two Dimensions of Normative Strength." *Erkenntnis* 59: 5–36.

Gibbard, A. (1990). *Wise Choices, Apt Feelings: A Theory of Normative Judgment*. Cambridge, Mass.: Harvard University Press.

Goldman, H. S. [now H. M. Smith]. (1978). "Doing the Best One Can." In A. I. Goldman and J. Kim (eds.), *Values and Morals*, pp. 185–214. Dordrecht: D. Reidel Publishing Company.

————. (1976). "Dated Rightness and Moral Imperfection." *Philosophical Review* 85: 449–487.

Graham, P. (2010). "In Defense of Objectivism about Moral Obligation." *Ethics* 121: 88–115.

Griffin, J. (1986). *Well-Being: Its Meaning, Measurement, and Moral Importance*. Oxford: Clarendon Press.

Hare, C. (2011). "Obligation and Regret When There is No Fact of the Matter About What Would Have Happened if You Had not Done What You Did." *Noûs* 45: 190–206.

Harman, E. (2009). "'I'll Be Glad I Did It' Reasoning and the Significance of Future Desires." *Philosophical Perspectives* 23: 177–199.

Harman, G. (1976). "Practical Reasoning." *Review of Metaphysics* 29: 431–463.

Harwood, S. (2003). "Eleven Objections to Utilitarianism." In L. Pojman (ed.), *Moral Philosophy: A Reader*, 3rd ed., pp. 179–192. Indianapolis: Hackett Publishing.

Heathwood, C. (2008). "Fitting Attitudes and Welfare." *Oxford Studies in Metaethics* 3: 47–73.

Heuer, U. (2004). "Raz on Value and Reasons." In R. J. Wallace, P. Pettit, S. Scheffler, and M. Smith (eds.), *Reason and Value: Themes from the Moral Philosophy of Joseph Raz*, pp. 128–152. Oxford: Oxford University Press.

Hieronymi, P. (2006). "Controlling Attitudes." *Pacific Philosophical Quarterly* 87: 45–74.

Hill, Jr., T. E. (2002). *Human Welfare and Moral Worth*. Oxford: Oxford University Press.

Holton, R. (2009). *Willing, Wanting, Waiting*. Oxford: Oxford University Press.

Hooker, B. (2000). *Ideal Code, Real World*. Oxford: Oxford University Press.

Horgan, T., and M. Timmons. (2010). "Untying a Knot from the Inside Out: Reflections on the 'Paradox' of Supererogation." *Social Philosophy & Policy* 27: 29–63.

Howard-Snyder, F. (1997). "The Rejection of Objective Consequentialism." *Utilitas* 9: 241–248.

Hurka, T. (2006). "Value and Friendship: A More Subtle View." *Utilitas* 18: 232–242.

Hurley, P. E. (2009). *Beyond Consequentialism*. Oxford: Oxford University Press.

————. (2006). "Does Consequentialism Make Too Many Demands, or None at All?" *Ethics* 116: 680–706.

Hursthouse, R. (1999). *On Virtue Ethics*. Oxford: Oxford University Press.

Jackson, F., and R. Pargetter. (1986). "Oughts, Options, and Actualism." *Philosophical Review* 95: 233–255.

Johansson, J. (2009). "Fitting Attitudes, Welfare, and Time." *Ethical Theory and Moral Practice* 12: 247–256.

Joyce, R. (2008a). "What Neuroscience Can (and Cannot) Contribute to Metaethics." In W. Sinnott-Armstrong (ed.), *Moral Psychology*. Vol. 3, *The Neuroscience of Morality*, pp. 371–394. Cambridge, Mass.: MIT Press.

————. (2008b). "Response to Nichols and Katz." In W. Sinnott-Armstrong (ed.), *Moral Psychology*. Vol. 3, *The Neuroscience of Morality*, pp. 419–426. Cambridge, Mass.: MIT Press.

Kagan, S. (1994). "Defending Options." *Ethics* 104: 333–351.

————. (1991). "Replies to My Critics." *Philosophy and Phenomenological Research* 51: 919–928.

————. (1989). *The Limits of Morality*. Oxford: Oxford University Press.

Kamm, F. M. (2007). *Intricate Ethics: Rights, Responsibilities, and Permissible Harms*. Oxford: Oxford University Press.

————. (1996). *Morality, Mortality*. Vol. 2, *Rights, Duties, and Status*. New York: Oxford University Press.

————. (1992). "Nonconsequentialism, the Person as an End-In-Itself and the Significance of Status." *Philosophy and Public Affairs* 21: 354–389.

Kavka, G. (1983). "The Toxin Puzzle." *Analysis* 43: 33–36.

Kawall, J. (2003). "Self-Regarding Supererogatory Actions." *Journal of Social Philosophy* 34: 487–498.

Kennett J. (2006). "Do Psychopaths Really Threaten Moral Rationalism?" *Philosophical Explorations* 9: 69–82.

Lawlor, R. (2009a). *Shades of Goodness: Gradability, Demandingness and the Structure of Moral Theories*. New York: Palgrave Macmillan.

————. (2009b). "The Rejection of Scalar Consequentialism." *Utilitas* 21: 100–116.

Levy, N. (2005). "The Good, the Bad and the Blameworthy." *Journal of Ethics & Social Philosophy*, http://www.jesp.org, vol. 1, no. 2.

Lopez, T., J. Zamzow, M. Gill, and S. Nichols. (2009). "Side Constraints and the Structure of Commonsense Ethics." *Philosophical Perspectives* 23: 305–319.

Lord, E. (2010). "Having Reasons and the Factoring Account." *Philosophical Studies* 149: 283–296.

Louise, J. (2009). "I Won't Do It! Self-Prediction, Moral Obligation and Moral Deliberation." *Philosophical Studies* 146: 327–348.

———. (2004). "Relativity of Value and the Consequentialist Umbrella." *Philosophical Quarterly* 54: 518–536.

McLeod, O. (2001). "Just Plain 'Ought.'" *Journal of Ethics* 5: 269–291.

McNamara, P. (FORTHCOMING). "Action Beyond Morality's Call versus Supererogatory Action: Toward a More Adequate Conceptual Scheme for Common Sense Morality." *Oxford Studies in Normative Ethics*.

———. (1996a). "Making Room for Going Beyond the Call." *Mind* 105: 415–450.

———. (1996b). "Must I Do What I Ought (or Will the Least I Can Do Do)?" In M. A. Brown and J. Carmo (eds.), *Deontic Logic, Agency and Normative Systems*, pp. 154–173. Berlin: Springer-Verlag.

Mellema, G. (1991). "Supererogation and the Fulfillment of Duty." *Journal of Value Inquiry* 25: 167–175.

Mill, J. S. (1991). [1861]. *Utilitarianism*. In J. M. Robson (ed.), *Collected Works of John Stuart Mill*. Vol. 10, pp. 203–59. London: Routledge.

Moller, D. (2009). "Review of Michael Zimmerman's *Living with Uncertainty: The Moral Significance of Ignorance*." *Ethics* 119: 606–611.

Nichols, S. (2008). "Moral Rationalism and Empirical Immunity." In W. Sinnott-Armstrong (ed.), *Moral Psychology*. Vol. 3, *The Neuroscience of Morality*, pp. 395–408. Cambridge, Mass.: MIT Press.

———. (2002). "How Psychopaths Threaten Moral Rationalism, Or Is It Irrational to be Amoral?" *The Monist* 85: 285–304.

Noggle, R. (2009). "Give Till It Hurts? Beneficence, Imperfect Duties, and a Moderate Response to the Aid Question." *Journal of Social Philosophy* 40: 1–16.

Norcross, A. (2006a). "The Scalar Approach to Utilitarianism." In H. West (ed.), *The Blackwell Guide to Mill's Utilitarianism*, pp. 217–232. Oxford: Oxford University Press.

———. (2006b). "Reasons without Demands: Rethinking Rightness." In J. Dreier (ed.), *Contemporary Debates in Moral Theory*, pp. 5–20. Oxford: Blackwell.

Oddie, G., and P. Milne. (1991). "Act and Value: Expectation and the Representability of Moral Theories." *Theoria* 57: 42–76.

Olson, J. (2009). "Fitting Attitude Analyses of Value and the Partiality Challenge." *Ethical Theory and Moral Practice* 12: 365–378.

Parfit, D. (2011). *On What Matters*. Vol. 1. Oxford: Oxford University Press.

———. (2001). "Rationality and Reasons." In D. Egonsson, J. Josefsson, B. Petersson, and T. Rønnow-Rasmussen (eds.), *Exploring Practical Philosophy*, pp. 17–39. Aldershot: Ashgate.

Pettit, P., and M. Smith. (1996). "Freedom in Belief and Desire." *Journal of Philosophy* 93: 429–449.

Piller, C. (2006). "Content-Related and Attitude-Related Reasons for Preferences." *Royal Institute of Philosophy Supplement* 81: 155–182.

Portmore, D. W. (FORTHCOMINGa). "Consequentialism and Moral Rationalism." *Oxford Studies in Normative Ethics*.

———. (FORTHCOMINGb). "Imperfect Reasons and Rational Options." *Noûs*.

———. (FORTHCOMINGc). "The Teleological Conception of Practical Reasons." *Mind*.

———. (2011). "Doing Our Best." Unpublished manuscript.

———. (2009). "Consequentializing." *Philosophy Compass* 4: 329–347.

———. (2008a). "Are Moral Reasons Morally Overriding?" *Ethical Theory and Moral Practice* 11: 369–388.

———. (2008b). "Dual-Ranking Act-Consequentialism." *Philosophical Studies* 138: 409–427.

———. (2007). "Consequentializing Moral Theories." *Pacific Philosophical Quarterly* 88: 39–73.

———. (2005). "Combining Teleological Ethics with Evaluator Relativism: A Promising Result." *Pacific Philosophical Quarterly* 86: 95–113.

———. (2003). "Position-Relative Consequentialism, Agent-Centered Options, and Supererogation." *Ethics* 113: 303–332.

———. (2000). "Commonsense Morality and Not Being Required to Maximize the Overall Good." *Philosophical Studies* 100: 193–213.

———. (1998). "Can Consequentialism Be Reconciled with Our Common-Sense Moral Intuitions?" *Philosophical Studies* 91: 1–19.

Postow, B. C. (2005). "Supererogation Again." *Journal of Value Inquiry* 39: 245–253.

Quinn, W. S. (1993). "Putting Rationality in its Place." In W. S. Quinn, *Morality and Action*, pp. 228–255. Cambridge: Cambridge University Press.

———. (1990). "The Puzzle of the Self-Torturer." *Philosophical Studies* 59: 70–90.

Rabinowicz, W., and T. Rønnow-Rasmussen (2004). "The Strike of the Demon: On Fitting Pro-Attitudes and Value." *Ethics* 114: 391–423.

Raz, J. (1999). *Engaging Reason: On the Theory of Value and Action*. Oxford: Oxford University Press.

———. (1975). "Permissions and Supererogation." *American Philosophical Quarterly* 12: 161–168.

Rønnow-Rasmussen, T. (2009). "On For Someone's Sake Attitudes." *Ethical Theory and Moral Practice* 12: 397–411.

———. (2007). "Analysing Personal Value." *Journal of Ethics* 11: 405–435.

Ross, J. (FORTHCOMING). "Actualism, Possibilism, and Beyond." *Oxford Studies in Normative Ethics*.

———. (2009). "How To Be a Cognitivist about Practical Reason." *Oxford Studies in Metaethics* 4: 243–282.

———. (2006a). *Acceptance and Practical Reason*. PhD diss., Rutgers University–New Jersey. Retrieved March 12, 2010, from Dissertations & Theses: Full Text. (Publication No. AAT 3249337).

———. (2006b). "Rejecting Ethical Deflationism." *Ethics* 116: 742–768.

Ross, W. D. (1930). *The Right and the Good*. Oxford: Oxford University Press.

Sachs, B. (2010). "Consequentialism's Double-Edged Sword." *Utilitas* 22: 258–271.

Scanlon, T. M. (2007). "Structural Irrationality." In G. Brennan, R. Goodin, F. Jackson, and M. Smith (eds.), *Common Minds: Themes from the Philosophy of Philip Pettit*, pp. 84–103. Oxford: Oxford University Press.

———. (2001). "Sen and Consequentialism." *Economics and Philosophy* 17: 39–50.

———. (1998). *What We Owe to Each Other*. Cambridge, Mass.: Belknap Press.

Scheffler, S. (1994). [1982]. *The Rejection of Consequentialism*. Rev. ed. Oxford: Oxford University Press.

———. (1992). *Human Morality*. New York: Oxford University Press.

Schroeder, M. (2010). "Value and the Right Kind of Reason." *Oxford Studies in Metaethics* 5: 25–55.

———. (2009). "Means-End Coherence, Stringency, and Subjective Reasons." *Philosophical Studies* 143: 223–248.

———. (2008a). "Having Reasons." *Philosophical Studies* 139: 57–71.

———. (2008b). "Value Theory." *The Stanford Encyclopedia of Philosophy* (Spring 2008), Edward N. Zalta (ed.), retrieved from http://plato.stanford.edu/archives/spr2008/entries/value-theory/.

———. (2007a). "Teleology, Agent-Relative Value, and 'Good.'" *Ethics* 117: 265–295.

———. (2007b). *Slaves of the Passions*. Oxford: Oxford University Press.

Sepielli, A. (2010). *'Along an Imperfectly-Lighted Path': Practical Rationality and Normative Uncertainty*. PhD diss., Rutgers University–New Jersey. Retrieved June 14, 2010, from Dissertations & Theses: Full Text. (Publication No. AAT 3397515).

———. (2009). "What To Do When You Don't Know What To Do." *Oxford Studies in Metaethics* 4: 5–28.

Shafer-Landau, R. (2003). *Moral Realism: A Defence*. Oxford: Oxford University Press.

Sider, T. (1993). "Asymmetry and Self-Sacrifice." *Philosophical Studies* 70: 117–132.

Sidgwick, H. (1966). [1874]. *The Methods of Ethics*. New York: Dover.

Singer, P. (1999). "A Response." In D. Jamieson (ed.), *Singer and His Critics*, pp. 269–335. Oxford: Blackwell.

Sinnott-Armstrong, W. (2005). "You Ought to be Ashamed of Yourself (When You Violate an Imperfect Moral Obligation)." *Philosophical Issues* 15: 193–208.

———. (2003). "Consequentialism." *The Stanford Encyclopedia of Philosophy* (Summer 2003), Edward N. Zalta (ed.), retrieved from http://plato.stanford.edu/archives/sum2003/entries/consequentialism/.

Skorupski, J. (2010). *The Domain of Reasons*. Oxford: Oxford University Press.

———. (1999). *Ethical Explorations*. Oxford: Oxford University Press.

Slote, M. (2001). *Morals from Motives*. Oxford: Oxford University Press.

———. (1991). "Shelly Kagan's *The Limits of Morality*." *Philosophy and Phenomenological Research* 51: 915–917.

———. (1984). "Morality and Self-Other Asymmetry." *Journal of Philosophy* 81: 179–192.

Smith, A. M. (2010). "Attitudes and Control." Unpublished manuscript dated April 12, 2010.

———. (2008). "Control, Responsibility, and Moral Assessment." *Philosophical Studies* 138: 367–392.

———. (2005). "Responsibility for Attitudes: Activity and Passivity in Mental Life." *Ethics* 115: 236–271.

Smith, H. M. (FORTHCOMING). "The Moral Clout of Reasonable Beliefs." *Oxford Studies in Normative Ethics*.

Smith, M. (2009). "Two Kinds of Consequentialism." *Philosophical Issues* 19: 257–272.

———. (2006). "Moore on the Right, the Good and Uncertainty." In T. Horgan and M. Timmons (eds.), *Metaethics after Moore*, pp. 133–148. New York: Oxford University Press.

———. (2005). "Meta-Ethics." In F. Jackson and M. Smith (eds.), *The Oxford Handbook of Contemporary Philosophy*, pp. 3–30. Oxford: Oxford University Press.

Sobel, D. (2007a). "Subjectivism and Blame." *Canadian Journal of Philosophy* 33 (Supplement): 149–170.

———. (2007b). "The Impotence of the Demandingness Objection." *Philosophers' Imprint* 7: 1–17.

Sobel, J. H. (1994). *Taking Chances: Essays on Rational Choice*. Cambridge: Cambridge University Press.

———. (1976). "Utilitarianism and Past and Future Mistakes." *Noûs* 10: 195–219.

Sosa, D. (1993). "Consequences of Consequentialism." *Mind* 102: 101–122.

Splawn, C. (2001). "The Self-Other Asymmetry and Act Utilitarianism." *Utilitas* 13: 323–333.

Steup, M. (2008). "Doxastic Freedom." *Synthese* 161: 375–392.

Stratton-Lake, P. (2005). "How to Deal with Evil Demons: Comment on Rabinowicz and Rønnow-Rasmussen." *Ethics* 115: 788–798.

Strawson, P. (1962). "Freedom and Resentment." *Proceedings of the British Academy* 48: 187–211.

Stroud, S. (1998). "Moral Overridingness and Moral Theory." *Pacific Philosophical Quarterly* 79: 170–189.

Sturgeon, N. L. (1996). "Anderson on Reason and Value." *Ethics* 106: 509–524.

Suikkanen, J. (2009a). "Consequentialist Options." Retrieved August 9, 2009, from http://www.colorado.edu/philosophy/center/RoME_2009_full_papers.shtml.

———. (2009b). "Consequentialism, Constraints and the Good-Relative-to: A Reply to Mark Schroeder." *Journal of Ethics & Social Philosophy* (March), http://www.jesp.org.

Tännsjö, T. (1999). "A Concrete View of Intrinsic Value." *Journal of Value Inquiry* 33: 531–536.

Taurek, J. (1977). "Should the Numbers Count?" *Philosophy and Public Affairs* 6: 293–316.

Thomson, J. J. (1990). *The Realm of Rights*. Cambridge, Mass.: Harvard University Press.

Van Roojen, M. (2004). "The Plausibility of Satisficing and the Role of Good in Ordinary Thought." In M. Byron (ed.), *Satisficing and Maximizing*, pp. 155–175. Cambridge: Cambridge University Press.

Vallentyne, P. (1989). "Two Types of Moral Dilemmas." *Erkenntnis* 30: 301–318.

———. (1988). "Gimmicky Representation of Moral Theories." *Metaphilosophy* 19: 253–263.

Velleman, J. D. (1989). *Practical Reflection*. Princeton: Princeton University Press.

Vessel, J.-P. (2010). "Supererogation for Utilitarianism." *American Philosophical Quarterly* 47: 299–319.

Wallace, R. J. (2010). "Reasons, Values, and Agent-Relativity." *Dialectica* 64: 503–528.

——. (2006). *Normativity and the Will: Selected Papers on Moral Psychology and Practical Reason.* Oxford: Oxford University Press.

——. (2001). "Normativity, Commitment, and Instrumental Reason." *Philosophers' Imprint* 1: 1–26.

——. (1994). *Responsibility and the Moral Sentiments.* Cambridge, Mass.: Harvard University Press.

Williams, B. (1973). "A Critique of Utilitarianism." In J. J. C. Smart and B. Williams (eds.), *Utilitarianism: For and Against*, pp. 75–150. Cambridge: Cambridge University Press.

Wolf, S. (1990). *Freedom within Reason.* New York. Oxford University Press.

——. (1986). "Above and Below the Line of Duty." *Philosophical Topics* 14: 131–148.

Woodard, C. (2009). "What's Wrong with Possibilism?" *Analysis* 69: 219–226.

Zimmerman, M. J. (FORTHCOMING). "Partiality and Intrinsic Value." *Mind.*

——. (2008). *Living with Uncertainty: The Moral Significance of Ignorance.* Cambridge: Cambridge University Press.

——. (1996). *The Concept of Moral Obligation.* Cambridge: Cambridge University Press.

——. (1993). "Supererogation and Doing the Best One Can." *American Philosophical Quarterly* 30: 373–380.

INDEX